International Perspectives on Rural Homelessness

Housing, Planning and Design Series

Editors: Nick Gallent and Mark Tewdwr-Jones
The Bartlett School of Planning, University College London

This series addresses critical issues affecting the delivery of the right type of housing, of sufficient quantity, in the most sustainable locations, and the linkages that bind together issues relating to planning, housing and design. Titles examine a variety of institutional perspectives, examining the roles of different agencies and sectors in delivering better quality housing together with the process of delivery – from policy development, through general strategy, to implementation. Other titles will focus on housing management and development, housing strategy and planning policy, housing needs and community participation.

Housing in the European Countryside
Rural pressure and policy in Western Europe
Edited by Nick Gallent, Mark Shucksmith and Mark Tewdwr-Jones

Private Dwelling
Contemplating the use of housing
Peter King

Housing Development
Edited by Andrew Golland and Ron Blake

Forthcoming
Rural Housing Policy
Tim Brown and Nicola Yates

Decent Homes for All
Nick Gallent and Mark Tewdwr-Jones

Planning and Housing in the Rapidly Urbanising World
Policy and practice
Paul Jenkins, Harry Smith and Ya Ping Wang

International Perspectives on Rural Homelessness

Edited by
Paul Milbourne and Paul Cloke

LONDON AND NEW YORK

First published 2006
by Routledge
2 Park Square, Milton Park, Abingdon, Oxon OX14 4RN

Simultaneously published in the USA and Canada
by Routledge
270 Madison Ave, New York, NY 10016

Routledge is an imprint of the Taylor & Francis Group, an informa business

© 2006 Paul Milbourne and Paul Cloke, selection and editorial; individual
chapters, the contributors

Typeset in Galliard by
HWA Text and Data Management, Tunbridge Wells
Printed and bound in Great Britain by
Antony Rowe Ltd, Chippenham, Wiltshire

British Library Cataloguing in Publication Data
A catalogue record for this book is available from the British Library

Library of Congress Cataloging in Publication Data
International perspectives on rural homelessness / edited by Paul
      Milbourne and Paul Cloke.
      p. cm. — (Housing, planning and design series)
      Includes bibliographical references and index.
      1. Homeless persons – Cross-cultural studies.   2. Rural men – Cross-
      cultural studies.   3. Rural men – Cross-cultural studies.
      4. Sociology, Rural.   I. Milbourne, Paul, 1966–   II. Cloke, Paul J.
      III. Series.
      HV4480.I68 2006
      362.509173′4—dc22   2005034190

ISBN10: 0–415–34372–0 (hbk)
ISBN10: 0–203–63963–4 (ebk)

ISBN13: 978–0–415–34372–5 (hbk)
ISBN13: 978–0–203–63963–4 (ebk)

Contents

Contributors

Neil Argent is Senior Lecturer in Human Geography in the Division of Geography and Planning at the University of New England, Armidale, Australia. His research interests focus mainly upon social, demographic and economic change in rural communities, and how communities interpret and manage these processes. Recently, he has written on the causes and impacts of bank branch closure on rural towns (with Fran Rolley) and, with Peter Smailes and Trevor Griffin, has investigated the role of population density in the changing character and fortunes of Australian rural communities. Apart from the homelessness research reported on in this volume, he is currently examining how differing levels, and changing rates, of rural population density affect rural people's social interaction opportunities, as well as their perceptions of isolation or crowding in the rural environment.

Laudan Y. Aron is Senior Research Associate with the Urban Institute in Washington, DC. She has over 16 years of experience researching public policies affecting vulnerable populations, including homeless people, people with serious mental illness, out-of-school youth, children with disabilities, and victims of family violence and human trafficking. She has co-authored two books issued by the Urban Institute Press, *Serving Children with Disabilities: A Systematic Look at the Programs* (1996), and more recently, *Helping America's Homeless: Emergency Shelter or Affordable Housing?* (2001).

Andrew Beer is Professor in the School of Geography, Population and Environmental Management at Flinders University. He is also the Director of the Southern Research Centre, Australian Housing and Urban Research Institute. Andrew's research interests include regional development and housing. His publications include *Home Truths: Housing and Property Wealth in Australia* (Melbourne University Press, 2000, with Blair Badcock); *Developing Australia's Regions: Theory and Practice* (University of New South Wales Press, 2003, with Alaric Maude and Bill Pritchard) and *Developing Locally: International Lessons in Economic Development* (Policy Press, 2004, with Alaric Maude and Graham Haughton).

David Bruce is Director of Rural and Small Town Programme, Mount Allison University. He has more than 15 years experience in a variety of rural housing policy research and community housing and planning. He has also been actively involved in a number of rural community economic development planning and programme developments in Atlantic Canada. David is a former editor of *Canadian Housing* (1995–2000), Canada's only national housing magazine, produced by the Canadian Housing and Renewal Association.

Pedro José Cabrera Cabrera is a Professor in the Department of Sociology and Social Work at the University of Comillas in Madrid. Specialist in topics of social exclusion and poverty, he has carried out several studies on homelessness, including 'Guests of the air: sociology of homeless in Madrid' (1998) and 'The social action with homeless people in Spain' (2000). He is also a member of the European Observatory on Homelessness of FEANTSA.

Paul Cloke is Professor of Human Geography at the University of Exeter, and Founder Editor of *Journal of Rural Studies* (Elsevier). His research interests include rural homelessness and poverty, but also homelessness in the city, and broader geographies of ethics. His recent books include *Handbook of Rural Studies* (SAGE, 2005, with Terry Marsden and Patrick Mooney), *Country Visions* (Pearson, 2003), *Tree Cultures* (Berg, 2002, with Owain Jones), and *Rural Homelessness* (Policy Press, 2002, with Paul Milbourne and Rebekah Widdowfield).

Paul Delfabbro is Senior Lecturer in the Department of Psychology, Univeristy of Adelaide, where he lectures in statistics, developmental pscyhology and learning theory. He has published extensively in the areas of out-of-home care and gambling, and has been a frequent advisor to State and Federal Governments in Australia on issues relating to these topics. His recent book, *Children in Foster Care* (with Jim Barber) was published by Taylor and Francis in 2004.

Charles Geisler is Professor of Development Sociology at Cornell University. His research examines the equity issues of land policies, including homelessness, indigenous land rights, biotechnology applications, and the dislocations of protected areas. Recent publications include 'A new kind of trouble: evictions in Eden', *International Social Science Journal* (March, 2003): 'Rethinking land reform in South Africa: an alternative approach to environmental justice', *Social Research Online* (2001, with E. Letsoalo) and *Property and Values* (Island Press, 2000, with G. Daneker).

Lance George is a Research Associate at the Housing Assistance Council (HAC) based in Washington, DC. HAC is a nonprofit organization that supports the development of affordable housing in the rural United States. Lance's research at HAC encompasses a wide array of rural housing issues and topics with recent interests in manufactured housing, high poverty rural areas, and rural Native Americans.

Sakari Hänninen is presently working as a research professor at the National Research and Development Centre for Welfare and Health STAKES (Helsinki). His research interests are focused on political theory, welfare politics, government of social problems and social exclusion. Recent publications include the following edited books: *Mitä yhdistykset välittävät* (*Associations as mediators*, Atena Kustannus Oy, 2003, with Anita Kangas and Martti Siisiäinen), *Lue poliittisesti* (*Reading politically*, SoPhi, 2004, with Kari Palonen), *Yhteiskunta seis – tahdon sisään!* (*Hold it society – I want to be included*, SoPhi, 2004, with Tuula Helne and Jouko Karjalainen).

Robin Kearns is Professor in the School of Geography and Environmental Science at the University of Auckland. He has published over 100 journal articles and book chapters as well as two books: *Putting Health into Place: Landscape, Identity and Well-Being* (Syracuse University Press) and *Culture/ Place/Health* (Routledge, with Wilbert Gesler). He serves on the board of the Centre for Housing Research Aotearoa/New Zealand (CHRANZ). His research investigates the connections between health and place, community response to institutional change, and the social relations of research.

José Antonio López Ruiz is a Professor in the Department of Sociology and Social Work at the University of Comillas in Madrid and in charge of the Laboratory of Sociology at the same university. Current research interests are depopulation in rural areas, social exclusion and digital divide and youth and social change. His main publication related to homelessness is *A Roof and a Future: Best Practice in Social Intervention with the Homeless* (Cabrera, Malgesini and López, Icaria, 2002).

Katherine MacTavish is Assistant Professor of Human Development and Family Sciences at Oregon State University. Since 1997 she has been examining how growing up in a rural trailer park shapes the developmental pathways of children and youth.

Paul Milbourne is Professor in the School of City and Regional Planning, Cardiff University. He has research interests in rural poverty and social exclusion, rural housing needs and homelessness, rural welfare, and nature–society relations. His recent books include *Rural Poverty: Marginalisation and Exclusion in Britain* *and the United States* (Routledge, 2004) and *Rural Homelessness: Issues, Experiences and Policy Responses* (Policy Press, 2002, with Paul Cloke and Rebekah Widdowfield).

Kristin Natalier is a lecturer in the School of Sociology and Social Work, University of Tasmania. Her research interests lie in the areas of housing, law, young people and risk. She has just completed an AHURI funded project on private rental assistance and is currently working on issues surrounding how young people make sense of their financial futures and plan toward them.

Susan Oakley is a lecturer in the School of Social Science at the University of Adelaide where she teaches topics on youth, work and gender. Her research interests include the impact large-scale urban waterfront redevelopments have on work, community and place. She is currently one of a team of researchers examining the dimensions of low pay from the standpoint of the worker, their family/household and community in Australia, which is being funded by the Australian Research Council.

Eoin O'Sullivan is a lecturer in social policy in the School of Social Work and Social Policy, Trinity College Dublin. He is the Irish correspondent to the European Observatory on Homelessness and his research interests include homelessness, housing policy and criminology. Recent collaborative publications include *Crime, Punishment and the Search for Order in Ireland* (Institute of Public Administration, 2004), *Crime Control in Ireland* (Cork University Press, 2001) and *The Changing Role of the State: The State and the Housing Markets of Europe* (European Observatory on Homelessness, 2004).

Jasmin Packer is currently a PhD student at the University of Adelaide and her dissertation examines community attitudes to environmental issues. Prior to her PhD, Jasmin worked as a Research Officer in the School of Geography, Population and Environmental Management at Flinders University, as well as working in the youth and social work sector. Ms Packer was a Project Officer with Lutheran Community Care in South Australia during the course of this study.

David Robinson is Professor of Housing and Public Policy in the Centre for Regional Economic and Social Research, Sheffield Hallam University, where he is co-ordinator of the housing research group. He has published widely on housing and homelessness in the UK. His research into rural homelessness has focused on developing more effective methods for estimating homelessness in rural locations and revealing the hidden and neglected situations and experiences of rural homelessness.

Fran Rolley is Senior Lecturer in Human Geography at the University of New England, Australia, where she completed her Ph.D. focusing on the health needs of rural residents and the problems associated with the provision of health care services to rural areas. Her current research interests include health inequalities in rural areas, socio-demographic change in rural Australia and the impacts of changes in service provision on rural residents and communities.

Sonya Salamon is Professor of Community Studies, Department of Human and Community Development, University of Illinois at Urbana-Champaign. Her latest book *Newcomers to Old Town: Suburbanization of the Heartland* examines small community change and received the 2004 Robert E. Park Best Book prize from the American Sociological Association's Community and Urban Sociology Section for the most distinguished research monograph in urban and community sociology. Her current research examines the effect of rural trailer park life on families and children.

Fiona Verity teaches community work and social policy in the School of Social Administration and Social Work at Flinders University. She has a background in community work and is active in community action and research.

Chapter 1
Introduction
The hidden faces of rural homelessness

Paul Milbourne and Paul Cloke

> Homelessness is a global problem from the streets of Brazil's largest city, São Paulo, to Amsterdam, New York, London, Rome, Melbourne, and beyond. Much of the current literature on the problem of homelessness has focused on narrow, nationally-based studies, usually done in the United States and England, with little cross-cultural analysis. There is a need for material that attempts to bring together studies conducted in different countries ...
>
> (Wright, 1997: 1)

> Rural homelessness. My experience? My take on it? In this area, it is a life situation that happens every day to all kinds of people for all kinds of reasons. It's chock full of the same values of homelessness in the city. And it remains, for the most part, invisible in the rural landscape.
>
> (Cairns, 2002: 3)

This book is concerned with providing the sort of critical international perspective on homelessness that is called for by Wright (1997) in the introduction to a previous edited international text on homelessness (Hutin and Wright, 1997). We share Wright's concerns about the limited coverage given to cross-national homelessness issues within the mainstream homelessness literature and agree that a need exists to develop new critical international accounts of the changing nature of homelessness and associated welfare responses. At the same time, we feel that assumptions made by the contributors to this book about the spatialities of contemporary homelessness are indicative of a wider neglect of the geographies of homelessness in different countries. While the focus of Hutin and Wright's book is on *homelessness*, what is apparent from the introductory extract included above and throughout many of the chapters included within the book is a narrower concern with the *metropolitan centre* as a case-study for homelessness research. While we would not want deny the academic value of this and other studies of homelessness in global cities, we do consider that their particular spatial foci leave unanswered some important questions about the differential visibilities and complex spatialities of homelessness within contemporary society. In particular, we feel that the continued focus on the city as the principal site of homelessness research and writing has downplayed the significance of other less obvious and less public forms of homelessness that occur in different spaces, most notably small towns and rural areas.

As the second quotation, from a speech by a woman who has recently been homeless in rural Canada, illustrates, homelessness represents an everyday phenomenon in particular rural areas, impacting on the lives of a broad range of people and displaying similar qualities to city-based homelessness. Yet the subject of rural homelessness has received relatively little academic scrutiny (and political attention) over the last couple of decades. While the dominance of urban-focused research and policy agendas has played an important part within this neglect, it is also the case that the nature of rural homelessness itself makes it a more problematic subject for research. As Cairns points out, rural homelessness remains 'invisible' in the rural landscape; concealed within the physical, socio-cultural and political fabric of rural space. The rural homeless tend not to be concentrated in visible public spaces (such as the shopping street) or obvious welfare spaces (for example, hostels and shelters), for these spaces are absent within many rural areas. Instead, homeless people are more likely to be dispersed across smaller rural settlements, living in precarious forms of housing, or experiencing more hidden forms of rooflessness in the natural environment. The rural homeless thus represent less identifiable and quantifiable research (as well as media and political) subjects than their urban counterparts.

These invisibilities compound, and are themselves compounded by, local policy neglects of homelessness in rural areas. In many ways, policy intervention depends on the easy identification and measurement of problems: if homeless people cannot be encountered and quantified then it becomes difficult to make political claims about the significance of rural homelessness and to secure policy resources to tackle such homelessness. The absence of key welfare services for homeless groups in many rural places, though, makes the task of identifying the rural homeless more challenging and the experience of being homeless in rural areas more difficult. As Cairns notes, in the description of her recent experiences of homelessness in rural Canada:

> ... even when I was in hospital, knowing that I was without housing, aware of how bent over in pain I was physically and emotionally, there was no response from any professional there. There were no social workers, representatives of social agencies, or churches notified on my behalf.
>
> (2002: 3)

Returning to Wright's (1997) quotation, her point about the narrow foci of recent studies of urban homelessness also holds true for academic work on homelessness in rural areas. While it is the case that there have been very few studies of homelessness in rural areas, those that have been undertaken have not only focused on single countries, but have been largely restricted to the two mentioned by Wright – the United States and England. Rural homelessness was first researched in the United States in the late 1980s and early 1990s, when attempts were made to highlight its statistical scale, geographies and profile (see Patton, 1988; First *et al.*, 1990). These analyses of rural homelessness were then deepened by Fitchen (1991, 1992) through her research on homelessness in upstate New York in the 1980s. This work highlighted important connections between low-income, housing disadvantage and homelessness in rural areas, with Fitchen claiming that:

> ... a growing number of rural low-income people have housing that is so inadequate in quality, so insecure in tenure, and so temporary in duration that keeping a roof over their heads is a preoccupying and precarious accomplishment.
>
> (1992: 173)

Fitchen further argued that these types of rural housing problems need to be reconceptualized as homelessness given that 'many rural residents who are living below the poverty line are potentially homeless much of the time, and an unknown number of them actually do become homeless' (1992: 173).

More recently, research has been undertaken on rural homelessness in England. While the first report on homelessness in rural England was published in the early 1990s, this was restricted to a spatial analysis of official homelessness statistics. The first major study of rural homelessness in England was conducted by ourselves between 1996 and 1998 (see Cloke *et al.*, 2002, for an overview of the project and findings). Based on spatial analyses of official homelessness data, interviews with homelessness agencies and detailed case-studies of homelessness in two rural areas, our research has provided an overview of the scale and profile of rural homelessness for England (see Cloke *et al.*, 2001b, 2001c), as well as detailed local accounts of the different cultures, experiences and welfare contexts of homelessness in particular rural areas (see Cloke *et al.*, 2000a, 2000b, 2001a, 2001d). More recently, the government's Countryside Agency has commissioned research on the development of new methods for identifying homelessness in rural areas (Robinson, 2002) and on good practice for tackling rural homelessness (Streich *et al.*, 2002).

The origins of this book lie in our study of rural homelessness in England and our frustrated attempts in the late 1990s to position findings from this work within a broader international context. With the exception of research in the United States, we were able to uncover relatively little published material on rural homelessness in other countries. While our search was focused on English-language publications, it was abundantly clear to us that, in research terms, rural homelessness was a non-issue in many countries. We became curious to discover why this was the case.

This edited text represents the result of our curiosity. The book provides the first ever international account of rural homelessness. It is based on 13 case-study chapters covering eight countries – the United States, Canada, United Kingdom, Ireland, Finland, Spain, Australia and New Zealand. Written by human geographers and sociologists, the chapters discuss the academic and policy neglects of rural homelessness, provide an overview of evidence on the nature and scale of homelessness in rural areas, and examine welfare responses to rural forms of homelessness in these countries. Three of the countries included within the book – United States, United Kingdom and Australia – are also covered by more than one chapter, allowing for more focused coverage of rural homelessness issues.

The chapters are geographically structured into three sections. The first focuses on rural homelessness in *North America*. In Chapter 2 Laudy Aron provides an overview of recent statistical evidence on rural homelessness in the United States. After considering existing evidence on the geographies of poverty in the United States, Aron draws on findings from the 1996 National Survey of Homeless Assistance Providers and Clients to provide a detailed account of the profile of rural homelessness. She also directs critical attention to the nature of existing welfare assistance programmes for homeless people in rural areas, and argues for the development of new models of welfare provision to meet the needs of the rural homeless in the United States.

The focus of the next couple of chapters narrows to particular elements of homelessness in rural areas. Charles Geisler and Lance George consider issues of rural homelessness as they relate to 'Indian country' in Chapter 3. Here, they argue that homelessness amongst Native Americans is closely bound up with issues of landlessness. Focusing on an Indian reservation in North Dakota, Geisler and George highlight that, while the condition of the housing stock in this reservation is adequate in normative terms, there exists a sense of homelessness linked to cultural displacement. This displacement, they suggest, results from the erosion of the reservation's land-base and the operations of agricultural policies and welfare programmes.

In Chapter 4 Sonya Salamon focuses on what she terms 'quasi-homelessness' associated with people living in trailer parks in rural America. While these parks may provide an affordable form of housing for low-income households, Salamon shows how they also present additional insecurities that increase their risk of homelessness. Three types of insecurity are considered – financial, structural and social – each of which, it is suggested, stems from the fact that most trailer-park homeowners rent the land on which their home stands. As in the previous chapter, landlessness thus becomes an important component of these situations of quasi-homelessness. Salamon draws on findings from case-study research on trailer parks in Illinois, New Mexico, North Carolina and Oregon to highlight how financial, structural and social forms of insecurity impact on different trailer-park communities.

Attention switches to rural homelessness in Canada in Chapter 5. Here, David Bruce provides an overview of recent research evidence and policy initiatives focused on homelessness in small towns and rural areas. After considering some key housing challenges faced by rural households, Bruce then sets out a range of statistical information on the scale of rural housing needs as a proxy measure of what he calls 'at-risk' homelessness in rural Canada. The chapter incorporates evidence from recent case-study research in New Brunswick to provide a detailed account of actual and at-risk homelessness in this rural area and the difficulties faced by welfare agencies in tackling rural homelessness.

The second section of the book is concerned with examining rural forms of homelessness in Europe. In Chapter 6, Paul Milbourne and Paul Cloke provide a critical review of recent studies of rural homelessness in the United Kingdom. They suggest that, until relatively recently, rural researchers in this country have been reluctant to engage with rural homelessness as a research area. While there have been studies of rural housing problems, little attention has been given either to the linkages between housing problems and homelessness, or to those groups locked out of formal housing markets in rural areas. The chapter draws on a broad range of recent statistical evidence from England, Wales and Scotland to explore the shifting scales, profiles and geographies of rural homelessness in the UK. Utilizing materials from recent ESRC-funded research on rural homelessness in England, the authors then provide a detailed account of the nature of homelessness in particular rural spaces, highlighting important connections between homelessness, local housing markets and local socio-cultural contexts, and the coping tactics employed by homeless people in rural areas. The chapter ends with a discussion of the shifting states of welfare provision for the rural homeless at national and local levels.

Particular aspects of rural homelessness in England are explored in Chapters 7 and 8. In the first of these, David Robinson focuses on what he terms the 'denied and neglected' components of homelessness in rural areas. Based on recent studies of homeless people in different areas of rural England, including several undertaken by the author himself, Robinson provides a range of evidence on the extent and experiences of homelessness in rural areas. He highlights how different methods of enumerating homelessness expose the scale of undercounting of rural homelessness within government statistics, and particularly within official counts of rough sleepers in rural areas. Robinson also explores the experiences of being homeless in rural England, focusing on the main factors that result in people becoming homeless, the coping strategies adopted by homeless people, and the pathways through which people move out of situations of homelessness in rural areas.

The experiences of homeless people in rural England are explored further by Paul Cloke and Paul Milbourne in Chapter 8. Drawing on the findings of ESRC-funded research focusing on rural homelessness in England, the chapter explores how homelessness is situated differently according to varying social, spatial and personal circumstances. In addition, it uses the first-hand accounts of interviewees to investigate different processes, practices and performances of homelessness in rural areas. This account ranges from rough sleeping in the countryside, to sofa-surfing and inadequate/temporary accommodation in rural places. Cloke and Milbourne suggest that the experiences of homeless people relate not only to their personal crises, but more generally to the denial of these crises both within rural communities and in wider rural cultures. Such experiences thus need to be understood as embodied and personalized everyday events in rural areas.

In Chapter 9 José Antonio López Ruiz and Pedro Cabrera Cabrera examine rural homelessness issues in Spain. While the last few years have witnessed an increasing number of social studies of homelessness in Spain, they highlight that little academic work has focused on homelessness in rural areas. Drawing on recent research undertaken by the authors, their chapter explores the extent and profile of rural homelessness in Spain. Key findings are presented from analyses of new data-sets of homelessness and interviews with members of organizations involved in rural development and social work in particular regions of rural Spain. Cabrera Cabrera and López Ruiz then position these findings on rural homelessness within broader sociological literatures on rural socio-economic change and welfare in Spain.

Sakari Hänninen provides a wide-ranging discussion of homelessness in rural Finland in Chapter 10. The chapter begins with a detailed account of the shifting scales and geography of homelessness in Finland, based on an analysis of official homelessness statistics. Attention is then shifted to the nature of homelessness in two rural municipalities. Here, material from interviews with homeless agencies and homeless people is utilized to explore key structures and processes associated with local rural homelessness. Hänninen ends the chapter by positioning issues of rural homelessness within the theoretical writings of Foucault and Latour, arguing that homelessness needs to be understood as a 'situated event', which is bound up with issues of disablement, dispossession, displacement and disaffiliation.

The last of the European chapters focuses on rural homelessness in Ireland. Eoin O'Sullivan highlights that the limited research conducted on homelessness in Ireland has focused on a small number of urban locations, and Dublin in particular. He suggests that this urban research focus is understandable, given that recent official statistical data indicate that the vast majority of homeless people in Ireland are located in a handful of urban areas. These official data, though, reflect the activities of different pressure groups and particular local interpretations of the meaning of homelessness, and so do not provide any 'scientific' assessment of the scale and geographies of homelessness in Ireland. The chapter moves beyond these official statistical indications of homelessness to discuss the neglect of homelessness in rural areas and findings from several small-scale studies of rural homelessness undertaken in different parts of Ireland.

Rural homelessness in Australia and New Zealand is explored in the third section of the book. In Chapter 12, Neil Argent and Fran Rolley examine the geographies of homelessness in rural Australia. While homelessness in Australia is largely represented as an urban issue, associated with literal forms of homelessness, they point out that statistics from the recent national censuses reveal high levels of homelessness in rural parts of the country. Their chapter commences with a review of recent research evidence on the shifting scale, composition and causes of homelessness in Australia. Attention then shifts to consider rural homelessness; first, by discussing the geographies of rural homelessness at the national level and in New South Wales, based on an analysis of the 2001 censuses, and second, by drawing on findings from two local case-studies of homelessness in New South Wales. This local work highlights the invisibilities of homelessness, important factors leading to homelessness and the inter-relations between homelessness, housing markets and welfare provision in rural areas.

Andrew Beer and colleagues provide a more specific examination of rural homelessness in Australia in Chapter 13, by focusing on youth homelessness in rural areas. The chapter discusses the distinctive features of youth homelessness in rural Australia, with attention given to the different pathways into homelessness amongst young people in rural areas and the impacts of rurality on their homeless experiences. The authors draw on key findings from recent in-depth research in two case-studies – one in Western Australia, the other in South Australia – to provide detailed explorations of young people's experiences of homelessness in rural areas. They also provide a powerful critique of current welfare provision for homeless youth in rural Australia.

In Chapter 14, Robin Kearns explores rural homelessness in New Zealand with a particular emphasis on the indigenous Maori population. He suggests that rural homelessness is doubly neglected in New Zealand; first by the limited policy concern for homelessness in the country, and second by the more specific neglect of rural homelessness by researchers. The chapter provides estimates of the extent of homelessness in rural areas, considers policy responses to precarious forms of housing and explores the connections between population movements, housing and homelessness in the Northland locality of Mangakahi. Population trends, empirical evidence, policy responses and concepts relating to metaphorical constructions of home with respect to Maori are reviewed. Kearns concludes that rural homelessness, as it impacts on Maori population, is as much associated with cultural constructions of home, housing and belonging in the country as it is with a lack of shelter.

In the final chapter of the book we draw out key themes that cross-cut the individual chapters. Attention is given to the important role played by dominant constructions of homelessness and rurality in reducing the visibilities of homelessness in rural areas. We also suggest that rural homelessness needs to be understood as an assemblage of practices and develop Hänninen's four components of homelessness – disablement, dispossession, displacement and disaffiliation – using case-study material from the different chapters. Finally, we turn our attention to policy responses to rural homelessness and identify key principles that we feel should be applied to the task of responding to homelessness in rural areas.

Chapter 2
Rural homelessness in the United States

Laudan Y. Aron

Like poverty, homelessness in rural America is "unseen, unacknowledged, [and] unattended" (Andrews, 2002). Yet the two fundamental causes of homelessness – a lack of affordable housing and an inability to pay for adequate housing – are clearly not limited to urban communities. This chapter reviews what is known about rural homelessness in the United States. It begins by considering how "rural" is commonly defined and how differences between urban and rural communities extend beyond such simple measures as size, density, and distance. After reviewing estimates of the extent of homelessness in rural areas and the characteristics of rural homeless people, the chapter turns to a discussion of whether current approaches to defining and studying homelessness – approaches that have generally been developed in urban settings – are appropriate for rural areas. The chapter concludes with a brief discussion of how what we have learned, and continue to learn, can contribute to our efforts to end homelessness in rural America.

Defining "rural"

A major challenge in studying homelessness in rural areas is that there is no single definition of "rural" for statistical and other purposes. Rural communities are generally thought to be places with small, low-density populations, often remote from larger cities and towns. In reality, these geographic characteristics exist on a continuum and there is no obvious dividing line between places that are "urban" and those that are "rural." Two of the most common definitions used in the US are based on standards developed by the federal Office of Management and Budget (OMB) and the Bureau of the Census. Both define rural areas as those that fall outside certain areas: "metropolitan statistical areas" (or MSAs) in the case of the OMB standard,[1] or "urbanized areas and urban clusters" in the Census definition.[2] MSAs are composed of one or more counties, and are defined based on population size and density, and the extent to which fringe counties are economically tied to core metropolitan counties.[3] Because county-level data are quite plentiful, MSAs and counties outside of MSAs are often used to compare urban and rural America statistically.[4] On the other hand, the Census defines "urbanized areas and urban clusters" by settlement size and density, ignoring county boundaries. The Census approach offers a somewhat purer measure of "rural" but is more difficult to use (Cromartie and Swanson, 1997; Hewitt, 1989).

Data from the 2000 census show that 21.0 percent of the nation's population (or 59.1 million people) live in rural areas according to the Census definition, while a slightly lower share, 17.4 percent (or 49.2 million people), live in nonmetropolitan areas as defined by OMB (Economic Research Service, 2003b). But the two groups are not identical: about half (50.8 percent) of all Census-defined rural residents actually live in counties classified as falling within an MSA. Similarly, among residents of counties not included in MSAs, 41.1 percent live in urban areas.

Why place matters

Whatever standard one uses to distinguish rural from urban areas, it is clear that the differences between them extend beyond size, density, and distance. Living in a rural community has important economic, social, and cultural implications. These affect how people experience poverty and homelessness and also how rural communities address these problems. Lawrence (1995: 298) has even argued that the ways in which "the rural" and "the homeless" have each been objectified – the former as a construct in which privacy, property, and independence are glorified, and the latter as a group "outside" of social space – make understanding the two together especially challenging:

> ... to speak of the "rural homeless" is to speak of something greater than the sum of its component terms, particularly insofar as commonly deployed ways of making sense of and assigning meaning to each component challenge their combination and leave them in unstable association one with the other.

Housing costs are often lower in rural areas, but so too are incomes, with the result that rent burdens in rural communities are often as high or higher than those in urban places. Within rural areas alone, housing costs have risen much more quickly than have incomes. As a result, affordability has replaced poor housing conditions as the greatest problem confronting low-income rural households in the US, especially rural renters (Housing Assistance Council, 2002b). The opportunities for raising one's income are often much more limited in rural areas: lower levels of educational attainment, less competition for workers among rural employers, and fewer high-skilled jobs result in lower wages and higher levels of unemployment, underemployment, and seasonal employment. In addition, low population density discourages the development of workplace supports and critical infrastructure such as education and training, childcare, and public transportation (Rural Welfare Policy Panel, 1999).

Many of these factors also explain why poverty and homelessness are not evenly distributed across rural areas. Higher than average levels of homelessness are found in communities that are primarily agricultural; regions with economies based on declining extractive industries (such as mining, forestry, or fishing), and areas with persistent poverty; and places experiencing economic growth (First *et al.*, 1994). Those with growing economies include communities with new or expanding industrial plants that attract more job seekers than can be absorbed, and areas on the urban fringe that attract new businesses and higher income residents which in turn drive up taxes and other living expenses to the detriment of long-time residents. These places include ski resorts, upscale retirement communities, and counties experiencing a boom in vacation home sales. In communities with persistent poverty such as Appalachia, young able-bodied workers often relocate to urban areas in search of employment, but return to their home communities when they do not find work and are then homeless. Other people in impoverished or primarily agricultural areas may become homeless because of changing economic conditions, including lower demands for farm labor as a result of mechanized and corporate farming, and a shrinking service sector because of declining populations. Finally, communities located alongside major transportation routes often receive homeless people literally "off the interstate" – people on the road looking for work or simply on the move who run out of resources. The scarcity of health and social services in many rural areas makes the burden of poverty in these areas even greater. The situation is further complicated by a long tradition of self-reliance, a reluctance to seek help, and an inability to maintain anonymity in many rural communities.

Poverty in the US is disproportionately rural, and it is persistent in rural areas. In 2001, 14.2 percent of people living in nonmetropolitan areas (or 7.5 million people) were poor. By contrast, only 11.1 percent of those living in metropolitan areas were poor. Poverty rates in nonmetropolitan areas have exceeded those in metropolitan areas since the 1960s when such data began to be collected (see Figure 2.1). Reflecting the growing economy over this period, poverty in nonmetropolitan areas fell from a high of 17.1 percent in 1993 to a record low of 13.4 percent in 2000. In 2001, with the end of the economic expansion, the rate began to climb again.

Areas across the country that are persistently poor – meaning places where poverty rates have exceeded 20 percent in every decennial census since 1960 – are disproportionately rural. In all, 383 counties meet this standard of persistent poverty and 95 percent of them are outside of metropolitan areas. Among all nonmetropolitan counties, 16 percent are persistently poor, compared to only 2 percent of all metropolitan counties (Miller and Weber, 2004). In addition to

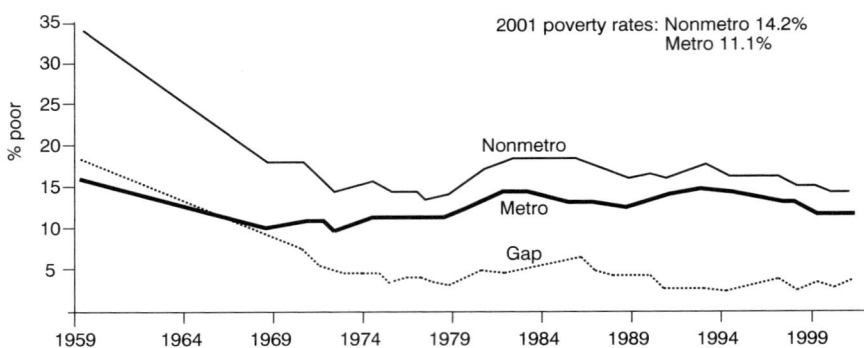

2.1 Poverty rates by residence, 1959–2001
Source: Prepared by the Economic Research Service using data from the US Census Bureau's
Current Population Survey, March Supplement. Reproduced from http://www.ers.usda.gov/
Briefing/IncomePovertyWelfare/ruralpoverty/.
Note: Metro status of some counties changed in 1984 and 1994. Metro and nonmetro rates are
imputed for 1960–8, 1970 and 1984.

being largely rural, high poverty counties are quite concentrated geographically:
they are found in the Black Belt and Mississippi Delta in the South, in Appalachia,
in the lower Rio Grande Valley, and in the Southwest (where Arizona, Colorado,
New Mexico, and Utah meet) and Upper Great Plains (see Figure 2.2). Rural
poverty rates are especially high in the South (17.6 percent) and over half all of
poor rural Americans live there (Summers and Sherman, 1997).

There are also striking patterns of rural poverty among specific racial and
ethnic groups. Areas of high longstanding poverty are largely the result of social
and economic conditions rather than individual-level factors, but understanding
the racial and ethnic typology of rural poverty can shed light on what strategies
may be most helpful for alleviating poverty in a given area. In Figure 2.2, Beale
(2004) shows how three-quarters of the 444 high-poverty nonmetropolitan
counties (based on the 1993 OMB nonmetropolitan definition and on 2000
Census data) are in fact reflections of low income among specific racial and
ethnic minority groups. Black (210 counties), Hispanic (74 counties), and Native
American (40 counties) high-poverty areas were identified based on one of two
criteria: (1) half or more of the county's poor population is from the given
minority group, or (2) over half of the poor population is white non-Hispanic
but poverty among the minority group in question is what pushes the county's
overall poverty rate above the 20 percent high poverty threshold. In addition
to the Black, Hispanic, and Native American high poverty places, Beale identified
high poverty areas in the Southern Highlands, where poor people are mostly
white and non-Hispanic. Only 27 high poverty counties fall outside this racial/
ethnic typology. Interesting differences emerge among these types in the

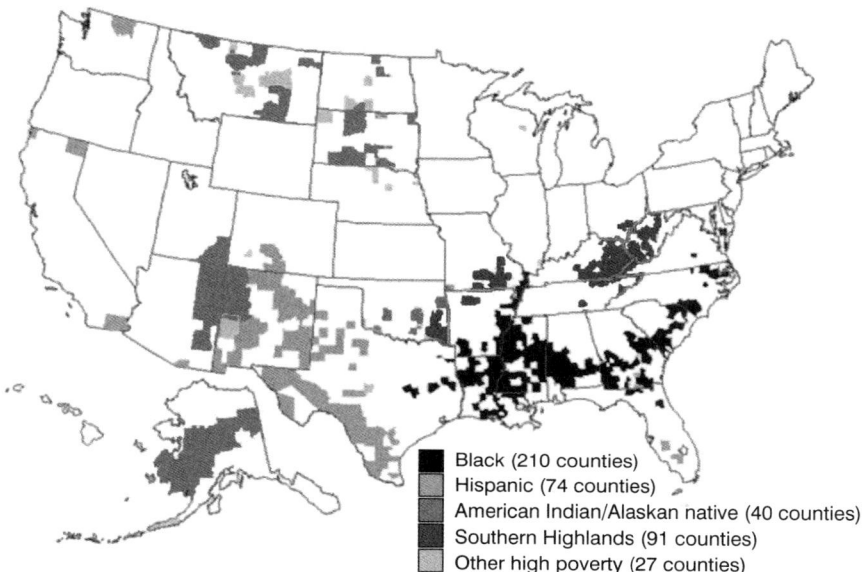

Black (210 counties)
Hispanic (74 counties)
American Indian/Alaskan native (40 counties)
Southern Highlands (91 counties)
Other high poverty (27 counties)

2.2 Nonmetro counties with high poverty, 2000
Source: Calculated by the Economic Research Service using Census data from the US Census Bureau. Reproduced from http://www.ers.usda.gov/Briefing/Incomepovertywelfare/ highpoverty/ which provides a colored version of the map.
Note: High poverty is defined as a poverty rate of 20 percent or more.

disadvantages they face (e.g., high shares of female-headed families, lack of a vehicle, low levels of education and language barriers, low employment, and high rates of disability). Duncan (1999) and Fitchen (1992) provide more sociological and ethnographic accounts of deep, persistent rural poverty in the US, including vivid illustrations of how such poverty puts people at much greater risk for homelessness. Based on her work in upstate New York, Fitchen (1992) identifies three distinct streams of poor rural residents: those who are part of an entrenched multi-generational cycle of poverty, those who have recently fallen into poverty following a loss of employment or death, disability, or divorce in the family, and new in-migrating poor people who have been squeezed out of high-cost metropolitan areas. She notes further that all three groups include people at risk of homelessness.

People homeless in rural areas

The most recent data on people homeless in the US come from the 1996 National Survey of Homeless Assistance Providers and Clients (NSHAPC). As the name suggests, the data are national in scope and include communities outside MSAs in addition to central cities and those in the "balance of MSA" (see Burt *et al.*, 2001 and 1999, for a detailed description of this study and its findings). NSHAPC used a service-based sampling strategy, meaning that it identified and counted only those homeless people who had contact with some type of homeless assistance program. Although NASHAPC included outreach programs, drop-in centers, and mobile food programs (i.e., programs that serve homeless people who are not in shelters), it is important to note that the survey very likely undercounted people homeless in rural areas.

Despite its limitations, NSHAPC generated a wealth of information on people homeless in the US, and the very large service system that has arisen to help them. The study revealed that an estimated 444,000 homeless adults and children used homeless assistance services during an average *week* of October and November 1996 (Burt *et al.*, 2001). Of this total, 69 percent were in central city areas, another 21 percent were in suburban or urban fringe areas of MSAs, and 9 percent (or about 41,000 people) were in rural areas (defined as living outside an MSA). In terms of *rates* of homelessness, the NSHAPC data indicate that anywhere between 7.3 and 13.9 people per 10,000 people in rural areas were homeless. Projections to the entire homeless population (not just those using services) increase this range to between 8.8 and 16.7 per 10,000. In all cases, these rates were about one-fifth those of central city locations, but were slightly higher than those of suburban/urban fringe locations.

Compared to poor people generally (about 23 percent of whom live in rural areas), service-using homeless people appear to be more concentrated in urban areas. But other findings from NSHAPC suggest that some of the homeless people found in urban areas may have originated in rural areas: almost half (44 percent) of the homeless people interviewed had left the community where their current homeless spell began, and only 28 percent of these "movers" began their current homeless spell in a central city. The NSHAPC data also show that these people tended to move from smaller communities to larger ones and that the smaller the originating community, the more likely they were to move to a larger one. Interestingly, the lack of shelters or other social services was *not* a major reason for leaving their home communities (losing housing and needing work were more important), but central cities were the primary destination of most of the movers and they *did* identify the availability of shelters and other homeless assistance services as a major draw to the community where they were interviewed for NSHAPC.

According to NSHAPC (see Table 2.1), over three-quarters of people homeless in rural areas are men, most are white non-Hispanics, the majority (64 percent) are between 35 and 44 years old, and another 23 percent are under age 35. Close to two-thirds have not graduated from high school, half are divorced or separated, and 18 percent live with their own minor children.

Table 2.1 Characteristics of currently homeless NSHAPC clients by urban/rural status (% of homeless people in given community with characteristics)

	Central cities	Suburb/ urban fringe	Rural
Sex			
Male	71	55	77
Female	29	45	23
Race/ethnicity			
White non-Hispanic	37	54	42
Black non-Hispanic	46	33	9
Hispanic	11	11	7
Native American	5	1	41
Other	1	1	–
Age			
Under 25 years	13	12	6
25 to 34 years	25	27	17
35 to 44 years	34	40	64
45 to 54 years	21	9	8
55 to 64 years	7	6	4
65 or more years	1	6	2
Educational attainment			
Less than high-school	36	35	64
High-school graduate/GED	34	40	13
More than high-school	30	25	23
Marital status			
Married	7	16	11
Widowed	2	8	3
Divorced	25	17	25
Separated	14	14	25
Never married	51	45	36
Living with own minor child/ren	14	16	18
Last 30 days			
Any paid work	40	49	65
Mean income last 30 days	$ 341	$ 422	$ 449
Median income last 30 days	$ 250	$ 395	$ 475
Any means-tested gov't benefits	46	45	35
ADM problems past month			
Alcohol problems (A)	39	30	48
Drug problems (D)	28	24	15
Mental health problems (M)	41	37	26
No ADM problems	33	36	33
Spent time incarcerated (including as juvenile)	55	44	68

Source: Tables 7.1 through 7.6 of Burt *et al.* (2001: 191–211).
Note: Data are drawn from weighted NSHAPC program data and represent program activities on "an average day in February 1996." The unusually high share of Native Americans in rural areas is a product of the sample weights. The *unweighted* data indicate that the shares of homeless Native Americans in central city, suburban, and rural areas are 82, 6, and 12 percent, respectively. Weighting the data to represent the nation as a whole changes these percentages change to 50, 3, and 47 percent, respectively. The change is due to very high weights attached to three Native American men interviewed in an emergency shelter in a rural area.

Almost two-thirds worked for pay during the past month, at a median monthly income of $475 (6 percent reported no income), and only 35 percent had received any type of government assistance in the prior month. Twenty-five percent of rural homeless people were on Medicaid, and 63 percent were uninsured. Nearly half of them had needed but were unable to see a doctor or nurse within the prior year. Two-thirds of them reported having a mental health, drug, or alcohol (ADM) problem during the past month: half had problems with alcohol, a quarter with mental health, and 15 percent with drugs. Only a third reported not having any ADM problems in the past month. Other NSHAPC data (not shown in Table 2.1) indicate that 60 percent of rural homeless people were homeless for the first time (44 percent for six months or less), with only 16 percent spending the night on the streets or in other places not intended for human habitation during the prior week.

Characteristics of homeless people vary by urban–rural location. As Table 2.1 shows, compared to other homeless people, those homeless in rural areas are *more* likely to be white, never married, and more heavily concentrated in the 35 to 44 year age range. Although they are less educated than their urban counterparts, homeless people in rural areas are *more* likely to be working and *less* likely to be receiving any means-tested government benefits such as food stamps, welfare, or supplemental security income (SSI). They are as likely as other homeless people to have a problem with alcohol, drugs, or mental illness (ADM) but the types of problems differ by community. Rural homeless people identified in NSHAPC are much *more* likely than their urban counterparts to have had recent problems with alcohol, and they are much *less* likely to have had recent problems with drugs or mental illness. Other NSHAPC results (not all shown in Table 2.1) indicate that people homeless in rural communities are more likely to have been incarcerated as juveniles and as adults; to be homeless for the first time and for a shorter period of time; to have no public or private health insurance; and to have needed, but not been able to see, a doctor or nurse in the past year. With the exception of the much higher rates of problems with alcohol, most of these findings are consistent with those of earlier smaller-scale studies of rural homelessness (National Coalition for the Homeless, 1999; Burt, 1996). Many rural communities also have disproportionately large shares of Native Americans[5] and migrant farm workers among their homeless populations (Burt, 1996).

The high rates of incarceration among rural homeless people documented by NSHAPC is of particular interest given the large numbers of rural communities that have turned to new prisons and other correctional facilities as a way of supporting their local economies (Kilborn, 2001; Beale, 1996). Without effective discharge planning, one unintentional consequence of these large and growing prison populations may be higher levels of homelessness in the communities where they are located. Discharge plans typically include an estimated discharge date, programs that prisoners complete while in prison, medical records, and making arrangements for post-release housing, medical and mental health care, and other community-based services. In some states this planning is the formal responsibility of corrections administrations, while in other states it is done more informally by correctional health providers, community-based social service providers, or other prison-based social services staff (Community Shelter Board, 2002). In the absence of effective policies and practices around discharge planning, many prisons simply release ex-offenders directly into local homeless shelters. Similar concerns have been raised about people being released from hospitals, treatment facilities, and psychiatric institutions.

Addressing homelessness in rural areas

In the late 1980s, discussions about rural homelessness were centered on how homelessness should be defined for rural areas (Kondratas, 1991). Because there are few or no shelters in rural areas and settlement patterns are so dispersed that even "living on the street" may not be possible, many rural homeless advocates and service providers called for expanding "traditional" definitions of homelessness to include people who are precariously housed (these are people who are "doubled up" with relatives or other families, or those living in abandoned homes or substandard or severely overcrowded housing) (Fitchen, 1992). But it is also true that many people living in urban areas are precariously housed, and while people literally homeless in rural places may not live "on the streets," many do live in their vehicles at campgrounds or in mountain hollows, desert canyons, farmers' fields, state parks, and highway rest areas.

Fortunately, debates about official definitions subsided, and attention turned to ensuring that restrictive definitions did not limit people's eligibility for critical homeless assistance services. Many people agreed that:

> ... in the final analysis, the total number of homeless persons, when homelessness has [such] a broad definition, is really less important than the segmentation of the homeless population into meaningful components, so that policy makers can design appropriate programs for specific groups.
>
> (Kondratas, 1991: 643)

Our best understanding of what programs are available to people homeless in rural areas comes once again from NSHAPC. The 1996 study documented almost 40,000 homeless assistance programs across the country, and a third of these were in rural areas (see Table 2.2). There were some interesting variations by urban–rural community within the four broad types of programs covered by NSHAPC. The majority (56 percent) of all programs distributing vouchers for

Table 2.2 Distribution of Homeless Assistance Programs by Urban–Rural Location (number of programs and % distribution by community)

Program	Estimated no.	Central cities	Suburb/ urban fringe	Rural
Total	39,670	49	19	32
Housing	15,890	50	20	30
Emergency shelter	5,690	50	21	29
Transitional housing	4,400	65	21	15
Permanent housing	1,920	53	18	29
Voucher distribution	3,080	25	19	56
Housing with vouchers	800	54	26	20
Food	13,000	46	23	31
Food pantry	9,030	39	25	36
Soup kitchen/meal distribution	3,480	65	20	15
Mobile food	490	52	15	32
Health	2,740	50	9	41
Physical healthcare	710	47	9	44
Mental health	800	50	10	41
Alcohol or drug	780	49	7	44
HIV/AIDS	450	59	13	28
Other	8,050	51	15	34
Outreach	3,310	59	16	25
Drop-in center	1,790	58	17	25
Financial/housing assistance	1,380	12	8	80
Other	1,570	59	17	24

Source: Table 9.2 of Burt *et al.* (2001: 248).
Note: Data are drawn from weighted NSHAPC program data and represent program activities on "an average day in February 1996."

emergency shelter were located in rural areas, but these same areas accounted for only 15 percent of transitional housing programs. Soup kitchens were much more likely to be found in central cities than in rural areas (65 versus 15 percent). These findings reflect fundamental differences in the social service structures of urban versus rural communities. Permanent housing structures and soup kitchens that rely on people walking through the door to get a meal are not efficient ways of helping homeless people in rural areas. The greater use of mainstream agencies by rural people, including public health programs and financial/housing assistance, is also confirmed by NSHAPC.

Over the past decade we also have learned a great deal about how best to study and serve people homeless in rural areas. Like NSHAPC, most studies of rural homelessness rely on identifying homeless people through various service agencies (Kentucky Housing Corporation, 2001; Koebel *et al.*, 2001). The absence of homeless-specific agencies in rural areas makes it essential that studies include broad-spectrum mainstream ones such as welfare and social services agencies, public and mental health departments, community action agencies, public housing agencies, Salvation Army centers, Legal Aid offices, and faith-based and other nonprofit organizations that serve poor people. Even for the NSHAPC study, an interesting deviation from the original sampling design had to be made in rural areas because there were so few homeless-specific service programs: the standard for inclusion in the study was expanded to include programs serving homeless *even if this group was not their intended population focus*, and about one-fourth of all rural programs in NSHAPC came in as a result of this expansion. The duration of the data collection is also important to consider. Some communities have replaced their one-night counts or "sweeps" of the shelter and street population with one- or two-month long periods during which service agencies collect information on all people they serve who may be homeless (they also collect unique but anonymous identifiers that allow one to "unduplicate" counts over time and across agencies so that the same homeless person is not counted more than once). This longer time period has been especially helpful in rural areas where homeless people are not as visible or easy to locate.

The organization and delivery of social services take different forms in rural communities and often vary according to the community's size and distance from urban areas, along with other factors. In places large enough to support health and social services, specific strategies include the use of community-wide partnerships linking formal and informal support systems, multi-service centers, and a hub-and-spoke model of outreach to (and referrals from) outlying rural and urban areas. More remote areas with very limited capacity to provide services must rely on mobile outreach units and, as a last resort, referrals to more urbanized areas with established homeless assistance services (Post, 2002). The US Department of Housing and Urban Development (HUD) recently sponsored a study profiling four different "model" approaches to developing homeless service systems in rural areas. The four partnerships included a county-level system in New York, a multi-county/regional system in Alabama, a rural statewide system in Arizona, and a statewide system in Ohio (Housing Assistance Council, 2002a).

A variety of other studies examining the delivery of health and social services in rural areas point to the need to develop new approaches (National Advisory Committee on Rural Health and Human Services, 2004; Rural Welfare Policy Panel, 1999; Burt, 1996). Another more general study discusses a tool known as "the rural prism" in which various characteristics of rural areas – characteristics such as isolation, low population density, mobility disadvantages, and scarcity of financial resources – are linked to their specific implications for service delivery and service deliver systems. It also suggests various options for overcoming barriers to effective service delivery, and can be used to design and evaluate the effectiveness of rural development efforts (see appendix A of Rural Welfare Policy Panel (1999) for a full description of this tool).

Understanding differences in the social service systems of urban and rural communities also has important implications for how federal programs and funding streams are structured. For example, applications from rural agencies to the federal government should not be rated poorly simply because they do not target specific subgroups of homeless people; such targeting may not make sense in many rural communities. It is also important to understand that some goods and services that are considered "nice extras" in urban areas may be absolutely essential for rural service agencies. In some rural places, for example, outreach may literally be the "front door" of an agency and without it many people would simply not be served. Other activities such as improving communications through more or better technology, and being able to transport agency staff and clients are also very important in rural communities (Burt, 1996). As these examples illustrate, it is important that public policies be systematically reviewed and revised with rural communities in mind. Several initiatives are under way to encourage a more widespread "rural proofing" of public policies (Countryside Agency, 2002; DARD Rural Proofing Unit, n.d.), which one source defines as

> a process which ensures that all relevant [Executive] policies are examined carefully and objectively to determine whether or not they have a different impact in rural areas from that elsewhere, because of the particular characteristics of rural areas: and where necessary, what policy adjustments might be made to reflect rural needs and in particular to ensure that as far as is possible public services are accessible on a fair basis to the rural community.
> (DARD Rural Proofing Unit, n.d.: 2)

Looking ahead

The US now has a "two billion dollar a year infrastructure designed to deal with the problem" of homelessness (National Alliance to End Homelessness, 2000). Some have argued that the country has done an adequate job of building up an emergency response system for homeless people and must now go beyond this by focusing on prevention and longer lasting housing and support services (National Alliance to End Homelessness, 2000; Burt, 2001). It is not clear from existing studies that an adequate emergency response system exists in rural areas, but few would argue that there is also a great need for prevention and longer lasting housing and support services in rural communities. Several new lines of thinking for how to "solve" the problem of homelessness may actually bode well for rural communities.

A major federal initiative has led to new approaches for ending chronic street homelessness. Chronic homelessness is certainly not limited to urban areas: indeed NSHAPC revealed that close to 40 percent of those homeless in rural areas were *not* experiencing homelessness for the first time, and the majority of these had been homeless for more than six months (Burt *et al.*, 2001). Chronically homeless people, many of whom have serious mental illness (SMI) often with co-occurring substance abuse problems, frequently shun traditional emergency homeless assistance.[6] Many providers consider them to be "resistant to treatment," in part because the multiplicity of their problems is challenging for single-focus providers and in part because providers have not been interested in trying to serve them, having enough easier people to serve. New approaches are clearly needed to engage these most vulnerable and disabled homeless people, bring them "to the front of the line" for the first time, address their multiple needs, and keep them housed over the long term.[7]

A new paradigm is emerging in which emergency shelters and other forms of short-term assistance (e.g. hotel vouchers) are reserved for people with acute needs who are homeless for the first time or as the result of a crisis such as a job loss or eviction (Burt *et al.*, 2004). Transitional settings, by contrast, are to be used for people under supervision (e.g. by the criminal justice and/or child welfare systems) and those who have been severely traumatized (e.g. victims of family violence). All other groups of homeless people, including those with chronic needs and serious mental illness, are offered the opportunity to move directly from "the streets" into permanent supportive housing. This direct link between the streets and permanent housing has come to be known as "housing first" because it provides housing immediately, does not require "housing readiness," and usually makes few or no demands for participation in mental health treatment, abstinence, and other types of care. Proponents of housing first argue that it is much easier to work on mental health and substance abuse issues when clients are stably housed than when they are on the streets or in a shelter. They also note that most homeless people with SMI are likely to need various treatment and support services for longer periods of time and at more intensive levels than are generally provided through emergency and even transitional housing programs. There is a growing recognition that permanent supportive housing, especially when it is made available under a housing first model, is a critical tool in truly ending chronic homelessness, and several studies suggest that it can be effective at keeping even the most disabled homeless people housed, and in a cost effective manner (Tsemberis and Eisenberg, 2000; Culhane *et al.*, 2002; Lipton *et al.*, 2000; Rosenheck *et al.*, 2003; Shern *et al.*, 1997). This reconsideration of the traditional homeless service model in which everyone goes from "the streets" into emergency shelter and then into transitional or permanent housing may be useful for rural areas which do not have elaborate homeless-specific systems to begin with. Of course developing permanent supportive housing is no easy task (Wilkins *et al.*, 2003), and the challenges are likely to be as great if not greater in rural areas. Still rural areas may offer some advantages over urban ones in terms of the availability and cost of real estate, and if the units are publicly subsidized, the challenges of affordability and credit access for individual people and families become less important. Housing first approaches still require resources and political will, and these are in short supply in both rural and urban communities.

Beyond these chronic homelessness initiatives, many policymakers and service providers are renewing their focus on the role of mainstream safety net programs in ending mass homelessness. These are programs such as Medicaid, public housing, and "welfare" that are intended to meet the needs of poor, elderly, and disabled Americans generally. It is important to remember that the system of targeted programs spawned by the McKinney Act in 1987 provides critical support for hundreds of thousands of homeless people each year, and this system was created largely in response to the failure of mainstream programs in meeting the needs of homeless people. There is a growing understanding, however, that genuine solutions to ending (and preventing) homelessness must involve mainstream programs, along with their much larger budgets and broader areas of focus. Unfortunately, many of the reasons these programs were failing to help homeless people in the first place remain and need to be resolved. These include limitations in program eligibility; inadequate funding levels resulting from state and federal budget decisions; barriers to enrollment and access due to bureaucratic complexity and inconsistent eligibility determination procedures; and service delivery systems that are insensitive to the needs of deeply impoverished, transient populations with multiple problems (National Health Care for the Homeless Council, 2003; US General Accounting Office, 2000). Nonetheless, strengthening mainstream safety net programs will clearly benefit many rural communities, including those affected by deep and persistent poverty and high levels of homelessness.

In both rural and urban areas, truly ending homelessness involves more than just "safety net" systems (mainstream or otherwise). The US needs comprehensive and effective policies on affordable housing, economic development, employment and training, and healthcare. But it is important to keep in mind that, because place really does matter when it comes to being poor and homeless, sound rural policies may not resemble those that have been successful in urban areas. Rural and nonmetropolitan communities have been largely neglected in public policy, and recent research on rural homelessness may help change this. Developing what has been called "a national rural public policy" (Castle, 2001) and committing adequate resources to implementing these policies can go a long way toward solving rural America's most persistent problems, including poverty and homelessness.

Notes

1 The general concept of a metropolitan statistical area is that of a core area containing a substantial population nucleus, together with adjacent communities that have a high degree of economic and social integration with that core. The exact terms used to refer to these areas have changed slightly over time: metropolitan areas were first defined by the Bureau of the Budget (predecessor of OMB) in 1949 under the designation "standard metropolitan area" (SMA). The term was changed to "standard metropolitan statistical area" (SMSA) in 1959, and then to "metropolitan statistical area" (MSA) in 1983. The term "metropolitan area" (MA) was adopted in 1990 to refer collectively to metropolitan statistical areas (MSAs), consolidated metropolitan statistical areas (CMSAs), and primary metropolitan statistical areas (PMSAs). Most recently, the term "core based statistical area" (CBSA) became effective in 2000 and refers collectively to metropolitan and "micropolitan" statistical areas (Economic Research Service, 2003a). Micropolitan statistical areas are nonmetropolitan areas with at least one urban cluster with a population between 10,000 and 50,000. The addition of this class of area is an important development in recognizing the diversity of nonmetro areas, and over the coming years more and more data will be made available based on the three-level "metropolitan/nonmetro micropolitan/nonmetro noncore" classification.

2 The Census Bureau classifies as "urban" all places within an urbanized area (UA) or an urban cluster (UC). These in turn are defined as densely settled territories that consist of (1) core census block groups or blocks with a population density of at least 1,000 people per square mile, and (2) surrounding census blocks that have an overall density of at least 500 people per square mile.

3 As the Economic Research Service explains: "Counties are typically active political jurisdictions, usually have programmatic importance at the Federal and State level, and estimates of population, employment, and income are available for them annually. They are also frequently used as basic building blocks for areas of economic and social integration" (Economic Research Service, 2003a).

4 The Economic Research Service (ERS) within the US Department of Agriculture (USDA) has developed several other county-based classification schemes: the 9-level rural-urban continuum (or "Beale") codes (Economic Research Service, 2004), and the 12-level urban influence (or UI) codes (Economic Research Service, 2003c). The Beale codes reflect a relatively richer set of metropolitan areas, while the UI codes include a richer set of nonmetro areas, leading some analysts to suggest the development of a hybrid of the two.

5 The share of Native Americans among the rural homeless population is unlikely to be as high as the NSHAPC data suggest (41 percent). As the note to Table 2.1 explains, this figure is most likely an artifact of the NSHAPC weighting scheme.

6 Note that in addition to traditional shelters, homeless people with SMI can come in "off the streets" to many other types of places: special programs for chronic public inebriates, residential detoxification facilities, medical respite care facilities, safe havens, and even permanent supportive housing programs.

7 Recall from Table 2.1 that two-thirds of rural homeless people in NSHAPC reported having had a problem with alcohol, drugs, or mental illness (ADM) within the last month. Other NSHAPC data show that 72 percent have had ADM problems within the past year, and 82 percent within their lifetime.

Chapter 3

Homeless in the heartland

American dreams and nightmares in Indian Country

Charles Geisler and Lance George

Introduction

For many Native peoples, landlessness begets homelessness but is conveniently glossed over. This formulation is central to the following narrative and, we suspect, to the ultimate effectiveness of efforts to counter homelessness among Indians in America.[1] Homelessness afflicts both urban and rural Indian populations, but, unlike the majority of the population, is particularly acute among the latter. In 1995, the US Department of Agriculture's unit on Rural Economic and Community Development held several conferences on rural homelessness across America in cooperation with the federal Interagency Council on the Homeless. Its report (Burt, 1996) noted the housing difficulties of Indians, on and off reservations, and provided grist for that year's Native American Housing Assistance and Self Determination Act. This legislation yielded block grants for American Indian housing through the US Department of Housing and Urban Development (HUD). Despite this attention, some claim there were roughly 100,000 homeless or near-homeless Indian families in the United States a year later (Hamilton, 1997; Hensen and Taylor, 2002; US Commission on Civil Rights, 2003: 51).

Being homeless in a nation which holds homeownership aloft as the ultimate form of security and status (HAC, 2002) and as integral to the American Dream is materially and psychologically devastating. But for non-urban Indians, the problem is still more serious. Because homelessness is widely viewed as an urban problem, attention to rural homelessness escapes notice. And because Indians make up a dwindling fraction of the rural population, their housing issues, if noticed at all, are last in line (US Commission on Civil Rights, 2003: 7).

There are additional problems in tracking the housing inadequacies of this invisible rural minority. Data bases characterizing them are unreliable and fall through the cracks of many federal agencies. And, just as urban and rural homelessness are different, the rural homelessness of Indian communities is in many ways unlike the rural homelessness of non-Indians, which itself is poorly understood (Fitchen, 1981, 1995). Housing construction and repair cost more in remote places; overcrowding is acute because of family structure and custom; the semi-absence of fee-simple ownership gives lenders "due cause" to withhold mortgages; and poor economic conditions (reservation poverty rates are more than double the national average) reduce the ability of tribal members to pay mortgages, rents, or repairs. The list goes on.

The present chapter is about the tragedy of rural homelessness experienced by Native Americans, but it is also about obscurantism. This refers to the systematic omission of official information vital to the welfare of a group or community. States, according to Scott (1998), have a crucial need to "see" as part of normal governance functions, and do so by making the complexity of the real world legible through information simplification of many kinds. But at times states elect not to see – perhaps the ultimate form of simplification. They obscure and omit, they erase and obfuscate. Unless one appreciates how states simultaneously see and don't see, the problem of Indian homelessness may well be insoluble.

We begin our analysis with an exegesis of available data bearing on Indian homelessness from government sources, assessing what is present, what is absent, and what the consequences are of this truncated account. We then move to the more nuanced view of Indian homelessness and consider the implications for housing providers and data keepers in and out of government. Our argument here is about the "other homelessness" – that is, homelessness that is more than the absence of shelter. We suggest that homelessness is not an either–or binary of shelter versus no shelter. Such reductionism confuses housing with home and thereby glosses over cultural, spiritual, and ideational meanings of "home" as a secure place to be. A subtle form of obscurantism, such reductionism sidesteps the degrees of homelessness that come with tenure insecurity, poverty, and compromised civil rights and legal identity. A legally sheltered person, in short, may be a de facto homeless person (HAC, 1987). The chapter summarizes past and present responses to Indian homelessness, only some of which recognize the sheltering role of land, and concludes with a comment on the trust obligations of the federal government.[2]

The narrative in numbers

Social science research on Native American populations has many challenges associated with it. These challenges in no way diminish when homelessness is at issue, in part because of the difficulties of defining and quantifying homelessness itself. Measuring homelessness is an extremely imprecise and often controversial undertaking in the US (Burt, 1996) and abroad (Cloke *et al.*, 2002; Gallent *et al.*, 2003). Estimates on the size of the total national homeless population vary widely (Hombs, 1994; Corday and Pion, 1997; Burt, 2000; Berg, 2003). Under the Stuart B. McKinney Homeless Assistance Act of 1987, the federal government defines a person as homeless who lacks a fixed, regular, and adequate nighttime residence, or lives in a shelter, an institution other than a prison, or a place not designed for or ordinarily used as a sleeping accommodation for human beings.

This definition is an example of the state "seeing" homelessness by imposing a simplifying definition of limited use in rural areas. It fails to accommodate populations with culturally divergent attitudes towards housing, home-place, and tenure rights. In many cases the rural homeless move from one extremely substandard, overcrowded, and/or cost-burdened home to another, often doubling or tripling up with friends and relatives. Their shelter is uncertain from one day to the next, creating a considerable shadow population of homeless who, for Scott's seeing state, are nonetheless reported as "housed" (Burt, 1996; GAO, 1999). Though such housing is precarious, the inhabitants are not officially homeless.

Currently, the government makes periodic estimates of the homeless or supports nongovernmental efforts to do this. But in relative terms the population of Native Americans remains small, undersampling is severe, and results are unreliable. Native American homelessness easily becomes a statistical problem to avoid rather than a human problem to understand. Here we consider two ways of understanding Indian homelessness. One is an indirect approach, using a mix of indicators to provide a partial picture of the problem and its proximate causes. In the second, we revisit the problem of homelessness in historical context and coax our understanding less from population, affordability, and housing quality data than from the foundational cause of homelessness, land disenfranchisement often officially approved by the state.

Population

Native Americans are an internally diverse ethnic group, consisting of members of an estimated 500 tribes in disparate locations across the United States (Figure 3.1). Census data describing them are aggregated in geographic areas determined by the Census Bureau (i.e. American Indian Areas, Alaska Native Areas, or Hawaiian Homeland Areas). Yet not all Native Americans live therein (HAC, 2002: appendix A). And, further complicating the picture, not all inhabitants of these areas are Native Americans. So to see people inhabiting Native Lands as homogeneous, or to assume that the demographics and housing characteristics of these places can be accurately compared over time results in a fallacy of composition. It is equivalent to assuming Europe is inhabited only by Europeans.

A useful starting point for quantifying Indian homelessness lies in the comparison of population and housing stock over time. The population data contain several important surprises. First, in 1900, the Census Bureau enumerated less than 250,000 Native Americans. According to the 2000 Census, however, approximately 2.5 million people reported their race as Native American, an

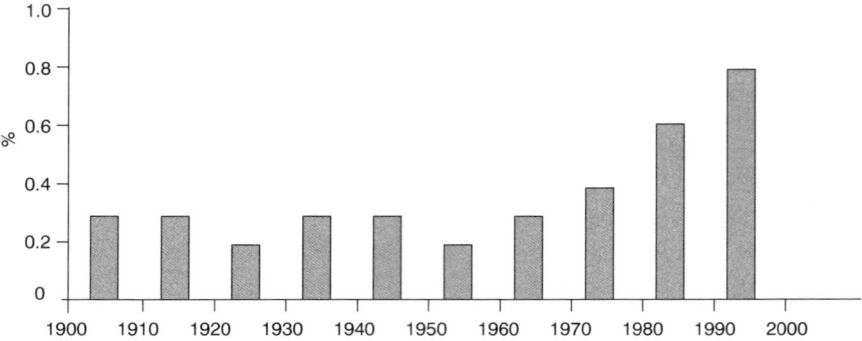

3.1 Native Americans as a percentage of the US population, 1990–2000

order of magnitude increase over the century (Figure 3.2). This growth is attributable to natural population growth and increased self-identification as Native American.[3] To drive this point home, compare the growth rates of the US population as a whole and Native Americans over the century. The former grew by 270 percent, Native Americans by 943 percent (Hobbs and Stoops, 2002). Second, more Native Americans are now urban than rural. As recently as 1990 only 38 percent were urban, compared with 60 percent today.[4]

A third surprise bears directly on Indian homelessness. For the US as a whole, 80 percent of the population is metro and the remaining 20 percent (rural) is growing nationally at a rate of 1 percent per year. But in the western US (where most nonmetro Indians live), overall population growth is more than twice the national nonmetro growth rate (HAC, 2002). If all or most nonmetro Indians lived on reservations, they might be buffered from the housing affordability effects of this growth. Often this is not the case, however. As shown in Figure 3.3, Native Americans constitute only 17 percent of the population on Native

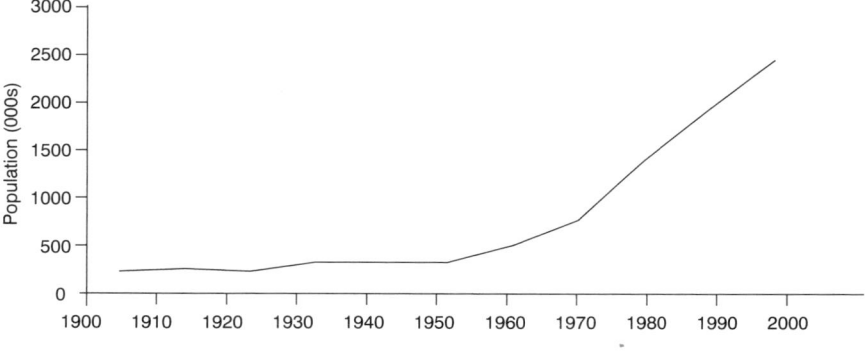

3.2 Native American population, 1990–2000

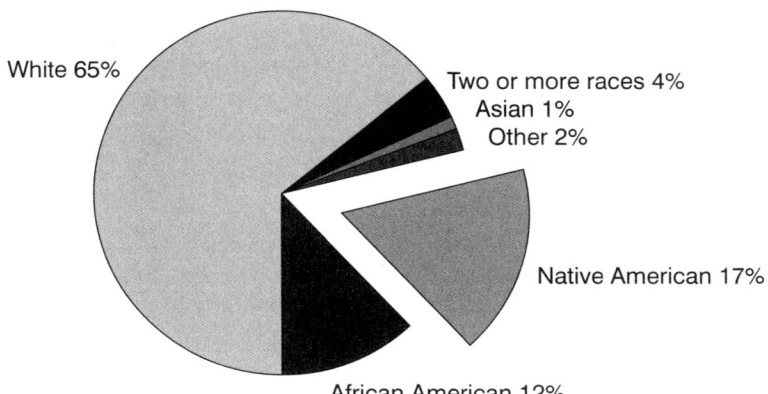

White 65%

Two or more races 4%
Asian 1%
Other 2%

Native American 17%

African American 12%

3.3 Race on Native American lands

lands, strongly suggesting that they must compete with other racial groups for housing and services.[5]

Poverty

Native Americans are historically one of the poorest groups in the United States. While the national percentage of individuals living below the poverty level is 12.4 percent, nearly one-third of Native Americans on Native American lands live in poverty (Figure 3.4). On nearly 64 percent of the Native American lands, poverty rates are higher than the national average (HAC, 2002). High poverty rates frequently go hand-in-hand with poor housing conditions and require further investigation.

For example, the seemingly insurmountable issue of poverty tends to be embedded in social problems such as substance abuse, lack of access to quality education and services, and persistent discrimination and cultural arrogance by the mainstream society. The poor social and economic conditions experienced on many Native American lands are directly related to historical patterns of exploitation, generations of neglect and abuse, and land title complexities that discourage investment in Indian communities. Some of the only economic activity on Native lands are extractive industries that are both hazardous and polluting (Kelley, 1979). Indian gaming enterprises are widely disparaged or viewed jealously by non-Indian jurisdictions (Mason, 2000). Trust fund annuities managed by the Bureau of Indian Affairs in the name of Indians are lost track of in ways that can only be described as legal negligence (NARF, 1996).

Impoverishment of this magnitude and duration has profound effects on housing opportunities among Indians as it does for other people of color (Figure

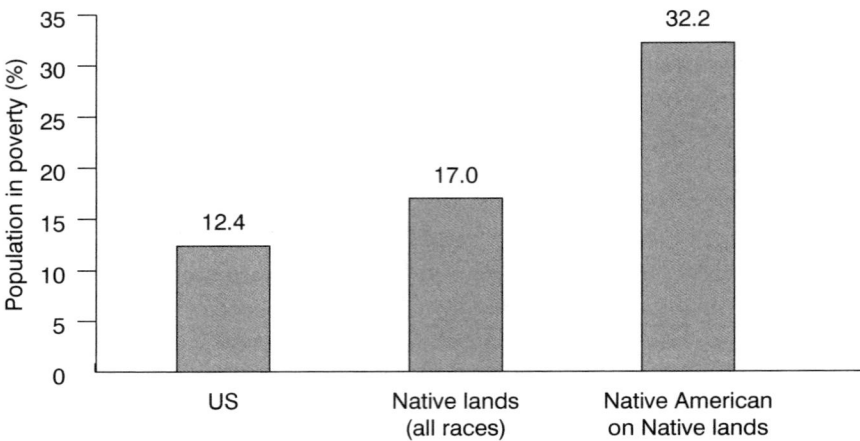

3.4 Poverty on Native American lands by race and Native American status

3.5). Not only does job and income insecurity translate directly to housing insecurity (e.g. inability to consistently pay mortgages, rents, repairs, and improvements), but housing insecurity means an inability to borrow and therefore to capitalize businesses, pay for education, or recover from emergencies. Home ownership, as is often said, is a cornerstone of wealth for many families and an ultimate form of social security, status, and power (Kruekeberg, 1995). At the community level, housing is a significant economic prop – an engine for employment, income, and family stability. Communities that are blocked from attaining their share of new and rehabilitated homes are blocked from the many individual and collective benefits packaged therein (Kalt, 1987; Harvard, 2003).

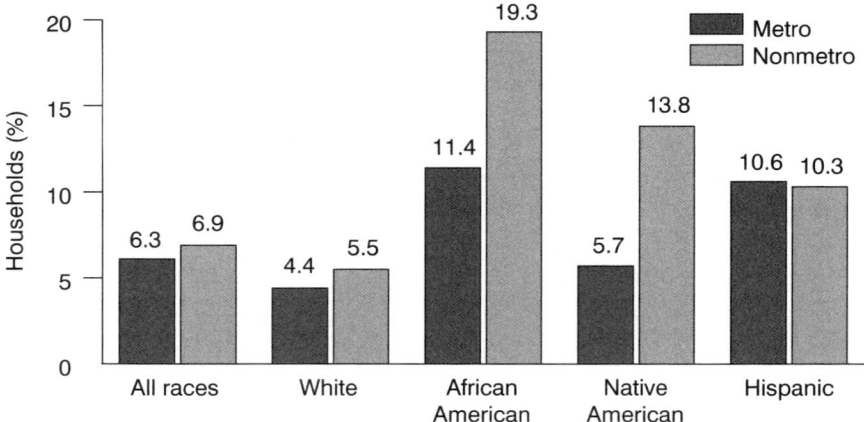

3.5 Substandard housing by race and residence

Housing

Of the 106 million occupied housing units in the United States, roughly 22 percent are in nonmetro areas. Of the latter, 72 percent are single-family owned. Over the past century, homeownership – the symbol of the American Dream – has swelled dramatically in accord with ongoing public and private sector promotion of this staple asset. In nonmetro America, homeownership now stands at 80 percent among households headed by whites and 61 percent for those headed by nonwhites (HAC, 2002). This gap appears to be closing faster in rural than in urban areas, except among minority-headed households and particularly those in poverty. These households resort to rental units, mobile homes, cluster housing, cohabitation with relatives or friends, or makeshift housing.

Notwithstanding high poverty rates noted above and the cluster housing sometimes seen on Indian reservations,[6] Native American homeownership in nonmetropolitan areas stands at 69 percent.[7] This percentage seems inconsistent with the case for disproportionate Indian homelessness and thus raises a question: Can the American Dream be "working" for Native Americans and at the same time be disguising widespread homelessness? We answer in the affirmative for several reasons.

First, mobile homes account for 15 percent of all housing units on Native American lands, almost double the nationwide percentage. This rate rises to 18 percent if only Native-headed households are counted on Native American lands. Mobile homes are often the most feasible form of housing in poor and remote areas (where many Native American lands are), where few contractors or developers are present, building supply stores have largely disappeared, and site-built housing is prohibitively expensive. They are a customary default "single-family-owned" option in a climate of lingering distrust by lending institutions over foreclosure options on trust lands (GAO, 1998).

Second, and perhaps ironically, crowding can and does occur in low-density places. The key is housing affordability. Crowded and unaffordable conditions often prevent poor families from moving beyond substandard housing. At present, the lack of affordable housing has reached crisis proportions in some Native communities. The dire housing conditions that result can be legitimately considered forms of homelessness and near homelessness (NAIHC, 2001), though officially they are neither. Densely populated housing or crowding is not new to Native American Lands (Figure 3.6).[8] Among Census enumerated reservations in 1970, nearly 60 percent of Native American households lived in units with more than one person per room, and 42 percent were severely crowded units of more than 1.5 persons per room. On certain reservations, crowding rates neared 90 percent. Although in the 2000 Census only 18 percent of American Indians and Alaskan Native households in Native lands lived in crowded units, this is three times the national crowding rate.

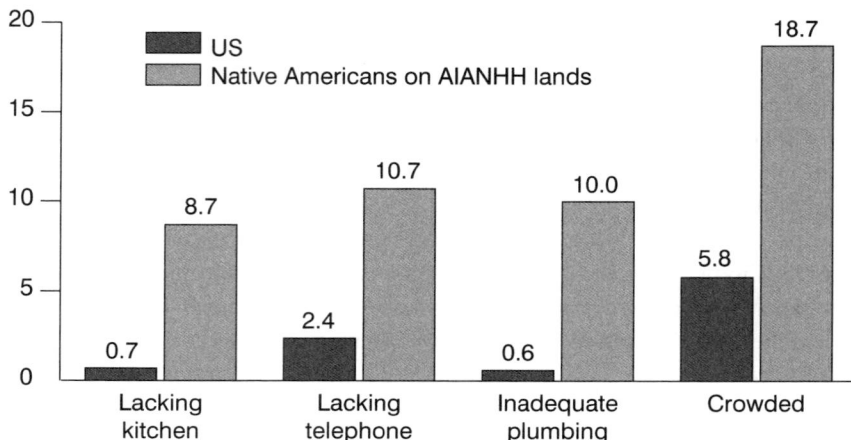

3.6 Housing quality on Native American lands by Native American status

Third, among Indian communities strong family, clan, and kinship ties dictate cultural behaviors that mask the extent of real homelessness. Native American communities are generally "more family oriented" than their non-Native American counterparts (HAC, 2002). Indian families have long depended upon extended families for child-rearing and economic benefits sharing. Grandparents, aunts and uncles serve as caregivers for children when parents are unable to fulfill this role, and are valued as elders. And if a clan member is indigent or in need, he or she can look to other clan members for shelter. Thus, multi-generational family arrangements are common[9] and a source of crowding within single-family, owner-occupied homes. Although crowding among rural Indian households has subsided since 1970, the remaining crowding is chronic and culturally complicated.[10]

Household crowding leads to a fourth reason. Intense use of home facilities and utilities shortens their life-span and depletes savings diverted for repairs. Kitchen facilities and household plumbing are inadequate in Native American nonmetro homes at roughly ten times the rate of US households (see Figure 3.7). Once again, these conditions are improving if compared to past Census records, but remain problematic today. Homes that suffer the "revenge effects" of crowding on their infrastructure deteriorate quickly, lose their resale value, and are not "homes" in the full sense of the official housing census definition.

Thus, the American Dream for nearly 70 percent of Native Americans who are "homeowners" is contradictory and anything but a firewall against homelessness and near-homelessness. For the 30 percent or more of rural Native Americans yet to attain the American Dream, other problems arise such as affordability. Overall, 18.4 percent of homeowners in Native American Areas are cost-burdened.

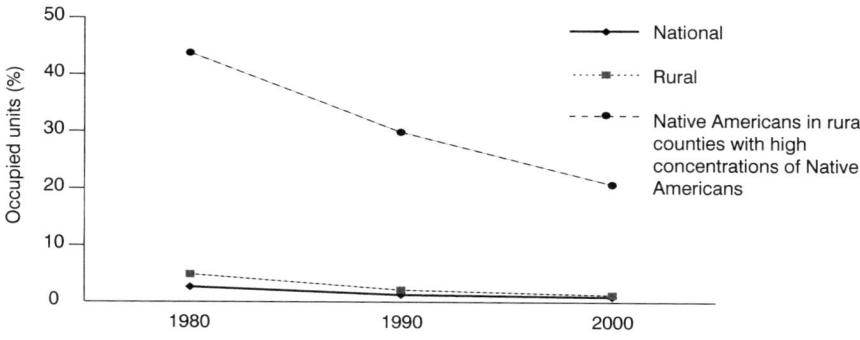

3.7 Inadequate plumbing, 1980–2000

This means spending over 30 percent of their households' income for housing each month. Among Native Americans, 32 percent on Native lands (mostly renters) are cost-burdened. And because affordability is a function of income, it can be a problem even where housing costs are modest. The Cheyenne River Sioux reservation in Ziebach County, S.D., for example, has considerable cost-burden problems among its population. In this area, and in many other Native American communities, incomes are so low that many residents cannot afford housing even though costs are much lower than the national average. When incomes and housing prices are both depressed, the quality of housing is also typically low (HAC, 2002).

Manufactured housing and mobile homes continue to be controversial forms of affordable housing. While their attributes of quality, safety, and size have dramatically improved in recent decades, the financing of manufactured housing is still fraught with difficulties. A vast majority of new manufactured homes is still financed as personal property loans through sub-prime lenders and companies specializing in manufactured housing credit. This form of financing is generally less favorable to the consumer than more conventional lending mechanisms (HAC, 2002) and swiftly eats up savings. Once again, what appears to be affordable housing may be an illusion that leaves its "owner" at higher-than-average risk of losing the asset.

To summarize this section, the information with which one might construct the canvas of Native American homelessness is informative but problematic. Its basic ingredients include: increasing population amid growing non-Native population and competition for space, housing stock, and financing; a changing census definition of "Indian"; an ongoing shift in Indian residence between metro and nonmetro areas; a strong official tendency to equate "home" with housing regardless of condition, crowding, affordability, or cultural nuance; and the fact that Native numbers remain small in relative terms, making them easily overlooked in the vast rural landscape by dispensers of housing services. The 100,000 families or so who are thought to be homeless are vulnerable to both obscurity and obscurantism. But even if all these vexing technical and definitional problems could be remedied, there remains another condition which stands between Indians and their homes. This is landlessness, the homelessness that is invisible to the state.

The "other homelessness"

A recent government report (USDA, 1996) concluded that rural homelessness is symptomatic of larger societal problems. Among these problems is landlessness (Geisler, 1988). The second part of this chapter suggests that Indian homelessness is embedded in Indian landlessness or the replacement of original homelands with meager reservation lands. Landlessness is infrequently considered, even in the most searching investigations of homelessness. Its obscurity is perhaps related to its notorious and controversial history and to government complicity therein. In what follows, we offer historical notes to emphasize this point. Homelessness, either as an official finding or a fact of life disguised as cultural preference, is apt to continue so long as the appropriation of Indian country by non-Indians remains unrecognized as de facto homelessness. We provide several examples of such homelessness in different regions and eras and then conclude the chapter.

Land loss

Homelessness among American Indians has been a source of continuing concern for several centuries. Between the explorations of Columbus and the 1930s, some 100 million Europeans migrated from the old world to the new, often with subsidies and encouragement from their respective governments eager to substantiate territorial claims. This European diaspora dislodged up to twenty million aboriginal peoples (Churchill, 1993), either annihilating them outright or removing them to western territories often claimed by other native or settler communities (Sheehan, 1973). From the outset, being dislodged from land quite literally meant dislodged from home and community – collective homelessness with enduring consequences.

This point bears further comment. Indian removal following US Independence began with Thomas Jefferson (Wallace, 1993), gained force with the Louisiana Purchase, and played out most severely in the administration of Andrew Jackson (Gibson, 1980; Terrell, 1972).[11] Large numbers of Indians (Ottawas, Pottawatomies, Kickapoos, Choctaws, Chicasaws, Seminols, Whyandottes, Winnebagos, Sacs, Delawares, Shawnees, Weas, Peorias, and others) were uprooted from homes and homelands east of the Mississippi and marched west to new homelands under terms of the Indian Removal Act of 1830 and other government policies. Between 1778 and 1871, Congress signed over 370 treaties with Indian nations, the former often canceling terms of the latter or grossly reducing their protections and land coverages (Gibson, 1980; Wolf, 1981).[12]

In retrospect, it is unimaginable that the dismemberment of Indian homelands in the nineteenth century has not been formally linked to the profound insecurities of Indian life on reservations and the de facto homelessness that accompanied them. The Homestead and Railroad Acts of 1862 were followed, after the Civil War, by westward forays of the federal army which in turn were followed by the cessation of treaties with Indians in 1871 and the intensification of Indian Wars in the west. The rigor mortis of Indian lands came with the Dawes Act of 1887. The Dawes (or Allotment) Act was a compulsory "homestead act" for Indians (Sutton, 1970). Compliance meant allotments and small annuities; noncompliance meant forfeiture of land, even if the holdings were within reservations.[13] Such measures were believed by eastern reformers to be the crux of Indian assimilation, civilization, and salvation (Ortiz, 1973). In 1900, the Commissioner of Indian Affairs said of the ongoing allotment process: "The true idea of allotment is to have the Indian select, or to select for him, what may be called his homestead, land upon which by ordinary industry he can make a living either by tilling the soil or in pastoral pursuits" (quoted in Seymour, 1923: 100).

But troubling provisions appeared in the fine print of the new law. For the first time in the history of US–Indian relationships, Indians were enumerated on the basis of their blood quantum and allocated land according to a definition of Indian determined by non-Indians using a racial criterion. In a single act, the United States reduced the genealogical complexity of 500 tribes to a blood formula for ease of land allotment and, as would soon became clear, for further land appropriation. Vast amounts of Indian land were thus declared surplus and vanished as Indian homelands. A few years after the Dawes Act, Indian land holdings fell to 2.5 percent of the continental United States (Churchill, 1993).

More land loss was to follow under the Indian Appropriation Act of 1904 and other legislation. In 1907, 20 years after the Dawes Act,[14] Congress passed laws authorizing the sale of allotments belonging to "incompetent" Indians (those who showed no interest in farming) at the discretion of the Secretary of the Interior (Hurt, 1987; McDonnell, 1991). The legislation was widely abused. At Minnesota's White Earth Reservation, for example, trickery and fraud led to a transfer of 95 percent of the reservation allotments or the timber on them. Describing these processes soon after the White Earth debacle occurred, Seymour (1923: 104) states that "The White Earth story is a flagrant example, it is true, but the conditions discovered there are in the essence typical of the situation everywhere." On the eve of the Indian Reorganization Act in 1934, Indian lands had plummeted from 150 million acres before the Dawes act to 48 million acres. John Collier, a reformer and later Commissioner of Indian Affairs in Washington, wrote that the General Allotment Act, originally intended to entitle Indians with individual holdings (the American Dream of that era), left them with fragments that could support neither family nor household (Collier, 1934).

So homelessness among Indians, often the result of federal land and settlement policies, is not new. The much-revered Homestead Act of 1862 (along with previous and subsequent Homestead Acts) provided "homes" for whites while displacing Indian homesteads. The so-called Indian Homestead Act aggravated this situation rather than correcting it (Wagoner, 1998). It is partially for this reason – land policies condoned by the federal government acting as Trustee to Indian people – that Native Americans hold barely more than 50 million acres of land today but, as noted earlier, retain less than a fifth of the land designated by the government as Native Lands (HAC, 2002: 96).[15]

Ghost Acres

Readers now have, in addition to the portrait of de facto homelessness ascribed to many nonmetro Indians in the first section, a brief historical account of the hollowing out of secure Indian tenure, first in the east and then in the west. Yet, the connection between homelessness and landlessness may seem abstract. Several abbreviated cases of coercive disenfranchisement will be summarized to provide further detail.

The Cherokee of Georgia were among the most advanced Indians in the east. Like the settler communities around them, they owned cattle, slaves, grist mills, saw mills, had a written language, published a newspaper, manufactured cotton and woolen clothes, and were widely Christianized. On more than one occasion they ceded thousands of acres to Washington in order to be left alone (Champagne, 1989). When they drafted a constitution for their nation in 1827, the state of Georgia vehemently protested and demanded their removal. This demand gained force with the discovery of gold on Cherokee lands two years later. Georgia quickly passed a law forbidding Cherokees to prospect or mine gold on their own lands and a stampede of over 3,000 whites followed (Gibson, 1980).

Despite constitutional immunity of Indian nations to state laws and a Supreme Court ruling (Worcester v. Georgia) in favor of Cherokee sovereignty, both Congress and President Jackson sided with Georgia. In 1834 the state surveyed Cherokee lands and disposed of the choicer parcels by lottery. The estates of Cherokee leaders were confiscated and given to white planters (Gibson, 1980). Over the next three years the Cherokee were dislodged from over 8 million remaining acres. The federal government offer for compensation and escort split the nation; those who failed to depart for Oklahoma were detained and brutalized by the Georgia militia – anything but willing sellers. In the end, 10,000 Cherokees were forcibly evicted and marched west in the 1830s, one in four perishing in the removal (Terrell, 1972). The dispossession of the Chickasaws, the Creeks, the Choctaws and Seminoles in the 1830s, less well known, were equally bleak (Gibson, 1980) and described by Alexis de Tocqueville (1840/1938: 363–6) as perpetual encroachments tolerated by the federal government.

Scattered across contemporary Wisconsin and Minnesota are the Anishinaabeg (Ojibwe) people, who ceded land first to the British and then to the United States and Canada in treaties from 1871 to 1929. Significant numbers of Anishinaabeg inhabited what is today Wisconsin, Minnesota and Michigan in previous centuries. The Northwest Ordinance, drafted to govern the Northwest Territory after the Revolution, made good-faith pledges to the native inhabitants. Statute 51 of the Ordinance of 1787 read as follows:

> The utmost good faith shall always be observed towards the Indians; their lands and property shall never be taken from them without their consent; and in their property rights, and liberty, they shall never be invaded or distributed unless in just and lawful war authorized by the congress, but laws founded in justice and humanity shall from time to time be made for preventing wrongs being done to them, and for preserving peace and friendship with them.
>
> (Hurtado and Iverson, 1994: 168–9)

But after Michigan gained statehood in 1837, followed by Wisconsin in 1848, the federal government sought to move the regional Anishinaabeg to northwestern Minnesota in 1850. Prior efforts having failed, four officials of the Taylor administration in Washington conspired to lure the "Lake Superior Chippewa" away from their homelands. This they did by moving the locus of annual annuity payments and rations west to Sandy Lake in central Minnesota in late autumn.

Over 3,000 Indians arrived, many in family units. But payments were stalled until winter arrived. Exposure, starvation, and disease led to the deaths of 170 Anishinaaleg and 270 more died returning to their homes (Clifton, 1987). Those who survived this treatment were dispossessed a generation later by the Dawes Act and amendments to other federal laws pertaining to Indian lands (Meyer, 1991). The Allotment Act steered Indians to farming, despite the unsuitability of soil conditions on most Minnesota reservations for this vocation. Timber companies and other interests were quick to manipulate the law to avail themselves of Indian lands and the federal government took more scenic lands for National

Forests and Seashores. Referring to the effects of the former, Peacock and Wisuri (2002: 56) write:

> There were other ways, too, in which the land was lost. Railroads laid tracks across reservations and acquired large sections of land as a result of condemnation. Timber barons used the allotment act to open up large sections of reservation land for clear cutting. Mineral seekers convinced the federal government to acquire, through treaty, large sections of Indian land to develop copper and iron mines in Upper Michigan and northern Minnesota. Throughout most of this period, our ancestors were powerless to stop the disintegration of their land base and, subsequently, their ways of being.

Indian lands not lost through abuses of the Dawes Act were substantially eroded by the Nelson Act, Minnesota's equivalent of the Dawes Act (Meyer, 1991).

In 1854, a year after 400 Anishinaabeg died waiting for their annuities in Minnesota, the US government entered into the first Fort Laramie Treaty with the Lakota, Cheyenne, Arapaho, Crow, and other tribes of the Great Plains. Its dimensions roughly followed that of the upper Missouri watershed and covered over 10,000,000 acres (or between 6 and 7 percent of the current lower 48 states (Churchill, 1993)). Gold and silver discoveries in Montana Territory spawned military forts along the Boseman Tail across the treaty lands within a decade, leading to the treaty's renegotiation in 1868. The new treaty committed the US army to preventing non-Indians from trespassing within these lands. The 1868 treaty unraveled when gold was discovered in the Black Hills. By 1875, some 15,000 miners had invaded the treaty region and a year later Custer's Seventh Cavalry met its demise within its boundary. The following year (1877), the federal government expropriated the Black Hills (7.7 million acres) in the treaty's heartland (HAC, 2002). Today, the treaty area is 10 percent of what it was in 1868 and two-thirds of this is leased by the Bureau of Indian Affairs to non-Indians (Churchill, 1993). The best agricultural land – the bottom lands along the Missouri River and its tributaries – is permanently flooded under terms of the federal Pick-Sloan Plan to generate electricity for western development (Lawson, 1994).

The consequences of treaty reversals, land invasions by miners and home-steaders, military fort expansion, roads, impoundments, and utility corridors have greatly reduced the wealth and buffering capacity of the land on which Indians depend. Buffalo County, SD, home to the Crowe Creek Indian Reservation, is the poorest county in the nation, with 56.9 percent of its population living below the poverty level. In fact, five of the ten poorest counties in the country are in South Dakota, and all five contain remnant Native American homelands. This pattern of land dispossession and poverty is found across the country. On nearly

64 percent of the Native American lands, poverty rates are higher than the national average (Figure 3.8). Life on marginal lands is predictably a prescription for indigence in the absence of employment and affordable housing.

Another South Dakota County, Shannon, is entirely within the Pine Ridge Reservation and home to the Lakota Sioux who were removed from the Black Hills. HAC researchers visited Pine Ridge in the early 1980s, in 1994, and again in 2002 to survey housing conditions. "The legacy," HAC reports (2002: 103), "left by more than two centuries of colonial subjugation and economic marginalization is still quite visible on the reservation." The poverty rate was declining but remained at 52 percent (almost four times the rate of South Dakota), unemployment ranged between 7.6 and 70 percent (depending on the source consulted), 39 percent of the housing was crowded (compared to 3.1 percent for the state), and acute homelessness was masked by families sheltering indigent relatives.[16]

Many more examples of the homelessness–landlessness connection could be cited. In California, some 25,000 Indians were drawn to Franciscan missions and thereafter not allowed to return to their homelands (Terrell, 1972). After statehood, according to John Collier (1947), the United States negotiated treaties with 119 tribes for over half the state's land in exchange for perpetual ownership of the remaining 7,500,000 acres. Bending to California pressure, however, the US Senate denied confirmation of the treaties but did not inform the Indians that their lands were unprotected until 1905. During this period, virtually all of the 7,500,000 acres were sold to non-Indians. Time and again, throughout the east, the mid-west, the high plains, and the far west, Indian culture and property rights were annihilated and Indians made outcasts on their land (Collier, 1947;

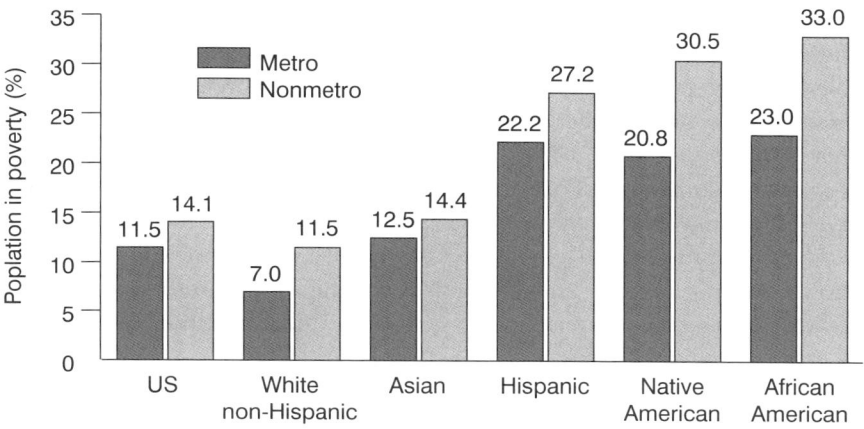

3.8 Poverty by race and residence

Mitchell, 1981). Local, state, and federal governments were complicit. Yet when it comes to explaining Indian homelessness today, it is commonplace to assign responsibility to rapid population growth among Indians relative to housing supply, to the upwards push of rural gentrification on housing markets, or to the risk of trust lands to lenders.[17] Policy solutions are shaped accordingly.

Federal responses to Native American housing problems

Housing assistance for Indians is not new.[18] Until the mid-1990s, tribes and Native American lands received a bulk of their federal housing funding under the 1937 Housing Act. These funds complemented the efforts of the Housing Improvement Program at the Bureau of Indian Affairs (BIA). In 1966, Congress passed the Native American Housing Assistance and Self-Determination Act (or NAHASDA), designed to provide federal housing assistance for Indian tribes in a manner that recognized the right of tribal self-governance.[19] Since the 1970s, the US Department of Housing and Urban Development took the lead in housing homeless and near-homeless Indians on and off reservations, particularly through HUD's Section 184 loan guarantee program (Williams and Leatherman, 1975). This authorized HUD to operate an Indian home loan guarantee program to stimulate access to private financing. Under HUD's Section 248 guarantee program, the Federal Housing Authority (FHA) insures mortgage loans for groups of Native Americans on trust lands whose higher incomes disqualify them from other federally subsidized housing programs. Yet another federally subsidized homeownership source for Native Americans is the USDA/Rural Housing Service (RHS). Most RHS housing finance for Native Americans falls under the Section 502 program, which provides direct homeownership loans for low-income families in rural areas.

Important as these and other measures are for thousands of Native Americans, one must ask to what extent they beg the question of "the other homelessness" posed in this chapter. Restitution for the historical injustices chronicled ever so briefly here is unlikely, as is an end to the denial that surrounds them. Our history books will continue to excuse if not praise Manifest Destiny and romanticize the moral havoc of the frontier. Yet on occasion federal courts have settled land claims in favor of Indian nations, and Congress has established commissions to indemnify and extinguish outstanding claims (Gibson, 1980). On occasion, the executive branch has moved to mitigate "the other homelessness" as well. Early in the twentieth century, western citizens petitioned the federal government to establish a secure place for homeless Cree, Chippewa, Meti, and Assiniboine on the Rocky Boy Reservation in Montana (Peacock and Wisuri, 2002). During the New Deal, President Roosevelt committed land to 150,000 homeless Indians in the Wheeler–Howard Bill of 1934 (Collier, 1934, 1947).

The Termination Era of the 1960s threatened the homelands of still more Indians, but was partially averted by President Nixon's signing of the Indian Restoration Act of 1971. History, if not reversible, has revocable moments.

Conclusion

Estimates of Indian homelessness are imprecise, whether urban or rural. Our research concentrates on the latter, artificial as this distinction is. Taken together or separately, the true extent of Indian homelessness is probably unknowable. This is not because arguments about technical complexities at present lack plausibility. The underlying problem, however, is both administrative and political. Administratively, this is the way states "see" their subjects, record their records, and construct their realities. Politically, this is the way they see when they are responsible for the problems they wish to remedy. Regarding Indian homelessness, the government is unlikely to count well if it has been unaccountable to its laws, treaties, and moral traditions. The historical record speaks for itself.

Early in this chapter we made reference to Scott's (1998) notion that states impose order and regularity on complexity and disorder in everyday life by effecting "legibility." While appreciating the broad applicability of Scott's insight, we have suggested that *illegibility* may also serve the state's purposes when legibility is contradictory or compromising (e.g. Dove and Kammen, 2001). Under such circumstances – and land conquest and occupancy are arguably defining cases – the state "sees" in a way that exonerates past policies or separates past from present. Both the legible and illegible side of homelessness must be considered if Native Americans are to be at home again in this society. Sight must be joined with hindsight.

Incorporating "the other homelessness" into contemporary policy towards Indian people is more than historical correctness. It is engrained in law and legal commitments. In its recent report on the unmet needs of American Indians, the US Commission on Civil Rights (2003: 61) makes the following observation:

> Advocates argue that it is important to distinguish between Native American housing and housing programs for low-income families. The federal government has a special trust responsibility to Native American peoples, and as such, programs for their benefit should not be grouped with those that benefit low-income or rural populations in general. Moreover, while Native Americans have many of the same needs as other low-income populations, they also confront additional challenges . . . Irrespective of the trust responsibility, the fact that Native Americans do not have the housing opportunities available to other low-income communities – and that therefore housing conditions remain substandard – raises civil rights concerns.

This formulation should perhaps go further. Central to the trust responsibility and widely echoed in treaties, statutes, and Supreme Court decisions is the government's pledge to not confiscate Indian lands and homes and thereby not alienate Indians materially and culturally. Short of this and creative efforts to remediate past breaches of honor, Indians will be homeless indefinitely.

Notes

1   The term Native American refers to Census-designated American Indians/ Alaska Natives. American Indians/Alaska Natives are people having origins in any of the original peoples of North and South America (including Central America), and who maintain tribal affiliation or community attachment. American Indian lands refer collectively to American Indian Areas and Alaska Native Areas, as used by the Census Bureau. They include American Indian Reservations, American Indian Off-Reservation Trust Lands, American Indian Tribal Subdivisions, Oklahoma Tribal Statistical Areas, State Designated American Indian Statistical Areas, Tribal Designated Statistical Areas, Alaska Native Regional Corporations, and Alaska Native Statistical Areas.

2   Sections of this quantitative overview rely heavily on HAC (2002) which draws its data from several sources: The 2000 Census of Population and Housing, the 2001 American Housing survey compiled by HUD and the Census Bureau, the 2000 Current Population Survey from the Census Bureau, Year 2000 data gathered under the Home Mortgage Disclosure Act, and other federal agencies.

3   The 2000 Population Census data on race and AIANHH populations are not directly comparable with data from earlier censuses because self-identification is new. For factors influencing self-identification, see US Commission on Civil Rights (2003).

4   For purposes of this paper, rural and nonmetro will be used interchangeably and refer to places defined by the Office of Management and Budget as nonmetropolitan in 1999. See Appendix A in HAC (2002).

5   A small part of this seeming incongruity is probably due to the "checkerboarding" of reservation lands going back to the Dawes Act. However, much of it comes from the BIA's Native American Lands classification for Alaska Native Villages and Oklahoma Statistical Tribal Areas. In these sizeable areas, land is not set aside in trust, and tribal land is mixed with that of the non-Indian community. For example, much of the entire state of Oklahoma is considered tribal lands.

6   Cluster housing is single-unit detached government-assisted rental housing built, for the most part, in small clusters. It was first offered by HUD in the 1960s. Even though Native Americans were accustomed to living on their

own parcels, many moved into cluster housing to have access to better housing and modern utilities. Now such housing has deteriorated and is often referred to as "reservation ghettos," with a full complement of ghetto problems (HAC, 2002).

7   This statistic may inflate Native homeownership somewhat. For example, HUD's Mutual Help housing program is a lease-purchase program. Many participants do not yet have title to these units but may identify themselves as homeowners. Were mutual-help occupants excluded, the homeownership rate for Native Americans on tribal lands would likely drop to significantly lower levels (HAC, 2002).

8   These 1970 crowding statistics were for Indian Reservations Identified by the Bureau of Indian Affairs with an Indian population of 2,300 or more. The data exclude Indians living on trust lands outside reservations. These crowding figures are not directly comparable with those of other censuses (US Dept. of Commerce, 1973).

9   On trust lands, 57 percent of family households that include a grandparent and a child under the age of 18 have grandparents acting as caregivers for their grandchildren (versus 42 percent in the total US population) (HAC, 2002).

10 Crowding surely reduces homelessness even as it brings new problems. A recent National American Indian Housing Council (NAIHC) study links domestic crowding and the substandard housing conditions that often accompany it to increased incidences of tuberculosis, pneumonia, gastrointestinal disorders, head lice, conjunctivitis, hepatitis, and various other infectious diseases that are easily transmitted in crowded spaces. Lower educational attainment among children and social problems like alcoholism, domestic violence, and child abuse and/or neglect are also associated with severely crowded living conditions.

11 Under the terms of the Louisiana Purchase, Jefferson's government pledged to protect "the inhabitants of the ceded territory...in the free enjoyment of their liberty, property and the religion they profess." Cited in Churchill (1993:40). See Smith (1957: Chapter 16) for the logic and legacy of this policy.

12 The treaties signed between 1778 and 1860 numbered 250 and accounted for over 450 million acres (Wolf, 1981), considerably more than all the land held today by the largest land-holding federal agency, the Bureau of Land Management.

13 Allotments to Indians – a transfer of small individual holdings in exchange for large collectively held domains – date back to 1633 in colonial times (Gibson, 1980). Exempted from the General Allotment Act were the Five Civilized Tribes, the Osages, the Senecas, the Miami, Peorik, Sac, and Fox (ibid., 498).

14 The Act contained a provision (probably copied by the Alaskan Native Claims Act of 1971) that froze all land transactions and gave Indian "owners" an opportunity to adjust to the new legislation.

15 This phenomenon is also explained by the fact these lands include large reservation and community lands that are not set aside in Trust, thus permitting non-Indians to purchase and settle at will. Tribal trust lands are held in Trust for the tribe by the Department of Interior, but ownership remains with the tribe. Allotted or individual trust land applies to land owned by individual tribal members but held in Trust by DOI. It is common for allotted Trust lands to be owned by several individuals.

16 Only 588 people of the full Pine Ridge population of 15,000 to 20,000 people were officially homeless. During 1999, Shannon County residents applied for a total of 228 mortgage loans. Nearly 78 percent of these applied to subprime or mobile home lenders, while only 22 percent of all applications were processed by lenders classified as mainstream or prime.

17 In the nineteenth century, tribes themselves often gave asylum to the remnants of other tribes, and occasionally Quakers and secular groups made provision for Indians severed from their homelands (Wallace, 1960).

18 Funds disbursed under NAHSDA have few restrictions. There are six eligible affordable housing activities which NAHSDA funds may be used for. Homelessness is not explicitly stated among these (NLIHC, 2003).

Chapter 4

Quasi-homelessness among rural trailer-park households in the United States

Sonya Salamon and Katherine MacTavish

Introduction

In the last three decades of the twentieth century mobile or manufactured home parks, typically known as trailer parks, became common across the rural United States. Trailer parks, particularly those parks catering to families with children (rather than those populated by the retired) house those of modest means and provide them access to their dream – an affordable separate, stand-alone home in a rural setting. In most US trailer parks homeowners rent rather than own the land beneath their homes. Owning a mobile home but being landless, or renting both home and land, is not a state of homelessness. But landlessness is central to why trailer-park homeowners or renters share *quasi-homelessness*. They have a home, whether shabby or plush, but due to specific financial, structural, and social insecurities connected with living in a privately owned trailer park and being landless, they are at risk of homelessness. We show that a rural trailer-park family can rapidly lose everything, particularly where there is scarce affordable housing. Such a threat makes people fear homelessness, despite owning a home – or at least owning a mortgage on a mobile home. Each of the three insecurities – financial, structural, and social – will be considered in turn as a potential risk of homelessness, for trailer-park homeowners as well as renters. Examples are drawn from field studies of trailer-park communities in Illinois, New Mexico, North Carolina, and Oregon. Finally, we conclude by considering the link between the potential quasi-homelessness status of mobile-home park dwellers in the context of evolving rural land tenure patterns. First, some basic information about US mobile-home or trailer-park communities.

A mobile-home community differs fundamentally from other rural communities of place because a park is the private property of a landowner who runs it as a profit-making enterprise. As private property, community governance is not democratic; who owns the land or manages a park for the owner makes and enforces the rules by which residents must live. Owners either regulate residents' lives with a code of rules or abdicate any responsibility for residents' behaviors. Yet, despite these constraints, a mobile-home park is a popular rural residential choice among those of modest means. Parks provide access to an affordable separate, stand-alone home in a small community for people who we found share a profoundly rural identity (Hummon, 1990).

A trailer park emerges when a land developer clusters individual mobile homes densely on one site. Because the US Census does not ask whether a trailer home is located in a park, park numbers are only a speculation. The proportion of all housing represented by manufactured or mobile homes across the US is represented in Figure 4.1. Almost half the nation's 8.8 million mobile homes (the fastest growing type of housing) are situated in what the industry estimates as the 50,000–60,000 mobile-home or manufactured-home communities that exist in the US (Consumer Reports, 1998; Ruditsky 1994; US Census Bureau, 2003). A mobile-home community or trailer park may have as many as 600 units, with a 1,500 resident population equivalent to that of a small town, but typically has fewer than 200 units. In the US about half of mobile-home communities are found in rural areas for several reasons (Geisler and Mitsuda, 1987). Urban zoning often excludes trailer parks and rural zoning and housing codes are notoriously more lax than city codes. These conditions and cheap land make rural places differentially attractive for park developers and investors.

Four types of mobile-home communities are found in the United States (Ruditsky, 1994; O'Hare and O'Hare 1993; US Census Bureau, 2003). First, are the *seasonal park communities* largely populated by retired couples in the Sun Belt who traverse a circular migration route from the South to the North on an annual basis in recreational vehicles (the self-propelled RV), or with trailers pulled by cars or trucks. Some seasonal parks house permanent residents. Second are the *rental mobile-home* communities in which the landlord owns the land and the homes, and rents to tenants – often the only affordable housing available to impoverished rural families. Found adjacent to railroad tracks, highways, junkyards and water treatment plants on the edge of small towns, rental parks are typically shabby. Popular media images liken the rental parks to a rural version of an inner-city ghetto, given the dense concentration of households with too few resources, too many children, and dogs who "don't just bark, they bite" (Dean, 1999: 134). Rental parks perpetuate the negative stereotype of trailer parks as transient places housing a fair share of "hard living," poor, less well-educated people subject to job and housing instability (Howell, 1973). The Oregon field study targeted such parks. A third type, termed a *land-lease park community*, mixes retired households and families with children in places where residents own their homes but the land on which they sit is rented from the park owner. These parks were the focus of the Illinois, New Mexico, and North Carolina field studies. Such parks may have large lots for newer, double-wide homes or have older, single-wide units on smaller lots. Finally, a newer variation of the third type is a form of *cooperative, or subdivision community*, where residents own both their home and the land. Rural rental parks and land-lease parks are the focus of this chapter –

Mobile homes as a
percent of all housing
by state

13.1 to 20.3
7.6 to 13.0
3.3 to 7.5
0.1 to 3.2

US percent 7.6

Mobile homes as a
percent of all housing
by state

33.3 to 60.5
20.6 to 33.2
7.6 to 20.5
3.3 to 7.5
0.1 to 3.2

US percent 7.6

0 ⊢——⊣ 100 miles

0 ⊢——⊣ 100 miles

0 ⊢——⊣ 100 miles

4.1 Mobile home prevalence by US county, 2000. Source: obtained from US Census Bureau (2003) *Structural and Occupancy Characteristics of Housing: 2000*; Census 2000 Summary File 3.

Note: American Factfinder at http://factfinder.census.gov provides census data and mapping tools. Data based on sample. For information on confidentiality protection, sampling error, nonsampling error and definitions see http://www.census.gov/prod/cen2000/doc/sf3.pdf.

residents of the other types are not likely to be threatened by the quasi-homelessness status.

Owning a home is in all likelihood the largest single investment most Americans make. In contrast to the European middle class who are often life-time renters, Americans share a high priority for homeownership (Perin, 1977; Tremblay and Dillman, 1983). Homeownership is favored by the US federal tax policies by privileging those who own a home over those who rent. After homeownership, the national housing preference is to own a conventional or 'stick' home (not manufactured), that is detached (stands alone), and has a private space (a yard or garden). Ownership of conventional housing is nationally equated with residential stability, financial worth, better communities, voting regularly, and more civic pride when compared with home renters (Putnam, 2000). Mobile-home owners, due to stereotypes about a housing form clouded by quasi-homelessness, are not awarded the same positive image as other homeowners. But the owned-home icon of the American dream also inspires mobile-home owners and renters.

Insecurities underlying quasi-homelessness for trailer-park families

Mobile-home owners and renters who live in rural trailer parks are at risk of homelessness for similar reasons to those housing trends identified for the rural poor in New York state on the edge of homelessness: supply and demand

4.2 Illinois land-lease park

imbalance, insecure tenancy, rising rent burden, proliferation of land-use regulations and housing codes, and higher uses for rural land (Fitchen, 1991, 1992). The last factor is also seen as fostering UK rural homelessness (Cloke *et al.*, 2002).

Financial insecurity

Homeownership as an ideology is fundamentally a desire for security against the dread of homelessness. The antithesis of homelessness is having a place where one is known and belongs (Stone, 1993). Self-worth is eroded by the inability to own a home in the US. At minimum, the desire for homeownership among the poor is a hope for social mobility of one's children. In rural communities, common knowledge is accurate about who owns or rents a home, or is homeless. Lacking the anonymity of the city, a rural family experiences great pressure to strive for homeownership, of any form. Circumstances, however, conspire to make mobile-home owners as insecure as renters. High interest mortgages, exploitative lot rents or eviction, capricious park management, or sale of park land for a "higher use" all foster household financial vulnerability, particularly when the land beneath the home is controlled by another.

First, lending practices are predatory for those of modest means (Berenson, 2001). Unlike conventional homebuyers, most homeowners (85 percent) purchase mobile homes with personal property or chattel loans rather than mortgages because these loans are easier to obtain. But chattel loans carry high interest rates (up to 13.5 percent) as they have no up-front costs and are financed by sub-prime lending companies or finance companies. Given these low-income buyers with few financial resources, 30-year mortgages are common. Conventional homes, as a real estate investment, tend to appreciate in value over time. In contrast, mobile homes tend to depreciate in value. After about three years the typical mobile home has a wholesale value of only about half its original price. After twenty years, a family accrues little value on their investment in a mobile home while paying more proportionately for it than a conventional homeowner. Such lending practices continue because the typical manufactured-home buyer is considered a risky investment. Repossessions climbed as high as 20 for every 100 sold in 2001 according to the industry, which acknowledges that loans were made to those who could not afford them (Fuguay, 2001). Additional factors exacerbate the financial woes of mobile-home owners.

Second, it is in the best interest of the mobile-home distributors, who are often also park owners, to lock in long-term tenants. Management practices therefore tend to foster owners' park maintenance goals rather than residents' goals for conventional homeownership. Park owners as distributors urge people to trade up, by financing a newer, more expensive unit. If like car dealers, mobile-home dealers keep monthly payments the same, residents do not feel financially more challenged by trading up. A park owner with newer units, of course, has a more attractive community to entice new tenants. A park owner in Illinois, where mobile homes comprise only 3.2 percent of all housing, sent his older, traded-in units to Kentucky or Tennessee where mobile homes are more prevalent (see Figure 4.1 and Table 4.1) and there is a market for used units (MacTavish, 2001). In North Carolina (where mobile homes constitute 16.4 percent of all homes) the county ordinances required units be ten years old or newer to combat used-market practices (Eley, 2004; US Census Bureau, 2003). Given the rarity of a park household fulfilling dreams of a conventional home, trading up to a better unit in the same park is the next best option. But the financial costs are high. Because of depreciation an owner receives little for a used unit. In the 1990s a loan was more than a unit's worth after just a few years.

Third, owners and tenants are captive to the whims of the park owner/landlord, with little recourse. Trailer homeownership is not conducive to accumulation of household equity or savings (Apgar *et al.*, 2002; Hurley, 2001). A mobile-home purchase or the trade-up option mires families in chronic debt. If a family falls on bad times due to a job loss or for another reason cannot make their mortgage payments, they can quickly lose everything. Because a mobile-home community is private property and few states have statutes regulating evictions, residents are subject to eviction without due process, in instances of conflict with the park owner or neighbors. A national scarcity of trailer sites has allowed absentee park owners or managers to act arbitrarily toward tenants by raising rents or enforcing restrictive regulations – from the number of pets allowed

Table 4.1 Prevalence of manufactured/ mobile homes in US by location

US Housing	Total	% Manufactured/mobile homes
All housing units	115,904,641	7.6
US Region		
Northeast	22,180,440	3.0
Midwest	26,963,635	5.4
South	42,382,546	11.6
West	24,378,020	7.1
Study states		
Illinois	4,885,615	3.2
New Mexico	780,579	18.6
North Carolina	3,523,944	16.4
Oregon	1,452,709	10.3

Source: Compiled from US Census Bureau (2003) *Structural and Occupancy Characteristics of Housing: 2000.*

to the color of homes or whether a car can be repaired in the driveway. Given the prohibitive costs for moving a trailer, owners have little choice but to relinquish their property rights or home if evicted by a park landlord according to residents in all four sites.

Owners of trailer parks look to the monthly site rental as an income source. (In the heyday of the 1990s boom, trailer parks were touted as an excellent investment for which owners need only drive by monthly and pick up the check, according to Ruditsky, 1994.) Park owners are known to dramatically raise lot rents or cancel leases, particularly if the land has appreciated in value due to urban sprawl (see Leland, 2003). Sudden and capricious lot rent increases in low-end rental trailer parks are devastating, where a change of 10 percent or $25 in the lot rent represents a substantial draw on household income. Likewise, the hidden costs of extra fees for children, parking, and pets can present insurmountable struggles that push a household toward transience or even over the edge into homelessness. Mobile-home owners squeezed between the expensive trap of the chattel mortgage, the escalating monthly rental costs for a park site, the restrictive regulations and codes used by management, and prohibitive costs of moving their home, have few options but to continue as land-lease park residents.

While not subject to predatory lending and chattel loans, rent-to-own home sales common in rental trailer parks also place low-income households in financial jeopardy. With a rent-to-own agreement, residents are told that, after a fixed period, often five years of paying rent, they will own the trailer. Rent-to-own is appealing to landlords as it essentially absolves them of maintenance for an aging trailer by transferring those often substantial costs to poor tenants. Households who, given their precarious financial situation, could never dream of home-ownership through more conventional means, are lured by these arrangements into assuming they will gain greater control over their housing. Yet, actual ownership rarely happens. The financial insecurities of tenants' situations ensure they will move well before the agreed ownership transfer is reached. When a tenant abandons a rent-to-own agreement, not only is the hope of social mobility lost, but investments of time, energy, and money on maintenance and repairs are lost as well. For others, however, the lack of ability to make repairs and the declining condition of the home encourages a move. In Oregon we found aging trailers in shabby rental parks that were "sold" over and over until finally too dilapidated to function as shelter.

Finally, high utility costs associated with mobile homes aggravate the financial insecurity of the rural poor. Energy costs in the US are a direct cause of homelessness among poor households (NEADA, 2004). For families receiving public assistance (Temporary Assistance of Needy Families), the monthly energy burden averages about a quarter (26 percent) of household income. In an aging

4.3 Oregon rental park

trailer with poor insulation, monthly energy bills topping $200 were not unusual in Oregon. Such costs consume a household's monthly income and force hard choices between paying the light and heat bill or the rent. Older and ill-maintained appliances, manufactured long before development of fuel-efficient units, only compound the problem. One urban study found a quarter of evictions due to electric and gas service termination and 40 percent to water cut-offs (Copeland, 1997). A social service worker explains how high energy costs push households toward homelessness:

> People get roped in before they realize how much it's going to cost to pay the bills. They don't earn enough to pay the rent and bills so they use the rent money to pay the electric bill. You can't live without lights or heat, right? Eventually, when they do this for long enough, they have to move out.

Housing affordability is a particularly pressing issue facing low-income rural renter households. Currently, over a third of rural renters fit the classification "housing cost burdened" or those whose housing costs consume over 30 percent of household income (HAC, 2003). For mobile-home renters, the housing cost burden rate climbs to 40.7 percent (see Table 4.2 for relative cost comparison by housing type). Renting a mobile home in the US on average consumes 32 percent of household income (US Census, 2001a). Thus, while attracted by the notion of affordability, people move into a rental trailer park only to find that, as in land-lease parks, hidden costs in reality make this housing form less than affordable.

Home structural insecurity

Consumer groups report a long history of serious home quality and safety problems generated by the mobile-home industry. Manufacturers resisted federal guidelines for manufactured home-construction to improve safety and construction, implemented in 1974. Rural families with children tend to buy lower-end or used models (the average owner-occupied mobile home was constructed in 1984) in comparison with retired households (one-third of the population) who more often can afford better construction and timely maintenance. Most builders offer only a one-year warranty on a new manufactured home. Yet even in newer homes – those less than five years old – we found homeowners to incur surprisingly high costs for repair or replacement of basic structural features: doors, windows, floors, and roofs. In a survey of mobile-home owners by Consumers Union (2002) many were satisfied with their home, but a majority (including those whose homes were less than five years old) had had a least one major problem. One-fourth had the particleboard subfloors swell when wet and break down, over one-third had plumbing problems such as leaky sinks and showers. Almost one-third had experienced leaking windows, doors and roofs. A major HUD study found that over a ten-year period, a manufactured home when exposed to normal wind conditions was five times more likely to incur structural failure than a conventionally built home. Because a manufactured

Table 4.2 Relative cost of US housing by type

	Owner-occupied units	Owner-occupied manufactured/ mobile homes	Renter-occupied manufactured/ mobile homes
Median purchase price	$68,945	$25,212	Not available
Median value	$123,830	$27,474	Not available
Median year acquired	1992	1995	Not available
Median monthly cost	$685	$394	$498[a]
Median cost as % of income	18.2	16.9	32.0
% Housing cost burdened [b]	23.5	25.1	40.7

Source: American Housing Survey of the United States: 2001.
Notes: a Median rental cost for mobile homes likely reflects lot rent as a portion of cost.
       b Housing cost burden occurs when a households spends 30 percent or more of monthly income on housing.

home must be transported to a site, structural damage may occur in transit or during installation (*Consumer Reports*, 1998; Zuckman, 1990).

Living in a trailer confers potential health risks from air pollution, fire and water, in addition to wind damage (Huss-Ashmore and Behrman, 1999). First, the structure and materials of the mobile home pose air pollution risks greater than those of a conventional home. Mobile homes typically are constructed with extensive use of pressed wood products such as plywood and particleboard. In the relatively small-sized mobile homes (most commonly a single-wide home), being airtight, as required by federal manufacturing guidelines, means higher concentrations of pollutants such as formaldehyde than in other home types. A large California survey of 1,000 mobile-home residents found elevated indoor formaldehyde levels related to the physical symptoms of burning eyes and skin, fatigue, sleeping problems, dizziness, chest pains and sore throat (Liu *et al.*, 1991). The negative effect held even when age, sex, smoking status and chronic respiratory or allergy problems were controlled for. If residents are also smokers, the airtight homes and the interaction of tobacco smoke with other common pollutants means the potential health risk for children in particular can be high, especially in seasons when residents are more often indoors.

Another prominent health risk in mobile homes is an elevated fire risk. Mobile homes have twice the rate of fire deaths than all other home types combined (Zuckman, 1990; Runyan *et al.*, 1992; Parker *et al.*, 1993; Mobley *et al.*, 1994). In a manufactured home the likelihood that fire is fatal is high. Smoke detectors in mobile homes, unlike conventional homes, give little protective effect. Mobile homes not only are small, but also are built with a high proportion of flammable materials that allow a fire to build quickly. If the home is older this increases the fire risk. If residents smoke or consume alcohol, the risk of a fire-related death is higher in all housing, including mobile homes. Of course, higher smoking rates are associated with the population drawn to a manufactured home for its affordability. Because of their propensity to burn quickly and to the ground, mobile homes built before 1974, common to rental parks, are often referred to as "matchsticks" or "firetraps" (Shanklin, 2003).

Across housing types in the non-metro US, renters are twice as likely as homeowners to live in housing deemed moderately to severely structurally inadequate (HAC, 2003). Compared to conventional housing with an expected useful life of hundreds of years, the manufactured housing industry reports an average useful life for manufactured homes of 57.5 years while other sources report a much shorter 22-year median life-span (Jewell, 2001; Meeks, 1998). Many of the structural issues found are exacerbated as a trailer ages. Holes caused by disintegrating particleboard flooring or deteriorated door, for example, are a direct danger and also make it hard to keep out rodents and pests. In some rental trailer parks (where the median home is likely to be over 23 years old), parents resorted to carrying young children at all times to protect them from various physical dangers, both structural and animal, in their aging rural trailer home (Edwards, 2004; US Census 2001b). Doubling-up or even tripling-up is a well-documented cost-saving strategy among renter families, but when employed in a trailer, over-crowding can be severe. The average size of a manufactured home represents half the living area of the typical conventional home in rural areas. Older single-wide units common to rental parks are on average much smaller, with second bedrooms being barely large enough to accommodate a single bed and a chest of drawers. Over-crowding, where there is less than one room per person, is reported for 9.2 percent of all renter-occupied trailers, as compared to 3.4 percent of all single-unit detached housing (US Census Bureau, 2001c; 2003). The challenge of maintaining sanitary living conditions for several families in such a tight space can exceed the limited resources of low-income families (Fitchen, 1992; Edwards, 2004).

Together, the high interest rates, the rapid depreciation and physical deterioration of homes, escalating site rents, high utility bills, and the expense of moving a home constitute substantial hidden costs for mobile-home owners and renters associated with financial and structural insecurities of mobile-home park residence. It is clear why many families regret being sucked into buying or living in a mobile home without understanding the financial obligations that make it less affordable over the long term than is initially apparent. What began as access to affordable housing can become for its owners or renters of modest means an "expensive trap" (Williams, 1998).

Social insecurity

Land-lease and rural rental trailer-park residence produce social insecurities that compound the poor's vulnerability. Rural people typically possess a strong sense of place and attachment derived from generations of the same families sharing a history and culture (Hummon, 1990; Salamon, 1992, 2003). Mobile-home owners and renters in our parks are uniformly self-identified as rural and small-town people, but lack attachment to the place where they live, despite its being rural (Hummon, 1990; Low and Altman, 1992). A park is not a source of place identity because residents prefer moving on to something better, epitomizing the US cultural ideal of social mobility. Their dedication to mobility – a sense of transience – exerts a distancing mechanism on daily life. Park residents are not rooted in place nor have a sense that their home is permanent (it is somewhat mobile after all). They do not want their children to live in a park as adults. Thus, lacking an attachment to place (other than the place of origin or the place of dreams) may prevent park families from developing the sense of permanence associated with rural life.

Mobile homes and trailer parks, as shelters and places, inherently are settings of transience, whether in reality or psychologically. Several medical anthropologists liken the impermanence and rootlessness trailer-park households live in to a "permanently transitional community" (Huss-Ashmore and Behrman, 1999). They argue that having an ideology of transition means a park environment has substantial social costs for families because a sense of place or centeredness on a home is essential for emotional well-being. In a study of Walla Walla, Washington, trailer parks Huss-Ashmore and Behrman (1999: 82) found similar to our parks that residents view their trailer home as "we are only here for now, until we can 'make it' and move on." They found that a sense of rootlessness has unfortunate health outcomes while an ideology of impermanence as "selecting for flexibility" allowed people to cope with their present situation as being only temporary. Other factors such as instability of jobs and the unpredictability of landlords cause even urban trailer-park dwellers to dream of moving into a rural area in a "real" home; the same dream held by our rural park dwellers. Without land ownership, trailer-park residents as tenants lack security against displacement from their homes, lack control over the form and uses of their homes, and of course are not full members of the wider community (Stone, 1993: 18).

Analogies to an inner-city ghetto, for the apparent power of place to shape family well-being and child development, readily emerge for rural trailer parks. While the popular media tends to overdraw the ghetto-like analogies, rental parks do attract a concentration of hard-living residents or what one Oregon social worker termed "the lowest of the low income – families that are half a check away from homelessness at best." Such parks are socially fluid places with the average household moving after only six to eight months in residence. In such a context, levels of mutual trust run low while fears about other residents abound. In an effort to counter perceived negative influences, parents employ child management strategies used in risky urban contexts (see Jarrett, 1995). They drastically limit their children's exposure to the neighborhood, keeping them indoors and off park streets when they are not in school (Edwards, 2004; MacTavish, 2001). Further, many parents limit their own social engagement in these park neighborhoods to avoid entering into potential dependency relationships they lack the resources to support. Day-to-day life within such contexts is vastly removed from the socially supportive community culture expected of rural, small town life.

Sharing a sense of impermanence we found trailer-park households, whether homeowners or renters, do not identify their park as a real community. Households showed an unwillingness to forge substantive links with neighbors, who they expect to move on (MacTavish, 2001; MacTavish and Salamon, 2001). Without a local social network, park households lack a sense of community – or a positive identification with where they live and their neighbors. Furthermore, lacking attachment to the park, people neither engaged in nor cared for the park's common areas in ways that would make their community a better place to live (Wilson, 1987). These traits are a contrast with the importance of community to the stable working-class where resources are exchanged among kin and friends for economic and social support (Kefalas, 2003). Without kin and neighbors as social or financial supports, recognized as important to survival of those who share their socioeconomic status, trailer-park households lack important ingredients to their social and economic well-being.

Faced with tight rural rental housing options, low-income families often make choices that meet their short-term housing needs but that socially imperil them over the long run. A rural social worker explains how some families move into a park rental situation expecting to be evicted:

> These families know they don't have enough to pay the rent and the utilities and afford anything else. They sign a contract for a place where the rent is 100% of their income. Then they can't pay the rent and the utilities not to mention food. But these are families who are in a constant state of crisis.

When an eviction occurs in a small town, a family reputation develops. A "ne'er-do-well" reputation only exacerbates a poor family's potential for integration in a rural community (Fitchen, 1991; Ziebarth *et al.*, 1997; Salamon, 2003). A rural housing authority worker explains the dilemma of rural renters, "We see it every day, landlords are getting pickier and pickier about who they will rent to. If you've been evicted you really can't find a place." A bad reputation as a renter in a small town thus can speed a family along a path toward homelessness.

Social insecurities are enhanced by how the wider community or region spatially treats residents of a rural trailer park. Several factors demonstrate that for trailer-park residents a system of spatial inequality operates to ensure that park residents remain persistently poor, despite their personal best efforts to shape their own destiny (Tickamyer, 2000). Social insecurities are constant for trailer-park residents who do not make community rules, who are subject to management whim, and who own or rent a home that is a financial entrapment.

Park residence is a stigmatizing category that to a certain extent makes families pariahs in a rural community – a mechanism that perpetuates inequality. Using the attribute of park residence as a stigma, members of nearby communities establish a stereotyped relationship between park living and categorization of residents as bad people (Goffman, 1963; MacTavish and Salamon, 2001). For example, in one case when Illinois park residents had their address discovered, former friends from the adjacent town stopped speaking to them and in another case a high-school couple was forced to stop dating when a youth's home was made known to the girl's parents. Townspeople consistently denigrated park residents as free-loaders who gain a fine education, although they do not pay for it (Salamon, 2003). Theft of items or deviant behavior was typically attributed to park residents. Such beliefs and actions contribute to a stigmatized identity and form barriers to better life chances, particularly for youth, despite being based on unverifiable innuendo. These boundaries effectively reinforce already existing unequal categories of class or ethnicity, and thus contribute to durable inequalities (Tilly, 1999).

Segregation in a rural trailer park, often on the edge of town, means that residents seldom cross paths with people who live in an adjacent community but differ by class. Without social contacts, stigmas based on lack of knowledge are enhanced creating the stigma of being "the other" that becomes more difficult to erase through personal knowledge (Goffman, 1963). The spatial barriers created when park families are excluded from the wider community foster a system of spatial inequality. Segregated families absorb the stereotypes associated with living in a trailer park. That they are defined as "trailer trash," despite having managed to buy a home, is a belief rampant in the parks. This stigma inhibits behavior among park families who feel marginalized through no action of their own (MacTavish and Salamon, 2001). That is, the rural park as a space, because it is a distinctive and segregated place and inhabited by those of modest means, represents social relations of power between residents and non-residents (including park owners) that disadvantages residents and limits their local opportunities and comparative outcomes (Tickamyer, 2000).

Social control by the wider community is enforced by excluding mobile homes through zoning, and lax legal systems regarding homeowners' rights with eviction and redevelopment of parks. Shabby housing or manufactured housing is not viewed as high use for rural land in a suburbanized landscape, particularly where the subdivisions developed are more upscale. Similarly, where second homes owned by affluent urbanites have consumed the housing that lower income rural residents might once have occupied, rural housing values increase. Rural gentrification creates pressures for land-use ordinances to exclude or marginalize new parks to areas of the county or other less well-off nearby communities (Fitchen, 1991; Leland, 2003). Thus trailer parks, as rural housing, in emerging ways spatially reflect new social divisions and/or persistence of previous social inequities in new contexts. Mobile-home parks, as the affordable housing in a rapidly transforming upscale, suburbanized area, tend to lodge the workers who occupy the service jobs that support a more affluent lifestyle of second-home owners, rural tourism, or retirees. The divisions may evolve into an equity issue of the center (those areas growing more upscale) versus the periphery (those areas housing the lower income service providers). In this way trailer parks reflect and represent visually the growing inequality between the classes in rural places. As places, the parks may be viewed as an expression of the power relations in the wider area that in a new way defines who belongs to a place and who may be excluded.

Rural trailer-park households along with their housing tenure-ladder ideology (see next section) share insecurity about keeping their homes. Their insecurity is underscored by an abiding dissatisfaction with achieving only half the American homeownership dream. Two sources fuel this sense of insecurity. First, because they live in a trailer park, families lack real financial and structural security about their sustaining a permanent site for their homes. Second, households who feel vulnerable about keeping their homes do not develop the strong sense of place that typically characterizes rural residents. They maintain a social insecurity or a sense of impermanence. These vulnerability factors inherent to mobile-home life reinforce a quasi-homeless status. They have a home but can lose it in a heartbeat if the park is sold, rents for lot or home are raised, or if the park management reneges on their right to live there.

The "agricultural tenure ladder" and a rural "housing tenure ladder"

> Tenancy has never been a desirable position for residents of the United States. The drive to own has obsessed the people from the yeoman farmer to the modern suburbanite. Being a tenant has never been part of the "American dream," the status of tenants in this society has never been secure or comfortable.
>
> (Heskin, 1983: xi)

Rural society once possessed a social structure fundamentally based on landowner-ship (Newby, 1980). In today's rural society, more suburban than agrarian, housing is the form of landownership that underlies the local social system (Salamon, 2003). We now turn to fascinating parallels between the ideologies of the agricultural tenure-ladder concept current in the first half of the twentieth century, especially among tenant farmers, that lie behind a proposed analogous housing tenure-ladder dream prevalent among trailer-park homeowners and renters.

Ownership of rural farmland was historically likened to an *agricultural or tenure ladder* whose rungs a farmer (and by implication the farm family) gradually ascended over the course of a lifetime (Spillman, 1919). Where land is expensive, such as in the Corn Belt, the high cost of farming ensured that the classical tenure-ladder metaphor, climbing the rungs from tenancy to full ownership of farmland, was never realized by a large proportion of farm families. Few mounted the agricultural tenure ladder without the assistance of inheritance or other access to family-owned land (Kloppenburg and Geisler, 1985; Salamon, 1992). In fact, the metaphor was abandoned after the 1950s as lacking explanatory value. It is clear the tenure ladder was an ideology about social mobility that never reflected reality about land tenure or rural social systems. The ideology was that hard work, competence, and diligence were essential to ascending the tenure ladder. But social inequalities based on access and control of land were and are almost impossible to overcome (Salamon, 1992; Strange, 1988). Kloppenburg and Geisler (1985) demonstrate conclusively that the tenure-ladder concept as a motivating ideology straddled a major transition in agriculture from family farms to an industrial model based on tenancy. The ideology smoothed the transition by giving hope to those mired at the ladder's bottom in the context of ongoing land and farm concentration.

We propose that a *housing tenure ladder* exists in rural trailer parks having close parallels to the ideology and social inequalities associated with the agricultural tenure ladder. Families, whether mobile-home owners or renters, we found desire to own a conventional home on owned land. Renters are socially equivalent to hired laborers on farms. Thus, a rented home in a trailer park represents the initial tenure-ladder rung, a tenure status that ranks above subsidized housing or apartment rental. Those families able to skip the bottom/rental rung have sufficient savings for an initial payment on a trailer; although during much of the 1990s little or no down payment was needed to obtain a mortgage (Berenson, 2001). Therefore, the second rung of this new rural tenure ladder involves mobile-home ownership via buying a used home on contract from the previous owner or purchasing a repossessed or trade-in older home from a dealer, but renting the land/site on which it sits in a trailer park.

Mobile-home owners assume ownership will help them accumulate the resources necessary to accomplish their mounting the housing ladder. Their work, given the bad jobs (minimum wage, few benefits, irregular schedules, often part-time) available in rural America and the insecurities outlined above, are real barriers to their achieving social or occupational mobility (Nelson and Smith, 1999). Like the farm families where land is expensive, most trailer-park families never mount the tenure ladder high enough to own a "stick" or conventional home and its land. In fact, due to the financial, structural and social insecurities outlined above, families are vulnerable to losing it all and falling downward on the tenure ladder.

The housing tenure ladder reflects the spatial inequalities in the post-agrarian countryside as did the agricultural tenure ladder in the agrarian countryside. For mobile-home owners, their American dream of homeownership remains a dream just as land ownership remained a dream for most farm hands and tenant farmers. Comparable to the agricultural tenure-ladder ideology, the housing tenure ladder has only one or at most two bottom rungs. Whether by virtue of class, gender, ethnicity or being down on their luck, the rural working poor must mount the ladder through dint of their own labor, as did the farm hired-hand. This new tenure ladder straddles a rural transformation from a productive, agrarian economy to a suburbanized economy based on consumption, just as the agricultural tenure ladder straddled two eras in the transformation of agriculture (Kloppenburg and Geisler, 1985; Ritzer, 2001; Salamon, 2004). Family status in small communities is now derived from where and in what home one lives rather than amount of farmland controlled (Brown and Lee, 1999). Having a mobile home in a trailer park therefore constitutes a new configuration of land as a marker of social inequality, and thus land is a persistent component of status in rural society.

Landless farmers according to Kloppenburg and Geisler (1985) were motivated and at the same time trapped by the ideology that hard work produced tenure-ladder ascension. Their social inequality therefore was persistent. Persistent social inequality is likewise intertwined with the "housing tenure ladder", but for different reasons. Mobile-home owners also believe that, by dint of hard work and saving, a move out of the trailer park and up into conventional housing is possible. Yet, few mobile-home owners realize their dream, and therefore their inequality is similarly persistent. Durable inequality for mobile-home owners, rather than being derived from lacking control over a value-producing resource, results from there being an asymmetrical relationship between them and the park owner. The relationship generates consistently greater advantages for landownership, especially when the landowner is also a mobile-home dealer (Tilly, 1999). A park owner's control of land tends to prevent the rights and dreams of his or her tenants.

The high priority for conventional homeownership we uniformly found among park families may be an expression or compensation for alienation from their bad work or class discrimination by the neighboring community. Their strong prioritization for conventional homeownership, however, serves as a control wielded indirectly by the wider community. Stone comments on the home-ownership ideology as a mechanism that undercuts those of modest means organizing on their own behalf:

> [T]he ideal of homeownership as an instrument of social control; and from the promotion and idealization of the home as a vehicle for marketing commodities to facilitate economic growth and profit [for others] – from houses, to cars, to furniture, to appliances …
>
> (Stone, 1993: 30)

A principal contradiction exists for trailer-park families who are homeowners. They have mounted the bottom rung on a housing tenure ladder and thus achieved some validation for their goal of social mobility. But a mobile home remains an imperfect home that can never completely satisfy their housing desires. Because they do not own the land for their home, the park as a community is in many ways also imperfect. They remain dissatisfied despite realizing half the American dream: they own a home but not any land. Rural park families see their inability to mount the housing tenure ladder as a personal failing, due to US society's pervasive ideology of individualism expressed in each household having its own responsibility for bearing the financing burdens for housing acquisition.

Mobile-home park life in an owned home on rental land does not assure a rural family with all of the qualities that satisfactory housing confers: security, autonomy, control, and affordability (Stone, 1993). Further, owning a mobile home is a relatively permanent rung on the homeownership tenure ladder that due to a variety of social and economic reasons does not foster social mobility, or ascension of the ladder. Attaining half the American homeownership dream is regarded as better than renting by the rural park households we interviewed. Yet, despite reaching the bottom rung and our households viewing themselves above those who live in subsidized housing and own nothing, once residence is established in a mobile-home park, a community spatially segregated and homogeneous by social class, it is difficult to mount higher rungs on the housing tenure ladder. Segregation by housing type and class, for primarily the insecurities outlined above, means that trailer owners are caught, just as were landless hired hands, in the conundrum that makes achieving the full American dream so challenging even for those who think by mounting the first rung of a tenure ladder gives them the chance.

Moving into a rental trailer park allows the rural poor to climb out of homelessness. Given the financial, structural, and social insecurities we described for park life, however, renters rather than homeowners are more likely to circle iteratively in and out of homelessness via tenure in a trailer park. Renters may become more secure by climbing the tenure ladder's next rung to homeownership via a windfall – such as inheritance of funds or a contract sale of a repossessed home as in North Carolina, where a dealer wanted to move his inventory. Yet more often, we found life events such as unpredictable jobs, divorce, drugs (for example, the widespread rural problem of methamphetamine), or high debt were related to the persistence of quasi-homelessness of renters more than owners. For homeowners, the liminality of quasi-homelessness was linked to personality clashes with management, and sale of park land, as well as the issues noted for renters. Being a trailer-park homeowner provides a bit more stability than renting a home. Inevitably, however, park residence sustains a rural family's vulnerability to those who control the land, and hence the potential is always lurking for instantly going from having a home to not. Trailers are a solution to a roof over your head but whether an owner or renter the liminal state of quasi-homelessness remains unless people are protected from the problematic consequences of landlessness.

Chapter 5
Homelessness in rural and small town Canada

David Bruce

Introduction

It is well-known that Canadians are a well-housed nation, and that the private market housing system works efficiently and meets the needs of most people. However, for about 16 per cent of the population in this country who fall into what is defined as core housing need, there are very real problems (Carter, 1997). Most of these people are at risk of becoming homeless. In a country where, with the exception of southwest British Columbia (and primarily the cities of Vancouver and Victoria) the weather and climate are particularly unfriendly and not conducive to 'living on the streets', the risk of becoming homeless for an individual or household is a frightening prospect.

Canada is also a very urbanized nation. The 2001 Census of Canada shows that 80 per cent of the population lives in cities, with only 20 per cent living in rural and small town Canada (Statistics Canada, 2003). Here, rural is defined as all incorporated municipalities of less than 10,000 population, plus all rural unincorporated areas not included within the commuter shed of urban centres with 10,000 or more population (du Plessis *et al.*, 2001). Thus, it is not surprising that the focus of homelessness research and programmes and interventions has a very strong urban flavour.

The problems of homelessness, particularly that of at-risk homelessness, in rural and small town Canada are often overlooked and underestimated. Very little has been written on this subject in the Canadian context (Bruce, 2003, Bentley, 1995). This is because many rural and small town households facing the prospects of homelessness move to larger centres in search of social and economic supports (Tota, 2004).

This chapter explores rural homelessness in Canada, with a particular focus on estimates of at-risk homelessness in rural and small town Canada. The chapter begins with a brief overview of the homelessness landscape in Canada, with an emphasis on the current public policy and research foci. I then discuss the general housing and related challenges facing rural households, followed by an assessment of national indicators of core housing need – to serve as a proxy measure of at-risk homelessness – in rural Canada. The chapter then uses evidence from a case study community – St Stephen, New Brunswick – in a rural region of Canada to provide estimates of at-risk homelessness, and to illustrate the challenges that small communities face in addressing the problem. I conclude with a discussion of present and emerging issues related to rural homelessness in rural and small town Canada.

For the purposes of this chapter, at-risk of homelessness refers to anyone at risk of not have their own place to stay because they are spending 50 percent or more of gross household income on shelter costs regardless of tenure, or because they lack security of tenure. Absolute homelessness refers to not having one's own place to stay for the night.

The landscape of homelessness in Canada

In 1999 the federal government established a new cabinet position – Minister Responsible for Homelessness. The minister's responsibility is to coordinate the government's efforts to address a wide range of homelessness issues. More than $600 million in new and reallocated resources was earmarked for the period 1999–2003 under a National Homelessness Initiative (NHI). One of the key elements of this was the Supporting Communities Partnership Initiative (SCPI), designed to create a more integrated and inclusive approach to homelessness. Targeted communities were provided with financial and administrative support for government, private sector and voluntary sector partnership in developing and implementing a local action plan. In addition, the communities were required to secure matching funds from other community sources, and were required to develop a long-term sustainability plan for the activities to continue after SCPI funds were exhausted. The objective of all plans developed under SCPI was to increase the availability and access to a range of services and facilities along the continuum from homelessness to self-sufficiency: emergency shelters – transitional/supportive housing – prevention (Government of Canada, 2003a).

SCPI funds amounted to $305 million over three years in 61 communities. However, 80 per cent of the funds were allocated to 10 major cities with the most serious problems (Vancouver, Calgary, Edmonton, Winnipeg, Hamilton, Toronto, Ottawa, Montreal, Quebec City and Halifax). The remaining funds were distributed across the remaining 51 communities. Each of the centres has a population of at least 10,000, and only Nelson (British Columbia), Wood Buffalo (Alberta), Thompson (Manitoba), Thunder Bay (Ontario), Chicoutimi (Quebec), Bathurst (New Brunswick), Summerside (PEI), and Cape Breton Regional Municipality (Nova Scotia) could be considered urban centres in predominantly rural regions (where the majority of the population in the region served by the centre live in low density, rural areas). Few, if any, of the plans have reached out into the rural and small town areas (Government of Canada, 2003b).

Rural communities lack the capacity to respond to homelessness issues. At-risk individuals and families often move to larger urban centres to access services, and this places a burden on the support within larger centres (Tota, 2004). In recognition of this, the federal government also established the Regional Homelessness Fund (RHF) within the NHI. This is a $13 million fund (over three years) to provide funding and support to proposals from communities not included within the 61 SCPI communities. The objective is to help small communities to establish support services to prevent at-risk individuals and families from becoming homeless and help stabilize their living conditions.

The National Housing Research Committee (NHRC) is coordinated by the Canada Mortgage and Housing Corporation (CMHC) and is designed to coordinate the sharing of research projects and information, stimulate exchange of ideas, and encourage partnerships in articulating, funding, and completing research projects. Membership includes all provinces and territories and major housing stakeholders, including municipalities, NGOs, and other federal departments. The NHRC meets semi-annually and is organized around a variety of working groups and discussion groups. One of these is the Homelessness Working Group, which was initiated in 1994. A review of the meeting notes from the 2000–3 period reveals very little discussion on rural homelessness among the research members (Homelessness Working Group, 2000–3). The concentration of discussion and research is related to pressing urban problems.

Finally, a review of CMHC's Policy and Research Division homelessness projects and activities shows that of the 39 ongoing, current, and completed projects (back to 1995), 17 deal with large urban-specific issues, and 6 deal with the interface between housing and other services (such as health, social services and others, for example, see Frankish *et al.*, 2003). A total of 13 deal with specific groups (such as Aboriginals, those with mental illness or families or the disabled). These categories are not mutually exclusive. There are two which deal with rural-specific issues related to homelessness (Bruce, 2003; Beavis *et al.*, 1997). Going back prior to 1995, a report commissioned by CMHC looking at housing programmes and projects addressing homelessness provided information on only four rural-specific related projects, and found no rural-specific programmes (CMHC, 1995).

The literature review by Beavis *et al.* (1997) on Aboriginal people and homelessness in rural areas noted that there is very little literature on the topic. Most of the research focuses on Aboriginal socio-economic conditions and housing, on urban Aboriginals and street youth, on Aboriginal health issues, and on the Aboriginal 'skid row' lifestyle, all of which point to the preponderance of homelessness as an urban issue. It also notes poor housing and severely depressed conditions on reserves (lands designated by the federal government for the specific purpose of collective Aboriginal settlement) and in remote communities, which lead to rural–urban migration in search of jobs, education and better housing, but leaves Aboriginals vulnerable to poverty, depression, addiction and crime. Continued attachment of urban Aboriginals to reserves may result in hypermobility, regular alternation between city (winter) and reserve (summer), necessitating regular searches for urban accommodation.

Housing and related challenges for rural households

Housing in rural and small town Canada is predominantly owner-occupied (82 per cent), mortgage-free (56 per cent) (Marshall and Bollman, 1999), and single detached dwellings. There is a real lack of housing choice in rural Canada. Bruce (2000a), in a study of rental housing in Atlantic Canada, found that the supply of rental housing is quite limited in rural communities (unincorporated places of less than 1,000 population), and mostly in the form of single detached homes (about 61 per cent of all rural rental supply). In small towns (incorporated places of less than 10,000 population) the profile is a bit more 'urban-like', with one-quarter of the rental stock being single detached units and 62 per cent in multiple unit structures. A study of homelessness in rural British Columbia also identified the lack of housing choice as a problem (VisionLink, 2002).

People on the margins in rural areas also suffer from a lack of transportation options and limited access to a broad range of social programmes and services (such as Legal Aid, emergency shelters), which are often managed and delivered centrally from larger urban communities. VisionLink (2002) noted that these were very real problems for the elderly and for those in abusive situations.

Aboriginal people in rural Canada either live on reserves or off-reserve among the general population. For Aboriginals on-reserve, the special designation of those lands for collective habitation means that there is a lack of security of tenure and the inability to own land or property (it is held in the collective). Furthermore, because there is limited public funding for new housing construction on-reserve to meet the rapid growth in Aboriginal household formation, many households live in crowded (38 per cent) conditions or in houses requiring major repair (35 per cent) (Spurr, 2001). For Aboriginals off-reserve in rural Canada, their housing conditions are quite similar to that of the general population.

Absolute homelessness in rural Canada

The study of low income persons living in rural areas (Bruce, 2003) did not provide evidence of rural homelessness in its case study communities. At best, informants[1] in those ten communities suggested there may be only one or two households or individuals who could be described as being 'absolute homeless' without a permanent place to call home. They would typically be living outside of a small town or community, in a very rural location, perhaps in a tent for part of the year, or in some other modified structure (such as a converted bus or camper). Most informants attributed the lack of absolute homelessness to a variety of factors, including the lack of services for such people in small towns and rural areas (and thus they move on to urban centres), the (usual) presence of an extended family network to help people who are in trouble (taking the form of temporarily 'doubling up' of families, or permitting individuals persons to 'couch surf' for a few days from one home to the next until a more permanent solution can be found), and the relatively lower costs associated with obtaining housing. In short, the informal networks of coping and care in rural areas helps to keep people 'off the roads' and 'out of the woods', masking the short-term presence of absolute homelessness. Individuals and families then either get back on their feet, or head to urban centres for services and help.

Informants did, however, identify the presence of households 'at-risk' of becoming homeless, barely making it from month to month. This has also been found in other case studies conducted in specific rural communities and small towns in Canada (for example, see VisionLink, 2002; Callaghan, 1999).

Core housing as a proxy for at-risk of homelessness

Most Canadian households live in dwellings that are adequate in condition, affordable in relation to their income and suitable in size. Core housing need, developed and defined by CMHC (1991, 1994), involves a two-step approach to determine needs. The first involves the following elements:

- An adequate dwelling does not, in the assessment of the occupants, require major repairs or lack (hot or cold) running water and has a full bathroom.
- The shelter cost for an affordable dwelling must be less than 30 per cent of household pre-tax income.[2]
- A suitable dwelling has enough bedrooms to provide the household with the required amount of space and privacy, taking into account the age and gender of the members using the National Occupancy Standards (NOS) as the measure of space requirements.[3]

Second, to be in core housing need, a household must fall below one or more of these housing standards and lack the financial means to access accommodation that would meet adequacy and suitability standards. The step compares 30 per cent of the pre-tax household income to the median annual rent for adequate and suitable accommodation. A household that pays 50 per cent or more of gross income and is in core need is considered to be at risk of homelessness. However, data are not available in general public tables, except through special tabulations from the Census of Canada, for this calculation, so for the purposes of this discussion, I look at the affordability problem related to the 30 per cent threshold as an indicator of potential to be at risk of homelessness.

In 1996 the percentage of rural households in core housing need was 14 per cent compared to 18 per cent for households in urban areas. It was 16 per cent among the Aboriginal off-reserve rural population. Looking only at those in core housing need, in rural areas, more than 78 per cent of households in core housing need fell below the affordability standard, either alone or in combination with one of the other standards. However, in urban areas that percentage was 95 per cent, and it was 96 per cent among the Aboriginal off-reserve rural population (CMHC, 2000).

Regardless of the type of household in a low income situation, the most common housing problem they face is one of affordability, especially in the private rental market. With limited incomes, a significant proportion goes toward rent and utilities, with little left over for other necessities. A total of 15 per cent of rural households faced affordability problems, as measured by the core housing need model, in 1996; 3.8 per cent of these households are not in core need, and 11.2 per cent of these rural households are in core need.

In a rural context, senior-led households were more likely than non-senior-led households to find themselves in a core housing need situation (which is mostly driven by affordability problems). Non-family households (such as people living alone or unattached individuals living together) are also more likely to find themselves in a core housing need situation. Rural renters are also more likely to be in this situation than rural homeowners (Table 5.1).

Table 5.2 examines incomes, shelter cost, and shelter cost-to-income ratios (STIRs) for rural households. In 1996, the household incomes of rural households in need were less than a third of households not in need ($15,200 as compared to $47,800). The difference in their shelter cost was less than eight dollars. Households in need paid on average $487 dollars a month compared to $495 for households not in need. This small difference in shelter cost combined with a

Table 5.1 Incidence of core housing need among rural households, by type and tenure, 1996, Canada

	Total	*Own*	*Rent*
All households	14.2%	10.3%	30.2%
Senior households	14.8%	10.9%	34.7%
Non-senior households	14.0%	10.1%	29.0%
Family households	11.2%	8.3%	26.3%
Non-family households	27.3%	22.5%	34.3%

Source: CMHC's HIC Database, based on 1996 Census.

Table 5.2 Average income, shelter cost and shelter cost-to-income ratios for rural households by need status, 1996, Canada

		Average income	Average shelter cost	Average STIR
All	Total	$43,160	$495	18
	Not in need	$47,794	$495	14
	In need	$15,156	$487	42
Owner	Total	$46,257	$504	16
	Not in need	$49,727	$504	13
	In need	$16,171	$493	40
Renter	Total	$30,297	$458	26
	Not in need	$37,481	$446	17
	In need	$13,716	$479	46

Source: CMHC's HIC Database, based on 1996 Census.

large difference in income led to a major difference in the average percentage of income going towards shelter. Households in core housing need spent 42 per cent of their income on shelter compared to only 14 per cent for households not in need. For Aboriginal households living off-reserve in rural Canada, the income, shelter cost and shelter cost-to-income ratio is much the same as for the general rural population. The average income of households in need was less than 40 per cent of that of households not in need

Renters in need had the lowest household income – $13,700 compared to owners $16,200. In fact, renters in need spent more on shelter than renters not in need – $479 compared to $446. As a result the renters in need were spending 46 per cent of their income on shelter.

The need for repair (adequacy) and crowding (suitability) are less frequently problems when compared to that of affordability. A total of 11.3 per cent of rural households have an adequacy problem, and only 4.4 per cent are in core need. Suitability is a smaller problem, with 4.1 per cent of rural households being crowded, and only 0.9 per cent being among those who are in core need.

Core housing need is not calculated for farm households, since it is not always possible to separate the residential expenditures from those related to the farm buildings and property. However, 8,680 (4.7 per cent) of all farm households live in unsuitable or crowded conditions. As well, 22,530 (12.1 per cent) of all farm households fall below the adequacy standard. For the oldest category of dwelling – those built before 1946 – the rate was 18 per cent (CMHC, 2000).

Problems with the rural housing stock

Most rural areas and small towns suffer from a lack of new rental housing construction (Bruce, 2003). The result is very little rental housing choice, characterized by low vacancies, relatively poorer conditions, and higher operating costs. Rental housing problems for low income households may also be compounded by public policies and programmes. For example, in provinces where there is a shelter component to social assistance, the shelter component amount poses some problems. While this is not necessarily a problem for households on social assistance, it does keep rents higher than the marketplace might actually dictate, posing greater affordability burdens on other low income households, namely the working poor. In provinces without a shelter component to social assistance, the total amount of money available to social assistance households is often insufficient to pay for housing and other expenses (Bruce, 2003).

As noted, ownership is the main tenure form in rural areas and small towns – even for low income households. On a relative basis, a smaller percentage of rural homeowners are in core need – 10 per cent compared to 30 per cent of rural renters – but their absolute numbers are higher, and they make up 59 per cent of all rural households in core need. In many cases ownership may be the only choice in a rural community, especially when rental housing is either unavailable due to low vacancies, or is at least as expensive as owning. One particular problem for low income homeowners, especially older widows, is the cost of maintaining their homes. This includes the costs of property taxes, high utility bills, and maintenance and repair (Bruce, 2003). With small fixed incomes, the rise in prices for oil and for property taxes can lead to people abandoning their homes or selling them off.

Estimates of at-risk homelessness: evidence from St Stephen case study

St Stephen is located in Charlotte County, a very rural but strategically located area within the Province of New Brunswick.[4] The county stretches from the Maine (USA)–New Brunswick border in the west to the outer edges of the Greater Saint John area in the east, along the Bay of Fundy. There are five municipalities (St Stephen, St Andrews, St George, Blacks Harbour and Grand Manan) and a total population of less than 30,000 people. St Stephen is the western-most town, located on the Maine border with a population of 4,667. There is no public transportation in the town or county. The time to travel to Saint John (a city of about 100,000) is almost 1.25 hours from St Stephen. Many people must travel to Saint John for specialty services (particularly health care related) not available locally.

St Stephen's population declined by 5.9 per cent from 1996 to 2001. The county has a very high ratio of people aged 65 years and over (about 19.5 per cent of the population), and about 43 per cent of seniors lived alone. The incidence of lone parent families was about 21 per cent.

Housing profile

Slightly more than two-thirds of the households are homeowners (Table 5.3). Most of the housing stock is older: more than half was built prior to 1946. Additionally, more than half of the stock is in poor condition: 17 per cent in need of major repairs, and 35 per cent in need of minor repairs (as self-reported in the Census). Single detached housing is the dominant form; however, small apartment structures are also important.

The private rental stock is dominated by older single detached houses which have been converted into three or more units, and small older duplexes. These

---

Economic and social development issues contributing to at-risk homelessness

- Shift in employment from seasonal and part time employment to full time, year round positions.
- Still many low paying and part time jobs (usually with no benefits) in the area which for many households serve as primary incomes.
- Lack of skilled labour force, especially among those looking for work.
- Lower education levels and a relatively high dropout rate from high school.
- Rising drug use and trafficking of prescription drugs.
- Out-migration of youth: about 75 per cent of young people leave each year.
- Mental health is a rising problem, in part because of deinstitutionalization.
- Teen pregnancies are a problem; in 1996, highest rate in Canada.
- 'Social blackmail' of lone parents – discriminated against in the workplace and less likely to be hired.
- No public transportation – low income households and seniors are dependent on others (extended families or friends).
- Health care services are under stress.
- Severe shortage of social workers, child care workers and child protection workers.
- Qualifying for income and housing assistance is a major problem for non-elderly singles.

Table 5.3 Housing stock profile, 1996 and 2001, St. Stephen (percentages)

	1996	2001
Homeowners	69.8	71.0
Renters	30.2	29.0
Built prior to 1946	55.7	54.4
Built after 1990	4.5	6.7
In need of major repairs	19.1	17.2
In need of minor repairs	28.7	35.4
Single detached dwellings	71.0	70.0

Source: Statistics Canada, 1996 and 2001 Census of Canada.

provide rental housing for all types of households but primarily lone parent families and the working poor. The general condition can be described as poor to fair, but those in better condition are generally rented to seniors. There is very little rental in the form of single houses, secondary suites, basement suites, or mobile homes. The cost of rental housing is high and vacancy rates are very low. Almost all units require the tenant to pay heat and utilities on top of rents charged, in rental units that are very hard to heat. Rents charged over time have increased more than incomes.

The rental stock is generally in poor condition. Estimates from informants suggest that between 50 and 85 per cent of the rental stock is in very poor shape, and that people should not be living in these units. One landlord summarized the crisis associated with the state of disrepair this way: 'someone [who eventually looked at one of our units and rented it] looked at 20 units and would not take a single one of them'.

Typical of most of the converted house properties are high ceilings, paper-thin windows, drafty conditions, little or no insulation, and poor flooring, all of which translates into high heating costs. Several informants, including those who visit low income households in their rental units when they make home visits or provide services to their clients, described many situations involving toilet leakages, septic backups, poor lighting, dangerous staircases, old oil-cloth floors, rodents, and mildew problems. The biggest problem, as one informant summarized, is that many rental properties are fire hazards and someone needs to address this immediately. While there is a perceived general lack of enforcement capacity, there is also recognition that the tradeoff is that, if many rental units were shut down, there would be few or no places for tenants to relocate to.

Landlords are generally unable or unwilling to repair or maintain their units, and thus it is common for low income households to shift from one rental property to another. They move into a unit and realize that the heating costs are high, so they move as soon as possible, often foregoing their damage deposit. At the same time, several informants including landlords and others noted that the poor condition of the rental stock is not entirely attributable to the landlords themselves. They identified a core group of 'problem tenants' who have collectively significantly damaged many rental properties and have created an environment where it is simply risky for landlords to rent to them. As one landlord noted, 'if you have a good unit, you don't advertise'.

Absolute homelessness in St Stephen

There was no evidence of absolute homelessness in this community. Several informants were aware of people living in hunting camps (their own or that of others) for parts of the year. In one exceptional circumstance, in the summer of 2000 a family of six in Canoose (a rural area outside of town) camped out for most of the summer when they could no longer afford to keep their rural home. Although this received some media coverage, it is generally thought that this was out of the norm. In general, the primary reason for the lack of use of 'other' housing is that there is a 'lack of demand' for these types of potential housing units. Instead, people in the area generally have a personal support network they can draw on for help and accommodation.

Low income households: the at-risk of homelessness

Although there are no official counts of the number of low income households, they can be quantified or identified in a number of different ways, and serve to identify households at risk of becoming homeless. The 2002 waiting list for social housing in the area included 43 family and 68 seniors households. These households have very low incomes and they likely live in deplorable conditions. Statistics Canada's measure of 'low income', which is based on incomes against a basket of expenditures for different types of rural communities, shows that low income situations have deteriorated recently for individuals but have improved for families (Table 5.4). Further evidence of low income problems can be seen in the high proportion of households using 30 per cent or more of their income for housing.

The local food bank is operated by the Volunteer Centre of Charlotte County, Inc., and provides services across the county but mostly to residents of St Stephen and the immediate rural area. Between April 2000 and March 2001 about half of the households in St Stephen used the food bank at least once, including most lone parent families and most people on social assistance. Usage patterns suggest a growing number of low income households at risk of becoming homeless, as there were 184 new clients over the previous year, including 75 new families, and the number of elderly accessing the food bank doubled.

Table 5.4 1996 low income profile, St. Stephen (percentages)

	1996	2001
Renters spend 30%+ for rent	39.3	37.2
Owners spend 30%+ for major payments	15.1	14.4
Individuals with low income	34.2	47.2
Economic families with low income	20.3	14.3
Total population with low income	22.5	18.6

Source: Statistics Canada, 1996 and 2001 Census of Canada.

The social assistance caseload provides yet another angle on the situation. There is no shelter component of the social assistance payment, as is the case in many other provinces. Most social assistance recipients spend most of their income on shelter, with little left for other necessities. There are an increasing number of people accessing social assistance because they have a long-term disability which makes them unemployable. Furthermore, there are more people accessing social assistance because they are getting assistance with defraying the costs of expensive prescription drugs. Single persons living alone (mostly boarders and renters, mostly over the age of 45) make up the largest group of recipients (28 per cent of all single persons are on social assistance). Lone parent families are the second largest group of recipients (62 per cent of lone parent families are on social assistance).

Youth without an income are a growing problem. There might be between 10 and 20 in the 16–21 age group who have no income and no education, and who have quit school. They have either left home or they have been 'kicked out' by their families. Their basic coping strategy has been to move from friend to friend for as long as possible. Other estimates suggest that about 25 youth per year present problems for the social assistance system because they do not qualify for programme support. Teen pregnancies are also a problem: in 1996 St Stephen had the highest teen pregnancy rate in the country. Today, the town has a lot of '20-year-old lone parent mothers with 3 kids'.

Many low income households have poor credit histories, which would pose problems for them if they were interested in purchasing or building a very modest home. One informant was aware of several households who qualified for assistance under the province's Home Ownership Assistance Program, but were unable to get mortgage financing because the banks in town felt they were too great a risk.

There are only about 90 social housing units (assisted housing or units occupied by those received subsidies) in the community, 60 of which are rented to low income elderly households. A general comment about the social housing stock in comparison to the private rental stock is that, although the social housing stock rents or housing charges do not include heat and utilities, the units are generally better insulated and therefore have lower operating costs.

There is only one small rooming house (6 units) in the town, although in the past there have been others operating. As there are 71 social assistance recipients from within the town who self-classify themselves as boarders, many single people are likely boarding with extended families and friends as a coping mechanism in the absence of a permanent housing solution.

There are few housing options under what would be classified as 'other' (such as motels, campgrounds, camps, etc.). There are two or three motels just outside the town which, over the years, have rented short- and long-term units to some households. However, there is less of this type of rental arrangement today because these facilities have experienced some damage to their units. The motels in town are not in the business of renting their rooms on a long-term basis, except to those families or individuals who are in the transition process of moving into town and require temporary accommodation. There is, however, some evidence of a small number of transients who pass through the area and who may rent for a short period of time in motels.

Collectively, individuals and households at risk of becoming homeless face many housing challenges or problems, including generally high rental charges relative to their very low incomes, and the associated high energy costs. There are some crowding issues for families (especially lone parent families) with children. In these cases it may be that lone parent families are forced into a one-bedroom situation; in other cases lone parents have moved back home with their parents, so there is an intergenerational sharing of housing in a crowded situation. Elderly homeowners have high maintenance costs. Many people in a low income situation simply do not have 'comfort'; no matter how high they turn up the heat in winter, they can't get warm because of the poor state of properties. There are too many dangerous properties in need of major repairs. Most tenants won't call their landlords with problems for fear of eviction; others have just given up trying. For victims in family violence situations, at least 40 per cent are in a crowded situation.

Emergency response mechanisms to help those at risk

There are some support mechanisms within the community to assist people with emergency housing problems. The Fundy Region Transition House assists women and their families escaping violence issues (providing at least one night's accommodation to as many as 150 different women and their children each year). The Charlotte County Group Home is available for youth, if they are placed by New Brunswick Family and Community Services (28 youth were provided with accommodation in 2001–2). There is a rentalsman in Saint John who provides services over the phone. However, since many tenants rent their places without a lease, and because their damage deposits are generally not held by the rentalsman, there is often little use of this service. The local food bank, operated by community volunteers, is regularly approached by individuals looking for help to find emergency housing. New Brunswick Family and Community Services does work with individuals to sort out problems associated with late or non-payment of heating bills, to help people avoid having their heat cut off. There is a relief bed at the local hospital, and there is also the possibility of 'social admission' to the hospital for people experiencing an immediate problem (such as a loss of power in a major storm). Furthermore, Lincourt Manor, the local nursing home, does have one extra bed for emergency situations. At the end of the day, when people find themselves in an emergency housing situation, they depend on informal family support.

Actions to address the problems

It is clear that the major concern for most people connected to those at risk of becoming homeless is that the incomes earned by the working poor, and the social assistance rates in general, are simply too low for people to act on an individual or collective basis to address their own housing problems. Something must be done to increase the income earned by individuals and households so that they have more 'purchasing power' in the housing marketplace, thereby increasing their security of tenure.

Related to the issue of low incomes are seasonal incomes, which may in fact be quite high during the period of employment. This is a problem because, without a consistent income over the full year, households run into budgeting problems, gaps in income while waiting for employment insurance payments, etc. This places them at risk of losing their housing.

Most informants recognized that improving people's incomes is not enough. There is a clear need to help people with household and budget management. General life skills and home skills are lacking. Many low income households have no family experiences with these. Furthermore, there is a need to help low income people improve their general attitudes and outlook on life (from defeatist and oppressed to being more proactive), and to help them understand the systems that affect them. Many people just do not understand how the economy works, how policy and programmes work, and so on. Changes on these fronts will help people cope better and to make better decisions.

With respect to seniors, there is a need to help facilitate their understanding of alternative housing solutions, especially as it relates to home sharing and sharing expenses. There are many seniors living alone who could benefit economically and socially if they chose to 'pair up' and live together. But there is a great deal of resistance to this in North American society.

Getting the housing issue onto the agenda of the local municipal council for action is a challenge. There is a need to build more empathy and acceptance within the community. Many people do not understand the problems that low income households face, especially those with multiple challenges associated with mental disorders, the youth and the working poor.

There is a need for additional public funding to offset the cost of modest, affordable, rental housing. Public investment is needed to support the construction of new social housing stock, primarily through existing organizations like the Charlotte County Housing Council. More cash for housing subsidies (rent supplements) for low income households to access better quality private sector rental units is also needed.

There was widespread agreement that an immediate change needs to take place with respect to the existing tolerance of slum landlords and poor quality rental properties. There needs to be a healthy minimum standard in the community for housing, and it needs to be aggressively and proactively enforced. There are simply too many loopholes in the present system with respect to how standards are enforced, how the courts deal with fines and penalties for contravening local bylaws, and much more. The net result will be a move towards ongoing upgrading of existing properties and better living conditions for tenants.

Conclusion

The faces of homelessness, be it absolute or at-risk, will likely vary from one community to the next, depending upon the unique local circumstances. The case study of St Stephen identifies seniors living alone, social assistance recipients (especially boarders and those with long-term disabilities), lone parent families and the working poor as especially vulnerable populations. It also suggests that the problem is getting larger, compounded by low paying jobs with no benefits, a centralization of services in larger centres and a lack of new subsidized housing being built to meet affordable housing needs and provide security of tenure. Although a variety of short-term coping strategies tap into extended family and friend networks, public funding for new housing or for rent supplements is needed.

On a broader scale, there is no comprehensive research on rural homelessness in Canada. There are some community-specific studies, developed in the context of preparing a plan to access federal government funds to support local interventions. Most of the research has an urban orientation, usually in relation to specific groups and to understanding the linkages and interactions among housing, services and homelessness. Given the highly urban nature of the Canadian population, and the fact that the problem of absolute homelessness is greatest in the major urban centres, this is not surprising. However, there are very real problems faced by youth, lone parent families, the working poor, those on social assistance and the elderly in rural areas. They live month to month with the reality of being at risk of becoming homeless. There is a great need to document the magnitude of the problem, to understand the underlying causes and influences, and to explore and develop rural and small town specific strategies and solutions.

Notes

1 'Informants' refers to the landlords, municipal employees, provincial employees, non-governmental sector representatives, and others, who were interviewed as part of the study.
2 Shelter cost for owners includes mortgage principal and interest, property taxes, condominium charges (if applicable) and utility payments (water, gas and electricity). For renters, the shelter cost includes rent and utilities if the latter are not included in the rent.
3 The elements of the National Occupancy Standards are as follows: Children under 5 years of age are expected to share a bedroom with one other sibling, regardless of gender. From 5 to 18 years of age, children are expected to share a bedroom with one other sibling of the same gender. Each adult (18 years of age and older) is allotted his/her own bedroom, unless they are part of a married or common-law relationship, in which case they would be expected to share a bedroom with his/her spouse/partner.
4 The material in this section is drawn from field work conducted as part of a larger project conducted by the author for CMHC (see Bruce, 2003, 2000b). Permission granted from CMHC to use the material for this chapter. Throughout this section 'informants' refers to the landlords, municipal employees, provincial employees, non-governmental sector representatives and others who were interviewed.

Chapter 6
Rural homelessness in the UK
A national overview

Paul Milbourne and Paul Cloke

Introduction: moving beyond rural housing needs

> There were young families living with their parents who had been on housing waiting lists for about ten years, whilst their children grew up in more and more cramped surroundings. There were parents who had ended up walking the streets with their children as a result of the homelessness policies being operated by councils in that area. There were families with young children who were living in winter let accommodation, gaining a brief respite of independence before eviction and a return to over-crowding and perhaps a caravan site over the summer. There were families living in rural slums, usually isolated privately rented cottages with no basic amenities ...
>
> (Larkin, 1979: 71)

Writing more than a quarter of a century ago about the state of rural housing needs in Dorset – a county in the south of England – Alan Larkin provides a graphic illustration of the types of housing problems experienced by disadvantaged groups of the rural population. Among the problems discussed by Larkin are overcrowding within households, the inadequate physical conditions of private rental housing and the difficulties faced by low-income groups in securing social housing. Reference is also made to literal forms of homelessness being faced by particular groups in this part of rural England. This is probably the first occasion that the issue of homelessness is discussed, albeit briefly, within the UK rural studies literature. Unfortunately, up until quite recently, it has remained one of only a handful of references to rural homelessness, as rural researchers in the UK have largely focused their studies on the problems faced by groups positioned *within* rural housing systems.

There has been a long tradition within British rural studies of research and writing on housing needs. Two main components of these rural housing needs have been emphasized. The first concerns the historical linkages between poverty and housing conditions in the countryside, and includes coverage of the crowded and damp condition of housing experienced by the rural poor, as well as the limited provision of essential household amenities, such as electricity, sewage and water services. The main focus of this area of work has been on the poor state of rural housing during the first half of the twentieth century and government interventions to deal with these housing conditions.

The success of these policies, together with the movement of new groups to the accessible and then remoter parts of the countryside from the 1970s onwards has meant that substandard housing in rural areas has ceased to be a significant concern for both researchers and policy-makers. In 1981, for example, only 7 per cent of the housing stock in rural England was officially categorized as substandard by government (Rogers, 1984), although it was suggested that particular groups of the rural poor were likely to remain trapped in inadequate forms of accommodation (Rogers, 1985). A survey of 3,000 households in 12 areas of rural England in the 1990s by Cloke *et al.* (1994) confirmed this general trend of improving conditions and an entrapped poor minority living in substandard accommodation. Their study revealed that while only 8 per cent of responding households were living in substandard housing in 1990–1, this figure rose to 17 per cent amongst those households living in or on the margins of poverty (Cloke *et al.*, 1994). Furthermore, poor quality housing remains a significant problem in particular rural areas. For example, a survey of housing conditions in Wales in 1998 revealed that three rural local authority areas had more than 10 per cent of properties in an unfit state.

During the mid to late 1970s, research attention on rural housing in the UK began to move from a concern with inadequate physical conditions to unequal processes of access to housing in the countryside. From being a symbol of poverty and population decline for much of the previous century, rural housing began to be viewed more as a desirable positional good that was attractive to urban middle-class groups. Identified first in peri-urban rural areas (see Pahl, 1966; Ambrose, 1974) and then in other areas of the countryside (Dunn *et al.*, 1981), increasing and unequal forms of competition for rural housing came to represent the most pressing housing issue for both research and policy communities. Two main factors were highlighted. First, an increase in the size of the rural population raised the overall level of competition for (and price of) housing in the countryside. In addition, it was claimed that in-moving groups were more affluent than the established rural population and thus could buy themselves into rural housing markets at the expense of 'local' groups. Second, the nature of social housing provision for low-income groups in the countryside was restructured by government housing policies introduced in the 1980s. These policies reduced the numerical significance of the social housing sector by selling off social rental properties and preventing local authorities from providing new social housing in their areas. In the countryside, where social housing provision had traditionally been limited (Rogers, 1976) and sales of social housing were proceeding at a rate that was higher than the national average across the 1980s (see Milbourne, 1998), concerns began to be raised about rising levels of unmet rural housing needs.

While early academic and policy coverage of these needs were distracted by the 'newcomer'–'local' dualism, whereby the categories newcomer and local became equated with high- and low-income groups respectively, it was widely recognized that low-income groups within rural society were finding it more difficult to secure affordable housing in their local areas. Various efforts have been made to measure the scale of these housing needs. Clark (1991), for example, used a sample of village surveys to estimate that 377,000 households in rural England were experiencing housing needs in the late 1980s. Drawing on findings from their survey of households in 12 areas of rural England, Cloke *et al.* (1994) highlighted that 68 per cent of respondent households considered housing affordability problems to be a significant issue in their areas, with young people identified as the most needy group. More recent work by the Countryside Agency (2004) has sought to measure the changing scales and geographies of housing affordability in rural England. By combining data on household incomes, house prices and mortgage rates, the Agency produced an index of local housing affordability for rural England. This index indicates that, in aggregate terms, housing is less affordable than that in urban areas (recording an income to mortgage cost index of 4.94 compared with 4.66 for urban housing in 2003). In addition, rural housing is shown to be less affordable in southern regions of England than in the north.

Problems of housing access have also been linked to the broader social and cultural sustainability of rural communities. In Wales cultural and linguistic consequences of uneven access to rural housing are very much evident (see Cloke *et al.*, 1997, 1998), while the Countryside Agency (2004) has pointed to similar impacts of housing need on the social make-up of English villages:

> ... people on modest incomes, including young and pensioner households and local first-time buyers, are being priced out of the many rural districts. This has implications for the maintenance of viable, inclusive rural communities ... The balance of communities is disrupted, families are separated, increased pressure placed on many rural services, and the local economy may be forced to decline.

While such studies have been useful in highlighting the scale and nature of rural housing needs, it remains the case that the focus has been on problems faced by groups positioned *within* the rural housing system, with virtually no recognition given to the fact that some of these groups have actually been made homeless – in a literal sense but also by being forced to reside in rather precarious housing situations, leaving them 'on the edge of homelessness' (Fitchen, 1992), such as short-term sharing with friends or family in crowded accommodation, living in badly maintained property and paying high housing costs that are likely to increase the risk of homelessness in the future. In this chapter we argue that it is important to relabel some these latter forms of precarious rural housing situations as homelessness in order to destabilize the dominant construction of homelessness as a problem that only exists in metropolitan centres, as well as do justice to the plight of those who are unable to access appropriate housing in rural areas. While other chapters within this book cover particular aspects of homelessness in the English countryside (Chapters 7 and 8), here we provide an overview of recent evidence on rural homelessness in the UK. We do this by analysing official statistics on the changing scales, profiles and geographies of rural homelessness in England, Wales and Scotland, and by drawing on findings from our own and other recent studies of the nature and welfare contexts of homelessness in rural areas.

The statistical visibilities of rural homelessness

For more than a quarter of century, homelessness has been recognized, recorded and dealt with by government as a specific aspect of housing needs. While the homelessness legislation may have changed over this period, what has remained constant has been the obligation placed on local authorities to provide statistical information on the scale and profile of homeless cases within their areas. It is therefore possible to highlight the shifting levels and profiles of homelessness at different spatial scales within the UK. It should be noted at this point, though, that these official data are based on rather narrow definitions of homelessness, which tend to prioritize the needs of families over other households and largely exclude particular homeless groups, such as young people.

The first attempt to explore the geography of homelessness in the UK was made by Newton (1991), who analysed official homelessness statistics from the late 1970s to early 1990s for London, metropolitan and non-metropolitan local authority areas in England. This work indicated that 26,200 households in non-metropolitan areas were recorded as homeless in 1978, representing 49.3 per cent of all homelessness in England for that year. By 1990–1 the level of non-metropolitan homelessness had risen to 63,200 households, although the non-metropolitan share of the homeless total had fallen to 42.7 per cent. The first study to focus specifically on rural homelessness statistics was undertaken by Lambert *et al.* (1992). Funded by the Rural Development Commission,[1] this work provided a detailed analysis of official homelessness data for rural, urban and London authority areas over the 1980s and early 1990s. Lambert *et al.* calculated that 14,590 households in rural areas were homeless and in priority need in 1989–90, a figure which translated to 12 per cent of the English homeless total. In addition, this analysis of official statistics indicated that levels of homelessness in rural areas had increased at faster rates than those in metropolitan and urban areas over the 1980s.

More recent spatial analyses of these official homelessness statistics have been provided by ourselves (Cloke *et al.*, 2001b). Using official homelessness data for the years 1992 and 1996, our work has provided a range of information on the scale, profile and geography of homelessness in rural England in the 1990s. In relation to the changing scales of rural homelessness, our analysis indicated that almost 16,000 households were accepted as priority homeless by English rural local authorities in 1996 – a figure that represents 14.4 per cent of the national total. When standardized for population sizes, though, the average rate of homelessness in rural areas (3.5 per 1,000 households) was much lower than the rates recorded for London (7.6 per 1,000) and urban areas (5.7 per 1,000). Highest levels of homelessness in 1996 were found in the South-West, East Anglia and the East Midlands regions, and lowest rates in the North. However, our analysis also suggests a more complex geography of rural homelessness, with local authority areas recording high and low levels of homelessness existing in the same regions (see Cloke *et al.*, 2001b for more detail).

While the standardized level of homelessness in rural areas were lower than that recorded in London and urban areas in 1996, rural forms of homelessness did become more significant over the decade. Between 1992 and 1996, for example, the rural share of the national homelessness total increased from 11.8 per cent to 14.4 per cent. In addition, while London and urban areas witnessed decreases in their homelessness totals of 27.3 per cent and 17.6 per cent respectively across this period, 'deep' rural areas – predominantly those located in remoter locations – experienced a 12.1 per cent increase. In fact, 29 per cent of rural authorities witnessed rises in their homelessness totals of more than one-quarter between 1992 and 1996, compared with only 10 per cent of London authorities. Again, highest increases in homeless totals were largely in areas located in the middle and southern regions of England.

In 1996, family households[2] accounted for the vast majority of rural and urban homeless cases, although families were more significant in rural areas (74 per cent compared with 66 per cent). The rural homeless population was less likely to comprise vulnerable groups, such as the young, people experiencing domestic violence, those with physical disabilities or mental illnesses, and people who had been sleeping rough or living in emergency accommodation. In fact, the elderly were the only vulnerable homeless group to be over-represented in rural areas. These contrasting profiles of rural and urban homelessness, though, are complicated by two factors. First, the data for these different homeless groups are not standardized, and so do not take account of the different totals of the non-homeless groups in rural and urban areas. Second, the average rural statistics hide a great deal of spatial variation in the profile of homeless groups within rural England. For example, some rural authorities recorded homeless rates for particular groups that were three to five times the rural average, while others had no recorded cases of these groups.

Four factors were responsible for almost nine out of ten cases of homelessness in rural England in 1996: a loss of rented or tied accommodation (33 per cent), a relative being unwilling or unable to accommodate the household (23 per cent), a relationship breakdown (21 per cent) and an inability to meet mortgage costs (11 per cent). While these four factors were also significant as causes of homelessness in urban areas, several differences are evident between the rural and urban homelessness profiles. First, the unwillingness of relatives to provide accommodation was less important as a cause of homelessness in rural areas. While this difference was seen by Bramley (1992) as a reflection of higher levels of social stress in cities, it is also the case that homeless people in rural areas are forced to place greater emphasis on the informal support of their families in the absence of emergency services (see later). Second, housing-related factors were a more significant cause of homelessness in rural areas, with higher levels of homelessness resulting from a loss of rental housing and mortgage arrears. This suggests particular problems with access to rental housing and the affordability of properties in rural areas. Third, a lower proportion of rural households were living in hostels or sleeping rough at the time they were accepted as homeless by local authorities, which can again be linked to the more limited provision of emergency accommodation for the homeless in rural areas.

While providing a useful indication of the scale and nature of particular types of homelessness in rural areas, it remains the case that these official homelessness statistics underestimate the true extent of rural homelessness, as only certain household types and causal factors are registered within the homelessness statistics. For example, of the 46,748 households that approached rural local authorities claiming to be homeless in 1996, 27 per cent were deemed to fall outside the homelessness legislation, 24 per cent were considered not to be homeless, 13 per cent as homeless but not in priority need and 2 per cent were deemed to be intentionally homeless (Cloke *et al.*, 2001b). As such, about two-thirds of those households approaching rural local authorities claiming to be homeless in 1996 were not classed as homeless. And while information on the situations of these households remains unpublished, it is reasonable to assume that a significant proportion were experiencing severe housing difficulties. It is also true that not all homeless people approach their local authority in an attempt to deal with their situations (see next section).

Given that our statistical analysis of rural homelessness in England was based on homelessness data for the 1990s, it is useful to provide an updated picture of the homelessness situation in rural England. The Countryside Agency has recently presented official data for the period 1999–2003, which demonstrate an increased statistical significance of rural homelessness since the late 1990s. Between 1999–2000 and 2002–3, the number of households accepted as homeless and in priority need by local authorities in rural England increased by 24 per cent, a rate of increase higher than that recorded for urban areas (21 per cent).[3] By 2002–3, almost 24,000 households in rural areas were officially classed as homeless, and rural homelessness comprised 18.3 per cent of all homelessness in England (compared with 14.4 per cent in 1996 and 11.8 per cent of homelessness in 1992). Within rural England, it is also evident that homelessness increases have again been higher in remote than accessible rural areas. For example, the incidence of homelessness rose by 29 per cent in remote rural areas over this period, compared with an increase of 21 per cent in accessible areas of the countryside.

These increases in homelessness totals, though, have not really impacted on standardized rates of homelessness in rural and urban areas. In 2001–2 the standardized level of homelessness in rural England was 3.5 per 1,000 households, the same level as that recorded for 1996. In fact, the official statistics indicate that the gap between standardized rates of homelessness for rural and urban areas has remained consistent since the mid-1990s. It can be suggested that key reasons for this are that the (non-homeless) rural population has continued to increase in size over this period, fuelled by (middle-class) in-migration, and some of the rural homeless population are forced to relocate to urban spaces (see Cloke *et al.*, 2001a).

Thus far the chapter has only considered homelessness in rural England. While our decision to follow this particular approach reflects the spatial focus of recent studies of rural homelessness, we now want to provide an account of the changing scales and profiles of rural homelessness in Wales and Scotland, based on new analyses of local homelessness data for these countries.

Of the three countries, it is Wales that has recorded the most significant rise in rural homelessness over recent years. Between 1996 and 2002 the number of cases of official homelessness in rural Wales increased by 115 per cent, more than double the rate of increase for Wales as a whole (54 per cent). In addition, homeless totals rose by at least 200 per cent in four rural authority areas – Ynys Mon, Gwynedd, Pembrokeshire and Carmarthenshire – over this period. Scotland has also witnessed significant rises in the number of households applying under the Homeless Persons legislation in its rural areas.[4] Official statistics indicate that homeless applications in rural areas rose by 29 per cent between 1996–7 and 2002–3, a figure that is more than three times higher than the increase reported in cities (8 per cent). Again, individual rural local authority areas were characterized by the largest increases in homeless applications, with seven authorities having increases of more than 50 per cent and one of these – Perth and Kinross – witnessing a doubling of its homeless population.[5]

In 2002, 1,868 households in rural Wales were accepted by local authorities as homeless and in priority need, representing 29 per cent of all homeless households in Wales. In Scotland, 11,659 homelessness applications were made by rural households (23 per cent of the national total) in 2002–3. As is the case in England, the standardized rates of rural homelessness in Wales and Scotland are lower than both the national and urban levels. In Scotland, for example, a recent study by Scottish Homes calculated the standardized rate of homelessness in rural Scotland to be 8 per 1,000 households, compared with 14 per 1,000 in urban areas (Scottish Homes, 2000). Similarly, the standardized level of rural homelessness in Wales in 2002 stood at 1.8 per 1,000 persons[6] compared with 2.2 for the country as a whole.

As in England, family households represent the most significant homeless group in rural Wales. However, at 51 per cent, the rural Wales average is much lower than that recorded for rural England (74 per cent). This means that there exist higher levels of other vulnerable groups within the rural homeless population in Wales. Three vulnerable homeless groups in particular can be identified as being over-represented in the Welsh countryside: those with a physical disability or mental illness (11 per cent); young people (13 per cent) and persons experiencing domestic violence (9 per cent). Turning to the causes of homelessness in rural Wales, 34 per cent of homeless cases in 2002 resulted from a housing-related problem, which is a higher level than that recorded for Wales (27 per cent) but much lower than that for rural England (44 per cent). While mortgage arrears levels were broadly similar, homelessness resulting from rent arrears in rural areas accounted for more than twice the proportion of homeless households than in Wales, while one-quarter of all rural homeless households had been forced to leave rented or tied accommodation for reasons other than rent arrears. Two other causes of rural homelessness can be identified: parents, relatives or friends being unable or unwilling to accommodate the household, which accounted for 24 per cent of all causes of rural homelessness (28 per cent for Wales); and a relationship breakdown with a partner, making up 26 per cent of rural homeless cases (compared with a national figure of 25 per cent).

Official data on the groups applying to rural local authorities in Scotland as homeless is also available and reveals that the profile of homeless groups in rural areas is broadly similar to that for cities. In each case, two groups make up the vast majority of homelessness applications: single person households and single female parent households. The former group comprised 60 per cent of rural applications in 2002–3, although this figure is lower than in the cities, where single person households accounted for 68 per cent of all applications. Single female parent households made up 21 per cent of applications in rural areas, a rate that is similar to that recorded in the cities (22 per cent). Within rural Scotland, though, there exists considerable variation in the profile of homeless households between local authority areas. For example, single person households made up 34 per cent of all homeless applications in Aberdeenshire and Angus in 2002–3, but 48 per cent in Argyle and Bute.

The nature of rural homelessness

These official datasets clearly demonstrate the increased significance of homelessness in rural Britain over the last couple of decades. However, these statistics provide only a partial picture of homelessness in rural areas; not only do they underestimate its incidence but little information is provided on the nature of homelessness in rural areas. To gain a broader understanding of rural homelessness we undertook a major study of the subject in the late 1990s.[7] The research project set out to examine the nature, experiences and welfare contexts of rural homelessness from a range of perspectives – including government, homelessness agencies and homeless people – and at national and local scales[8] (see Cloke *et al.*, 2002, for further details of the study). In this section and the next couple of sections of the chapter we discuss key findings on the major components of homelessness in rural areas that emerge from this study. Where appropriate we highlight findings from other research on rural homelessness in the UK undertaken since our own study was completed.

The statistical significance of rural homelessness revealed in the previous section is also reflected in the responses received to our national survey of homelessness officers in rural areas. Three-fifths of responding homelessness officers in all rural areas, and four-fifths of those in 'deep' rural areas, regarded homelessness as a significant problem within their authority. A similar proportion of rural officers stated that local homelessness was also considered a significant problem by other officers and councillors in their local authority, although only 12 per cent of rural authorities used the term 'rural homelessness' in any official documentation. The lesser visibility of rural homelessness was identified by half of rural officers as a key reason for it having a lower profile than its urban counterpart. Others also pointed to particular aspects of this reduced visibility, including the dispersed nature of rural homelessness, the lack of street homelessness and the tendency for media attention to concentrate on urban areas (see Cloke *et al.*, 2001c, for further details).

Our interviews with national and local homeless agencies clarify a number of important findings, especially that official statistics relating to statutory homelessness provide an extremely partial picture of the scale and spatiality of homelessness. Clearly, the official homelessness statistics do not include the many other homeless households who fail to approach their local authority for assistance.

In the national survey of homelessness officers, 65 per cent of officers in rural areas considered that certain groups of homeless households tended not to contact them for help with rehousing, with young and/or single people regarded as particularly unlikely to seek local authority assistance. Furthermore, a more recent study of homelessness in North Yorkshire reveals that only half of homeless people staying with a friend or relative had approached their local authority claiming to be homeless (Robinson and Coward, 2003) and, of those who had made an approach, just 20 per cent had been recorded as homeless.

Our research reveals that national and local agencies do recognize the potential for homelessness to exist in rural areas. This was ascribed to commonly acknowledged factors such as: the loss of a job, or of income (leading to rent or mortgage arrears); a crisis such as relationship breakdown, domestic violence, family disputes or disputes with landlords; deinstitutionalization from care, prison, the armed forces or mental health services; and benefit restrictions which limit access to accommodation, especially for young people. Other factors, relating to the changing geographies of rural areas, were also considered important in causing or contributing to homelessness, notably the gentrification of local housing markets, reducing the availability of affordable housing, low wages and limited employment opportunities, and transport difficulties, which hinder access to the jobs and housing that are available.

However, recognition of potential problems is not often converted into an acceptance of rural homelessness *per se*. In local and national policy documents, and in the wider public sphere, recognizing the potential for homelessness in rural areas has not generally led to an acceptance that rural homelessness is a problem that requires an urgent policy response. Some homelessness officers expressed frustration at the failure, particularly at a national level, to appreciate that, while the absolute number of people experiencing homelessness might be lower than in urban areas, particular features of the rural environment – including lack of affordable accommodation, poor transport and little or no emergency provision for homeless people – make homelessness in rural areas particularly difficult to resolve.

Our research also highlights a tendency for a 'non-coupling' of rurality and homelessness. This can be attributed to two principal factors. First, there is the limited visibility of homelessness in rural areas. In the main, rural homelessness is not about rough sleeping (indeed, this is true of homelessness more generally) but about people living in a range of inadequate and insecure situations. Street homelessness is limited and a lack of facilities for homeless people such as hostels, drop-ins and other potential 'points of congregation' tends to hide homelessness from public view. Furthermore, where rough sleeping does occur, it tends to have a less visible presence than its urban counterpart, as the following comments illustrate:

I think that it's a lot greater than we know about. You don't see the rough sleepers like you would in a place like Taunton. You don't see people sitting in shop doorways etc.

(Homelessness officer, Somerset)

… people will not be sleeping rough in the same way that people sleep rough in a city, it will not necessarily be in shop doorways or shopping precincts but is going to be in more secluded spots, hedgerows, barns, caves, cars, caravans …

(Crisis)

A second factor that leads to the non-coupling of homelessness and rurality is the dominant construction of rural living in England. Continuing notions of idyllic rural lifestyles set amongst close-knit communities and picturesque landscapes tend to cloak out social problems – such as crime, poverty and homelessness – which offer a challenge to these popular constructions of rural life. This was reflected in the comments of a number of the local authority survey respondents.

There is, I think, not only a false perception that homelessness is primarily an urban problem but also an accompanying idealised image of the non-problematic nature of rural living.

[Rural homelessness] is not as visible and therefore not perceived as a problem which is significant in rural areas. There is also an idealised image of rural life as tranquil, peaceful and problem free.

Thus middle-class rural residents, local and national politicians and policy-makers, and even some of the people experiencing what would normatively be recognized as problems of homelessness, will tend to deny the very existence and certainly the pressing priority of homelessness as an issue. This seems to be especially the case in areas heavily dependent on tourism. As one interviewee from Shelter – a national homelessness charity – commented:

I think its the way communities like to present themselves, especially in an area, if the rural area … has a lot of tourism say … it has a lot to lose if you start raising issues about levels of poverty, levels of deprivation, levels of housing and homelessness.

Indeed, in order to retain the confidence of the local community in setting up a number of schemes to tackle youth homelessness in one rural county, Shelter took the decision to refer to two of the schemes as *housing* rather than *homelessness* projects.

It is possible to identify three key distinctions in relation to the spectrum of rural homelessness situations revealed by our study. The first is between *local and in-migrating forms of rural homelessness.* Local people in rural areas will often have experienced a personal family, financial or medical crisis which means that they are no longer able to, or cannot afford to, stay in their previous home. While lack of alternatives forces some people to remain in unfit or otherwise inadequate housing situations despite risks to their health and/or safety, for others – for example, households evicted from accommodation or served a notice to quit – 'sticking it out' was not an option. In such circumstances, the first step for some households was to go to the local authority for help. Others, however, failed to approach the council for assistance in the belief that they would be unable or unwilling to help them or that any accommodation offered would be 'miles away' from home. Such impressions, whether correct or not (and many were generally confirmed to us by local homelessness officers), reproduce local cultural constructions of the futility of applying to the local authority unless one conforms to a certain stereotyped pattern of need.

For those who have to move out, the options are often far from ideal. The homeless people interviewed had experienced a range of one or more insecure and/or inadequate living arrangements including: staying in bed and breakfast accommodation, in bedsits, on a succession of friends' floors, in a caravan or a tent and, in some instances, interspersed with periods of sleeping rough. On the other hand, people fortunate enough to obtain rented accommodation of reasonable quality often find themselves struggling to pay the rent. Officers noted that restrictions on the amount of housing benefit paid by government have led to a large number of households having to make up a shortfall in the rent from their own resources. This often has disadvantageous consequences, with households having to make a choice between cutting back on essential items – such as food and heating – or running up arrears which could lead to eventual eviction.

Rural homelessness also involves non-local people, with some rural areas attracting people from outside the area in search of work or simply drawn to the environment and lifestyle, who subsequently encounter problems of homelessness. Such attractiveness can be localized and specific, for example, in one of our case study areas, young people from all over England were attracted by the prospect of work at a major holiday centre. Many chose to stay in the area when jobs failed to come to fruition or when contracts ended. With residential restrictions debarring many of these young people from access to social housing, and affordable privately rented property difficult to obtain, it is not surprising that some found themselves with nowhere to live. A number of the young homeless people we interviewed spoke of sleeping in bus shelters along the sea front and staying with a succession of friends who had managed to acquire a tenancy, moving every few days or so to avoid outstaying their welcome.

There is a tendency for non-local forms of homelessness to be constructed as less deserving than their local counterparts (see Cloke *et al.*, 2000b). This tendency is evident from a recent discussion of homelessness in Ceredigion, a rural local authority area in west Wales, which has witnessed a dramatic increase in the number of households applying to the council as homeless over the last couple of years. Rather than this increase being discussed as a general welfare problem, the council leader chose to make a clear distinction between local and non-local homeless groups. Referring to figures that show that only one-quarter of recent homelessness applications were from people who had been born in the area, the council leader made the following comment:

> These homeless people are moving to Ceredigion month after month and all we can do is throw money at them. This can't carry on or the structure of our community is going to be spoilt forever. If a council house becomes vacant that house will invariably go to a homeless person who has come into the area with social problems.
>
> (BBC News, 2004: 1–2)

The second distinction that can be made about rural homelessness is that between *settled and transient forms of rural homelessness*. This is an uneasy distinction to make in that many of the homeless people interviewed had lived in such a way as to alternate constantly between settling and moving on. It is clearly evident from the research that homelessness occurs across a wide spectrum from those who are settled in a place (and require resettling) to those simply seeking a temporary stopping point within a more general pattern of mobility. The research also identifies different kinds of mobility amongst homeless people. It is clear from the housing histories analysed that, in line with popular perception, many people do leave rural areas and head for the perceived work/housing/life experiences of urban centres. This migration clearly reinforces perceptions of homelessness as an *urban* problem. However, interviews also reveal movements from urban to rural areas, as well as movements of homeless people through rural areas as part of wider 'circuits' of movement encompassing key towns and cities such as Winchester, Oxford, Bath and Brighton.

Our final distinction is between *visible and invisible forms of rural homelessness*. Homeless people will often engage in 'tactics' of invisibility in rural settings. Rural homelessness often only becomes visible when people believe they might receive a positive response from local authorities or advice agencies, or when some external factor – such as a flood – can be blamed for their crisis.

However, local people who are in crisis may well be regarded by the community around them as undeserving, and will thus attempt to hide the crisis from local gossip, or will move away to another place (often an urban location) to escape the visibility that their crisis would bestow upon them. The hiding or relocating of homelessness in this way, renders the problem of homelessness in rural areas invisible both to generalized public and political discourses, and to the imaginings of local rural people.

In addition, as with rural poverty, there is often a reluctance to acknowledge one's difficulties and our research suggests that many rural people who would be defined normatively as homeless do not accept that label for themselves. Many of the homeless people interviewed (especially those contacted outside of formal facilities for the homeless, or who were encountered in advice centre case files), did not want to be identified as homeless. To do so would be to stand out visibly as unable to sort out their own problems, and as having lost control over their life. This elective invisibility through refusing the label 'homeless' occurs throughout the spectrum of people interviewed, and adds significantly to the hidden nature of homelessness in rural areas. Such invisibility hinders the development of initiatives to tackle the problem. It is difficult to engender a response to homelessness in rural areas when it is hard to visually point to its existence and where people are reluctant to make their needs known (see Cloke *et al.*, 2001a, b, c).

Welfare responses to rural homelessness

Welfare responses to rural homelessness in the UK need to be considered at different spatial scales. Overarching policies of support for particular groups of homeless people have been in place for more than a quarter of a century. This means that people experiencing homelessness have been protected by national legislation and have been dealt with by local authorities in largely consistent ways. While national homelessness policy has been altered by different governments since the mid-1970s, these changes have generally been minor ones (see Hutson and Clapham, 1999; Kennett and Marsh, 1999; Cloke *et al.*, 2001a). The introduction of the 1996 Housing Act, though, brought with it more sweeping changes to the ways that homelessness was dealt with by government. This Act sought to reduce the role played by central and local government in responding to homelessness by adopting a more restrictive definition of homelessness, reclassifying homelessness as a component of housing need and pushing policy responses to homelessness into the private housing sector. The election of the New Labour government in 1997 led to a dilution of the key components of the 1996 Housing Act and national homelessness policy that is largely in keeping with the spirit of the original legislation. While the private sector still plays a role in state responses to homelessness and the definition of homelessness remains restrictive, homelessness has been treated more seriously by the present government.

It is also the case that the devolution programme implemented by New Labour in the late 1990s has introduced new complexities in the ways that welfare policy is developed and delivered in the different countries of the UK. While brevity prevents any detailed discussion of these changes as they relate to homelessness policy, it is clear that different welfare responses to homelessness are emerging in England, Scotland, Wales and Northern Ireland.

Our research points to the importance of local systems of welfare in meeting the needs of homeless groups in rural areas. For example, our examination of the impacts of the (then current) 1996 Housing Act on our case-study areas indicates the important role played by individual local authorities in mediating some of the key changes to the national homelessness legislation. Local authorities were shown to be able to work within this new national policy context by making changes to particular policies so that they continued to deal with homeless groups in similar ways (see Cloke *et al.*, 2001a). Such actions would appear to lend support to other accounts of the British welfare system that stress the continued importance of local government in shaping welfare policies at the local level (see, for example, Cochrane, 1994).

In addition to considering these changing national contexts of homelessness policy, findings from our study indicate considerable spatial unevenness associated with agency responses to homelessness within rural areas. Local authorities continue to interpret national homelessness policy in different ways, meaning that homeless people experiencing similar conditions are treated differently by different rural local authorities. More generally, the increased number of agencies drawn from the voluntary sector now involved in the provision of welfare services for homeless people at the local level has introduced a greater degree of complexity, and particularly spatial complexity, to the delivery of such services. For example, we highlighted important differences associated with partnership working between state and voluntary sector agencies to deal with homelessness in our two study areas, as well as the continued significance of local government within new networks of local welfare delivery. While rehousing homeless households in priority need remains the primary response to homelessness at a local level, many rural authorities are also involved in a range of inter-agency schemes which focus on tackling housing and homelessness issues. Notwithstanding this complexity, partnerships between statutory and voluntary agencies are often particularly important for single people and other homeless persons who fall outside the definition of priority need. Decent housing advice, rent deposit schemes and landlord forums emerged as especially valuable in facilitating access to private rented accommodation.

Recent studies also highlight the difficulties bound up with delivering welfare support for homeless people in rural areas. Our national survey of homelessness officers reveals that 43 per cent of officers in rural areas and 71 per cent of those in 'deep' rural areas stated that households in rural areas find it difficult to access advice services. Poor transport and limited outreach services were viewed as significant barriers, particularly given the tendency for advice facilities to be concentrated in larger centres of population. More generally, welfare agencies pointed to a series of difficulties associated with responding to homelessness in rural areas, including identifying the extent of the local homelessness problem and dealing with local political and cultural denials of homelessness (see Cloke *et al.*, 2001e, 2002; Streich *et al.*, 2002). Similarly, the Countryside Agency (2004) highlights the limited provision of temporary accommodation as a particular problem facing homeless agencies in rural areas. In 2002–3, 51 per cent of homeless households were in temporary accommodation, compared with 76 per cent in urban areas. Again, this problem appears to be more pronounced in remote rural areas, where only 44 per cent of homeless households were in such accommodation.

Conclusion

Rural life as we know it is under threat. The severe and growing shortage of affordable housing is polarising communities, forcing families out of the countryside, and removing a labour force needed to sustain rural life. There is a real danger that living in the countryside will become the preserve of the wealthy and the diversity of rural communities will be undermined. Unless action is taken now to replace the affordable homes lost through Right to Buy and rocketing house prices, rural life, as we know it, will be lost.

(Shelter, 2004)

This quotation, taken from a recent report on the rising costs of rural homes by the homeless organization Shelter indicates important linkages between access to housing and social cohesion in rural areas. While the focus on rural issues by this major UK homeless charity should be welcomed as belated recognition of the scale of housing problems in the countryside, it is strange given the types of evidence presented in this chapter (and others in this book) and the nature of Shelter's work (on homelessness) that so little coverage is given to rural homelessness within this report. Again, we see critical attention being directed towards problems of housing accessibility and affordability, without any real acknowledgement that many of those experiencing such problems are effectively locked out of formal housing systems and thus living in varying states of homelessness.

It is also true that while rural homelessness in the UK has been taken more seriously by researchers over the last few years, the subject remains a marginal concern amongst rural scholars and homelessness researchers. Academic publications on homelessness in rural areas have failed to act as a springboard for further research in this area and any review of the mainstream texts on homelessness will reveal scant attention given to rural forms of homelessness. Clearly, there is much more work to be done before rural homelessness is awarded the significance that it deserves by policy and research communities in the UK. We end this chapter by pointing to three important deficits in our current knowledge of homelessness in rural areas.

The first relates to the uneven spatial coverage of recent studies of rural homelessness in the UK, with almost all of the research undertaken being focused on rural areas in England. There remains a real need to examine in much more detail the different scales, profiles and geographies of rural forms of homelessness in the other three countries of the UK. Local in-depth studies of the experiences of rural homelessness have been restricted to only a handful of localities in England and it would be useful for a larger number and broader range of places to be included in future studies of homelessness in rural areas. In addition, the different models of welfare provision resulting from recent processes of devolution in the UK require further attention from researchers in order to explore their impacts on rural homeless groups in each country.

The second gap in our knowledge of rural homelessness relates to statistical indications of homelessness. While acknowledging that the official homelessness data published by government provide useful information on the shifting levels and profiles of homelessness in rural areas, they also represent a rather frustrating set of statistics for homelessness researchers. Not only are they based on a rather restrictive definition of homelessness but the detailed information on homelessness is supplied for just one-third of households who make applications under the homelessness legislation – those households who are accepted as homeless. Analyses of unpublished data relating to the circumstances of the remaining two-thirds would certainly provide a better indication of the 'real' scale of homelessness in rural areas. Furthermore, alternative measurements of rural homelessness, based on statistical information collected by other local welfare agencies, may offer opportunities to develop more meaningful counts of homelessness in particular rural places (see, for example, Everitt and Wright, 1997; Robinson, 2002).

Third, we still know relatively little about the processes and experiences bound up with homelessness in rural areas. Few researchers have actually engaged with homeless people to produce accounts of rural homelessness that are shaped by the voices of homeless people themselves (see Evans, 1999; Cloke *et al.*, 2002). The viewpoints of the rural homeless are typically collected second-hand from representatives of welfare agencies. While there are understandable research reasons for the adoption of this approach, given the difficulties encountered in locating homeless people in rural areas, we need to develop more first-hand accounts of rural homelessness through in-depth place-based studies of homelessness and homeless people in a range of rural areas. By doing this we will be able to generate more compelling narratives of the socio-cultural contexts of rural homelessness, the spatial and temporal dynamics of this homelessness and the coping strategies employed by different homeless people in rural areas.

Notes

1   The Rural Development Commission was a government agency concerned with the social and economic conditions of rural England. It became part of the Countryside Agency in the late 1990s.

2   Families include households with dependent children or a household member who is pregnant.

3   The definition of priority-need homelessness was widened by the 2002 Homeless Act.

4   Time-series data on homelessness in Scotland could only be obtained for homeless applications.

5   The rural local authority of Moray also recorded an increase of over 100 per cent, but this was due to flooding in the area in 2002.

6   The standardized rate of homelessness in Wales is presented in relation to persons rather than households, even though all other homelessness statistics are household based.

7   The study was funded by the ESRC (grant number R000236567) and involved a co-worker, Rebekah Widdowfield.

8   The research involved a national survey of local authority homelessness officers, interviews with representatives of national homeless and rural agencies, and detailed case studies of rural homelessness in two counties in south-west England, which involved interviews with agencies and homeless people as well as ethnographic work.

Chapter 7
The hidden and neglected experiences of homelessness in rural England

David Robinson

Little is known about rural homelessness in England. Despite the suggestion that one in five of all homeless people live in rural areas, and analysis pointing to a recent increase in rural homelessness (Cloke *et al.*, 2001a; Countryside Agency, 2004), the incidence, extent and experiences of homelessness in rural England remain points of conjecture rather than conviction. Discursively denied, politically neglected and hidden from view, rural homelessness is invisible in accounts of homelessness in England.

The mere possibility that homelessness might exist in rural England challenges deep-rooted idealized notions of rural life which have been upheld and reasserted as a natural and essential constant within English national identity and values. As Cloke and Milbourne point out in Chapter 6, these discourses of the rural have had a persistent and pervasive influence on discourses of homelessness, informing the attitudes and understandings of homelessness among rural residents and serving to confirm homelessness as an 'out of place' behaviour in rural space. Relayed into local and national political discourses, these notions have legitimized a policy agenda rooted in the concomitant notion that homelessness is an urban phenomenon. This chapter challenges this denial of rural homelessness in England. Breaking free from the clutches of what Cloke (1995: 354) refers to as the 'pervasive yet obfuscatory influence' of notions of the rural idyll on the recognition of poverty and social problems in rural areas, it seeks to make visible the denied and neglected experiences of homeless people in rural England. Mining a small but growing body of research on rural homelessness, glimpses are provided into the incidence and extent of rural homelessness and the hidden and neglected situations, circumstances and experiences of homeless people in rural England. Integral to this review is consideration of how rural spaces, and their particular geographies of provision and opportunity, render rural homelessness a unique and particular experience.

Making rural homelessness visible

Compared to the very visible presence of homelessness in major towns and cities, homelessness in rural areas is hidden from view and often goes unnoticed. The symbolic markers of contemporary homelessness – people bedded down in shop doorways and underpasses, *Big Issue* vendors on the high street, people begging for spare change – are largely absent from rural areas. The emergency support, advice and accommodation services for people threatened with and experiencing homelessness – hostels, day centres, health care facilities – that draw homeless people together and serve to make homelessness more visible, are also largely absent from rural areas (Cloke *et al.*, 2000; Robinson and Coward, 2003; Robinson and Reeve, 2002; Wright and Everitt, 1995). Faced with the practical difficulties of being homeless in the service-poor spaces of rural England, many homeless people actively choose to get out and migrate to larger towns and cities that are able to offer both targeted support and more general opportunities essential to surviving and negotiating an escape from homelessness, including affordable housing, relevant health and social care provision, employment opportunities, and advice and support services. Homeless people who stay put and make do in rural areas, meanwhile, are often forced to adopt tactics of invisibility to avoid the stigma and persecution that can flow from being homeless in a space where homelessness is deemed inappropriate behaviour.

This invisibility of rural homelessness in England raises major challenges for counting and estimating the extent of homelessness in rural areas. As we will see, official homeless statistics have largely failed to acknowledge or address these challenges and underestimate, almost to the point of denial, the extent of homelessness and rough sleeping in rural England. New and innovative methods are being developed, however, more capable of quantifying the scale and nature of rural homelessness and, as the case study example below reveals, exposing homelessness and rough sleeping to be major problems in rural England.

Official perspectives on rural homelessness

It is difficult to state with any certainty how many homeless people there are in any particular district or region of England. The homeless population is often hard to reach, can be hidden from view and is ever changing. The best that can be hoped for are estimates, and two main sources of data inform understanding of the incidence and extent of homelessness in England: statutory homeless statistics based on actions taken by local authorities under the homeless legislation, and rough sleeper headcounts.

England, along with the rest of the UK, is unusual in having time-series data on the number of homeless people available at the local, regional and national level. Derived from systematic counts of homeless people compiled by central government on a quarterly basis, these data record households recognized by local authorities as being statutory homeless and having 'justiciable' rights of access to accommodation, originally spelt out in the Housing (Homeless Persons) Act 1977 and reasserted in the Homelessness Act 2002. The statutory homeless statistics have been criticized for underestimating the overall scale of homelessness. Critics have pointed to various failings, primary among which are the fact that the statistics only count homeless people who express a 'felt need' and approach a local authority for assistance, employ a restrictive legal definition of homelessness which excludes many homeless situations and groups, count households not individuals and refer to the number of households recognized as becoming homeless during a particular timeframe, rather than the stock or total number of people homeless at a particular point in time (Cloke *et al.*, 2001a; Robinson, 2002). Despite these failings, the statutory homeless statistics represent the most comprehensive data source on homelessness and it has been suggested that they take account of the majority of homelessness in England (Burrows, 1997).

According to analysis of official homeless statistics (Table 7.1), 23,798 households were recognized as homeless and in priority need (having the justiciable right of access to secure accommodation) in rural England in 2002–3 (Countryside Agency, 2004). Official figures reveal rural homelessness to be on the rise, a 24.2 per cent increase in statutory homelessness being recorded in rural areas between 1999–2000 and 2002–3, compared to a 21.1 per cent rise in homelessness in urban areas. In what the Countryside Agency (2004) refers to as 'remote' rural areas, the increase has been even greater, the number of households recognized as homeless and in priority need rising by 29.4 per cent. The official rate of homelessness in rural districts is still far lower than in urban districts, however, 38.3 households per 10,000 being homeless in 2002–3, compared to 68.3 households per 10,000 in urban districts.

Reflecting on these figures, it is important to remember that the statutory homeless statistics are a socially constructed dataset. They reflect different policy and practice frameworks, developed by local authorities within the context of their statutory duties under the homeless legislation, but also informed by local political, socio-economic and housing circumstances (Hutson and Liddiard, 1994). These different local practices result in geographical inconsistencies. In particular, evidence has been revealed of rural specific undercounting of homelessness within the official homelessness statistics (Cloke *et al.*, 2001a).

Rural authorities have been revealed to be more draconian in the interpretation of their duties under the homelessness legislation, accepting a lower proportion of applicants as statutory homeless than their urban counterparts and being less likely to recognize single people as homeless (Cloke *et al.*, 2001a; Pleace *et al.*, 1997). Perhaps because of low expectations about the help they will

Table 7.1 Households accepted as homeless and in priority need in England (1999–2000 to 2002–3)

	Number of homeless households				Change in number (%)
	1999–2000	*2000–1*	*2001–2*	*2002–3*	
Rural	19,161	21,021	21,445	23,798	24.2
Accessible rural	11,386	12,182	11,919	13,735	20.6
Remote rural	7,775	8,839	9,420	10,063	29.4
Urban	87,451	94,060	95,972	105,955	21.2
England	106,612	115,081	117,417	129,753	21.7

Source: Countryside Agency 2004

receive, the limited provision of housing advice, or because of the reluctance among homeless people in rural areas to recognize that they are homeless (Cloke *et al.*, 2001a), homeless people in rural areas are less likely than their urban counterparts to approach a local authority for help (Robinson and Coward, 2003). It also appears that some homeless people in rural areas, given the dearth of opportunities to access affordable housing and the limits of homeless services in rural areas, are driven to migrate to larger towns and cities to present themselves as homeless, thereby rendering their homelessness visible as an urban phenomenon (Centrepoint Eden Valley, 1998; Lockwood, 1996).

The scale of rural undercounting of homelessness within the statutory statistics is difficult to establish. A number of small-scale studies have, however, cast some light on the phenomenon. A comparative study of hidden homelessness in rural and urban locations, for example, which involved 165 interviews with homeless people in three case-study locations – the rural district of Craven in North Yorkshire, the city of Sheffield in South Yorkshire and London – found that only 54 per cent of all homeless people surveyed in the rural case study had approached a local authority as homeless, compared to over 80 per cent of homeless people in the city of Sheffield (Robinson and Coward, 2003). Homeless people in the Craven area were found to have few expectations about the help they were likely to receive from the local authority, were cynical about their chances of being recognized as homeless and receiving help and assistance, and often failed to recognize that the local authority had any role to play in helping them escape homelessness (Robinson, 2003). These opinions would appear to be well founded, less than half of the homeless people who approached the local authority being recognized as homeless, compared to almost two-thirds of homeless applicants in Sheffield. In total, therefore, only 26 per cent of the homeless people surveyed in the rural case study had been recognized as homeless by the local authority, compared to 61 per cent in Sheffield. Everitt and Wright (1996) report similar findings from their work in Boston, Lincolnshire. Comparing the number of statutory homeless cases recorded by the local authority with the number of homeless people approaching various service providers in the district over a six-month period, they report that the local authority only recorded as homeless 23.4 per cent of the cases recorded by other agencies.

The other main source of data informing understanding of the incidence of homelessness in England is rough sleeper headcounts. Whereas official homeless statistics are prone to underestimate the incidence and extent of homelessness in rural England, rough sleeper headcounts have been revealed to deny the very existence of rough sleeping in rural England. This failing is of significance, not because rough sleeping is, in numerical terms, a major dimension of the homeless experience in rural England, but because it is an extreme and, in urban areas, a very visible situation, which, as Cloke *et al.* (2001b) point out, has been adopted both as an iconographic representation of homelessness and identified by successive governments as a policy issue deserving particular attention.

In 1999 the government established and charged the Rough Sleepers Unit (RSU) with meeting the Prime Minister's target of reducing the number of people sleeping rough in England by two-thirds. The RSU targeted its efforts on 30 towns and cities identified as particular concentrations of rough sleeping through the local application of the government-approved method for counting rough sleeping. On the basis of successive counts undertaken in these 30 towns and cities, the government claimed in December 2001 that the Prime Minister's target of reducing rough sleeping had been met (DTLR, 2001a) and the work of the homeless directorate has subsequently focused on maintaining reduced levels of rough sleeping in these locations. The very particular geography of problem recognition legitimizing the focus of the government's rough sleeper programme on London and a small number of larger towns and cities relies, however, on evidence collected through the inconsistent application of a questionable method of limited relevance and practical use when applied in rural areas (Robinson, 2004). First, central government does not require local authorities to undertake counts of the local rough sleeper population, merely suggesting that authorities do so if they perceive there to be a problem with rough sleeping in their local area. Published headcount data reveal rural authorities to be far less willing than their urban counterparts to explore the incidence of rough sleeping through headcounts of the number of people sleeping rough within their district. Second, the government-approved method for counting rough sleeping – which involves teams of enumerators visiting known haunts of rough sleepers on a particular night and counting people bedded down in order to generate a snapshot estimate of the number of people sleeping rough in an area – is insensitive to the particular difficulties of counting rough sleeping in rural locations.

Although underestimating the incidence of rough sleeping, the government has claimed that the headcount method provides a relative measure of the scale of the problem in different locations. Rural spaces serve to hide homeless people, however. There are few obvious points of concentration for homeless people in rural areas, resulting in people 'bedding down' in a more diverse range of situations and locations when sleeping rough – barns, out-houses, garages, parks, cars and such like (see Table 7.2, p. 105). There is also an absence of specialist agencies to inform and assist with headcounts, whilst the 'stigmatic visibility' associated with homelessness in rural areas can lead homeless people in rural areas to adopt strategies of invisibility (Robinson, 2004). Headcounts undertaken in rural areas have therefore tended to return low or zero counts of rough sleeping, 28 of the 30 rural local authorities detailed by the Minister for Housing in 1999[1] as having undertaken rough sleeper headcounts returning counts of less than 10, compared to 25 out of 67 urban authorities (Robinson, 2004). In subsequent years, local authorities returning estimates of less than 10 have not been included in the rough sleeping figures and only figures relating to towns and cities with the highest headcounts have been collated and made publicly available (Robinson, 2004). Rural rough sleeping is therefore rendered invisible by official evidence, when, as we will now see, it is in fact a common experience among homeless people in rural England.

An alternative estimate of rural homelessness: a case study example

Official statistics are a notoriously unreliable measure of homelessness in England, but are particularly prone to underestimate rural homelessness, which has largely remained statistically hidden. Recognizing that if a problem is not observed and measured it is unlikely to attract the attention of policy or be the target of resources, the Countryside Agency (the statutory agency charged with conserving and enhancing England's countryside and promoting social and economic opportunity for the people who live there) recently funded a project to develop a cost-effective method for more accurately estimating homelessness and rough sleeping in rural areas, which could be used by officers, rather than specialist research staff, would demand minimal resources and could easily be implemented on a regular basis.[2]

The method developed represents a relatively simple enumeration exercise, with information being collected through the implementation of a basic screening tool by agencies who come into contact with homeless people during a specified time period. Potential outputs include a count of the stock of homelessness (number of people homeless at a particular time) and an estimate of the hidden homeless population. The method was piloted in North Lincolnshire – a rural district with a population of 150,000 located south of the Humber estuary, centred around the town of Scunthorpe and including the market towns of Brigg and Barton-on-Humber – and proved capable of providing important insights into the previously hidden and denied experiences of rural homelessness in the district.

The first step of the method is to establish what is already known about homelessness in the local area, the limits of current understanding and the need for more detailed and accurate information. In the North Lincolnshire study, this involved a review of service user records of agencies working with homeless people, which immediately revealed a credibility gap between the number of homeless clients referred to three key services in the district working with homeless people, and official estimates of homelessness and rough sleeping in the district. In particular, service user records suggested high levels of homelessness among groups traditionally neglected by official statistics, such as young people and single person households. For example, a housing advice agency for young people reported working with 408 young homeless people in the previous year, and a resettlement service for single homeless people reported receiving 287 applications from homeless people during this same year, 105 of which were from people aged between 18 and 25 years old. Official statistics for this year, meanwhile, only recognized a total of 308 households as homeless in the district.

The quality and rigour of data collected by service providers cannot be presumed and the insights provided are limited by the application of different definitions of homelessness and sleeping rough. The credibility gap between the evidence provided by the service user records of front-line agencies and the official statistics proved, in North Lincolnshire, however, a revelation for many in the district and was vital in helping secure the commitment of the local authority and other service providers to the count exercise. The commitment of local agencies to the count was critical, given that the method relies on service providers implementing a specially designed screening tool capable of collecting basic information about the current accommodation situations of clients. It is also important to secure the involvement of a wide range of agencies, given the relative dearth of targeted services for homeless people in rural areas and the consequent reliance of homeless people on a wider range of statutory, voluntary and community sector services, as well as networks of kith and kin, to satisfy their material needs and secure the help and assistance they require (Robinson and Coward, 2003). There is also a need to look beyond homeless-specific services located in larger towns, to minimize the potential bias associated with the genderized and spatialized nature of provision for homeless people (Cloke *et al.*, 2001b). Nine local agencies were involved in the count in North Lincolnshire, working with various client groups and located across the district: a young person's housing advice service; a day centre for people in distress and vulnerable situations; an accommodation referral service for single homeless people; Connexions officers (the government support service for young people aged between 13 and 19 years old); two housing associations; and the local authority youth service, housing department and local one-stop-shop offices.

Central to any count exercise is the screening tool, which needs to be capable of collecting information about the current accommodation situation and personal details of service users, while being easy to understand and quick to administer. The screening tool piloted in North Lincolnshire contained 13 questions focusing on a respondent's current accommodation, any recent experiences of sleeping rough, the location of their last home and where they are currently living, age, gender, ethnic origin, main reason for leaving last home, and case identifier information to allow the eradication of double counting. Homelessness was defined as living in an insecure housing situation (sleeping on a friend's or relative's floor or sofa, squatting, staying in a bed and breakfast hotel or a short or long stay hostel, staying as a guest in someone else's home or sleeping rough). Rough sleeping was defined as sleeping on the street, in a doorway or stairwell, in outbuildings, a barn or garage, in a building or caravan without services such as running water, in a bus shelter, a railway station or in some other roofless situation.

Implementation of the count in North Lincolnshire took place during the calendar month of October 2001. Front-line officers were requested to ask, wherever practical and possible, all clients during this month to answer the anonymous questionnaire. The count took place in October on the advice of local service providers, who reported that the homeless and roofless population was at its greatest during the autumn months and were keen to record homelessness at its seasonal peak. Completed questionnaires were collected from the participating agencies, the data was cleaned (incomplete and invalid cases removed), double counting eradicated through analysis of the case identifier information and counts of the homeless and rough sleeping population generated.

During the *single* month of October 2001 the alternative count recorded 91 people as homeless in North Lincolnshire (Robinson and Reeve, 2002). The statutory homeless statistics for the fourth quarter of 2001, the three-month period including the month of the count, recorded a total of 63 homeless households. A repeat count was undertaken in the district in April 2003 by council officers and recorded 130 people as homeless in the district during this single month, compared to an official count for the second quarter of 2003, the three-month period including the month of the count, of 98 homeless households. Even allowing for the fact that official statistics count households and measure flow (the number of households officially recognized as becoming homeless during a time period), while the alternative method counts individuals and measures stock (the number of people homeless at a particular time), the alternative count paints a picture of homelessness in the district clearly at odds with the official position. Even more startling, however, were the insights into rough sleeping provided by the count exercise.

Table 7.2 The situations of homeless people in North Lincolnshire (October 2001)

Accommodation situation	Number	Percentage
Sleeping rough	**21**	**23.1**
Street	6	6.6
Doorway/stairwell	2	2.2
Outbuildings/barn/garage	3	3.3
Car	3	3.3
Bus shelter	5	5.5
Park	2	2.2
Living in insecure accommodation	**70**	**76.9**
Friend's/relative's floor or sofa	43	47.2
Vacant property/squatting	1	1.1
Bed and breakfast hotel	1	1.1
Hostel	7	7.7
Guest in someone else's home	6	6.6
Being evicted from own home	7	7.7
Escaping violence at home	3	3.3
Other homeless situation	2	2.2
Total	**91**	**100.0**

Source: Robinson and Reeve (2002).

A previous headcount of the rough sleeping population in North Lincolnshire had recorded three people sleeping rough (Natress, 2000) and the government has accepted a zero estimate of rough sleeping in the district. During the month of the October 2001 count exercise Table 7.2), the alternative method recorded 21 people as sleeping rough. In addition, a further 30 homeless people reported that they had slept rough for at least one night in the previous month (Robinson, 2004). In total, therefore, 51 people reported a recent or ongoing experience of rough sleeping. This relatively high incidence of periodic rough sleeping was confirmed by the April 2003 count, which, despite one agency failing to adequately detail the specific accommodation situations of 47 homeless people, revealed 20 people to be currently sleeping rough in the district.

The importance of this enumeration exercise, and other such efforts to shine a light on the incidence and extent of rural homelessness, is that they expose a problem previously unseen, often denied and consistently neglected within the policy response to homelessness. Evidence that homelessness is a lived reality for many people in rural England also raises the question to which I now turn: what does it mean to be homeless in rural England?

Rural dimensions of the homeless experience

Homeless people in rural England are little different from their urban counterparts. Although it appears that the age profile of the homeless population in rural areas might be younger than in urban areas (Robinson and Coward, 2003), comparative analysis of the family backgrounds of young homeless people has found the personal circumstances and vulnerabilities of homeless people in rural areas to be essentially the same as their urban counterparts (Smith and Ing, 2001; Streich, 2000). The comparative study of hidden homelessness found similar proportions of homeless people in the rural and urban case studies to have spent time in local authority care, to have been subject to probation service supervision, to be suffering from mental health problems and to be coping with a drug dependency problem (Robinson, 2003). Other problems – alcohol dependency and time spent in prison – although less common within the rural homeless population surveyed were still prevalent experiences (Table 7.3). Homeless people in rural areas, it would appear, exhibit many of the same vulnerabilities as a result of age, health and personal history as homeless people in urban locations. The circumstances, situations and experiences of rural homeless people are rendered distinct and unique, however, not only by the socio-cultural peculiarities of rural life discussed by Cloke and Milbourne in Chapter 6, but also by the particular structural conditions and associated opportunities available in rural England, as revealed below.

Rural areas have experienced dramatic recent changes in the nature of employment, resulting in rural residents being faced with a more restricted choice of jobs, limited training opportunities, constrained job progression and lower rates of pay than their urban counterparts (Chapman *et al.*, 1998; Shucksmith *et al.*, 1996; Townsend, 1991). Opportunities to extend travel to work areas, meanwhile, are often hampered by the limits of public transport provision (Rugg

Table 7.3 Personal problems and challenges experienced by homeless people (%)

Issue	Craven (n=35)	Sheffield (n=47)	London (n=82)
Mental health problem	31.4	38.3	28.0
Learning disability	0.0	8.5	12.2
Drug dependency	25.7	36.2	19.5
Alcohol dependency	11.4	25.5	17.1
Probation service supervision	34.3	40.4	31.7
Prison/young offenders' institute	17.1	46.8	34.1
Time in local authority care	22.9	21.3	25.6

Source: Robinson and Coward (2003).

and Jones, 1999). The potential impact of these factors on household incomes, poverty levels and, consequently, security of tenure and the incidence and duration of episodes of homelessness has been compounded by the shortage of affordable housing in rural areas. House prices have been pushed up, often by growing demand from affluent in-migrants and through the purchase of second homes (Chapman *et al.*, 1998; Diaz and Colman, 1997; Ford *et al.*, 1997; Shucksmith, 1990). The social rented sector is small and shrinking, as the new build programme now delivered by the housing association sector fails to keep up with the sale of council properties to sitting tenants through the right-to-buy programme. By 2004, the social rented sector accounted for only 13.4 per cent of the housing stock in rural districts, compared to 22.4 per cent in urban districts (Countryside Agency, 2004). The private rented sector, although relatively large in rural areas, has increasingly catered for the tourist trade and provided short-term seasonal lets and seen an associated rise in rent levels. The opportunities for escaping homelessness are therefore severely restricted, while the targeted support and assistance, commonplace in urban areas, is conspicuous by its absence. Becoming homeless, and surviving and escaping homelessness in rural England is consequently rendered a spatially unique and particular experience.

Becoming homeless

People become homeless for various reasons. Typically, however, homelessness is triggered by a particular event or incident that people struggle to cope with because of personal vulnerabilities and inadequacies in available support and provision. These personal vulnerabilities represent aspatial at-risk indicators of homelessness, being common in rural and urban areas and including an experience of living in local authority care as a child, time spent in prison or a young offender institute, long-term unemployment, mental and physical health problems, alcohol and drug use problems, debt, including a record of rent arrears, and a poor record of educational and training achievement. The particular triggers and pathways into homelessness in rural England, however, appear to be distinct and unique.

The triggers of rural homelessness commonly include relationship breakdown, family or friends no longer being able or willing to accommodate, being required by a landlord to leave rented accommodation, and financial problems (Cloke *et al,*, 2001a; Evans, 1999; Robinson and Coward, 2003; Robinson and Reeve, 2002; Sawtell, 2002; Wright and Everitt, 1995). These factors have also been revealed to be the principal triggers of homelessness in urban areas, but a number of subtle and important rural–urban variations have been revealed. First, the loss of private rented or tied accommodation is of increased importance in rural areas, possibly reflecting a reduction in the pool of rented accommodation as a result of seasonal lets to accommodate the tourist trade and reductions in the number of properties tied to employment in the agricultural sector (Cloke *et al.*, 2001a). By 2001, according to the Countryside Agency (2004), there were 135,000 second and holiday homes in England in 2001, 64.1 per cent of which were located in rural districts, with second homes accounting for 2.5 per cent of the total dwelling stock in 'remote' rural areas. The private rented sector is therefore unable in many rural locations to provide accessible and affordable accommodation for people on low incomes and in receipt of state benefits, as we will see when considering the particular challenges of escaping homelessness in rural England.

A second rural–urban variation is the higher level of mortgage arrears recorded in rural districts, perhaps reflecting limited opportunities for renting and the forced reliance of lower income households on house purchase if they want to remain in the area, at a time of above average house-price rises in rural locations (Cloke *et al.*, 2001a). According to the Countryside Agency (2004), by 2003 one-third (36.8 per cent) of the rural population were required to spend more than 50 per cent of their household income per month on mortgage repayments to purchase a home in their local district. The hidden homelessness study also revealed more general financial difficulties to be an important trigger of homelessness in rural areas, one in five homeless people in the rural case study of Craven citing financial matters as the main reason for leaving their last secure accommodation, compared to just 2.4 per cent of homeless people in Sheffield (Table 7.4).

Table 7.4 Reasons for homeless people leaving last secure accommodation (%)

Reason	Craven (*n=35*)	Sheffield (*n=47*)	London (*n=82*)
Dispute/relationship breakdown with parents	15.4	12.2	23.6
Parents no longer able to accommodate	7.7	2.4	1.4
Relationship breakdown with partner	11.5	43.9	23.6
Dispute with other occupants (not parents or partner)	3.8	0.0	2.8
Eviction	7.7	4.9	5.6
Financial reasons	19.2	2.4	11.1
Overcrowded	0.0	2.4	0.0
To seek employment	3.8	0.0	11.1
To live somewhere else	3.8	2.4	0.0
Other	26.9	26.8	20.8
Total	**100**	**100**	**100**

Source: Robinson and Coward (2003)

The hidden homelessness study also found that, despite the young age profile of the rural homeless population surveyed and the fact that 40 per cent reported living with parents immediately before becoming homeless (compared to only 18 per cent in Sheffield), a relatively small proportion reported leaving home as a consequence of a dispute or relationship breakdown with a parent or guardian. More in-depth discussion with respondents suggested that young people in rural areas were often compelled to leave the parental home by problems their parents were encountering, such as financial difficulties, eviction or mortgage repossession, rather than a breakdown in relations.

The common pathway into rural homelessness appears to involve people staying with family and friends as the first port of call upon becoming homeless (Robinson, 2003). Reliance on family and friends was explained by homeless people questioned in the hidden homelessness study with reference to the difficulties of accessing alternative provision at short notice, given the dearth of affordable housing opportunities and the limited provision of emergency accommodation, and limited awareness about what accommodation was locally available (Robinson and Coward, 2003). Young people, in particular, were found to be unclear and uncertain about how they might go about securing a tenancy with a private or social landlord in a bid to avoid homelessness, and unaware whether temporary accommodation was available in the local area. Liam is 24 years old and was interviewed in the rural case study as part of the hidden homelessness study. Before becoming homeless Liam lived in a council house in a small market town with his mother, who gave him just one week's notice that she was giving up her tenancy and moving out of the area and that he would have to find somewhere else to live. Liam was keen to stay in the town where he had grown up, had family and friends and employment, but was uncertain how to go about finding somewhere to live. He reported wanting to take over his mother's council tenancy, but was unclear how to do so and was worried that he could not afford the rent on his current salary. In the event, unaware of any temporary accommodation available locally and not knowing if and how the local authority might be able to help, Liam saw no option but to move in with his sister and her family, sleeping on the sofa in the living room:

> I did not know about it [local authority]. It was a case of, I was naïve. I had never done this before, never tried to get a place of my own before, so I did not know how to approach it. I was more scared of making a complete and utter arse of myself than anything else.

Liam, like many young people threatened with homelessness, was unsure about available opportunities and how to secure alternative accommodation. The hidden homelessness study also uncovered a degree of scepticism among homeless people in the rural case study about the help they were likely to receive from the council housing department, scepticism that would appear to be well placed, given, as revealed above, the reluctance of the local authority to recognize homeless applicants as statutorily homeless and in priority need for accommodation. Hayley, for example, whose case is discussed in detail in Robinson and Coward (2003), is 19 years old and has been homeless three months. Told to leave, without warning, by her mother and step-father, Hayley chose not to approach the local authority for help. Asked why, Hayley explained that she had previously been homeless and had approached the local authority, but had been told that she would have to wait a number of years for a tenancy and could only be offered temporary hostel accommodation outside the district:

> I went to the Council. They just said 'no' basically … They said it can take anything up to two years, and unless you are actually on the streets they can't deal with it. And because of my age and I was still at College I was better going to a Housing Association.

With little time to seek advice, having received no warning that she was going to have to leave her mother's, and unaware of possible alternatives, Hayley went straight to a friend for help:

> I know there is an emergency room [temporary accommodation] in Skipton … somewhere … My mum just told me to go, and I had nowhere to go so I went to my friend's … she was quite willing. She knows what arguments were like with my mum …

In the three months since becoming homeless, Hayley has spent all her time staying with friends, although she reported that her preference would be to move into temporary accommodation where help, assistance and advice might be available. In Craven, however, as in many other rural districts, there is a dearth of such temporary accommodation.

Surviving homelessness

Many people are thought to leave rural areas upon becoming homeless and to migrate to larger towns and cities. It appears that a large proportion of the homeless people who move away are keen to return to their home rural area and that such movements are often forced – by the lack of emergency accommodation and targeted assistance for homeless people, the limited availability of social housing and inaccessibility of private renting – rather than driven by choice. Many homeless people, however, are resistant to moving and choose to stay put.

There is also evidence of homeless people moving into rural areas, drawn by the greater anonymity, privacy and freedom and hoping for a better quality of life in a more problem-free living environment (Cloke *et al.*, 2003; Evans, 1999; Robinson and Reeve, 2002). The rural homeless condition, however, is far from problem free, although it is certainly distinct from the experience in urban locations, the virtual absence of emergency support, advice and accommodation for homeless people and the limits of more general opportunities, including affordable housing, employment, public transport, health service provision and social care, forcing homeless people in rural areas to adopt very different survival strategies.

Rural homelessness is largely contained within civil society. Most homeless people are forced to rely on family and friends for a place to stay because of the dearth of alternatives, other than sleeping rough (Centrepoint, 2000a; Evans, 1999; Robinson and Reeve, 2002; Wright and Everitt, 1995). The accommodation histories of 165 homeless people collected during the hidden homelessness study, however, revealed staying with friends and relatives to be a common homeless experience across England; 77 per cent of all homeless people in the rural case study of Craven had stayed with family and friends since becoming homeless, but so had 72 per cent of homeless people in Sheffield and 69 per cent in London. Significantly, however, over two-thirds of the homeless people in Craven had only ever stayed with friends and relatives since becoming homeless, compared to just 13 per cent in London and 4 per cent in Sheffield (Robinson and Coward, 2003).

Staying with family and friends might be presumed to be a comfortable and problem-free situation, allowing homeless people to avoid the risks and hazards associated with living in hostel accommodation, for example. The hidden homelessness study, however, revealed staying with family and friends in response to homelessness to often be a problematic situation (Robinson and Coward, 2003). Many people complained about the lack of personal space or privacy associated with sharing a room or sleeping on a sofa. Various limits and restrictions on behaviour, lifestyle and movements were also reported. Homeless people, for example, reported rarely having a door key when staying with a friend or relative, their movements and use of the accommodation therefore being restricted by their reliance on their friend or relative to let them back in every time they left the property. Carol and her two children, for example, left home in the middle of the night after Carol was the victim of a violent assault from her partner. Initially staying with a friend, Carol and her children soon moved in with her mother and father. While staying with her parents, Carol shared a single room with her two children, sleeping on the floor, while her eldest child slept in the bed and her young daughter slept in a cot. Carol was unable to pay board, having no income other than what she received in Incapacity Benefit, but did pay for food and reported trying to help out around the house, by cooking meals and helping with housework. Without a key, Carol was unable to come and go as she pleased and reported leaving the house each morning and not returning until the evening, spending the day visiting friends and walking around town:

> I used to get up before they did so I could use the bathroom. I would get the children up and be giving them their breakfast when my dad came down. Then I would take them to school and nursery. A lot of friends were very good, inviting us for lunch and things because they knew the situation. Other than that we were trailing around until we picked Ben up at half three. Then I would go back and make tea for everybody … then I would be just sat upstairs. I did not have a television or anything so I would just be sat in the room. But it was a hell of a lot better than what I had left.

People staying with family and friends rarely have a room or bed of their own, the familiar euphemism 'sofa surfing' accurately capturing the reality of staying with family and friends for most homeless people. It can therefore prove difficult to get a good night's sleep, as Matt, who is 23 years old and has been homeless for almost a year, reported. In Matt's case, these difficulties were reported to have caused problems at work, ultimately leading to him losing his job:

> I fell out with my mum and moved to my aunty's, then my friend asked me if I wanted to stay at his house, and I had to sleep on the settee. I would be coming home from work, I would be that knackered I just wanted to go to sleep, but I couldn't because they [friend] would just sit up talking until about three in the morning. So my body clock was all wrong … it made it difficult to work. I started having days off and I ended up getting the sack because I was so tired.

Staying with family and friends is also a highly insecure situation. Reliant on the goodwill of their friend or relative, homeless people can be asked to leave at any time, without reason or explanation. As Andrew, a 27-year-old man who was interviewed in the rural case study as part of the hidden homelessness study, pointed out:

> … you are always having to think 'where am I going to go next'? It is always in the back of your mind. You might be alright tonight, but what about tomorrow? You are never sure who is going to say yes. It's just really unsettled.

Andrew has a drug dependency problem, a history of time spent subject to probation service supervision and is currently unemployed. Since leaving home two months ago following an argument with his mother, Andrew has stayed with eight different friends, moving from one friend to another every two days, in the hope of not overstaying his welcome:

> A couple of people offered, but I did have to ask. You don't want to put yourself on anyone. I felt really bad. They have no problem with me stopping, it was just me. I did not feel right, you know what I mean, and that is why I was only stopping for a couple of nights even if they said I could stay another night. I thought if you get too comfy and into the place I am not going to want to go ... I pretty much avoid that by not staying there that long. If you stop a week or so you start getting under people's feet. So that is what I was quite keen to avoid. So I stayed two days, that is not long enough to get sick of someone. I could always ask to go back.

Relatives are a finite resource and homeless people are less able to call on family members for help the longer they are homeless. Friends are a more renewable resource, but arrangements can still break down, given the inevitable tensions and practical difficulties associated with staying as a guest in often cramped and overcrowded conditions. Over half of the stays with a friend analysed in the hidden homelessness study were found to have been less than a month. Stays with a family member were found to last longer, but were far less common and increasingly infrequent the longer people were homeless. The dearth of emergency accommodation, the consequent reliance of homeless people in rural England on family and friends for shelter and the relative insecurity of these arrangements therefore appear to be rendering the rural homelessness experience one of frequent, short-stay moves.

The longer people are homeless, the further these moves appear to extend, as people widen their search for accommodation opportunities when agreements with friends and relatives break down. So while many moves appear to be very localized, a detail that Cloke *et al.* (2003) have related to the very 'localness' of local in the rural context, necessity can demand that homeless people move increasing distances in search of shelter and the assistance they require. This does not necessarily mean, however, that people migrate to larger towns and cities. Many of these moves remain within the rural context. The North Lincolnshire study, for example, found evidence of movements between villages and towns within the area: one-third of the 91 homeless people counted as homeless in October 2001 having moved within the district since becoming homeless and over half of people with a recent or ongoing experience of rough sleeping having moved within the district since becoming homeless (Robinson, 2004).

Dispersed within the frequent moves of rural homeless people appear to be intermittent periods of rough sleeping, as and when arrangements with family and friends break down, as Andrew's experience illustrates: 'Only once have I been stuck. That was when his [friend's] family were coming to stay. I had to leave. That is when I had to leave. I ended up in Skipton on a park bench.' Many incidences of rough sleeping in rural areas are therefore relatively short lived, lasting only as long as it takes people to negotiate to stay with another friend or relative. Hence, 38 of the 51 homeless people in the North Lincolnshire count who had slept rough in the previous month had done so for one week or less and 16 had slept rough for no more than one or two nights (Robinson and Reeve, 2002). As opportunities to stay with family and friends are exhausted, however, incidents of rough sleeping become longer and more frequent, 13 of the 51 people with a current or recent experience of sleeping rough in the North Lincolnshire count having slept rough for more than one week in the previous month, and six having slept rough for more than two weeks.

Just as the unique and particular geography of accommodation opportunities in rural England informs the strategies adopted by homeless people to finding a place to stay and avoiding sleeping rough, so the very different geographies of support and provision have driven homeless people to adopt very different patterns of service use to their counterparts in urban areas. These distinctions are well illustrated by the study of hidden homelessness in England, which compared service use among people staying with family and friends in London, Sheffield and the rural district of Craven (Robinson and Coward, 2003). In London and Sheffield, homeless-specific services played an important role in the lives of many homeless people, including those staying with family and friends. Although there was a distinction in the pattern of service use depending upon how long a person had been homeless and how aware they therefore were about available provision, day centres were found to be very important resource for homeless people, providing cheap food, a place to shower and wash clothes, as well as to meet people, socialize and share and learn from each other's homeless experiences. People who had been homeless longer were also heavily reliant on support and assistance provided by homeless-specific services including medical services and advice centres.

In sharp contrast, few homeless people in the rural case study reported any contact with a homeless-specific service, reflecting the virtual absence of targeted provision for homeless people in the area. Given the dearth of specialist services, homeless people in the rural case study were more likely to have sought help and been assisted by generic, non-specialist service providers, including hospitals, advice centres, the probation service and college staff. A resourceful response to the lack of targeted provision for homeless people, reliance on mainstream service providers, however, raises a number of problems. First, homeless people can encounter problems accessing mainstream provision, the lack of a fixed address, for example, being a major constraint in accessing publicly funded health care provision (Robinson, 1998). Second, sector-specific service providers, such as health care specialists, probation officers and college staff, will likely struggle to comprehend and respond effectively to the complex, multiple needs of homeless people, a fact that has led in urban locations to the provision of discrete homelessness services. Third, the reliance of homeless people in rural areas on broad networks of kith and kin for accommodation and mainstream service providers for help and assistance serves to render the experiences of rural homelessness susceptible to what Cloke *et al.* (2003) refer to as 'discursive scattering', whereby the situations and needs of homeless people in rural areas are comprehended as a host of problems other than homelessness. Finally, without an obvious point of congregation and concentration, homeless people in rural areas can often be invisible to each other and are therefore unable to tap into the informal support, camaraderie, advice and assistance that has been recognized as so important to surviving and negotiating an escape from homelessness (Robinson, 1998).

The difficulties associated with surviving homelessness in the service-poor spaces of rural England were recognized by a respondent to the hidden homelessness study who had experience of being homeless in Craven, as well as in the nearby city of Leeds. Jack is 30 years old and has been homeless for three years, since terminating his tenancy with a social landlord in a bid to escape problems with his tenancy and his neighbours. Jack reported drug use problems, poor health and periods spent in prison following a number of convictions for drug-related crime. Jack identified various distinctive aspects of being homeless in a rural area, compared to a large city. Integral to the distinctiveness of the rural homeless experience was the dearth of formal assistance and targeted service provision:

> It wasn't like I was really dirty person. I would get washed in the morning in the toilets … There are places in Leeds that can help you, like St Ann's [centre for homeless people] and that, you can wash your clothes. There's a doctor at St Ann's … It's bad being homeless here, in somewhere like Skipton where there is nothing for you. It's bad news, you know what I mean? There is a soup kitchen two days a week now… . As I say, there is no catering for the homeless, apart from the soup kitchen. You can't even get a blanket. If you had to sleep out for the night you could not get a blanket.

Jack also alluded to the socio-cultural policing of homeless and rough sleeping in rural areas, discussed by Cloke and Milbourne in Chapter 6, and reflected on the very different range of informal opportunities available in rural areas:

> If you tried to sleep in a doorway you would probably be arrested. They don't want people like that in Skipton, they don't want people like me in Skipton, but why shouldn't I when I was born in Skipton?

Jack had spent much of his three years in Leeds squatting in abandoned properties but reported opportunities to squat being few and far between in rural areas, a situation confirmed by a recent study of squatting in response to homelessness, which found more than one in four homeless people in urban areas to have some experience of squatting since becoming homeless, while no homeless people in the rural case study had squatted in response to homelessness, with respondents referring to the absence of both the social anonymity and the required opportunities provided by abandoned or empty properties (Reeve and Coward, 2004).

Escaping homelessness

The more restricted opportunities in rural England to negotiate an escape from homelessness have already been touched on. Key among these is the continued contraction of the already small social rented sector, which has historically played a key role in freeing people from homelessness through the allocation of housing to people in need. Sales through the right-to-buy programme, through which sitting tenants are able to purchase their home at discounted prices, continue to outstrip the new build programme now delivered by the housing association sector. The more restrictive interpretation by rural local authorities of their duties under the homeless legislation therefore comes as no surprise, as they struggle to manage demand for a depleting stock base. Nor is it surprising that homeless people in rural locations have few expectations about the help they are likely to receive from the local authority, are cynical about their chances of being recognized as homeless and, consequently, see little point approaching their local authority for help (Robinson and Coward, 2003). Failure to approach the local authority, however, cuts homeless people off from what in many rural areas is the only source of advice about local housing opportunities, local authorities having a statutory duty to provide advice to homeless people.

The failure of the social rented sector in rural areas to provide an adequate and accessible escape route out of homelessness forces many homeless people to look to the private rented sector for accommodation. Government policy has increasingly emphasized the role that the private rented sector might play in accommodating homeless people, and the sector is relatively large in rural areas. Issues of availability, accessibility and affordability, however, prevent many rural households from entering the sector (Cloke et al., 2001a). Wright and Everitt (1995) report, for example, that more than half of the 250 homeless people surveyed in Boston, Lincolnshire, had tried to access private rented accommodation but had failed, the down payment of a deposit and the rent levels of available accommodation barring entry.

Respondents in the hidden homelessness survey had also often tried to access private rented accommodation in a bid to escape homelessness, but found access was restricted by the blanket exclusion by many landlords of people claiming benefits and the requirement that new tenants put down a deposit or bond payment. A local bond scheme had been established in Craven in recognition of these problems and had provided bond guarantees for some of the homeless people surveyed. Entry to the private rented sector is still effectively barred for many young homeless people less than 25 years old by the vagaries of Single Room Rent Restriction (SRRR) applied to Housing Benefit (the rent rebate paid by local councils to people on low incomes) (Kemp and Rugg, 1998; Streich, 2000; White and Levison, 1999). The SRRR limits the Housing Benefit paid to single people less than 25 years old to the average market value of a single room with shared use of a living room, kitchen and bathroom. As evidence to the House of Commons Select Committee on Social Security tabled by Centrepoint (2000b) points out, there is a lack of available accommodation matching the Single Room Rent definition in many areas of the country, including rural areas. The accommodation is often in poor condition and when young people manage to access accommodation, they are often left facing a shortfall between the rent charged and the Housing Benefit paid, which they will get into debt trying to make up. According to Centrepoint, in some areas young people are increasingly relying on hostel accommodation because of difficulties affording their own tenancy, raising concerns about the capacity of the private rented sector to provide a realizable escape route out of homelessness for young people. In rural areas the picture is even bleaker, a move into hostel accommodation rarely being an option and the long term prognosis being continued reliance on friends and relatives for shelter and the possibility of more frequent and longer lasting periods of rough sleeping.

Sustaining an escape from homelessness is not only about accessing bricks and mortar. Homeless people have complex personal and social problems and can often require support and assistance to successfully sustain a tenancy and escape homelessness (Robinson and Hawtin, 2002). The assistance required can range from intensive or specialist services required by people with community care needs, through to practical assistance and advice about welfare rights, money matters and the practicalities of managing a tenancy. Joe's story is detailed in the North Lincolnshire study (Robinson and Reeve, 2002) and illustrates the numerous difficulties that homeless people can encounter managing and sustaining their escape from homelessness. Joe is 20 years old and was sleeping rough for six months before being allocated a property by the council. Joe reported that the property was not furnished when he moved in and that he had no furniture or cooking facilities. The lack of furniture and other basic goods, such as a fridge and cooker, have been recognized as increasing the likelihood that homeless people will abandon properties soon after moving in (DTLR, 2001b). In response, furniture schemes have been set up with the aim of limiting the likelihood of tenancy abandonment and repeat homelessness. One such scheme exists in North Lincolnshire, but Joe was unaware of its existence and reported relying on a nearby drop-in centre for hot food: 'I scrape through. I use the Forge [drop-in centre] for meals, but that's only a couple of days a week. The rest of the time I just scrape through.' Joe also reported that his flat is located in an unpopular neighbourhood, where drug use and dealing is rife: 'One day I came home and there were lads shooting up in the flat. I did know them, but they weren't friends. They'd kicked the door in and were using the flat.'

This represents a particular problem for Joe, who is currently on a methadone programme in an attempt to address his own heroin use. Joe reported that the council were aware of his record of drug use when they offered him the property, but apparently did not consider or act on the possibility that living in this area of town might undermine Joe's efforts to tackle his drug use and could put him at greater risk of repeat homelessness. Joe also reported that his house had been broken into 12 times since he moved in, the most recent incident involving the theft of the hot water boiler. Joe was reluctant to report the incident to the council, fearful of the consequences:

> No I haven't reported it yet because the council are going to blame me aren't they. They know I've been a drug user and they're going to think I did it for drugs. They might evict me then.

Joe is currently facing eviction for rent arrears accumulated during the administrative delay in processing his Housing Benefit claim. Recently, however, he has been in touch with a local advice service for young people, who have advocated on his behalf with the local authority and succeeded in negotiating a suspension of eviction proceedings for the time being.

Joe's case study graphically illustrates why relevant advice, support and assistance are considered so important to helping people secure an escape from homelessness. Since 2003, housing related support services have been resourced through the Supporting People programme, through which central government allocates resources to local authorities to distribute to service providers in response to recognized local needs. The implications for the resourcing of service provision targeted at the needs of homeless people in rural areas have not been explored and require urgent attention. There are, however, two immediate concerns. In the short term the Supporting People programme is focusing on maintaining existing provision, thereby maintaining the inadequacies in targeted provision for people in rural areas experiencing and struggling to escape homelessness.

More worrying, however, is the likelihood that the discursive denial and political neglect of rural homelessness will be relayed into the strategic planning and future commissioning of local housing related support services and serve to reproduce these inadequacies over the long term. This scenario would appear to be an inevitability if the development of what is supposed to be a more strategically planned model of local service provision that provides appropriate support in the right place at the right time is built on an understanding of local needs that fails to look beyond official statistical evidence that underestimates to the point of denial the incidence and extent of homelessness and rough sleeping in rural areas.

Conclusion

In 2002 the government heralded the arrival of a brave new era in the policy response to homelessness. The first national homeless strategy was launched, the Homelessness Act 2002 was introduced and the homelessness directorate was created and located in the Office of the Deputy Prime Minister to push forward the policy response to homelessness. Policy continued, however, to invest heavily in the notion that homelessness is an urban phenomenon. The Homelessness Act 2002 reasserted the 'justiciable' rights of homeless people to permanent accommodation, if recognized as meeting statutory criteria. It failed, however, to challenge the restricted availability of these rights in rural areas. The Homelessness Act 2002 also required all local authorities to formulate a comprehensive, multi-agency response to homelessness, but the local reviews of homelessness on which strategies are built rely on counts and estimates of homelessness and rough sleeping that systematically underestimate the scale of the problem in rural areas. The first national homeless strategy – 'More than a Roof' – was championed by the Secretary of State as representing a shift toward focusing help and assistance as much on the people as on the places where they live (Byers, 2002). The only reference in 'More than a Roof' to rural homelessness, however, relates to the purchase of properties in rural areas as second homes or by long-distance commuters, which is driving up house prices in rural locations and resulting in a shortage of affordable housing for local people on average incomes (DTLR, 2002). Rural homelessness is once again recognized as an unfortunate consequence of the popularity of rural life, rather than a manifestation of wider social problems. The activities of the homelessness directorate, which was established in 2002 and set the task of developing more strategic approaches to homelessness and strengthening help to people who are homeless or at risk of homelessness, have consequently focused on tackling homelessness in urban England.

Research and analysis has been largely complicit in the denial and neglect of rural homelessness by policy. Countless reports emerge each year addressing different aspects of the homelessness problem in England,[3] but rarely has analysis focused on or been sensitive to the particulars of rural homelessness. In part, this lacuna reflects the reliance of housing and homelessness research on state funding and the consequent focus of studies on the obsessions of contemporary policy, which certainly do not include rural homelessness. As this chapter has shown, however, there is an emerging body of work that is actively challenging the discursive denial and political neglect of homelessness in rural England and making visible the incidence, extent, circumstances, situations and experiences of rural homelessness.

Homeless people in rural locations encounter many of the same vulnerabilities and personal problems as their urban counterparts, but rural homelessness is a unique and specific experience, informed, in large part, by the particular geographies of housing supply, accommodation provision and service delivery in rural England. The triggers of rural homelessness are subtly different and distinct. Surviving rural homelessness involves drawing on a very different network of support and assistance to that available to homeless people in larger towns and cities. Traditional escape routes out of homelessness, meanwhile, are often blocked, opportunities to access affordable housing in the social and private rented sectors being limited and the advice and support that many people require to negotiate a successful escape from homelessness being unavailable. Within this context, it is hardly surprising that many homeless people choose to get out and migrate to larger towns and cities. Many homeless people remain in rural England, however, and further work is urgently required to more fully appreciate and understand the spatially specific situations and experiences encountered by different sections of the rural homeless population (young and old, men and women, single people and families, people with health problems and disabilities and minority ethnic groups) and their structural, social and cultural antecedents. What can no longer be denied is that rural homelessness is a major problem in England, demanding the urgent attention of policy and the targeted assistance of housing and social care agencies.

Notes

1 Comprehensive data on more recent counts have not been made publicly available.
2 A detailed review of the method and its application is provided in Robinson (2002).
3 For a review of recent research on homelessness in England see Crane and Warnes 2003; Fitzpatrick *et al.*, 2000; Fitzpatrick and Lynch, 2002; Sterling and Fitzpatrick, 2001.

Chapter 8

Knowing homelessness in rural England

Paul Cloke and Paul Milbourne

Researching rural homelessness

This chapter draws on a research project in the UK which sought to establish the significance of homelessness in rural areas (Cloke *et al.*, 2002). The project took as its underlying assumption that popular and political discourses of homelessness in the UK have largely been confined to the sites and sights of the city. After all, media focus on the problems of homelessness has been built around images and ideas relating to the on-street homeless people in major urban centres – the 'beggars' and 'rough sleepers' of London, Birmingham, Manchester, Bristol and so on. This public consciousness of homelessness in the city has been linked with highly publicized policy responses, such as the Rough Sleepers Initiative (see May *et al.*, 2005), which have served to reinforce the links between homelessness and city spaces.

Rural spaces, by contrast, have been linked with social constructions of idyllism – they represent places of close-knit community where it is possible to enjoy the benefits of proximity to nature and distance from the problematics of the city. The idyll-ization of rural areas has brought with it the implication that rural life can be problem-free (Cloke, 2005), and as a result it has been incredibly difficult for discourses of 'poverty' and 'homelessness' to take root in rural space – such phenomena are urban issues, and if rural people somehow get caught up with poverty or homelessness, the popular misconception is that they will inevitably migrate to urban areas, where their problems can be properly 'serviced'. Rurality and homelessness have therefore become almost mutually exclusive (Cloke *et al.*, 2000a, 2000b) in contemporary British society.

In undertaking our research, we had a number of objectives in mind. We were interested not only to present evidence for the existence of rural homelessness, but also to suggest how and why such homelessness is hidden away, out of sight and out of mind. We were fascinated by the propensity of the state to regard issues of rural homelessness under the category of 'housing' rather than 'homelessness', and why the simplification of state functions had led to particular forms of management of rural people. We were concerned to understand the tactical agency of homeless people in rural areas where not only was their freedom severely curtailed by the practical difficulties of being homeless, but their very freedom to *be* homeless was being curtailed by being rendered invisible by discursive refusals even to contemplate the *idea* of rural homelessness.

Our research involved two main phases of empirical endeavour. First an extensive phase involved a broad mapping of available local authority level statistics on homelessness in rural areas (Cloke *et al.*, 2001a) and surveys of central and local government policy-makers to ascertain both top-down and bottom-up appreciations of the issue of rural homelessness (Cloke *et al.*, 2000c, 2001b). Second, in an intensive phase of the research we addressed localized case studies in the counties of Somerset and Gloucestershire in South-West England, including ethnographic encounters with some 40 people who were or had recently been homeless in these rural areas, and access to a further 44 sets of anonymized case notes from local authorities and local homelessness charities. In this chapter, we draw on this evidence to illustrate the circumstances, experiences and mobilities of homeless people in rural areas, and begin to offer some responses to our initial research questions about the invisibility, discursive slipperyness and illegibility of rural homelessness.

The circumstances of rural homelessness

An obvious starting point in charting the circumstances and experiences of homeless people in rural areas is to confirm that in many ways the formation and reproduction of homelessness can be regarded as aspatial. As is made clear in contemporary accounts of homelessness in western society (see, for example, May, 2000; Pleace *et al.*, 1997), people become homeless because of a broad-brush background of impoverishment and more specifically because of particular crises associated with the loss of work and income, with the breakdown of family relationships, with a variety of processes and practices of deinstitutionalization, and with the gap between state benefit provision and the cost and availability of affordable housing. Our encounters with homeless people in the rural areas of Somerset and Gloucestershire reinforced the significance of these issues, and in particular highlighted four common sets of circumstances which undergirded the experience of rural homelessness.

First, rural areas are by no means immune from family breakdown, which was regarded by the manager of one youth housing project in our study areas as 'the main cause of youth homelessness'. Disintegration of family relationships causes young people to leave home, and often to live without the support networks provided by family members. We interviewed 16-year-old 'Laura' in a young people's housing project in Gloucestershire. She told us of a series of family rows which led to her leaving home and moving in temporarily with a friend.

I didn't want to get violent, but I did. My mum used to say 'Oh fuck off somewhere' and I would, and then she'd ring me at my mate's house and tell me to get back. She did that a couple of times, and then I left and I lived at my friend's for a month. But they were finding it hard to pay for stuff for me as well, so I moved in here.

Laura's story of the potential risks of a radical reorganization of parental relationships (in this case the introduction of a step-father along with step-brother and sister) was repeated in many of our interviews, as was her solution of temporarily 'sofa-surfing' between different friends before seeking more manageable accommodation. Such crises are by no means restricted to young people, as illustrated by the story of 'Charles', a retired man who until recently lived and ran a successful business in rural Somerset. Following his wife's death, Charles moved into a flat, and then moved in with his son, with whom he shared his business. Then, however, his son became seriously ill, and the business collapsed:

> Because of this ... his income wouldn't pay the mortgage and the endowment policies he had ... so he had no option but to go for a smaller house with lower costs. So of course, this puts me in the position of being homeless ... I couldn't come on to him for any money back that I'd loaned him, because of the simple fact that he hadn't got it.

Charles sought help from his local authority, but they would not prioritize his case, so he ended up in emergency halfway-house accommodation.

Some narratives of family breakdown involve the hidden and desperate circumstances of domestic violence, which is often tolerated in rural areas (as elsewhere) in order to present a fiction of normality, but which ultimately will often lead to tragic circumstances of distress and upheaval for women and children. 'Angela' told us of the kind of experiences in a rural home which represent an extremely serious aspect of the causality of homelessness

> To start with he was brilliant. Then he started working and that is when the grief started – he'd go out drinking. If he'd had a really bad day at work that was it – we were in for it when he got home ... It got to the stage when we just couldn't cope with it. I called the police out ...

Angela got advice from a local charity, and ended up in a women's refuge in the nearest city, but continued harassment from her partner meant that she had to move on several times before ending up in our rural study area in bed and breakfast accommodation.

Second, rural homelessness can be linked to different forms of deinstitution-alization. Although the institutions concerned – prisons, army bases, psychiatric centres, care homes and so on – are often located in urban centres, the issues of homelessness associated with release from these institutions spill out into rural areas. 'Peter', for example, endured several periods of imprisonment, but after release his life history is punctuated with periods of sleeping rough in rural settings:

> Living on the streets you are just trying to stay alive until the next day, but in the country it's quite easy – because I went poaching. I didn't have to go out and rob ... I was sleeping in a hay barn or under the stars.

Another of our interviewees was 'Elsa' whose life had involved several sojourns in different rural locations. Receiving treatment in a psychiatric institution to overcome problems of alcohol addiction, Elsa drew on her previous fears and experiences to try to work out where she could go after her release. She had previously slept rough in rural areas, and stayed in a variety of bed and breakfast accommodation, where she had frequently been robbed. Having left an abusive relationship with her alcoholic ex-husband, she was extremely keen to find a safe quiet place in which to live, well away from groups of men, and where she could receive visits from her three children. Rural places seemed to Elsa the most suitable for her circumstances. Clearly, people such as Elsa who find themselves in vulnerable and sensitive circumstances tend to get trapped into difficult cycles of relapse and recovery, but what is also important about her story is that these cycles are not contained within cities, but stretch out into seemingly idyllic rural communities.

Third, our interviewees told us about a series of other personal crises which had dumped them down into homelessness. It seems that depression and other expressions of 'not being able to cope' are not uncommon features of living in country locations, and can lead to homelessness. So too are addictions to alcohol or other drugs. Again, these are most commonly linked with homelessness on city streets, but our interviewees such as 'Dave' and 'Suzy' offer a different geographical perspective. We met them in a small Gloucestershire town which has a recently opened youth housing scheme. Dave was on probation following a court appearance, and had been instructed to attend alcohol counselling. He denies that he has a 'problem' with drinking, but Suzy tells us that he will consume at least four cans per day of the strongest beer he can find, provided that he can get the money to buy it. Suzy is in a relationship with Dave, but fears the consequences (both personal and potentially criminal) of his drinking. Many of our interviewees spoke freely of the importance of drugs and alcohol in their lives, convincing us that addiction is just as much a part of rural homelessness as it is in big cities.

Fourth, rural homelessness is associated with particular lifestyle circumstances which attract people to particular places, and ultimately place them at risk of being homeless in rural settings. For example, one of our study areas in Somerset is associated with summer tourism, and offers a range of holiday accommodation which can be rented out of season but where short-term and uncertain tenancies, along with a variety of housing conditions, can lead to housing vulnerability and homelessness. At the cheapest end of the market, people are sometimes forced to live in unfit conditions, as in the story of 'Mrs Clark'.

> There's no windows at the back of the house at all ... half of the house is under the hill ... the walls are really really damp ... I get mould all over my clothes ... they get ruined ... upstairs the walls are black. There's an electric heater, but that's too expensive to run ... At this time of the year I just can't sleep upstairs – it's too cold and damp.

Such unsatisfactory accommodation, and the associated problems of ill health and vulnerability, are fundamental aspects of living in or on the edge of homelessness. When we interviewed her, Mrs Clark was unable to secure priority status for rehousing by her local authority, so she had to 'stick it out' in clearly unfit housing conditions.

Elsewhere in the Somerset case study area, there is a substantial Butlins holiday centre, which attracts in-migrants seeking work, but who are at risk of becoming homeless in the area if they fail to secure employment, or if they are laid off at the end of the season. As the manager of the local information bureau told us:

> People come to Butlins thinking there is a job ... they hitch-hike down there ... and that's a whole category of homeless people that we get. People will hang around here and find a floor to sleep on and try to get themselves established down here.

Equally our Somerset case study area is close to Glastonbury which acts as a magnet for people in and around the traveller scene. These congregations of travellers produce localized experiences of homelessness, as people decide, or are forced, to 'settle' in the area. For example, 'Heather' left home at 14 and had been a traveller for 28 years, but was finally forced to seek accommodation in rural Somerset because of the threat to take her daughter into care:

> But because I lived on a bus – I put her into school because I thought every kid ought to have every opportunity ... And they found that a little bit difficult to accept. And in the end they brought social services in and they said they didn't think it was right the way [her daughter] was living.

These different kinds of circumstances associated with homelessness in rural areas reflect a complexity which can render generalization problematic, but this information from our research suggests a number of simple conclusions: there is clear evidence of single homelessness in rural areas; this particularly affects young people, especially those ineligible for benefits, but older people are also involved; there is also evidence of sleeping rough in rural areas; rural homelessness is not restricted to single people, nor is it a solely masculine experience; women suffer particularly from forms of homelessness associated with unfit housing and domestic violence; and we found no evidence of women sleeping rough in the countryside. These findings would be unsurprising if it were not for the broad perception that there is <u>no</u> homelessness in rural Britain. Our research not only contradicts that assumption, but it also explores how rural space influences the practices and flows of homelessness in particular ways. We therefore now turn to a discussion of how different implications in mobility conjure up sometimes particularly rural forms of homelessness.

Mobility and rural homelessness

Thus far we have interrogated some of the causes of rural homelessness, noting how some of our interviewees have 'ended up' in rural areas. However, the life histories of the people we talked to present clues to a more fluid mix of journeys and pauses which impact on rural areas in different ways, and which reflect different meanings and codes of rurality. In presenting an account of these mobilities associated with homelessness, we note two assumptions about mobility and rurality more generally. First, people experiencing extreme socio-economic problems in a rural setting are assumed simply to migrate to urban areas (see Cloke *et al.*, 1995, in the case of rural poverty). So, it is often assumed that poverty and homelessness do not exist in rural areas because the impoverished and the homeless will have been forced to move away. Second, mobility appears to be deeply implicated in the moral cartographies of rural areas. Ideas of home, rootedness and boundedness receive positive moral codings (Cresswell, 1996) while mobility can signify an absence of responsibility and attachment. More specifically, it is certain kinds of mobility which attract negative moral codings. As Cloke *et al.* (2003: 23) have suggested:

> It may be that some styles of mobility – for example the sofa-surfing practices of staying with friends – are more appropriate than others. By contrast, where the mobility of homelessness becomes visible to the public gaze, involving more transgressive embodied modes of presence in the rural scene, it is more likely to be 'inappropriate' and thus serve as a signifier of the absence of responsibility and rootedness.

The negative moral coding of inappropriate mobility in rural areas is very significant to understanding why rural homelessness often appears to be hidden or invisible. Where homelessness does become visible, it represents a transgression of the 'order' of rurality, thereby threatening the core reliance on home and community for other rural residents (Takahashi, 1998). Homelessness can therefore become out of place in the purified space of rurality (Cloke *et al.,* 2000a), and the tactical responses of homeless people will often serve to avoid or render incognito any such transgressions.

In our research we posed two key questions about the mobilities associated with homelessness. First, is out-migration the principal signifying mobility of homeless people in the countryside, and to what extent do other forms of mobility occur? Second, what forms of moral coding are mapped onto different mobilities of homeless people, and how do such moral codes become associated with different strategic necessities or technical decisions about being 'visible' or 'invisible' in rural settings? Here, we address these questions in terms of four different types of mobility.

Moving out of the rural

Our interviews with local authority homelessness officers and other professionals confirm that homeless people often do have to migrate away from their local rural area. The paucity of local social housing means that anyone becoming literally homeless has little chance of being housed locally by their local authority:

> if you are homeless from a rural area, the chances of you being allocated anywhere near that rural area are remote because in some of our villages where we've got stock, we've got right-to-buy rates of over 50%. (Homelessness officer, Somerset)

In addition, private rental costs tend to be high in rural areas, given competition from affluent commuters and tourists. So whether it is for rehousing, or to make use of the emergency accommodation services located in cities, people becoming homeless will often be forced to move out and take advantage of the opportunities offered by surrounding urban locations.

Our interviewees reflected that this enforced out-migration was often accompanied by an extreme visibility of their plight, as the small scale of the built and social environment and the restricted nature of housing and employment opportunities tend to throw a very public spotlight onto the experience of homelessness. As a local vicar in a Devon village told us, 'if you're homeless or unemployed in [village name] it sticks out'. 'Janice', a homeless women who had been living in a different village in Devon, confirmed this sense of being in the spotlight:

> When I lost my place, it was like my position in the village changed. I was one of them, like, but then everyone knew about me and I was like an outcast – sticking out like a sore thumb.

So, the specific problems of homelessness can become compounded by the identifiable isolation of being known as homeless in a rural place. The response to these issues is often to leave that place. Local homeless people can therefore become rather shadowy figures in the local sociocultural and political consciousness. Being known and recognized as homeless can be stigmatizing, presenting homeless people in rural areas with a narrow range of tactical choices: to survive in place by whatever means possible; or to move out to somewhere where homelessness is more in place. Neither of these tactics disrupt or transgress the idyllized and purified living environments of rurality.

Moving within the rural

Our research uncovered a considerable resistance amongst people in or on the margins of homelessness to move away from their local area. Indeed almost all of the homelessness officers and agency workers we talked to suggested that homeless people exhibit a strong desire to stay in their 'home' area. One officer in Gloucestershire told us:

> it is where they identify with … if you have lived in an area and you feel you have got connections and close ties in the area then any other area is going to be somewhere that you would not really want to go.

Moreover the desire to stay put tends to emphasize the localness of the local in rural areas, with people in different parts of a district reported as feeling more comfortable with some local places but not others:

> [P]eople from W will not live in M, people from M will live in W, and similarly, people who live in C will come to M but they won't go to W, and people in Wn will go to W but they will not come to M. And you get all that kind of, it's almost incestuous really, there is us and there is the rest of the world. (Probation officer, Somerset)

> If they live in L then they wouldn't want to live in D which is only a little way up the road, because it's totally different. They belong to L so therefore they do not need to live in D. So you've got that sense of people's opinions of where they should be and where they shouldn't be. (Homelessness officer, Somerset)

Perhaps it is unsurprising, given that broader ideas of rural politics and culture areas are often framed by local–newcomer distinctions, that homeless people will also subscribe to the value of their locality. In the case of homeless people, however, their 'local' is especially rich because it offers access to practical help through family and friends, and because the non-local 'other' represents a place of fear. For example we were told of a young man who spent three weeks sleeping under a bridge in a village because he was too frightened to go into the nearest market town to get help.

Although such rough sleeping does occur in rural areas, our research suggests that perhaps a more common coping strategy for dealing with homelessness without leaving the vicinity is to move around between friends or different members of the family:

> … you have people moving from one place to the other just to keep a roof over their heads without outstaying their welcome. (Agency project worker)

> I think there is an awful lot of people sleeping on people's floors, an awful lot of that, and they move from friend to friend and they outstay their welcome … then move on again sort of thing. And that's a really common story. (Agency project worker)

These homeless movers largely consist of young single people who have been forced to (or chose to) leave the parental home and circulate around a local group of friends. However, because they rarely approach the relevant authorities for help, they again represent rather shadowy figures on the rural stage, conveying a rather uncertain kind of absence rather than presence, and hence they become underdetermined in the public imagination. While some of these homeless people will adopt tactics to make themselves invisible, most exist in material and cultural circumstances which reinforce their hiddenness.

Moving into the rural

Contrary to the hegemonic assumption that homeless people will migrate out of rural areas, our research suggests that there is also a notable movement of homeless people *into* rural areas. So while the lack of anonymity in rural settings constitutes a reason why some people seek answers to their homelessness away from the rural, there is a curious reverse effect occurring, with rurality for others offering a greater privacy and freedom to conduct a homeless lifestyle. For example, David, a homeless man in his 20s, told us:

> I don't mind towns and I don't mind cities but I prefer the country because it's quiet and you can do what you want out there – you know, you haven't got people nosing about and seeing what you're up to.

A part of this in-migratory movement reflects homeless people seeking to escape from what they see as the dangers of the homeless city, notably relating to violence, and being caught up in the drugs scene. However, our interviews with agency officers suggested not only that rural areas are far from being free from these problems of violence and drugs, but also that these rural areas were now attracting through in-migration the kind of people and problems other in-migrants were attempting to avoid.

There is also evidence that the expectations of in-migrant homeless people were often not fulfilled in rural settings, and that their movement tended to be a somewhat temporary relocation:

> ... a high proportion of such (homelessness) applications eventually return to their previous areas once the reality of living in a rural areas sinks in. (Homelessness officer, Somerset)

> I generally find that people from inner cities don't settle very well in a rural country, You know they are here for two or three weeks and it's nice and it's refreshing and it's a change but then they soon quickly gravitate either back to their home inner city area or gravitate to another inner city area. (Probation officer, Somerset)

Aside from these instances of in-migration in order to escape some of the problematics of the city, other in-migrants are attracted by the opportunities for casual employment in rural settings. As 'Jake' told us:

> ... in the countryside, there's wooding, there's logging. You know, there's always work, farm work. There's always picking of some sort, you know. You don't have to sign on.

The nature of some homeless lives reflects a restlessness which militates against putting down roots in a particular place, home or job. Such shifting mobility is well served by short-term periodic work, and remains important in agricultural and tourist areas. This restless mobility is also reflected in key New Age centres such as Glastonbury which attract myriad travellers as well as festival-goers (see the story of 'Heather' above).

The 'non-local' status of these in-migrant homeless people induces clear morally coded responses from local people about homelessness which is out of place. These 'outsiders' are regarded as interrupting the social order of rural space and responsibility for them is consistently denied by local people.

Moving through the rural

Some of the people who seem to be moving *into* the rural might more properly be described as moving *through* the rural. Our agency interviews noted that the homeless population in rural areas included a number of transient people:

> [T]here is a whole bunch of people coming from elsewhere in the country and it's kind of circulating, masses come and go … and they are all age groups. We had a guy turn up in Taunton a couple of weeks ago who had walked all the way from Kent. (Probation officer, Somerset)

> [W]e get a very transient society particularly in the summer months; we get a lot of new age travellers and people that pass through the area and stop in the area, for the summer. (Homelessness officer, Somerset)

Our interviews with homeless people confirm that some travel around 'circuits' of homelessness (see Crane, 1999; Deacon *et al.*, 1995) involving relatively short periods of residence in several locations. 'Syd' told us about his connections with our Somerset study area:

> I've been here for the last five years on the trot. So I do, I do every sort of city or town I like in the country more than once a year, sometimes up to four or five … the longest (stay) will be, probably about four or five weeks – which will be here, or Canterbury in Kent.

A key facet of this transient moving through the rural is a wish for freedom and anonymity:

> [W]hen I walk down the street I want to be a stranger, d'you know what I mean? Like somebody you walk past and you do not notice … I don't want to be pre-judged all the time, I just want to meet people and be who I am, instead of being what they think I am.

Such anonymity, however, is unlikely to be available when walking the streets of smaller rural settlements, so homeless people employ tactics of visibility. 'David' told us that by wearing camouflage trousers and military boots, he could make people unaware that he was sleeping rough:

> I just blended right into the countryside … If I see a rabbit I'd shoot it and find somewhere that was nice and isolated and then start cooking it, and then once I'd eaten it stay around for five, ten minutes and then destroy the fire, make sure it looked like no-one had a fire, and then disappear.

These transient homeless people perform different tactics in different kinds of rural places. However, their non-local status again means that they become inscribed by particular moral signifiers which can lead to a denial both of their 'homeless' status, and of their 'place' in the rural area concerned. They are often dismissed as 'travellers' or (when made visible on the streets of a rural town) 'drunken beggars'; in both cases their identity is over-determined so as to make them easily knowable in the public imagination. Our research in the town of Taunton, for example (Cloke *et al.*, 2000d), demonstrates how a very negative response to homelessness can develop in these kinds of circumstances.

Making rural homeless people known

Although the distinctions deployed in this chapter between 'rural' and 'urban' will for some oversimplify the complexities of making and remaking social space, we have retained this distinction for two reasons. First, in terms of understanding homelessness, the unquestioning use of the category 'urban' has tended to overpower the rural other, to the extent of encouraging the assumption that homelessness does not exist in the rural. Second, the unprompted responses of our interviewees have suggested that the 'rural' continues to be a spatial category which informs discourse and imagination in Britain. By framing spatialities in terms of 'living in rural areas', 'moving out of rural areas', 'hanging around in the countryside' and so on, these discourses suggest that rurality both informs the spatial imaginaries of individuals, groups and agencies associated with homelessness, and is implicated in the life experiences, mobilities and politics which are informed by those imaginaries.

Our research, therefore, presents evidence with which to contradict the conflation of homelessness and the urban. The idea that rural homelessness is simply being transposed into a city problem through the auspices of out-migration fails to capture the complexity and multidimensionality of homelessness in rural areas. Out-migration of homeless people to service-rich urban places undoubtedly occurs, but homeless mobility also involves movements into, within and through rural space. The public acknowledgement of connections between rurality and homelessness, then, needs to get beyond the picture of rural homeless people ending up begging on city streets, and to include: locally homeless people making short distance moves in rural areas, seeking out rented housing, or sofa-surfing around local friends; transient homeless people involved in more wide-ranging circuits movements which include moving across and stopping within rural spaces; the longer term movements of homeless people into rural space to find work or to enjoy holidays or the environment, and so on. These different mobilities suggest that homeless people cannot be regarded as a static categorization, but need to be understood as moving, becoming beings. Their homelessness shifts over times and spaces, often charting complex cartographies involving not only journeys and routes but resting places and accommodations.

Within these cartographies, journeys and pauses are overlaid by axes of moral coding which are active in processes and practices which make homeless people knowable, both locally and in wider discourses. This process of making people known, as Hetherington (2000) has argued, vacillates between under-determination and over-determination of homeless people within the public imagination. Where the experiences of homeless people are hidden away or ignored, homeless people become a shadowy and uncertain absence in the collective consciousness of rural people and the culture politics or rurality. Where the experiences of homeless people (in this case often categorised discursively as something other than homeless) are rendered visible, they can become an over-determined caricature, ripe for vilification in both consciousness and politics. This is not to suggest some kind of fixed moral order in rural space, for both the out-of-placeness of homeless people and the practice of purification of rural space are fluid phenomena. However, both the under-determination of homelessness leading to hiddenness, and its over-determination leading to visibility, conspire against the discursive recognition of rural homelessness.

In this broad context, the knowing of homeless people is also associated with particular axes of moral coding, of which three deserve brief mention here. First, there does seem to be differentiation along local/non-local lines. Local people will often find ways of 'making do' rather than making their homelessness public. By staying in unfit housing, or enduring unacceptable family circumstances, or relying on the charity of friends or family, people who otherwise would be declaring their homelessness tend to conform to social constructions of rural self-help and community cohesion founded on traditional domesticity and familism. In so doing, power is exerted over them (as Lukes, 1974, argues) through the discursive shaping of perceptions, cognitions and preferences in such a way as to produce an acceptance of the existing order of things. Being local, in this sense, equates with a disavowal of the problem of homelessness and its social causes. We did also find cases where local people experienced life crises caused by external factors and where the resultant homelessness was viewed as 'deserving' by the local community that rallied around to help. Equally, we met other local people whose circumstances were regarded as 'undeserving' and were denied this kind of community help.

What is clear from our research is that non-local people seemed automatically to be branded by moral codings of 'undeserving', being seen as outsiders scrounging from local people. For example, with reference to the in-migration of workers to the Butlins holiday centre in Somerset (mentioned above), one local resident told us

One of the problems about the girls that come down to Butlins, and they have a good time, and they have too much to drink and they get themselves pregnant, and then just dump themselves on the local council. The problem is that they've got more priority then any of us … the locals are the last priority for the council.

The undeserving nature of non-locals is exaggerated here by the notion of unjust priority and preference – the morally unacceptable idea that need rather than belonging might shape local resource allocation.

The second axis of moral representation is related to the first and concerns the differentiation between being 'settled' or 'passing through'. In Britain's socially constructed rural idyll, the importance of the settled home is an axiomatic indicator of rural ways of life. Homelessness, by definition, transgresses this expectation of being in a settled home, although in our research respondents often distinguished between situations where homeless people were somehow in the process of being settled, and where homeless people performed aspects of transience and restlessness. In fact, our encounters with homeless people in rural areas revealed an array of different facets of being 'unsettled'. 'Kirsty' told us about her wish to stay 'settled' in an area, and how that wish meant that she passed through the four different forms of accommodation in a short period of time.

I was living in a one-bedroom flat in [Somerset village], it was damp and everything. I worked at Butlins, but they shut down for three weeks every year, so I went on the dole for three weeks … my claim [for housing benefit] was then treated as a new claim, and cut to £40 … so I could no longer afford my rent there … I stayed until March, but couldn't afford to live there any more. I moved because it was stressing me out. And all I could do was to move into a bed-sit, but from there I got made homeless. The landlady sold the house and they gave us notice to leave [Kirsty went to stay with a friend in another let, but this property too was sold]. From there on, the council put me in this hostel.

Others of our interviewees appeared to exhibit a much deeper sense of restlessness, connecting journeys and pauses in the countryside into a wider account of being emotionally adverse to settling. Whether through the force of circumstances, or inner emotional prompt, the lack of a 'settled' lifestyle acts as a moral code within the homeless population in rural areas, characterizing the people concerned as unfit for, or transgressive of, the expectations of living in a rural community.

The third axis of moral coding refers to whether homeless people are visible or invisible in the rural scene. Again there are a host of circumstances in which homelessness remains out of sight: the fear of being regarded as undeserving; the unobtrusive stays with friends, relations or even people they have just met; the putting up with unacceptable family or housing conditions; the siting of mobile or temporary accommodation in lonely, out-of-the-way places; the deliberate tactics of remaining incognito when sleeping rough and so on. One of the most significant reasons why rural homelessness remains invisible is that homeless people will often refuse to identify themselves with the category 'homeless'. As a local advice worker in our Somerset case study area told us:

> The difficulty is identifying people who will define themselves as being homeless. I mean, most people have an image of what it means to be homeless and that means sleeping in a cardboard box. So, you get people saying 'Oh no, I'm not homeless.' So you say 'where are you living?' And they say 'Oh I'm staying with a friend'. They are clearly homeless but don't actually identify themselves.

To be identified as homeless would be to announce to the community that they were unable to sort out their own problems. Instead, by electing to remain invisible by refusing to be labelled as homeless, people collude with a broader picture that homelessness does not exist in rural settings.

Knowing and being known

In his book *Seeing Like a State*, James Scott (1998) discusses how modern states manage people and structures so as to make populations more legible – more readable, more intelligible, more identifiable. This process of rending legible serves to simplify the normal functions of the state through processes of standardization, abstraction and codification. Local knowledge to the contrary is sacrificed in the valorization of universally valid legibility. Part of Scott's thesis was that by such means other people are rendered illegible, less readable, less intelligible, less identifiable. In the context of homelessness the counting of rough sleepers in city centres, and the wider cultural equating of urban on-street begging with the visibility of homelessness, seem to be mechanisms of legibility. The risk is that not only will other homeless people in other areas – notably rural areas – be rendered illegible by these self-same processes, but also that homeless people ensconced in the orthodoxies of rural living will conspire to proliferate their own illegibility, by succumbing to imagined geographies of homelessness involving sleeping rough in a cardboard box in an inner city location.

Distinctions and moral codings around local/non-local, settled/passing through and visible/invisible, each contribute to how homelessness is made illegible in rural locations. The local/settled/invisible gains more acceptance, but rarely achieves the sort of contact with state bureaucracies that allows enumeration and therefore legibility. The non-local/passing through/visible is least likely to be accepted by these localized bureaucracies as having priority need, leading once again to a situation in which homeless people displaying these characteristics 'don't count'.

However, local knowledges of rural homelessness *are* crucial in counteracting the standardized coding of the state, but making rural homeless people known also means counteracting the moral impulses of cultural constructions of the rural. Visibility is crucial here. By staying hidden, homeless people in rural settings become a shadowy absence in the cultural politics of rural people; an absence to be denied, or transmogrified into another discursive categorization. By choosing to be invisible, rural people effectively deny themselves the possibility of help with coping with their homelessness. Attributes of 'being local' or 'being settled' can result in a more sympathetic acceptance of a homeless person's deserving nature, but the crises associated with becoming homeless will often involve the competing interests of other local people – partners, parents, landlords, employers and so on – who will also be wanting to represent themselves in terms of 'being local' and 'being settled'. Such competition can often reinforce the moral otherness of a homeless person within their own local community. Certainly, attributes of 'not being local' or 'not being settled' equate with moral codings of 'undeserving'. Local discourse recognizes such people as 'outsiders', whose moral contamination is likely to prompt efforts to repurify the rural space concerned, and in so doing further overshadow the needs of less visible and supposedly more deserving cases.

Researchers attempting to render rural homelessness more visible may in fact simply be making homelessness known in an unknowable way. Recognizing the problem of rural homelessness is an important first step, but it is only a first step. We now need urgent action from the state to make the rural homeless legible, and to direct appropriate resources into suitable responses to their problems. Equally, there is a need for alternative and critical socio-cultural constructions of rural life which release the regulatory power of the purifying idyll, and promote core values of compassion for the poor and the homeless in rural settings.

Note

We gratefully acknowledge the financial support of the ESRC for our research (award number R000236567) and we thank Rebekah Widdowfield for her contribution to the project reported on here. We are also grateful for helpful comments from Charles Geisler in his book review of *Rural Homelessness* in *Journal of Rural Studies*, which have shaped some of our interpretative conclusions here.

Chapter 9

International perspectives on rural homelessness

A sociological perspective on homelessness in rural Spain

José Antonio López Ruiz and Pedro Cabrera Cabrera

Rural areas in Spain: poverty and exclusion

Probably the most serious social problems affecting Spanish rural areas today are probably those related to their demographics – that is, they experience both extremely high levels of an aging population and the depopulation of the medium and small-sized rural centres. This phenomenon is what some authors have classified as an extreme demographic landscape (Camarero Rioja, 2002: 63) because, while the rest of the Spanish population gradually ages, the degree of aging in rural areas is quite pronounced. Demographically, the clearly regressive population is characterized by the depopulation of towns due to out-migrations – whose numbers had been maintained up until the 1990s – and by the high rate of mortality due to the aging of the population and the very low birth rate. As such, Spanish rural areas have all of the factors that characterize a sustained demographic recession.

In this context, what are the conditions of poverty, limited quality of life and social exclusion related to the situations of those that are homeless?

We must begin by stating our definition of a 'rural area'. In terms of characterizing rural areas, recent OECD studies address various demographic criteria – such as growth and unemployment rates, the region's relative participation in the national product and activity, and, among others, social and environmental variables – in order to finally define rural areas as those in which the population density is less than 150 inhabitants per square kilometre (Abad and Naredo, 2002: 37–8). We will take this (limited) definition as a starting point in order to elaborate with comments that reflect the singularity and heterogeneity of the rural spaces of Spain from a sociological and not an entirely demographic perspective.

Therefore, a rural area is, now more than ever, a social system that is deeply connected to an urban system. From a sociological perspective, we do not believe that a rural society can only be defined by the size of its population and the predominant mode of economic production.[1] In a complex society such as our own, there are clearly some mid-range forms in between what is understood as rural and urban in pure forms; without a doubt, the definition of what is rural is not as tightly limited today as in the past. However, we must keep in mind – besides population size and the predominant mode of economic activity – factors like the distance from or proximity to the centres of activity, how the residences are spread out, which includes both the layout of the homes and the small scattered groupings of houses on the outskirts of towns and, lastly, the dependence of the main economic activities on the region's characteristics (Zárraga Moreno, 2000: 60). Combining the size of the population (understood from a demographic perspective) with variables like the proximity to or distance from the active urban centres, the ease or difficulty of communications and the greater or lesser economic prosperity, a town in Spain of 5,000 inhabitants can be considered a city, while another one totalling 15,000 may appear more like a town trapped in the past. Taking all of these factors into account, characterizing communities as more rural than urban solely according to the size of their populations would be a simplification of the analysis, which, while true from a demographic perspective, is not operationally valid for a sociologist.

Moving to the analysis of poverty and exclusion, we state that the ways of living have changed extensively in rural and urban environments over past decades. If poverty used to be more readily associated with the countryside, and wealth with cities, the end of the twentieth century confirmed the tendency for poverty and social exclusion to be most evident in urban centres, at least in their most heart-wrenching and extreme forms. For some, this phenomenon is the reason why a 'progressive urbanization of the sociological discourse on poverty, social exclusion and social marginalization processes' has taken place (Izcara Palacios, 2002: 459).

Recent sociological studies on poverty and territory show that 18 per cent of the total population living in poverty reside in rural areas, while 'four out of five poor people live in non-rural population centers' (Renes Ayala, 2000), which are those that have more than 5,000 inhabitants. There are other more or less recent studies (Pereira Jerez, 2004) in which we can find data broken down for each of the 17 Spanish autonomous communities: upon differentiating the data by community, it shows that the proportion of the population living in conditions that we could call rural impoverishment is much greater in some of them than in the average of the entire territory. Extremadura, with 57 per cent of its poor population living in rural settings, and Castilla-La Mancha and Castilla-Leon, with 55 per cent and 49 per cent respectively, are the most extreme regions in this regard (Alguacil Gómez, 2000: 160–4). The problem that we find upon reviewing the aforementioned studies is that the research has gathered data from housing surveys, along with censuses, town registries and other official statistics; the homeless, due to their living situations, are systematically excluded from the observations.

In order to move beyond this initial challenge, we will try to extrapolate from the profile of the homeless in rural areas (drawn from interviews with people living in impoverished conditions) some generalizations about how they viewed themselves, the general causes of poverty and the problems that hinder them from overcoming such conditions. We begin with the hypothesis that the following data might not be far from the conceptions and idiosyncrasies that are unique to some of the homeless, since they are based on the opinions and attitudes coming from the *personal experiences* of those immersed in the poverty. Thus, among the causes that they believe have led them into poverty, the subjects interviewed highlight three main impediments to getting out of poverty: educational deficiencies, lack of work and, surprisingly, laziness. In the smallest towns, with less than 500 inhabitants, poverty is blamed on educational deficiencies or a lack of education – 52 per cent of those questioned agreed with this – while 60 per cent of those in towns with populations between 500 and 1,000 did not agree with this explanation. Lack of employment is the most common argument in all types of populations, with 90 per cent of those polled agreeing with this explanation. With regard to laziness, it must be stated that, while 70 per cent of those questioned do not agree that this attitude is an original cause of poverty, the remaining 30 per cent show a big difference from the opinion observed in the poor homes in urban areas, since the smaller the population area, the higher the correlation attributed by those interviewed to the relationship between laziness and poverty.

Beyond poverty – understood as insufficient income – exclusion appears linked in research to the 'breakdown of both deeply-rooted social mechanisms and integration and insertion processes' (Castel, 1995; García Roca, 1998). In accordance with this linkage, it is clear that family support networks, seasonal job opportunities and the prospect of better conditions in terms of housing accessibility mean that people in rural areas tend to fall less often into situations of extreme exclusion than is the case in the cities. Rural impoverishment is more of a moderate economic poverty linked to situations of instability, rather than an extreme poverty linked to social exclusion and uprooting: 'extreme poverty levels are very low, around 2 percent, and the severe poverty levels that stand out further down the poverty ladder are in the Autonomous Communities of Murcia (27 percent), Extremadura (18 percent) and Galicia (14 percent)' (Fernández Such, 2000b: 373).

It must be taken into consideration that economic and educational standards in Spanish rural areas continue to be reported as inferior to those found in urban areas. The number of people experiencing severe economic hardship is proportionately lower in rural areas than in cities, given that rural poverty mainly affects older people whose retirement pensions do not meet a sufficient amount of income in order to rise above the conventional poverty line (60 per cent of the median of average incomes in the country), as well as younger generations unable to access job markets in favourable enough conditions.[2] Nevertheless, rural 'poverty' from the perspective of the objective incomes that enter the home can be accompanied by some general living conditions that, from both a subjective point of view and in terms of quality of life, are much better than those of many urban homes (García Serrano *et al.*, 2001).

Added to the factors of exclusion common to both urban and rural communities are those that are specific to the latter; for example, the importance of tradition and the scattering of the population and of activities.[3] Generally speaking, it is a proven fact that population dispersement along with the progressive disappearance of social living spaces (cafés and other meeting places) as a result of the depopulation of many rural areas leads to isolation. Frequently, even the building of family ties becomes difficult; the exotic cases of some towns in the Pyrenees where 'women caravan' outings have been organized in order to try to formalize some marriages respond to this difficulty. But reduced demographic density has consequences also for policy from the perspective of political options. As the electoral importance of rural areas is low, macroeconomic and macropolitical decisions reinforce the tendency to concentrate on a common centre, both in terms of population and employment services. Current training and employment insertion policies, for example, are aimed at encouraging specialization. However, this objective is practically incompatible with the multi-activity imposed by job instability in rural areas (activities of a markedly seasonal nature in agriculture, tourism, etc.).

On the other hand, the persistence of long-standing traditions in rural societies and the cultural difference with regard to the forms of integration into modern society can foment some exclusionary factors in rural communities. For example, the fact that employment was generated traditionally within the framework of protected family spheres causes rural populations to be ill-prepared to enter into anonymous job markets. Rural youths, whose 'traditional-rural' identity is constantly compared to the 'modern-urban' identity, thus feel displaced.

This difference between tradition and modernity affects women in particular. Historically, in rural areas, women's employment depended almost always on activities that complemented agricultural exploitation, which frequently required knowledge for which there is little demand nowadays, especially in certain sectors of craft production. Currently, rural women encounter specific difficulties related to employment, especially in regions where agro-tourism and other new activities carried out by women have yet to be established.

On the other hand, let us remember that there are major differences in the social and economic development of the different predominantly rural regions; the distribution of jobs and incomes is significantly unequal among autonomous communities and within them among the different regions and geographical areas.[4] In a single region, some valleys are notoriously richer than other adjacent ones because, while they had similar natural resources, historically some were cut through by major inter-regional roads and others were left isolated. In other rural regions the secular farming wealth has marked the differences in incomes, similar to what occurs on the cereal and livestock plateaus and along the banks of major rivers.[5] It is the most remote valleys, the least fertile lands and the territories used for livestock or specialized agricultural production that have had to modify their exploitations because of the EU Common Agricultural Policy (CAP) where the most deprived depressed populations are found.[6] In another mode of analysis, we can find regions in which there is considerable prosperity, albeit with traditional economic activities or through those that have been more or less recently established – like the various manufacturing industries or the different forms of tourism – where isolated cases of homelessness can be found, as examples of the known unyielding pockets of poverty in wealthy regions.

In Spain, the fact that territorial differences are extremely accentuated has been thoroughly studied, distinguishing between disparate demographic evolution and economic criteria in the regions that are administratively demarcated as autonomous communities. While there are regions with a traditionally agricultural base with incomes well below the European average, such as Andalusia and Extremadura (less than 60 per cent), other regions, such as Madrid, Catalonia, the Balearic Islands and the Basque Country, with broad industrial and tourist zones, far exceed this. These last few regions have the lowest poverty indices in the country.

The homeless in Spain

There is no universally accepted definition of homeless people. In the political context, the term refers not so much to forms of personal conduct – which are more abstract and have variable concepts – as to a specific situation characterized by a lack of adequate housing according to the social standards in each society, and which includes all of the people that do not manage to access and maintain it, albeit because of social barriers that are difficult to overcome, or for personal circumstances, which in turn requires the aid of some type of social support service (Cabrera Cabrera, 2000). Another definition that we take as a point of reference for this study is the one that has been popularized by the European Observatory of Homeless People, and that has been used up until recently by FEANTSA, according to which the following are considered homeless:

> All those people that cannot access or maintain adequate housing that is adapted to their personal situation, permanent and provides a stable living framework, albeit for economic reasons or other social barriers, or because personal hardships arise that hinder one from leading an autonomous life.

In Spain, we have hardly any official data that document the homelessness issue; the basic study of reference at the state level continues to be the one done by Cabrera (2000) for Caritas[7] with funding from the Ministry of Social Affairs. Beyond the data provided by this research there are only the local studies carried out in some large cities with varying methodological assumptions (Muñoz Lopez *et al.*, 1995; Vega González, 1996; Cabrera Cabrera, 1998; Jansa *et al.*, 1999; Muñoz Lopez *et al.*, 2003; Moreno Rebollo *et al.*, 2003; Cabrera Cabrera and Rubio, 2003). However, a report was published by the National Institute of Statistics (Instituto Nacional de Estadística (INE) 2004) that will allow us to include for the first time some information on homelessness in Spain that comes from official sources. It is a postal survey that gathers data from 555 homeless centres in Spain. Even though the main objective of the survey was to describe the characteristics of the network of centres and not those of the homeless, it will still allow us to present some data of general interest and approximations about the problem in question. Unfortunately, many of the places that attend to the most excluded people in small towns and in rural areas, and which are often tied to initiatives led by parish volunteers or which are small-scale services provided by the municipal authorities, are not collected in this INE survey, as they are not considered centres that specifically attend to the homeless. Therefore, we will also use the data from the Caritas survey in order to try to describe the issue of rural homelessness.

From the data obtained by INE at the beginning of 2003, we can confirm that in Spain there are 12,585 housing places for homeless people in serious need, which had an average occupancy level of 82 per cent throughout the year. This means that on any given day there were about 10,300 homeless people housed in the emergency network (albeit in collective shelters, state-subsidized rooming houses or state-owned apartments). If we take into account that not all homeless people turn to the housing services, preferring to fend for themselves and sleep in improvised quarters – in the street or in a car – we can raise this figure by about 30–50 per cent, which would lead us to refer to about 15,000 homeless people on any given day in 2002. The INE study points towards an average daily figure of 17,600 people for 2002 and raises the estimate to 18,500 people for the number of housing places obtained, from the note made on 5 November 2003 (13,439 places).

Taking into account all of its limitations, we can therefore accept that on any given day there are about 18,500 homeless people in Spain, for which there are some 13,500 emergency housing places.

It is true that the image received of homelessness from these data cannot be independent of the institutions that handle them, and so there is considerable risk of an institutional bias. Nevertheless, we do not have other means with which to approach it. In Spain it is not possible to exploit other channels like censuses and registries, or the administrative registers of applicants for public housing and social services, given that they either do not contain information on homeless people, or they are organized according to diverse criteria and from social intervention programmes that follow very disparate objectives. This fact is reinforced by the structure of the public administrations, as both social services and the organizations responsible for housing in Spain are decentralized and their organization is different for each of the 17 autonomous communities.

From the data so far available, we are going to attempt to describe the main characteristics of the network that attends to the homeless in Spain.

1 For the most part, it is a privately owned network. The great majority of the centres (73 per cent according to INE, 79 per cent according to Cabrera) are social initiatives and dependent upon religious bodies. Caritas alone controls approximately 40 per cent of the assistance centres for the homeless in Spain. This fact reflects in part the relative youth of our welfare regime (Esping-Andersen, 2000: 122), since the first laws to develop a public social services system in Spain are from the mid-1980s and there has hardly been any opportunity to fully develop the system due to the economic crisis of the last quarter century. In this sense, it is not surprising that, in dealing with issues of extreme exclusion and homelessness, we find ourselves facing a public welfare project that is continuously forgotten and postponed, which has only slowly been given a truly modern framework, created as a result of the recognition of social rights for all citizens and guaranteed by government.

2 Assistance to the homeless continues to be focused on survival (providing food, bed and clothing); in addition, in the past decade they have begun to develop newer kinds of initiative that go beyond immediate needs, such as, for example, vocational workshop and labour programmes, street intervention teams, and day centres in which social skills and cultural and leisure time aspects are addressed. However, this kind of approach is almost exclusively found in big cities; in rural areas, the traditional approach continues to dominate. The importance of history is still very strong. This is reflected in the predominance of centres oriented towards the traditional transient population (a single male, frequently an alcoholic or mentally ill, and socially marginalized), which does not include a broader profile of young adults, women, immigrants, family units and children. Likewise, their opening hours are inconvenient, the buildings used are often not properly adapted and hinder the type of work that is currently required, which is more personal and individualized.

3 In general, the network suffers from a chronic shortage of economic resources and qualified personnel, which makes the volunteer staff extremely important. According to data from INE, out of a total of 12,757 people working in the

network only 29 per cent are salaried employees, the rest are either volunteers (65 per cent) or another type of unpaid personnel (6 per cent), such as members of a religious order, interns, etc. While the majority of salaried personnel work full time (79 per cent), almost half of them handle administrative tasks and auxiliary services; the technical staff consists of a total of 1,263 people in the entire country. From data obtained in our previous study (Cabrera Cabrera, 2000), while salaried personnel in rural centres comprise only 10 per cent of the total, the number hovers around 20 per cent in the centres located in cities of more than 20,000 inhabitants. Taking into consideration that this shortage of qualified professionals is greater in the centres that are private, smaller and in rural areas, we find that a lower technical quality of the assistance provided in rural communities is widespread.

Up until recently, the public administration's involvement has been quite limited, which is reflected in the lack of coordination between its different departments and particularly between those that deal with social issues and those that are in charge of housing, employment and health policies. For this reason, we have requested on several occasions that a Comprehensive Plan of Action be made in each autonomous community. However, most of the funding comes from public funds (57 per cent according to INE, 54 per cent according to Cabrera). Of these public funds, the majority come from the municipalities themselves (40 per cent) and from regional governments (39 per cent), while national government pays the remaining 21 per cent – only 12 per cent of the 118.44 million euros a year that are used in Spain for the homeless (INE, 2004: 44). This means that – if we accept the estimate of 18,500 homeless – we are spending an average of €17.50 per day to attend to all of each homeless person's needs (housing, food, clothing, psycho-social care, training, etc.), while three years before, Cabrera (2000: 112) estimated the daily cost per person was between €14 and €18.[8] These figures give us some idea of the degree of poverty that we are dealing with in this area.

4   A last common trait of the network of centres that support the homeless in Spain is its essentially urban character. From the data shown in the INE survey, 85 per cent of the centres are located in population centres of more than 20,000 inhabitants. This means that only 15 per cent of the centres are found in towns of 20,000 or less inhabitants, while 34 per cent of the Spanish population lives in these places.

Rural homelessness in Spain

Even though we have more recent data from the INE study, we are going to use Cabrera's survey carried out for Caritas for the analysis of rural areas, given that it did not exclude the small support mechanisms located in rural regions, unlike the INE survey of centres. These kinds of centres, in rural areas, can be of great importance. In towns there are more of these kinds of services or voluntary services than professionalized services. We are referring to mechanisms that are often linked to a parish, a religious convent or a small group of volunteers. Including them in the recount, we find that the proportion of points of assistance in rural centres is greater than the one provided in the survey done by INE: 26 per cent. For our analysis of rural/urban homelessness, we will take this database of responses from 450 support centres for the homeless as an empirical starting point (Cabrera, 2000: 15).

With regard to the distribution of public ownership of centres (Figure 9.1), no major differences are observed according to the habitat, albeit rural or urban; the public centres make up about 17–18 per cent. However, there are significant differences in the internal make-up of the non-public sector. In general, the centres linked to religious congregations are quite homogeneously distributed, while in the rural areas the assistance is linked above all to Caritas parish groups. The greater importance of the private services in the cities is explained by the concentration of non-denominational, secular, social initiatives linked to non-religious, civic associations, which have usually been established quite recently. In contrast, it is more frequent in small towns for the centres to have mixed ownership, shared between town hall and some historically and traditionally settled religious entity in the town.

As reflected in Table 9.1, within the general trend of the network – which is markedly assistance-minded and oriented to satisfying the most basic needs of subsistence – there are conditions in the rural centres, such as a shortage of resources, limited professionalization and lower technical competence, which

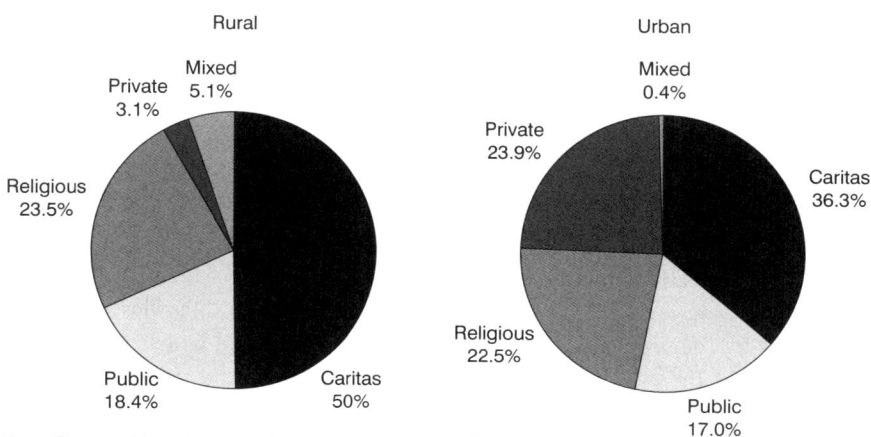

9.1 Ownership of support centres (Source: Cabrera 2000).

Table **9.1** Centres providing one of the following services (%)

	Rural	*Urban*
Information and admission	77	82
Clothing	73	55
Dining hall	87	81
Housing	73	68
Hygiene services	50	66
Health services	42	52
Addiction treatment services	3	15
Psychological support services	8	32
Mental health services	1	3
Education services	7	17
Documentation services	18	50
Job search	12	26
Vocational workshop services	17	41
Labour services	9	20
Project coordination services	2	8
Field work	0	7
Total	100	100

Source: Cabrera 2000.

make the assistance given appear even more like welfare and emergency. Except in providing clothing, food and a bed for a few nights, the centres in urban settings are generally ahead in terms of providing specialized services like, for example, addiction treatment (15 per cent of the urban centres as opposed to only 3 per cent of those located in rural areas), psychological attention (32 vs 8 per cent), job hunting (26 vs 12 per cent) and vocational workshops (41 vs 17 per cent). Of course, the modern and innovative methodology of street work is exclusively found in cities, with nothing similar found in rural areas.

This fundamental difference in work styles between rural and urban zones is clearly reflected by analyses of the different types of shelter in the two settings (Figure 9.2). In rural regions, the overwhelming majority of shelters are those that we refer to as emergency shelters, in which it is possible to stay for less than a week (84 per cent of the rural shelters, as opposed to only 37 per cent of the urban shelters). This is the model called the 'rotating door' which has left a pile of personal biographies linked to itinerancy and nomadic lifestyles that were reinforced by the very characteristics of the support system, which, on the one hand, allowed them in, before throwing them out onto the street even more forcefully than before, on the other.

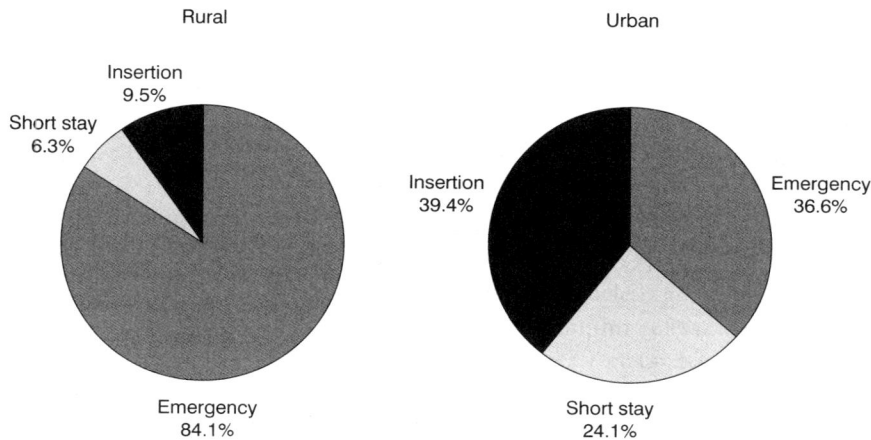

Rural

Urban

Insertion
9.5%

Short stay
6.3%

Insertion
39.4%

Emergency
36.6%

Emergency
84.1%

Short stay
24.1%

9.2 The different types of shelter in rural and urban settings (Source: Cabrera 2000).

Short-stay shelters where one can spend a period between two weeks and three months are much scarcer (6 per cent) in towns. This type of centre is much more frequent in urban zones where they represent 24 per cent of all centres. Lastly, the type of centre that offers housing without a set time-limit, because its aim is to try to carry out a personalized social insertion process – in which it is impossible to determine the duration of stay beforehand – is clearly an essentially urban reality; 39 per cent of urban shelters operate under this philosophy, as opposed to 10 per cent in rural areas. In fact, the average duration of stay in the rural shelters is 29 days while in urban shelters it reaches almost 90 days on average.

Likewise, some characteristics of shelter services are different according to the habitat: while a third of urban shelters have individual rooms – which allow for a higher degree of privacy for the users – the proportion only reaches 25 per cent among rural shelters. It is also true that in big cities it is more frequent to find large establishments inherited from the past where it is still common to find collective rooms, whereas in towns, due to their smaller size, it is much more infrequent to find this type of institution. In fact, rural shelters are much smaller; around 8.7 per cent of all emergency housing places for the homeless in Spain are in towns with less than 20,000 inhabitants (8.4 per cent according to the INE survey). On average, rural centres have nine housing places available, while those that are located in cities with more than 20,000 inhabitants have an average of 36 places. In one case almost 400 people are housed; naturally, this type of institution is unthinkable in a rural area. The usage is also higher – surpassing 80 per cent – in urban shelters than in rural ones, where the average is up to 20 percentage points lower.

Considering the descriptive data we can say that, in general, while the attention given in the urban setting is more professionalized, modern and technical, it also runs the risk of becoming more overcrowded and overwhelmed by the number of people to attend to and it therefore is in danger of increased depersonalization.

With regard to *dining services*, we find that it is typically an urban service. Of all dining places 96.4 per cent are found in cities. This probably does not mean that one cannot receive a meal in one of the many places in the rural areas, but it is something that is most certainly carried out in a much more informal and non-institutional manner. Where a poor person is seen begging, either the local solidarity networks of neighbours will be activated or the person will be attended to on an individual basis, without the need to set up an organized dining service. It is very probable that we are looking at the inheritance of the great famines that devastated the lower strata of the cities in the early days of industrialization and that consequently brought about the creation of an infinite number of charity and social assistance institutions (economic kitchens, dining halls for the poor, etc.) to deal with urban pauperism.

Due to the characteristics of the services, the seasonal nature of the peaks of assistance provided by the centres is also typically an urban phenomenon as the harshness of street life in a big city during the winter months makes a lot more people choose to seek refuge in shelter institutions then. In contrast, the attention provided in housing centres in towns appears to be more regular and constant. The seasonal nature of agricultural work – a phenomenon that causes difficulties in a lot of towns and rural areas, but that is only secondarily linked to the traditional assistance network of transients and homeless people – will be discussed in greater detail when we address the research on the homeless in La Rioja.

INE survey of centres

In the survey carried out by the National Institute of Statistics (INE) on the assistance centres for the homeless,[9] some information was collected that could complement what has been stated so far. Let us look at some data: according to INE, in towns of less than 5,000 inhabitants only 3.2 per cent of the centres responded to the survey; in municipalities between 5,000 and 20,000 inhabitants, there is a greater representation, of 12.1 per cent. At the opposite extreme, the cities of between 100,000 and 500,000 inhabitants, or more than 500,000 inhabitants, total about 60 per cent of all of the centres reported at the national level (41.1 and 20.4 per cent, respectively). The total number of rural centres from which information was obtained in this survey is 85 if we include the combined localities with less than 20,000 inhabitants.

The profile of the people supported by the centres in rural areas still corresponds generally to individual men and women, even though there are also some couples and children, although to a lesser extent (Table 9.2). Of the problems associated with the groups of people attended to in small towns (with less than 5,000 inhabitants), none of the 'classic' problems that are normally classified in the provision of services stands out, while more centres in larger localities attend to a population with problems related to the consumption of toxic substances and alcohol, as well as some that have specialized in attending to the immigrant population with housing problems (Table 9.3). The levels of specialization and diversification of services that these centres provide (Table 9.4) are much lower in the smaller towns than in medium-sized towns (between 5,000 and 20,000 inhabitants). If we extended the comparison to larger urban areas, the disproportion would be even more notable, a fact that confirms the trends pointed out in the previous section with data from the Caritas study (Cabrera, 2000).

Table 9.2 Percentage of the centres that attend to different segments of the population according to the size of the municipality (base = 85 centres)

	Total (%)	*Less than 5,000 inhabitants (%)*	*5,001–20,000 inhabitants (%)*
Men	86.7	100.0	98.5
Women	80.9	77.8	85.1
Couples	48.1	55.6	64.2
Children	30.5	33.3	29.9
Total	100.0	100.0	100.0

Source: INE 2004.

Table 9.3 Number of centres that primarily attend to certain segments of the population in municipalities with less than 20,000 inhabitants (base=60 centres)

	Less than 5,000 inhabitants	*5,001–20,000 inhabitants*
Ex-convicts	2	6
Drug addicts	2	7
Alcoholics	3	8
Battered women	0	5
Immigrants	3	13
Others	4	7
Total	14	46

Source: Based on data from INE 2004.

Table 9.4 Percentage of the centres that provide services according to the type of service offered and the size of the municipality where the centre is located

	Less than 5,000 inhabitants (%)	5,001–20,000 inhabitants (%)	Total (%)
Information and admission	77.8	77.6	79.6
Orientation	50.0	70.1	73.2
Housing	100.0	76.1	73.9
Restoration	72.2	50.7	69.7
Primary education	11.1	4.5	4.0
Professional training	11.1	4.5	2.5
Vocational workshops	27.8	16.4	22.5
Insertion workshops	11.1	11.9	15.3
Adult education	22.2	6.0	11.2
Art activities	27.8	10.4	23.8
Medical care	33.3	11.9	20.5
Psychological support	33.3	22.4	32.8
Legal assistance	16.7	13.4	22.5
Regularization of documents	27.8	19.4	23.2
Clothing	61.1	43.3	43.8
Childcare	0.0	7.5	7.4
Others	5.6	19.4	23.4
Total	100.0	100.0	100.0

Source: INE 2004.

Homeless people in the autonomous community of La Rioja

Over the course of 2001–2, we carried out a study on the situation and characteristics of transient and homeless people in La Rioja, in which we observed some of the existing circumstances in that autonomous community, which – with due interpretative precautions – can be extended to other territories of rural Spain (Cabrera Cabrera *et al.*, 2000).

The main primary sources of information for that work came directly from the non-governmental organizations operating in the region, namely Caritas and the Red Cross, as well as from the Social Services Department of Logroño (the region's capital).

La Rioja has a surface area of 5,000 km² and a population of about 263,000 inhabitants, almost half of which live in Logroño and only 3.6 per cent reside in the mountainous areas, which nevertheless represent 42 per cent of its territory. The population density is 52 inhabitants per square kilometre, a figure that is somewhat less than the Spanish average and half of the demographic density registered in the European Union; however, throughout the region there are mountainous areas that are scantly populated. The demographic evolution (growth and birth rates) registers values that are slightly inferior to those of the European Union as a whole over the past decade.

In terms of age distribution, and in comparison with Spain's population pyramid, a greater relative weight of the population over 64 years old is observed, with a lesser presence of under-25s. La Rioja is a region in which there has been a certain tradition of itinerancy since earlier times, as a region of passage for those that travelled between the Castilian plateau and the Basque Country. It is also traditionally a region of pilgrimages (the Road to Santiago crosses it) and seasonal agricultural jobs, which bring about a large contingent of labourers, especially for the grape harvests. The itinerancy and seasonal nature of the day labourers, associated with the agricultural cycles, are processes of great importance in the region's demographic dynamics.

Rural areas make up 84.7 per cent of La Rioja's territory – that is, all of the mountainous areas in the autonomous community and the 144 nearby municipalities – but only a third of the region's population lives in them, totalling 78,357 people. For the most part, they are areas of limited occupancy; only three (Arnedo, Alfaro and Santo Domingo) have more than 5,000 inhabitants.

The European Union has allocated budgetary funds for rural development in this region through its European Regional Development Fund (ERDF), the European Social Fund (ESF) and the European Fund for Agricultural Orientation and Guarantee (EFAOG) between 1989 and 1993 and, subsequently, through the different phases of the LEADER II and LEADER+ programmes.[10]

The limited demographic density that characterizes these rural territories, worsened by the rural exodus, presents an array of problems, the most severe of which being the difficult access to basic services. For a population that already suffers hardships, as in the case of the homeless, this problem is even worse. This would partly be the reason why homeless labourers tend to group together in somewhat larger communities, like the administrative centres, where some resources can be found. In the case of La Rioja, the only shelters and permanent dining halls for the homeless are in Logroño, the capital, where homeless people cyclically pass through both transiently and as a permanent ('chronic') way of life.

We must not forget that among the causes that lead groups of different people to a state of homelessness, several originate in economic, social, personal and familial circumstances: regional economic crises, the high levels of *unemployment* of the previous decade, the difficult socio-labour re-entry process of those that have been unemployed for a long period of time, the rise of *alcoholism and drug-dependency*, the changes in the *system of treating the mentally ill* (their return from medical institutions to families), the situation of *ex-convicts*, the *emergence and spread of HIV/AIDS* as an illness that provokes exclusion, the *changes in family structures* (women who are victims of abuse, or female heads of households without resources, elderly who live alone and children and adolescents who are alone). Added to this is the yearly incorporation of hundreds of thousands of *immigrants and asylum and refugee applicants*, who also go to La Rioja in search of work. This causes a multitude of new and often conflicting situations to deal with one day to the next. For example, the people who currently attend the largest charity kitchen in Logroño, which was founded at the beginning of the nineteenth century, is mostly made up of Moroccans who work in the fields but go to this canteen – run by religious people – for dinner as a way of lowering their living expenses; this means that the menu must be modified so that it does not include the omnipresent pork in the meals common in the Spanish countryside; furthermore, it is perfectly possible to find in that dining hall 'for the poor' reminders to turn off mobile phones, etc.

The professionals interviewed in rural areas of La Rioja gave us a very detailed description of the past and present situation. In the 1980s, about 800 transient people were counted to have annually passed through Caritas's parishes in the province without permanent addresses, especially along the railroad route and in the administrative centres. It was there that temporary shelters, places that 'took in every person that arrived to the town for about two or three days', emerged. The criteria used for the assistance were based on two predominant social profiles: that of the itinerant transients who went from shelter to shelter – who were normally male alcoholics uprooted from their families – and that of seasonal workers.

In the late 1990s, however, another type of classification began to be used in accordance with the amount of time experienced without a home and the degree of use made of the network, thereby distinguishing between: *new users*, those that were taken in for the first time in rural areas that year (164 in 1999); *common users*, those that had used the services for two years in the rural areas (47 in 1999); and *chronic users*, those that repeated over the course of more than three years (151 in 1999).

Moreover, it became necessary to differentiate between Spaniards and foreigners, which shows how the rural communities have experienced the influx of foreigners – something that has also taken place in the urban areas – which were most often transient passers-by associated with seasonal labour.

As a result of all of these circumstances, we see that if we apply the definition of a homeless person to the rural setting it must be made more flexible than in urban habitats. We could have two definitions applicable to rural areas: a strict definition, in which immigrant seasonal workers and people living in substandard housing are not included; and a broader one, in which they are included, given

Table 9.5 Proportion of foreigners in Spain

	Spaniards	*Foreigners*	*% foreigners*
1993 (12 towns)	1,912	n/a	n/a
1995 (12 towns)	1,647	387	23.5
1996 (20 towns)	1,996	845	42

Source: Cabrera *et al.* (2000).

Table 9.6 Seasonal workers without housing using Caritas's rural services

Town	*No. of workers*
Alfaro	261
Calahorra	245
Casalarreina	15
Cenicero	117
Fuenmayor	138
Haro	32
Huércanos	No data
Navarrete	15
Rincón de Soto	37
San Asensio	Service not available
Santo Domingo	30
Total	890

Source: Cabrera *et al.* 2000.

that they are important phenomena in this matter. As we see in Table 9.5, the proportion of foreigners had reached almost 50 per cent in 1999, according to data from a total of 20 towns. Today, the foreigners will surely be the overwhelming majority.

The importance of this mass of seasonal labourers, who in fact are homeless, is demonstrated by the fact that – taking the premise of 10 towns with seasonal agricultural campaigns or that are 'passing through localities' in order to get to them – between June and October 2000 Caritas's rural services attended to 890 people that lived without acquiring housing, in emergency housing, improvised camps on the borders of the fields, etc. (Table 9.6). It should be acknowledged that these months correspond to the highest agricultural activity. From analysis carried out on this group of seasonal labourers, we can point out some of their characteristics: they are generally victims of subcontracting, driven 'by the fear of not having work or any means of subsistence'. But in some cases they are people that are 'more on the fringe, that is, undocumented immigrants, a long-time unemployed person who is middle/older-aged or one who has an alcohol problem, etc.' to whom some type of support can be provided by municipal or regional social services.

With regard to immigrants, there is a noted increase in the poverty that undoubtedly affects housing and social dignity problems but, once again, here economic factors come together that also overwhelm the administration's abilities. For example, cases have come up such as the non-payment of wages after carrying out a job, or underpaying what was agreed to, between €21 and €30, the withholding of documentation, or in cases of those in irregular situations, they were given the documentation of other immigrant workers with work permits; with regard to housing conditions, we find people in subhuman housing, living with overcrowding and lacking minimum living standards. Or in the case of people that have been arbitrarily taken to work in very different localities, they have become victim to threats or of noncompliance with agreed conditions, and have even suffered verbal and physical abuse on occasions (despite this, no one reported the subcontractors to the authorities).

Under such circumstances, the assistance these people receive usually comes from NGOs like the Red Cross or Caritas. For example, the Red Cross works mostly with the immigrants and asylum seekers, as well as with the gypsy population, which is relatively large in the area, especially Portuguese gypsies, who work on the harvests. The housing problem is a central theme in the assistance programmes for these people, given that they generally have serious difficulties paying market prices to access a decent residence, or simply do not find any landlord that would accept them as tenants. There is the paradigmatic case of eastern Almeria (the area of El Ejido), where racism and xenophobia have been widely documented and have turned into violent outbursts against the Moroccans. In the case of the immigrants, it is quite common for them to be homeless or housed in extremely precarious conditions when they move to work as seasonal labourers. Naturally, the solution to the housing problem of the seasonal workers should come from compliance with the legislation that governs these kinds of employment contracts and not from measures of assistance.

For its part, Caritas's programmes for seasonal workers and homeless people in La Rioja attended to almost 2,300 people in 2000, the majority of which were immigrants. The information collected directly in interviews with professionals and volunteers from the organization – chosen to provide a closer vision of the changes and situations occurring on the ground in terms of homeless assistance – shows us that three profiles stand out among the types of homeless people that receive special attention from Caritas: seasonal workers, passers-by and 'chronic users'. As general criteria of the action-intervention apply, there is a need to coordinate with the municipal social work units in the administrative centres, for which various agreements with the town governments have been established in the past years. They are diverse and not uniform, because the conditions involved are distinctive in each case, with different degrees of participation by and responsibility for each side. Among these agreements, those entered into with the town governments of Haro, Alfaro, Santo Domingo and Calahorra stand out. In general, Caritas defends the need to offer services from a *single and coordinated point of assistance* in the different populations. This would mean coordination between Social Services and an NGO, which is why the project has major difficulties in terms of its implementation.

Caritas is trying to address the problems of the *seasonal workers* through coordinated action and campaigns with the unions, mainly the UGT (Unión General de Trabajadores, the General Workers Union).[11] The basic premise is to *promote that the workers enter into contracts*, and that the contracts envisage housing needs being met by the employer. Throughout the interviews, those in charge of management and coordination for Caritas frequently made reference to the National Agreement of Seasonal Workers, the result of negotiations between unions, agricultural federations and municipal federations, which – from their perspective – should be the real legal framework in which contractual relationships are established, including all of the economic and social conditions. The problem is that action is not always carried out within this framework. Therefore, the seasonal workers' problems have both social and economic dimensions. With regard to the economic issue, it is the responsibility of the farmers to provide better for the workers, so that the shelters are not charged to taxpayers. With regard to the social issue, the consequences and responsibilities relate to the public services (town governments).

In general, in terms of the detection of *urgent needs* regarding assistance to the homeless, the heads of the organizations interviewed insist on the need to establish a service of permanent shelters in various rural areas, at least in the three administrative centres, which would cover the needs of almost the entire territory.

Within the programmes and projects developed by Caritas, emphasis has been placed for many years on prevention of the various problems at hand. However, with regard to homeless people, this objective turns into quite a difficult task as it frequently involves extreme situations caused by multiple factors that almost always go back many years in the lives of each individual person. Therefore, they frequently direct some people to *rehabilitation programmes*, which may be led exclusively by Caritas or by the public services. The latter would be some social/labour insertion workshops, like those in Santo Domingo, Najera, Alfaro and Logroño. In terms of the public services, there are programmes in the town hall's municipal shelter; however, according to the experience of those in charge at the regional level of Caritas, one cannot speak with much optimism about the success of the rehabilitation programmes for the homeless. As an example, we were informed that in the last three years only a mere three to five people had entered the programmes and only one of them found a job; the ray of hope is that this person was then working and had a home, even if they still had major economic difficulties.

Conclusions

In analysing the geographic distribution of the assistance network for the homeless, according to the size of the populations in which the centres are located, we observe that there are still major differences between urban life and life in rural areas, which must logically be reflected in our subject of study.

It is useful to keep in mind that in Spain, which comprises a total of 8,098 municipalities, there are almost 6,000 (5,932 to be exact) that have less than 2,000 inhabitants. An array of resources feature less in these small municipalities; consequently, the proportion of centres that attend to homeless people is also less.

Frequently, it has been thought that the exclusion of the homeless is an urban phenomenon. This belief is aided by the fact that homelessness in the city is doubly shocking and more visible. The image is of homeless figures as solitary and slovenly people moving from one place to the next, pushing a shopping cart full of bags and with evident signs of mental disorder. From this archetypal model, a conception is built of what homelessness is, in the assumption that it relates to a phenomenon linked to anonymity and solitude, which reigns in the big cities. However, this represents less than 5 per cent of the homeless in big cities.

If we accept a more exact definition of a homeless person, and go beyond the most notorious and attention-grabbing appearances, then it is easy to understand that homelessness – far from being an urban phenomenon – is also found in rural areas, even though it naturally occurs with distinct connotations compared to homelessness in the big cities. Seasonal workers, many of whom are foreign immigrants, are one of the characteristic forms of the homeless in rural zones. Precarious and substandard housing is also prevalent in some rural areas; if we applied current standards of what can be considered a dignified place to serve as housing for human beings, many people from rural areas could become part of the homeless population or be 'at risk' of being homeless, even though technically speaking they are not.

In any case, as reflected in Figure 9.3 and Table 9.7, the overall majority of the centres are in cities of more than 5,000 inhabitants. Of the total Spanish population, 15.54 per cent reside in towns of less than 5,000 inhabitants and only 9.43 per cent of the centres that attend to the homeless can be found in towns of that size.

In this sense, the effort made by the large capitals, Madrid and Barcelona, do not appear to be more than the corresponding proportional weight of the population that lives in them (10.93 per cent of the Spanish population and

Table 9.7 Proportion of centres and municipalities by population and size

	Centres	%	Population	%	Municipalities	%
Madrid and Barcelona	73	10.93	4,375,655	11.03	2	0.02
500,000 or more	43	6.44	2,594,979	6.54	4	0.05
250,000–499,999	72	10.78	3,071,282	7.74	10	0.12
100,000–249,999	145	21.71	6,159,153	15.53	39	0.48
50,000–99,999	65	9.73	3,982,633	10.04	60	0.74
20,000–49,999	86	12.87	5,195,495	13.10	178	2.20
5,000–19,999	121	18.11	8,124,523	20.48	853	10.53
2,000–4,999	35	5.24	3,129,220	7.89	1,020	12.60
Less than 2,000	28	4.19	3,036,454	7.65	5,932	73.25
Total	668	100.00	39,669,394	100.00	8,098	100.00

Source: INE 2004, prepared by authors.

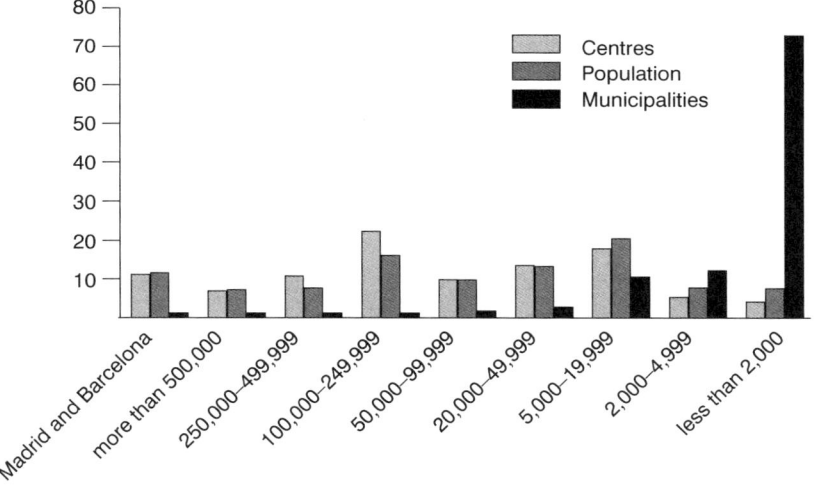

9.3 Proportion of centres and muncipalities by population and size (Source: INE 2004, prepared by authors)

11.03 per cent of the centres). From this perspective, the greatest effort is made in the provincial capitals, cities of between 100,000 and 500,000 inhabitants, which, while gathering only 23.27 per cent of the population, provide 32.49 per cent of the country's centres.

Nevertheless, the most notable imbalance is observed by comparing the percentage of centres in each area not so much with the percentage of the population but rather with what would be the percentage of municipalities that are part of it. Thus, while the two major cities have 73 centres, we find that there are 5,932 towns of 2,000 inhabitants or less that have only 28 centres among them.

This absence of centres in small towns can be explained to a certain extent by taking into account the shortage of resources in the municipal coffers in some cities surrounding the big capitals, which have experienced spectacular growth in recent decades, as is the case in the cities of southern Madrid (Getafe, Mostoles, Alcorcon, etc.), which have gone from being small towns to having more than 100,000 inhabitants.

But not only is the distribution of the centres very irregular between urban and rural areas, the condition – private or public – of the entities that work in them also varies. To summarize and conclude this chapter, we highlight the following differential characteristics.

1 The public sector is particularly present in both extremes, in the smallest towns and in the two largest cities, Madrid and Barcelona.
2 Caritas is mostly found in the largest towns and the smallest cities, between 5,000 and 100,000 inhabitants.
3 The private centres of religious congregations and associations are principally established in centres of more than 250,000 inhabitants.
4 The strictly private (non-denominational) centres find their most favourable environment in the cities, especially in the provincial capitals with between 100,000 and 500,000 inhabitants.

The most recent sociological studies on poverty and living conditions of the population living under the poverty line at the national level include a descriptive analysis of these situations in rural areas (Cabrera, 2000). But the principal objection that we find is that they are based on data gathered from housing surveys, thereby leaving the homeless completely out of the field of analysis.

By analysing the situation of the population with regard to housing from the data collected in the previous studies, we can extract some information, even though it is not very illuminating. It is said that there are fewer problems to access housing in rural areas (EDIS, 1998: 184), mainly because there are more chances of acquiring land ownership, which creates opportunities to build and expand the residence over time in accordance with one's economic possibilities.

Since there are no specific studies on homeless people in rural areas (compared to issues of poverty and exclusion) beyond the study presented here on La Rioja, one must ask about the technical means that would be required in order to monitor the population movements of homeless people in this type of habitat at a given moment, in order to be able to continue collecting data in longitudinal studies. We would certainly need a different methodology than the one used to gather information in the major urban centres. On the other hand, making observations at various times of the year and in different years could allow for more detailed description of the activity flows and links of homeless groups. Even more precise explanatory analyses could then be presented from which more adequate intervention and prevention policies could be developed.

Notes

1 For more information on the systemic concept of what is rural, see Hervieu (1996) or Ramos and Romero (1995), works cited in Ramos and Romero 2000: 49.

2 For more information on the distribution of rural poverty, there are more or less up-to-date studies (Renes Ayala,1998; 2000) from which we unfortunately cannot extract any information in order to study the situation and conditions of the homeless. This is because they defined the poverty line, classified different types of levels of poverty and applied these categories of analysis to all homes, while taking data from the existing population and housing censuses (INE Census, 1991, 2001).

3 Rural Europe, *Lucha contra la exclusión social en el medio rural.* 2000. http://www.rural-europe.aeidl.be/rural-es/biblio/exclusion

4 More on this information can be found by consulting the data and indexes published by the National Statistics Institute in the 2001 Census. It maintains a website from which a large part of the information can be accessed free of charge (www.ine.es).

5 In order to understand the regional and territorial differences in Spain, it is important to take into account, as well as the historic factors related to economic and political development, that this is a country that is geographically enormously diverse. Two determining characteristics are: the vast extension of the mountainous regions – it is one of the European countries with the highest mountainous proportions after Switzerland and Austria – and the problems regarding access to water in dry regions.

6 With regard to the CAP, there is an extensive and diverse bibliography available on the economic analysis of the contemporary rural area; Miren Etxezarreta, Lourdes Viladomiu, Martínez Alier and José Manuel Naredo are some of the authors to keep in mind.

7 Caritas is a non-governmental denominational organization, linked to the Roman Catholic Church, which is the predominant religion in Spain. Its initiatives in social work, the social studies that it has supported and in which it has participated, as well as its widespread presence throughout the territory make it a key reference point to understanding poverty and social exclusion in Spain.

8 It is enough to state that, in 2001, the available family income per inhabitant in Spain was roughly between €9,700 and €10,650, which is about €27–€29

a day. (Economic Yearbook of Spain 2003. Barcelona: La Caixa. http://www.anuarieco2003.lacaixa.comunicacions.com)

9 The survey of assistance centres for homeless people was published by INE on 19 May 2004. http://www.ine.es/prodyser/pubweb/epsh_052004/epshcen_0504.pdf

10 The LEADER II program has been applied since 1994 in the rural areas of Objective 1 regions, those of less economic development from the European Union, and those of Objective 5b, the areas with fragile rural systems. The concession of grants is also accepted within the programme to the regions bordering such areas, while the maximum limit of resources that can be granted to these regions is 10 per cent of the programme's total budget. The population of each of the different areas of activity cannot surpass 100,000 inhabitants. La Rioja's case is that of Objective 5b while in many other Spanish regions the zones fall under Objective 1. LEADER II was followed by LEADER+ for the development of rural areas in Spain between 2000 and 2006. In Spain, LEADER+ is articulated in one national programme and 17 regional programmes. More information is available at: http://redrural.mapya.es/web/temas/presentacion_leader/normativa_ leader+.asp.

11 For more information, see UGT online: http://www.ugt.es.

Chapter 10
Are there any homeless people in rural Finland?

Sakari Hänninen

Introduction

To speak about rural homelessness in Finland today sounds like a provocation. Since the seminal work by Pekka Haatanen on rural poverty in Finland (Haatanen, 1968), the topic of rural homelessness has not really been on the research agenda. I share the contention with Cloke *et al.* (2000) that rurality, on the one hand, and homelessness, on the other, have been constructed in such a manner that their linkages have become difficult to recognize. I shall not seek a recoupling of rurality and homelessness by way of a simple conceptual extension of their meanings. My writing strategy is not to start with a critique but rather to end with a challenge.

An outline of the profile and transformation of homelessness in different regional contexts in Finland provides the background for more focused explorations. The insight, developed in the next section, that the reduction in the 'official' number of homeless persons in rural Finland cannot be seen solely as a policy outcome, demands a more complex view of rural homelessness as a situated event. Homelessness is multi-dimensional; representing a kind of heterogeneous assemblage conceivable in terms of government (in the Foucauldian sense as the conduct of conduct). A more versatile picture of rural homelessness in Finland is made possible by analysing this event in terms of disablement, dispossession, displacement and disaffiliation.

Best practice in Finland

When Finland was asked by the EU Commission to propose Finnish examples of best practice for peer review in the field of social inclusion policies, the proposal thus made prioritized the Programme for the Reduction of Homelessness. The results of the two national programmes justified this proposal since the estimated number of homeless persons was halved during the first programme (1987–91), and in the next programme period (2001–3) there has also been a modest decrease. The Finnish proposal, however, did not convince the EU Commission, which selected Finland's second proposal – the citizen's social support networks (HYVE), a model for regional action to further welfare – to be an example of best practice for peer review. The Commission selected the homelessness eradication strategy in the UK as another example of best practice with which Finland should also be more closely acquainted.

The reasons for turning down Finland's proposal have not been publicized. The selection of the homelessness eradication strategy in the UK as an example did not leave room for another case. Traditional efforts to eradicate homelessness in Finland deviate from the mainstream governmental rationality adopted in the EU social inclusion policies. The public sector has carried the crucial responsibility for providing and organizing housing services for homeless people in Finland according to the principle of universalism characteristic of the Nordic welfare regime. This task is the responsibility of municipalities. The role of NGOs as providers of social services to the homeless is important, but only a secondary and complementary one compared to that of the local authorities. Voluntary organizations usually receive a large share of their funds from local authorities (on the basis of client contracts) and state budget funds from the Finnish Slot Machine Association (Kärkkäinen, 2003). The role of private providers of services for the homeless is still quite marginal in Finland.

In the 1980s, the governmental regime to combat homelessness was reconstructed. A strategic effort emphasizing homelessness as houselessness was made (Taipale, 1982) in order, for example, to neutralize the stigma of homeless persons. The force of the civil movement of the 1960s and 1970s against homelessness was exploited with the strategic aim of overcoming the disjointed nature of this movement. In 1987, controlling homelessness as houselessness became the focus of policy formation. In this regime of government, housing became the necessary point of departure, which made it possible to concentrate institutional action on this very point. The responsibility of the municipalities was to provide a home of a minimum standard for every homeless person in need of housing services (Kärkkäinen, 1998: 21). An outcome of this governmental reconstruction was that controlling homelessness became linked more directly with sectoral housing policies, which were then being co-ordinated with other sectoral policies such as welfare policies and regional policies. However, this regime of government soon had to confront the depression of the 1990s and was again challenged and hybridized by new governmental demands. The reduction of homelessness – and the practices of counting homelessness – since the middle of the 1980s must be situated in the context of controlling homelessness as houselessness. Rural homelessness in Finland, however, transcends this context.

The Housing Market Survey

Since 1986, a survey of homelessness has been carried out in Finland as part of the Housing Market Survey, first by the National Housing Board and, since 1994, by the Housing Fund of Finland. This survey is said to provide annual estimates of the total extent of homelessness. In the Housing Market Survey, the homeless include the following categories (Kärkkäinen 1999: 165, 171–2; Valtion Asuntorahasto, 2002):[1]

- persons living outdoors or in temporary shelters;
- persons living in night shelters or other shelters for the homeless;
- persons living in institutions or institutional homes either temporarily or permanently due to lack of housing;
- persons soon to be released from prison who have no housing;
- persons living temporarily with relatives and acquaintances due to lack of housing;
- families who have split up or are living in temporary housing due to lack of housing.

The first five categories refer to the number of single homeless persons, while the sixth category refers to families or other bigger households. The share of the sixth category has been about one fifth of the total number of homeless persons. This survey is not a sample; it attempts to outline the overall extent and distribution of homelessness and houselessness in each municipality (Kärkkäinen, 1999: 174–5).

Methodological precautions

In reading indications of homelessness, several methodological issues about surveying should be noted. The information about homelessness contained in the Housing Market Survey is provided by local authorities in each municipality. The number of homeless persons is one item in the survey that the Housing Fund has asked the municipal housing authorities, in collaboration with the social welfare authorities, to specify. This requested item is meant to provide information about the actual situation, since it is gathered on a daily basis so that it shows the total extent of homelessness on a certain day. The survey has been carried out either in the spring or in the autumn (Kärkkäinen, 1999: 173–6) but not during the summer, when the extent of homelessness may increase in the rural regions. The role of estimates is significant in the production of this data. Therefore, the results of the survey are 'a combination of register data, exact statistics, and estimates' (Kärkkäinen, 1999: 180).

Social welfare authorities systematically estimate the number of homeless persons to be higher than is approximated by the housing authorities. Social welfare authorities have a more encompassing conception of homelessness than the housing authorities, who tend to interpret it simply as a lack of housing. They may read the instructions of the survey in a different fashion.

The difficulties and variations in the municipal procedures of gathering information on homelessness are well known to the responsible authorities in the Housing Fund (Tiitinen, 2004; Asunnottomuustyöryhmä, 2001), and some measures to overcome these difficulties have been taken on in the process. If the municipal information delivered is diagnosed as out of date or the information significantly deviates from that of the previous year, then the information given is checked by contacting the municipal authorities (Kärkkäinen, 1999: 173–4). These measures can correct the most obvious misunderstandings.

A number of municipalities (55 altogether), where the annual variations (during 1992–2003) in the number of homeless persons were remarkably uneven, were approached (Displacement, 2003) to find out the reasons for this fluctuation. This was done by the researcher Juha Peltosalmi, who carried out the interviews by phone. The discussions with the local authorities revealed that, in some cases, the sharp variations in the numbers were due to changes in the mode of inscription. A new person responsible for delivering this information may have interpreted the instructions in a slightly different way. Young people living at home and waiting for housing were sometimes counted and sometimes not. People living in institutions or institutional homes were sometimes counted and sometimes not. These fluctuations are quite understandable since these boundaries are very much floating. The same persons may sometimes have been counted twice. It was also admitted that there were small mistakes in the figures.

The mapping of the distribution and development of homelessness in Finland is illustrative. The quality of information on homelessness provided by the Housing Market Survey varies from municipality to municipality. Each year, a very small number of rural municipalities do not answer the Housing Market Survey. The standard presupposition that in small rural municipalities the homeless are personally well known to local authorities cannot always be taken for granted. These people can come and go. These data give a cross-section of homelessness, but not a view of the actual flow.

The survey results of homelessness

What does the Housing Market Survey tell about the development of homelessness in Finland since 1987? Over 18,000 persons altogether, single persons and families, were counted as homeless in 1987. In 1996, this figure, for the first time, dropped to fewer than 10,000 persons. In subsequent years, the number of homeless persons slightly increased. In November 2002 the number of homeless persons was estimated to be 9,600 single persons and 775 families. In November 2003 it again dropped to fewer than 10,000 persons, including 8,200 single persons and 415 families (Tiitinen and Ikonen, 2003, 2004). The Housing Market Survey also illustrates how homelessness in Finland is concentrated in cities. More than half of the homeless persons are now in Helsinki. The survey points out that the most severe problems of homelessness are also situated in other city regions: Tampere, Vantaa, Espoo, Turku, Lahti, Kuopio, Joensuu, Jyväskylä, Lappeenranta, Oulu. According to this survey, in 2003 there were about 6,400 single homeless persons in these cities, which constitutes 78 per cent of the total number of single homeless persons in Finland.

Since the Housing Market Survey covers all Finnish municipalities, it maps the development and distribution of homelessness across the country. All the municipalities will be classified here into the following categories according to criteria of urbanization: urban centres, semi-urban municipalities, rural areas near cities, rural areas proper and sparsely populated rural areas. The Housing Market Survey results on the development of homelessness in Finland, during 1992–2003, can be seen in this classification (Table 10.1) (Valtion Asuntorahasto, 1992–2003).

Table 10.1 maps the relative number of single homeless persons in Finland (homeless families are left out for technical reasons), and illustrates how the degree

Table 10.1 Share of single houseless persons as permillage of municipal population in different regional categories (yearly average %)

	Urban centres	*Semi-urban municipalities*	*Rural areas near cities*	*Rural areas proper*	*Sparsely populated rural areas*	*All*
1992	1.83	1.13	0.66	0.50	0.87	0.78
1994	1.61	1.12	0.59	0.44	0.75	0.69
1995	1.73	0.84	0.61	0.39	0.55	0.62
1996	1.64	1.11	0.52	0.37	0.56	0.60
1997	1.64	1.01	0.55	0.38	0.38	0.55
1998	1.59	1.06	0.68	0.40	0.33	0.57
1999	1.51	1.08	0.58	0.37	0.39	0.55
2000	1.38	1.08	0.64	0.31	0.31	0.50
2001	1.33	1.03	0.58	0.31	0.27	0.48
2002	1.31	0.99	0.48	0.26	0.19	0.41
2003	1.19	0.94	0.43	0.23	0.22	0.38
N	39	18	74–82	157–174	112–123	402–436

of homelessness has developed in different regional settings. The most rapid decline in the relative number of homeless persons has taken place in sparsely populated rural areas, i.e. in remote countryside. In these areas, the permillage (‰) of homeless persons to municipal population has decreased from 0.87 to 0.22 during 1992–2003. This is a very low figure in comparison to urban centres (where it was 1.19 in 2003) and to semi-urban municipalities (where it was 0.94 in 2003). The decline has been significant, although much more moderate, in rural areas proper (from 0.50 in 1992 to 0.23 in 2003). This profile of transformation does not really change even if we pay attention to different dimensions of homelessness. (See Tables 10.2, 10.3, 10.4, at the end of this chapter.)

Homelessness as a complex assemblage

The regime of government which has obliged local authorities to provide housing for those in need has naturally played a significant role in the reduction of homelessness in Finland. This fact alone does not explain the regional variations and fluctuations in the figures. The differences in the capabilities and willingness to actualize the obligations could make these variations more intelligible. Municipalities have naturally differed in meeting their obligations. However, the practices governing homelessness cannot be reduced to mediation between society and individuals (the homeless), obligations and needs, or supply and demand. Since homelessness is not just a lack of housing but an intricate historical event, it can always be approached from many different perspectives and lead to intervention through different governmental practices. The moment when something – like decent living – breaks down and is destabilized as an assemblage, the associations and connections multiply and are individualized, and the chances of intervention become more contingent (Lehtonen, 2000: 279). By applying the Latourian spatial imaginary (Latour, 1993: 51, 58), the dimensions and limits of the regime of governing homelessness as houselessness might be schematically outlined.

Figure 10.1 is based on the conviction that the one-dimensional frame of reference must be abandoned if homelessness as a historical event is to be properly mapped as an object of government. In the one-dimensional diagram, homelessness as houselessness can be pictured only as a kind of meeting point between individuals and society, demand and supply, needs and resources, skills and structures (Latour, 1992: 276–7). Such a mapping always invites disputes and quarrels about the essence of homelessness. It either emphasizes the subjective (intentional) or the objective (structural) reasons behind the events. Therefore, a second dimension has to be introduced. If the one-dimensional yardstick allows one to position any entity or event along the subject–society line, the second dimension makes it possible to specify the degree of stabilization (value of the

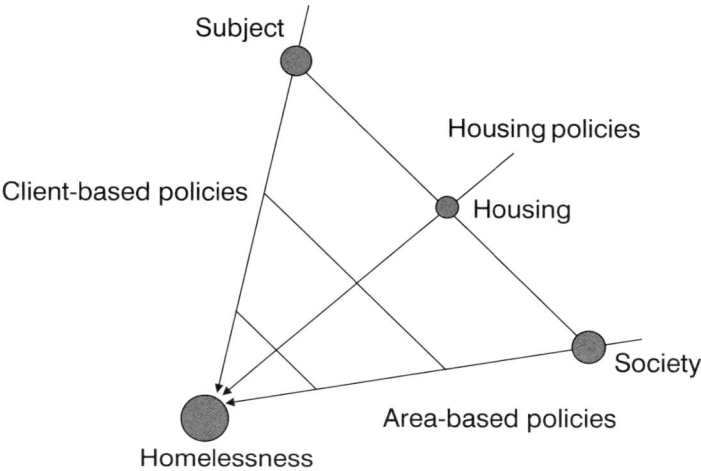

10.1 Policing homelessness

stabilization gradient) associated with the entity or event in question (Latour, 1992: 284–5). By situating homelessness (as existential) on this dimension, it becomes possible to problematize it in terms of such questions as why are we all not tied together? Why do there appear to be disorderly events? How is it that the same social links may weaken, strengthen or disappear altogether as we shift from place to place? (Latour, 1991: 3).

For the hard core of homeless persons, events are characterized by a low value of the stabilization gradient. It is meaningless to argue if such destabilized and disjointed events are generated by subjective or objective causes. They must be conceptualized in variable ontologies so that, in their mappings, points become lines (Latour, 1992: 286). For this reason, I have described situations of homelessness as complex assemblages, whose trajectories might be defined in terms of associations, connections, modalities, quasi-objects and so on (Latour, 1992: 286). In these terms, our coming together, the way we are tied together, is not only constituted by social forces, but as Latour says '(w)e are held together by loyalties but also by telephones, electricity, media, computers, trains, and planes' (1991: 16). But are we all thus tied together? What about the homeless? The life situations of homeless persons are in various ways characterized by a lack of such connectivities, and not only in terms of a dwelling, which would guarantee that the person is able to make good use of society's relations and institutions (Brandt, 1992: 11–12). Events of homelessness are assembled by associations and connectivities, which produce very fragile and individualized situations of a low degree of stabilization. These situations can also be characterized by a multiplication of a different set of connectivities, or quasi-objects, which bring together principles, strategies, techniques, instruments, diagnoses, resources, truth-claims, etc. One can visualize situations of homeless persons with multiple problems which can be penetrated by multi-agency efforts.

Latour makes the important point that the 'more the quasi-objects multiply, the greater grows the distinction between the two poles' (1992: 58). The multiplication of quasi-objects would mean that such situations become more and more mediated and saturated by connections, associations, attachments and interventions of various kinds. In situations of homelessness, the growing distinction between the poles of subject and society means that it also becomes more and more difficult and challenging to co-ordinate different sectoral policies in the governing of homelessness. The more the quasi-objects multiply, the greater is the awareness of the difficulties of sectoral policies and of the need for integration. The more mediated and multiplied the situations of homelessness become or are seen, the more the distance grows between area-based regional policies, housing policies and client-based welfare policies in the government of homelessness, and the more necessary it becomes to try to integrate their efforts. This may sound paradoxical, even contradictory, but the paradox is a real one. Interventions of sectoral policies can produce effects that challenge their own rationality. There is a strange tension between governmental efforts and effects. Since previous interventions can make further efforts even harder – the challenge of the hard core of homeless persons as a complex assemblage – there is a definite urge to leave matters as they are. It is possible to get a faint insight of the paradoxical logic of governing homelessness if one looks at this government as a process from area-based, resource-based and client-based policy perspectives.

Area-based perspective: intra-regional differences

The Housing Market Survey data portray quite well the housing situation in Finland during 1987–2003. It is evident that the validity and reliability of this data is weakened when it is used to inform about situations of homelessness of specific municipalities, or in comparing specific municipalities with each other. With this reservation in mind, it is worthwhile looking more closely at the regional distribution of homelessness, since it gives a much more complex picture than the one seen from a distance.

Even if the degree of homelessness has been (1992–2003) comparatively high in the urban centres, and especially so in Helsinki, there are a number of rural regions – in sparsely populated rural areas (e.g. Ilomantsi, Sodankylä, Eno, Kangasniemi), rural areas proper (e.g. Lumijoki, Uurainen, Orivesi, Vammala, Nivala, Toholampi, Sauvo), and rural areas near cities (e.g. Kiihtelysvaara, Forssa, Perniö, Nokia, Sipoo, Kempele) – where this degree is also relatively high according to the Housing Market Survey. Even in the sparsely populated rural areas, there are municipalities where the relative number of homeless people has not decreased but rather increased during these years (e.g. Kitee, Kemijärvi, Posio, Jaala). Similar examples could also be picked from other rural regions. The annual variations in the number of homeless persons can also be distinct in many rural municipalities, and for quite contingent reasons. There are many rural municipalities where the degree of homelessness has fluctuated from year (1992) to year (2003) in quite an irregular fashion (e.g. Kuusamo, Eno, Keuruu, Lieksa, Parkano, Kangasniemi, Asikkala, Ylistaro, Vihti, Vieremä, Valtimo, Valkeala, Vaala, Uurainen, Utajärvi, Ulvila, Rantasalmi, Oulainen, Harjavalta, Maaninka, Luoto, Kokemäki, Kaustinen, Inkoo, Inari, Ii, Haukipudas, Haapavesi, Eura). These figures warn us against making too hasty generalizations. There are many municipalities in the rural regions of Finland where the number of 'officially recognized' homeless persons is significant and may have even increased. The rural regions constitute a spatial mix, and the Housing Market Survey reflects this variation.

The inter- and intra-regional differences in the number of homeless persons may be a sign of a governmental failure. The Nordic regime of welfare practices in Finland was originally designed to reduce regional differences in living conditions. Implementation of the welfare practices has been the duty of municipalities. The welfare state has set the constitutional framework for municipal tasks, which was also monitored. Since the financing of these tasks has been based primarily on taxes and payments collected by municipalities, the state has shared in the statutory tasks of municipalities in order to equalize their differences in resources. Therefore, up until the 1980s, the system of government grants and subsidies was developed sectorally for one task at a time (Pihlajaniemi, 2003: 266). In this regime of welfare practices, different sectoral policies were co-ordinated with each other, or, at least, intersected each other so that regional policies – and even agricultural policies – had a definite welfarist dimension. However, in the 1990s, the welfare state regime in Finland was restructured so that state regulation, i.e. guidance by norms, in social welfare and health tasks of municipalities, has drastically diminished. At the same time, the state grant system has undergone several reforms in order for municipalities to have more liberty in organizing the management of their tasks (Pihlajaniemi, 2003: 267). As a result of this restructuring, municipalities can be in very different positions in the management of their welfare tasks. The future of municipalities in the sparsely populated regions can be especially vulnerable in this respect.

The restructuring of the welfare regime has been accompanied by a transformation of area-based regional policies. It can be claimed, in spite of the new rural policies, that the officially stated governmental goal to keep the whole country inhabited has been abandoned in Finland (Silvasti, 2003: 301–29). The outcome of this transformation has been radical. Since the early 1990s, in-migration to certain urban centres (Helsinki Metropolitan area, Turku, Tampere, Oulu, Jyväskylä, etc.) has really started to accelerate. The rural areas have been the regions of fast population decrease (Seutukunta- ja maakuntakatsaus, 2003: 31). In the remote rural regions in eastern and northern Finland, population decrease has been unexceptionally fast.

In this situation of rapid inter-regional migration, it seems to be an official conviction that the automatic mechanisms of exit and market forces will produce a desired state of equilibrium. This kind of governmental rationality marginalizes the role of voice – i.e. politics as a recuperation mechanism. This mode of governance does not invest in loyalty as a means of holding exit at bay (Hirschman, 1970: 78). There seems to be no urgent need to focus any particular political attention on the clearly recognized social problems of the remote rural regions. As far as rural homelessness is concerned, this seems to be a non-existent need. It is rather assumed that out-migration from the rural regions will displace this problem altogether.

Inter- and intra-regional variations in the degree of homelessness are crucially conditioned by migration flows. The inter-regional migration flows in Finland deviate significantly from the demographic patterns of more densely populated, advanced market societies, where small cities may have grown faster than large cities and small towns may have grown faster than larger towns. Intra-regional variations, due to decentralization and deconcentration of labour markets, can be much more significant than inter-regional differences (Urry, 1995: 80, 83).

In contrast, in Finland it was estimated (in 2001) that out of 452 municipalities, some 143 are municipalities where population decrease in the next ten years will be rapid. In the more far-reaching population prognosis (2000–30), it is estimated that municipalities situated in rural areas will lose 13 per cent of their population by the year 2030, while the population in municipalities that incorporate the urban centres will increase by 9 per cent during the same period (Seutukunta- ja maakuntakatsaus, 2003: 37).

Resource-based perspective: policing homelessness

In the 1960s, homelessness in Finland was connected with alcoholism, unemployment and vagrancy. The housing authorities did not consider homelessness to be of their concern until the 1970s. It was then that the first links between the housing authorities and social welfare and health authorities were established. It was in the 1980s that the elimination of homelessness was articulated as a policy issue, 'the primary goal being to provide normal homes' (Kärkkäinen, 1998: 16–19). The reduction of homelessness was translated into a housing policy problem that required specific measures. In this effort to eliminate homelessness in Finland, housing policy has not only been supported by social welfare and health policies, but has also been supplemented by regional policy measures. Even if Finnish housing policy has been criticized for being inefficient, it has, together with social welfare and regional policies, been effective in reducing the number of homeless persons in Finland since the mid-1980s (Kärkkäinen, 1998: 15), including within the rural regions. However, rural homelessness was dismissed as a relevant housing policy issue in the 1990s – if it was ever considered a specific one – due to increasing out-migration, the 'urbanisation' of regional policies and the restructuring of the welfare regime.

The non-issue of rural homelessness can clearly be seen if we read the recent government report on housing policy in the out-migration regions (Ministry of Environmental Affairs, 2001). The parallel decrease in both population numbers and the number of homeless persons in rural regions is ground for the conclusions of the above-mentioned report. The basic anxiety is that due to fluctuations in out-migration and employment opportunities, many municipalities will, in the near future, be in great financial difficulties because of over-investment in housing and other infrastructures (Ministry of Environmental Affairs, 2001: 28). It has been suggested that many of these municipalities will be compelled to pull down part of the housing stock so that the costs of maintenance will be reduced. In some Finnish municipalities these measures have already been implemented. This is just the beginning if Finland follows the example of Sweden, where in 2000–1 about 10,000 rental apartments were pulled down in 106 municipalities (out of a total of 288 municipalities). In the remote rural areas in northern Sweden (Norbotten), these measures have been especially radical (Ministry of Environmental Affairs, 2001: 48).

Rural homelessness has not been an issue on the public agenda in spite of the national programmes for the reduction of homelessness (1987–91, 2001–3). Homelessness is officially conceived as an urban issue in Finland. A starting point of the Programme for the Reduction of Homelessness (2001–3) was the concentration of homelessness in Finland in the urban centres, especially in the metropolitan area where about half of the homeless live (Asunnottomuuden vähentämisohjelma, 2001: 10). There is a similar emphasis in the Finnish National Action Plan against Poverty and Social Exclusion for 2003–5, which also reflects the view of the NGOs associated with the EAPN (European Anti-Poverty Network). There is not a word in these reports directly addressing rural homelessness. Many of the measures proposed in these reports, though, are also aimed at coping with problems of homelessness in the rural areas. The silence about homelessness and social welfare and health issues in general is also characteristic of the ongoing rural policy programmes (Ihmisen maaseutu, 2000).

Indifference to rural homelessness as a relevant housing or regional policy issue is connected with the increasing individualization of this condition. Occurrences of homelessness in the rural regions exemplify complex and unstable events. It is sometimes admitted that there is a noticeable antinomy between norms (interventions) and order (stability) in the government of the complex events of homelessness. However, conciliation between norms and order, interventions and stability, must remain a dream (Foucault, 1988: 162). Unsurprisingly there is a tendency to approach rural homelessness as a client-based problem of individual conduct.

Client-based perspective: homelessness and life-management

The Housing Market Survey provides indications of the number of homeless persons across the country. The survey does not pay attention to the life-situations of the homeless people; it does not reveal the duration of homelessness and it does not give reasons for these situations (Kärkkäinen 1999: 181). Homelessness cannot, however, be reduced to a lack of housing or to market disequilibrium. Homelessness is not just a market relation between commodities. It is basically a relation between persons and commodities but also between different people. Homelessness may sometimes have more to do with capabilities and functioning than with resources and commodities. There can be homeless persons in situations where there are plenty of dwellings available. Difficulties in the relations and dispositions of homeless persons with other persons and themselves can be crucial. This is a problem of subjectification, which addresses the interaction between oneself and others – ultimately how individuals act upon themselves (technologies of self). It is also a governmental issue, which addresses the contact between the technologies of 'conducting the conduct of others' and those of the self (Foucault, 1988: 19).

The emphasis on the life-management aspects of homelessness often makes individuals responsible for their homelessness. Such an outlook neglects to see homelessness as a complex assemblage of connections and associations. Empirical studies of governmentality, on the contrary, should not simplify but generate complexity (Rose, 1999: 277). The existence of homelessness in situations where there are dwellings available may signal many things. There are dwellings available but the potential clients are insolvent; the potential clients are otherwise unable to live in them; the dwellings are too big, unfit for habitation or they are situated in improper places; there are no supporting services to make life more manageable; there are no employment opportunities to avoid out-migration; the municipality cannot afford to keep up the dwellings; living in them is either too controlled or too dangerous; they are outside (im)proper social networks, and so on. Only some of these situations might be directly conceived as manifesting a 'governmental failure' in the sense that governmental efforts, 'technologies of citizenship' (Cruikshank, 1999: 438–42, 467–86), to 'help people to help themselves' have failed. These situations are already complex since they are penetrated by trajectories of rule and resistance. On the other hand, it is often claimed (Christensen *et al.,* 1998: 31) that living in the rural regions is characterized by a certain stoicism that entails 'just getting on with it'. Even if appropriate, this characterization need not to be taken as a sign of a specific cultural ethos or habitus. This interpretation can too easily contribute to idealizing rurality – for example, that there is no homelessness due to the life-management skills of the people – and can neglect to recognize that 'just getting on with it' is an imperative dictated by the social and collective compulsions of the situation, which condition the conduct of different people in different fashions.

Homelessness can be approached as an individual, collective and soci(et)al event. Not only individual, but collective and soci(et)al contexts can be the focus of an analytics of the government of homelessness. It is understandable that, as regional and housing policies retreat, the demand for welfare policies may increase. It is also understandable that, as universal welfare policies retreat, the role of client-based welfare policies, i.e. activation policies, can increase. This process is under way in Finland. Activation can naturally mean many things and take various forms depending on the political orientation: the 'orthodox consensus' vs reflexive activation (Van Berkel and Roche, 2002: 212). Activation is a contestable concept and practice whose meaning and content are under dispute. It can also mean the reduction of welfare services, with the provision of new, more tailored services. The current events of rural homelessness in Finland prove that the lack of supporting welfare services, due to the financial difficulties of municipalities, can be the crucial factor in explaining why the provision of housing alone does not suffice to eliminate homelessness.

A closer look at rural homelessness

Rural homelessness cannot be adequately recognized if we only look at the availability of dwellings or even at the incidence of supply and demand of dwellings. It is true that in the rural regions of Finland the utilization rate of dwellings is much lower than in the urban centres. Already in the late 1990s, in the rural regions, the utilization rate of state-subsidized rental dwellings was only 86.9 per cent, while in the Helsinki metropolitan region it was 98.3 per cent (Ministry of Environmental Affairs, 2001: 17). However, different situations of homelessness in the rural regions can be hidden behind these and similar figures. It is possible to make a double claim. In spite of the availability of dwellings, in the rural regions, there may be both people without proper housing and dwellings without proper people to inhabit them. A closer look at rural homelessness can disclose how this can be the case. A standardized view of Finnish rurality without homelessness has, naturally, to be challenged. This kind of standardized view of rurality – and homelessness – easily neglects to conceive that there can be multiple and complex associations between rurality and homelessness (Cloke *et al.*, 2000: 715–35; 2001: 438–53; Cloke, 1997: 252–71). Events of rural homelessness can be like intrinsic singularities existing in a fluid and dynamic space, in which homeless persons as 'others' are easily out of sight, hidden in multiple folds.

Even if cases of homelessness are like singularities in a fluid and dynamic space, one must apply formative concepts to perceive and analyse what is going on in these events. Homelessness could be interpreted as an instance of social exclusion. In terms of social exclusion, however, homelessness is too easily seen as a passive process, a kind of stepwise life-course. Homelessness is rather a relation of power, a social relation. Homelessness is constituted in a strategic field of molecular power relations. This need not mean that power produces homelessness. Homelessness need not be defined ostensively but performatively. Homelessness is performed through everyone's efforts to define it (Latour, 1986: 272–3). Homelessness, as a relation of power, is an effect or a consequence of numerous practices which constitute it as an assemblage. The naming of these practices is always a situated choice, which can be made from different perspectives.

I want to distinguish four dynamic aspects of homelessness: disablement, dispossession, displacement and disaffiliation. All of them can be interlinked in multiple ways and each of them can elicit different power effects. Disablement (disempowerment) refers to practices which inhibit or pre-empt the will to take care of oneself, aggravate the regulation of one's conduct, downplay reflection and predispose to risks. Dispossession has more to do with the political technologies of individuals than with the technologies of the self (Foucault, 1988: 18–19, 146). Dispossessive practices thwart the recognition of ourselves as part of a social entity, society, nation, state (Foucault, 1988: 146), or as part of a definite market society. A market society is not what holds or links us together, it is what is held together by financial and social connectivities (MacKenzie, 2004: 83–101) and transactions as possessive practices (Latour, 1986: 276). It is the 'cash nexus' which links us together in a market society. Dispossession refers to a break or a disconnection in the cash nexus. Dispossessive and disconnective practices are also immanent to the market. They cannot be reduced to externalities or market failures.

Displacement is a territorial practice of transformation. Displacement makes it impossible to find, know, dwell in, keep and hold on to one's place as usual. Displacing practices make something or someone take the place of something else, move somewhere else, change the direction, prevent access, even to transform into something else. A displaced person is out of place, in-between. A displaced situation is out of joint. Disaffiliation, finally, refers to 'a particular mode of dissociation of the social bond' (Castel, 2000: 520). In contrast to dispossession, disaffiliation does not specifically express the lack of something (money, housing, medical care, education …) but refers to practices which prevent social belonging, bonding, integration and interaction, or radically fold their configurations. Practices of disaffiliation destabilize sociabilities and social connectivities (mutual susceptibility, trust, imitation – MacKenzie, 2004) and generate experiences and feelings of detachment, isolation and indifference. It should be remembered that disaffiliation can also be intentional.

I consider disablement, dispossession, displacement and disaffiliation to be constitutive or generative practices of homelessness (D-matrix). They are not always easy to distinguish from governmental practices. For this reason, it might be possible to speak about disablement/empowerment, dispossession/possession, displacement/placement, and disaffiliation/integration as definite governmental dimensions. Different events of homelessness are hybrids whose configurations and trajectories are drawn by these practices. Even if this hybridity or complexity of assemblages must be recognized, it is possible to classify events of homelessness into these four types. Such classificatory thinking quickly meets its limits (Castel, 2000: 519). However, I would rather lean on ideal-types than end up drawing endless lists of all kinds. Besides, cartographic mappings are always ideal-typical descriptions, like Figure 10.2.

In Figure 10.2, rural homelessness is pictured as an assemblage that is constituted by the four practices of disablement, dispossession, displacement and disaffiliation. Unlike government (in the sense of conducting conduct) policy can never become immanent to the object of its measures but must act at a

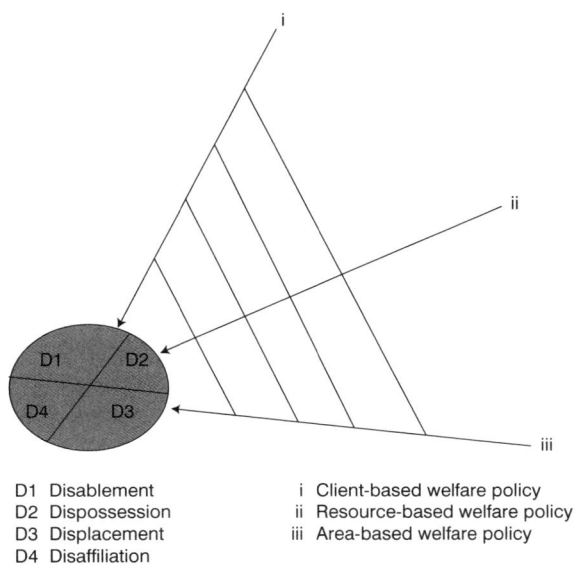

D1 Disablement
D2 Dispossession
D3 Displacement
D4 Disaffiliation

i   Client-based welfare policy
ii   Resource-based welfare policy
iii Area-based welfare policy

10.2 Governing homelessness

distance. Different sectoral policies cope with different constitutive aspects of homelessness: client-based welfare policies can deal with disablement, housing policies with dispossession, area-based regional policies with displacement and perhaps educational policies with disaffiliation. Even if crude, this mapping helps to conceive that the growing complexity of homelessness demands policy integration. Such integration is not an easy task to accomplish, since it generates further complexity.

Rather than examine the hybridization of the regime of practices as an effect of integrative policy efforts, I shall explore more closely the many aspects of rural homelessness in Finland in the context of the D-matrix. If rural homelessness is approached from the point of view of the constitutive practices of homelessness, the descriptions and characterizations of events and cases of rural homelessness should preferably be based on direct experiences and first-hand observations. What is needed is local or situated knowledge (Haraway, 1991) of governing and experiencing homelessness. This kind of knowledge can be provided by different participants involved as eye-, ear- or hand-witnesses in the government of homelessness: municipal authorities, voluntary workers, clients, researchers. Some of these persons use writing pads to record their observations and remarks, others do not. Both natural sources and constructed data can provide local knowledge on rural homelessness. An assistance application to the Finnish Red Cross is an example of a local, natural source, while interviews with municipal housing and social welfare authorities on rural homelessness are an example of locally constructed data. The Housing Market Survey and the qualitative comments on housing and homelessness of municipal authorities attached to this survey (Valtion asuntorahasto, 2003) are not as easy to position in this respect. All these sources and data are used in this article to empirically underpin the conclusions.

I have used the Housing Market Survey data as background information. The distinction between disablement, dispossession, displacement and disaffiliation is already inspired by my reading of the Finnish Red Cross assistance applications and the interviews with and comments of local authorities and voluntary workers on (rural) homelessness. The applications for voluntary help of the Finnish Red Cross (in 2003) have been made by persons in very severe living difficulties. Many of these persons in need have been diverted to the Finnish Red Cross or other voluntary organizations by social welfare offices, whose means and willingness to take care of them have drastically diminished. Besides the municipal survey on housing (Kysely asuntoasioista, 1998) and the attachments to the Housing Market Survey (Valtion asuntorahasto, 2003), in which the respondents were invited to write down the most crucial housing policy issues and problems in their municipality, a number of municipalities in the rural regions of central Finland were contacted – by Juha Peltosalmi in my research project (Displacement,

2003) – in order to achieve a more detailed picture of homelessness. Nine municipalities altogether were contacted: Keuruu, Korpilahti and Viitasaari in the sparsely populated rural areas; Laukaa, Kinnula, Saarijärvi and Uurainen in the rural areas proper; and Jyväskylän maalaiskunta and Muurame in the rural areas near the city of Jyväskylä. In each of these municipalities, local authorities and voluntary workers involved in the governing of housing deprivation were interviewed (in spring 2003).

In a closer reading of rural homelessness, I shall concentrate on each dynamic aspect of rural homelessness individually. This reading strategy is justified not only by a certain perspectivism but also by the information value of different data and sources. The natural sources (the Red Cross applications) can be used as a check on material for constructed data (the interviews), since they can open perspectives for those aspects (personal experiences) of rural homelessness which are often neglected by the more standardized views. My reading is an exercise in the analysis of the constitutive practices leading to homelessness in the rural regions. It is not a qualitative analysis of personal experiences and events of homelessness. The empirical material is used, in this article, in a diagnostic or symptomatic fashion.

Disablement

Respondents to the Housing Market Survey have, yearly, written down their comments on the most crucial housing policy problems in their municipalities. Their views have been annually collected as a qualitative supplement attached to the survey. This information (from 2003) can be supplemented with the municipal survey on housing in 1998 (Kysely asuntoasioista, 1998). Housing problems were, in this material, typically linked with the availability, size, location and quality of dwellings, dilemmas of housing policy, insolvency and rental prices, and with specific groups of people. It is conspicuous of this commentary that homelessness was recognized in the latter context. Respondents of the rural regions clearly connected homelessness with specific groups of people such as insolvent persons, those dependent on alcohol or drugs, mentally ill or disordered, disturbers and other 'problem-dwellers', helpless aged persons, young people leaving home. During the last decade, homelessness is claimed to have involved not only single middle-aged men with problems of alcohol abuse but, more often than before, persons with psychiatric problems, drug addicts and so-called 'double outcasts'. Lately, in these groups, there have been more young people who have been ready to move from place to place. Homelessness is seen also as a problem of young persons and couples who are leaving home and cannot find a suitable, affordable or available dwelling. Their situations remind us that in many municipalities – including in rural regions – there is a shortage of small apartments.

A similar picture of homelessness can be drawn from the interviews with local authorities and voluntary workers involved in the government of homelessness in the nine selected rural municipalities of central Finland. Homelessness was also connected, in these interviews, with definite groups of people, such as persons who are mentally ill, ex-convicts, long-term unemployed, young people leaving home, drug addicts, those dealing with problems of abuse and persons who are so-called 'double outcasts'. Homelessness was seen as an effect of other problems, rather than a problem in itself. It was argued that all the cases of homelessness were known to local authorities and voluntary workers, who were willing to apply targeted measures to these situations.

The interviewees emphasized that there is municipal rented housing and other dwellings available. Therefore, the housing needs of everyone could be met with the proper arrangements. It was, though, emphasized that there might be a lack of supported housing facilities for specific groups of people such as addicts. People at risk of homelessness not only needed housing, but support services that were not always organized or provided by the municipalities. All singular cases of homelessness in these municipalities (numbering in 2002 from 0 in Kinnula to 18 in Jyväskylän maalaiskunta) were said to be only temporary. If the risk of homelessness concerned families or people with children, the municipality was obliged to provide a dwelling without delay. Low incomes or a lack of money was not considered an ultimate cause of homelessness. It was pointed out that there were some persons who refused to be accommodated by the municipality, because they would then have been obliged to undergo some form of rehabilitation. Some interviewees did not hesitate to speak about intentional homelessness. The principal conclusion was that the main reasons for the events of homelessness have to be sought in the life-situations and life-management skills of the homeless persons. Rental arrears and evictions, although due to lack of money, were said to always go hand-in-hand with life-management deficiencies.

Homelessness, in the rural regions too, is certainly a life-management problem generated by numerous practices of disablement. Governmental experiences of local authorities (and voluntary workers) point to a number of these practices such as dependence, dissipation, derangement, defiance, disruption and derailment. All of them express difficulties in taking care of oneself and regulating one's conduct. In order to succeed, the government of homelessness therefore has to challenge these practices by reconducting the conduct of the persons involved. Such a challenge is acute and often voiced today. But it is not the only challenge to governing homelessness in Finland and is true even more so in the rural regions.

Dispossession

Although the previous observations have been made by eye-witnesses, or almost eye-witnesses, they should be read critically. Eye-witness observations can also be conditioned and framed by standardized viewpoints, governmental conventions or professional prejudices. A poverty of distinction (Thompson and Wildavsky, 1986: 163–99) can be a characteristic of professional thinking habits that proceed by way of classifications and dividing practices. It is seductive to recognize rules and regularities of conduct even where there are only random and singular events. It is often forgotten that homelessness can be a contingent effect. Sensitivity to details and differences is paramount for an understanding of how homelessness can be actualized in a world of uncertainty and risks.

Illustrative and instructive examples of the play of contingencies in the context of homelessness can be read in the applications for the voluntary help of the Finnish Red Cross, made by people in very severe living difficulties. Applications for unofficial assistance from the Finnish Red Cross (Finnish Red Cross, 2003) have come from all over Finland. The rural regions are well represented in this material which can be used as a natural source for the 'diagnosis' of rural homelessness. All the applicants for assistance are situated on the edge due to severe deprivation. The Finnish Red Cross is their last or next to last (the Church) place to turn to for help. In the rural regions, where 'everyone knows everyone else', it is sometimes much easier to turn to such voluntary associations for help than to go to the municipal social welfare office.

Among the applicants there are people coming from various disadvantaged life-situations who are driven by different motivations. A great number of their worries are connected with housing problems: the loss of home, over-indebtedness, personal security, house-selling chain, forced sale, fire, back rents, water and mould damage, eviction, etc. It is typical that people may have squeezed their everyday consumption to an extreme minimum, even far beyond the official poverty line, in order to keep their home by paying loans or rents. However, it is quite usual that people have lost their home due to their loans or unpaid rents. The applications to the Finnish Red Cross, coming from the rural regions, include many such cases where the forced sale of the home and the remaining debts are the reason for asking for assistance.

The radical decline of the property values of farms, estates and dwellings, especially in the remote rural regions, has greatly weakened the financial position of many municipalities, institutions and individuals. This has had a powerful impact not only directly on the situation of indebted home owners but also indirectly on people facing the risk of homelessness due to pressures to deregulate municipal housing policies and social welfare services. This situation has been further aggravated by the chop and change policy of the state (desultoriness). All the most severe problems of housing in the rural regions are in one way or another linked to indebtedness or unpaid rents.

By far the most common reason for applying for assistance from the Finnish Red Cross in 2003 – which is the last year of this domestic aid practice – has been rent arrears. This applies to more than half of the cases. The threat of eviction, even due to a few months' rental arrears, is a final alarm signal. People are then compelled to seek unofficial help. The applications make clear that unpaid rents can be triggered by various unexpected and often contingent factors which shake the vulnerable economy of the persons involved. Even small additional expenses of daily life, like car repair costs which cannot be avoided in remote areas, can ruin an already tight budget. These difficulties are most often a result of an acute crisis such as divorce, somatic or psychiatric illness, fire, unemployment, a death in the family.

Even though rental arrears and the consequent threat of eviction are the most common reasons for the Red Cross applications in the rural regions, the number of outright homeless persons among them, as defined earlier, is quite limited. They include ex-convicts, persons with psychiatric problems and problems of alcohol abuse, victims of domestic violence and persons living temporarily with acquaintances or moving on from place to place. Even in the case of eviction, the municipality has been, so far, practically obliged to arrange a new dwelling for these people, sometimes in a tripartite manner so that rental arrears are taken care of together with the Finnish Red Cross and the Church. While this arrangement is being reconsidered, it is misleading to claim that homelessness has more to do with personal life-management deficiencies than with low incomes and lack of money.

It is quite impossible to speak of homelessness as an either/or condition. All of the often contingent triggers of homelessness intersect so that causes cannot be easily distinguished from effects. The constitutive practices of homelessness perforate each other and are hybridized into a complex assemblage. Disabling practices supplement and reinforce multiple dispossessive practices: deprivation, default, depreciation, desultoriness and deregulation. These two again are intertwined with displacement and disaffiliation.

Displacement

From the point of view of the official housing policy, the principal dilemma of the rural regions is seen to be the lack of solvent demand for the available housing facilities. There is especially a lack of demand for particular kinds of housing, such as large facilities. On the other hand, it is pointed out that, even in the remote rural regions, there is a need for small apartments either for old people or for young people leaving home. This policy is naturally based on the demographic statistics which point out that in the (remote) rural regions, the average age of inhabitants demanding housing services is constantly increasing. Therefore, it is concluded that the existing stock of dwellings also has to be partly reconstructed to better meet this demand.

The contingent nature of homelessness is not only brought about by uncertainties in the life-situations of people but by the conditions of the dwelling. In the voluntary assistance applications to the Finnish Red Cross, there are a great number of cases each year in which the personal crisis situation is generated by a sudden recognition of damaged housing – not just fires, but failures in the damp proofing, waste drainage or water pumps, the discovery of mould, the breakdown of water pipes due to freezing, etc. These difficulties and unpleasant surprises are more common in the rural regions of Finland. Difficulties in housing can emerge there without explicit damage. An exceptionally cold winter can accelerate the costs of heating so that one cannot manage the bills without financial support.

A special group of people among the voluntary assistance applicants were those who lived in the remote rural regions in dwellings of a very low quality. In the 1980s, when municipalities were motivated to collect and provide information on the quality of living conditions in order to receive earmarked state grants for the fundamental improvement of housing stock, some studies based on available statistics were made which also examined regional differences in the quality of housing (Vesanen, 1988; Kärkkäinen *et al.*, 1989). These studies made clear (Vesanen, 1988: 44–5; Kärkkäinen et al., 1989: 75) that the share of persons living in inadequate dwellings was much higher in small municipalities in the rural regions than in urban centres, which had much better resources and housing programmes available. Even though, since the 1990s, no focused studies on the subject have been made, there is reason to believe that this situation has not changed. The available statistics confirm this trend.

The Housing Market Survey responses have pointed out that, even if dwellings are available, they may be in an unsuitable location, they may be badly equipped or they may be in very poor condition. Statistics of living conditions in Finland make clear that the relative share of persons living in very badly equipped dwellings in different regional contexts is very much higher in the rural regions of Finland than in the urban centres or semi-urban municipalities. This share has been highest in the sparsely populated rural areas where the percentage of persons living in badly equipped dwellings was about 18 per cent in 1990 and was still nearly 14 per cent in 2000. In the rural areas proper, these shares were about 17 per cent in 1990 and about 13 per cent in 2000. In contrast, in the urban centres, the number of people living in badly equipped dwellings was about 5 per cent in 1990 and under 4 per cent in 2000. In the semi-urban municipalities, these percentage shares were somewhat higher, slightly over 6 per cent in 1990 and about 5 per cent in 2000 (Karvonen and Rintala, 2004: 162; Rakennukset, 2003: 141–54).

Not only dilapidation (dereliction), but also environmental degradation can accompany desertification which, now, characterizes many (remote) rural regions. In these conditions, there is an even greater potential supply of badly equipped dwellings than those in use. There are naturally a number of different reasons why people have to, or do not want to, out-migrate from rural regions. The lack of support services for people whose capacity for independent living has greatly diminished, or is altogether nonexistent, can be one reason to move elsewhere. In small municipalities in the rural regions, it may be much easier to get municipal rented housing (in municipalities with under 6,000 inhabitants, about 80 per cent of the applicants for such housing are approved) than supportive services for the homeless (the addicted, mentally ill, etc.), which are far less often available than in cities or rural regions near cities (Pitkänen *et al.*, 2004: 4, 7–8, 10, 13–14). These issues are connected with the mobility of homeless persons and persons at risk of homelessness.

In small municipalities in the rural regions, decisions to move elsewhere are frequently forced rather than voluntary. They are also often cases of diversion. Municipalities, even adjacent ones, have very different political histories that condition their governmental conduct. Municipalities have various means of influencing the selection of their inhabitants. If a municipality is keen on gate-keeping, it can quite effectively influence the inflow but also the outflow of specific groups of citizens. In this way, it can influence the degree of homelessness too. There is hardly any systematic knowledge about these municipal gate-keeping mechanisms, partly because they are not officially recognized to exist. The diversion of homeless persons to other municipalities was, however, admitted to exist unofficially in the interviews, though their mobility was not emphasized. In smaller municipalities in the rural regions, targeted measures of diversion or dispersion are applied in some situations (e.g. housing of ex-criminals). Much more extensive effects of diversion can be achieved, however, by indirect means. Housing and social welfare authorities in different municipalities can apply more or less stringent criteria for reorganizing the life-situations of people with rent arrears and other disturbances in housing which possibly affect mobility.

Displacement can be claimed to generate – often quite indirectly – homelessness in a number of different ways: desertification, diversion, dispersion, dilapidation, degradation. Displacement consists of practices which disclose that the linkages between homelessness and rurality can be rhizomatic and complex. On the one hand, homelessness could be understood in such an encompassing sense (Edgar *et al.*, 2003: 7) that, for example, inadequate housing is definitely understood as a form of homelessness. On the other hand, homelessness – as a displacement effect – need not be seen to be located at the place of its generation.

Both of these points, naturally, emphasize that rural homelessness might be recognized in much more dynamic terms than is ordinarily or officially done.

Disaffiliation

Homelessness is a process which can be triggered by multiple factors. Rent arrears are often the most immediate risk leading to homelessness, but there may be more fundamental reasons behind them. In the Finnish Red Cross applications, including ones from the rural regions, the following factors behind back rents are emphasized: divorce, illness (including dependence on alcohol or drugs), leaving home, forced change of residence. A person's economy can be seriously destabilized or even totally damaged by any of these factors. A divorce or a chronic disease can bring about so many unexpected and sudden expenses without the possibility of sufficient compensation, that the person can, in a very short time, lose their grip on the management of finances and life. A similar course of events with the risk of homelessness can take place when leaving home, or being forced to change residence. Young people leaving home – who are not necessarily very competent in their household management – can easily fall into debt and thereby face the possibility of losing their new residence if they have to get through it by themselves. Recent employment can force a person to change residence and may involve extra expenses which threaten the personal economy. Of course, this state of affairs is rather temporary, while unemployment can be permanent. A forced change of residence can be the result of the desire to escape violence, most often a violent husband or male companion. A dwelling that is detrimental to health can also force one to move. In these cases, there may be no alternative to a change of residence.

The impact of a divorce, chronic disease and forced change of residence on the risk of homelessness is not only directly due to disadvantage and deprivation but to disaffiliation, which fuels dispossession. All of these and similar misfortunes can accompany disaffiliation, which can lead to 'a series of breakdowns in belonging and failures to establish bonds, which finally throws the person concerned into a floating state, a sort of social no-man's-land' (Castel, 2000: 529). If disaffiliation is coupled with dispossession, or the rupture of social bonds – and belonging is joined with impoverishment – the end of this process can be destitution (Castel, 2000: 520). The classical characterization of homelessness was of a destitute, a vagrant, who represents 'the extreme rupture of all forms of social belonging; the figure of the stranger, excluded everywhere and condemned to roam in a sort of social no-man's-land' (Castel, 2000: 523).

Vagrancy is no longer an officially recognized condition in Finland. However, it wasn't until 1987 that the Vagrancy Act – according to which living as a vagrant had been punishable – was abolished (Kärkkäinen, 1998: 21). There are still many persons drifting in a kind of floating state from place to place, who may be also homeless passers-by in the rural regions. In their situations disaffiliation meets with displacement. These persons include young alcoholics, drug addicts, ex-convicts, and depending on the perspective, also gypsies and immigrants. They are not always recognized or counted as homeless because of the unforeseeable nature of their movements.

Can homelessness be intentional? Even in cases when a person refuses to be accommodated by the municipality, homelessness is a forced choice; perhaps, a desperate attempt to retain one's way of life. Such a condition cannot be called freedom, even if it challenges normalcy and demonstrates dissidence or deviance. Such events remind us that disaffiliation can be deliberate. Living in the rural regions in very badly equipped dwellings can be a deliberate choice and an expression of disaffiliation. Disaffiliation alone does not generate homelessness but only in conjunction with disablement, dispossession and displacement. In order to incur homelessness, drifting, divorce, deviance and dissidence have to be recoupled with these practices. Destitution is already such a conjunction, and a condition which truly characterizes homelessness.

Conclusion

There is no universally valid and inclusive definition of either homelessness or rurality. If homelessness is seen as performed by everyone's efforts to define it, it is easy to understand the contestable character of the concept. This applies even more so to rural homelessness. Different perspectives and definitions of homelessness easily emphasize certain aspects of homelessness at the expense of others. The dominant political rationality of the governing of homelessness in Finland too often tends to translate homelessness into an incapacity to function as a dweller. This is a governmental tendency which was recognized to rule professional discourse already in the early 1990s (Jokinen and Juhila, 1991). The reason for such an emphasis may be the correct conclusion that governing homelessness as houselessness is not sufficiently efficient without supporting welfare services. However, in this way, one aspect of homelessness, disablement, also can be exaggerated as a cause of homelessness. This would be an expression of a governmental bias due to a too one-dimensional conception of homelessness. By exaggerating the role of disablement, the significance of dispossession, displacement and disaffiliation can be belittled. The successful governing of homelessness demands the recognition of the complex character of the phenomenon.

The new operational definition of homelessness suggested by the European Federation of National Organizations Working with the Homeless (FEANTSA) is an important move, though it is articulated from the perspective of housing and houselessness. In this definition, homelessness includes the following five categories: rooflessness, houselessness, insecure and inadequate housing (Edgar *et al.*, 2003: 7). This definition does take into account different aspects of displacement, i.e. the risk of homelessness. By following this definition of homelessness by FEANTSA, a more accurate picture of rural homelessness in Finland might be obtained, since the rural regions of Finland are particularly characterized by inadequate housing. This is a challenge to both the research of and collection of data on homelessness. A first step towards this direction is the appraisal made on the applicability of the new FEANTSA categories of homelessness in Finland in the light of the existing knowledge base (Kärkkäinen, 2004).

If homelessness is seen as a social relation of power, then the new FEANTSA definition of homelessness is not so satisfactory. A contrast with Peter Brandt's portrayal of homelessness helps to clarify this point. He depicts homelessness in the following manner (1992):

> A person is homeless when he or she does not have a place to live that can be considered to be stable, permanent, and of a reasonable housing standard. At the same time, this person is not able to make use of society's relations and institutions (understood in the broadest sense, such as family networks and private and public institutions of all kinds) due to either apparent or hidden causes relating to the individual or to the way in which society functions.

Brandt's depiction of homelessness captures quite well all four aspects of homelessness outlined in this chapter. An important paragraph is Brandt's argument that a person is homeless when she or he is not able to make use of society's relations and institutions due to the way in which society functions. In the rural regions of Finland, where the support services for people at risk of homelessness have been reduced, this disadvantage is of great significance. This argument, however, points to an even more crucial association: the way we understand and approach homelessness is dependent on how we understand society. Since not only homelessness but society at large is performed by everyone's efforts to define it; since society is made and shaped before our eyes by our collective action, society no more than the individual can explain homelessness (Latour, 1986: 272–3). For this reason, I have approached homelessness from the point of view of associations (Latour, 1986: 277).

Table 10.2 Share of persons living outdoors, in temporary shelters or in night shelters etc., as permillage of municipal population in different regional categories (yearly average %)

	Urban centres	Semi-urban municipalities	Rural areas near cities	Rural areas proper	Sparsely populated rural areas	All
1992	0.42	0.23	0.11	0.07	0.18	0.15
1994	0.23	0.22	0.10	0.05	0.11	0.10
1995	0.23	0.22	0.08	0.06	0.11	0.10
1996	0.25	0.16	0.10	0.04	0.09	0.09
1997	0.22	0.20	0.08	0.04	0.06	0.08
1998	0.27	0.15	0.08	0.04	0.06	0.08
1999	0.19	0.15	0.08	0.04	0.07	0.07
2000	0.23	0.15	0.10	0.04	0.03	0.07
2001	0.27	0.23	0.07	0.05	0.03	0.08
2002	0.27	0.19	0.05	0.03	0.03	0.06
2003	0.27	0.13	0.04	0.02	0.03	0.06
N	39	18	74–82	157–174	112–123	402–436

Table 10.3 Share of persons living in institutions or institutional homes either temporarily or permanently due to lack of housing, or persons soon to be released from prison who have no housing as permillage of municipal population in different regional categories (yearly average %)

	Urban centres	Semi-urban municipalities	Rural areas near cities	Rural areas proper	Sparsely populated rural areas	All
1992	0.52	0.25	0.14	0.14	0.25	0.21
1994	0.47	0.22	0.08	0.10	0.12	0.14
1995	0.48	0.16	0.12	0.05	0.15	0.14
1996	0.50	0.24	0.08	0.07	0.12	0.13
1997	0.52	0.25	0.08	0.07	0.09	0.13
1998	0.46	0.22	0.08	0.07	0.09	0.12
1999	0.46	0.18	0.08	0.08	0.05	0.11
2000	0.38	0.21	0.07	0.07	0.03	0.09
2001	0.35	0.17	0.09	0.06	0.02	0.09
2002	0.37	0.22	0.10	0.04	0.03	0.09
2003	0.34	0.26	0.09	0.06	0.04	0.09
N	39	18	74–82	157–174	112–123	402–436

Table 10.4 Share of persons living temporarily with relatives and acquaintances due to lack of housing as permillage of municipal population in different regional categories (yearly average %)

	Urban centres	Semi-urban municipalities	Rural areas near cities	Rural areas proper	Sparsely populated rural areas	All
1992	0.90	0.64	0.41	0.30	0.43	0.43
1994	0.92	0.69	0.42	0.30	0.52	0.46
1995	1.01	0.46	0.41	0.28	0.30	0.38
1996	0.89	0.71	0.34	0.26	0.36	0.38
1997	0.89	0.56	0.40	0.27	0.22	0.35
1998	0.87	0.69	0.52	0.29	0.18	0.37
1999	0.85	0.75	0.43	0.25	0.28	0.37
2000	0.76	0.73	0.47	0.21	0.25	0.32
2001	0.72	0.63	0.41	0.21	0.22	0.32
2002	0.67	0.59	0.33	0.19	0.13	0.26
2003	0.59	0.55	0.29	0.15	0.15	0.23
N	39	18	74–82	157–174	112–123	402–436

Acknowledgement

I want to especially thank the researcher Sirkka-Liisa Kärkkäinen (The National Research and Development Centre for Welfare and Health) for her many valuable comments on this chapter.

Note

1 There is now a more up-to-date version of this classification in use:

Persons staying outdoors, on staircases, in night shelters, etc.;
Persons living in other shelters or hostels or boarding houses for homeless people;
Persons living in care homes or other housing units of social welfare authorities, rehabilitation homes or hospitals due to lack of housing;
Prisoners soon to be released who have no housing;
Persons living temporarily with relatives and acquaintances due to lack of housing;
Families and couples who have split up or are living in temporary housing due to lack of housing.

(Valtion asuntorahasto, ohjeet; Kärkkäinen, 2004)

Chapter 11
Homelessness in rural Ireland

Eoin O'Sullivan

Introduction

In attempting to write about homelessness in rural Ireland, a number of difficulties arise. Definitions of homelessness, and consequently the quantification of 'homelessness', are problematic, contested and emotionally charged (Jacobs *et al.*, 1999; Edgar *et al.*, 2003; O'Sullivan, 2003), and a similar complexity exists with the use of, and understanding of, the term 'rural' (Tovey, 2002; McDonagh, 1998). In Ireland, it can be argued, the term 'rural' is vested with a range of symbolic meanings, which are routinely invoked to articulate particular belief systems and the importance and, often, superiority of rural life over urban life. Indeed, rural Ireland was symbolically constructed as an Arcadian utopia by both nationalist and Catholic ideologues from the late nineteenth century onwards (Devereux, 1991; O'Dowd, 1987). This particular articulation of rural Ireland culminated with the Taoiseach (Prime Minister) Eamon de Valera's vision of the 'good society' in his oft-quoted St Patrick's day speech in 1943, a key element of which entailed a countryside 'bright with cosy homesteads' (Cusack, 2001: see also Doherty and Keogh, 2003), a vision that seems inimical to homelessness.

In contrast, the city was seen as an 'alien institution' (Daly, 1985: 192). Rural Ireland, or more simply the countryside, was idealized as a site where the family farm could harmoniously integrate its various members in a seamless web of family and community obligations and reciprocations (McCullagh, 1991). Not surprisingly, given the fact that the realization of this idealized vision was premised upon a series of exclusionary practices, including emigration and institutionalization, alternative visions of the 'good society' were offered, but until the late 1950s, an idealized vision of rural Ireland dominated political discourse. Despite a fundamental reorientation of Ireland's economy and society since the 1960s, a lingering sentimentality regarding the positive attributes of the 'rural' over the 'urban' remains significant and finds concrete expression in recent debates on once-off housing (i.e.not part of an integrated housing scheme) in rural areas.

The well-known ethnographic work in rural Clare of the 1930s by the Harvard anthropologists, Conrad Arensberg and Solan T. Kimball gave qualified academic support to the policies that de Valera was espousing with their description 'of an integrated set of relationships within families, and between families, kin groups and neighbours in rural Ireland' (McCullagh, 1991: 201). Although neither the theoretical nor the empirical substance of this thesis was left unscathed by the end of the 1970s (Gibbon, 1973; for an overview of these debates, see Tovey, 1992 and Byrne *et al.*, 2001), the belief in the positive attributes of the 'rural' over the 'urban' remained important and has real consequences, although Tovey cautions against talking about rural Ireland 'as if it is some sort of coherent entity' (2002: 171; see also Tovey, 1999; Crowley, 2003). For example, McCullagh (1999) in his analysis of rural crime highlights the fact that three unrelated murders in January 1996 provoked a disproportionate response by the Irish state, which included armed Gardai (police) operating roadblocks and helicopter patrols. While rates of crime had increased in Ireland since the late 1960s, much of this was recorded in urban centres and the popular view was that crime, particularly violent crime, was an urban phenomenon. These three murders challenged the idealistic view of rural Ireland and '[i]f violent crime could come to such areas, then crime really was a serious problem and one that needed an urgent response' (McCullagh, 1999: 35). These deaths along with two other unrelated murders contributed to the introduction of 'zero-tolerance policing' in Ireland and a substantial increase in the Irish prison population (O'Donnell and O'Sullivan, 2001, 2003).

Thus, it may be argued that, despite the revisions and rejections of the Arensberg and Kimball thesis, alongside the detailed historical studies of the lived experience of inhabitants of rural Ireland, a certain ideological attachment to a belief in the superior attributes of the rural over the urban remains. Indeed, in one of the first academic studies of homelessness in Ireland, homelessness was described as 'an Irish urban disorder' (Kearns, 1984), suggesting that homelessness was a consequence of the structure of urban life and was one of the disorders resulting from the recent urbanization of Irish society. The first social science studies of homelessness emerged from the early 1970s and were primarily conducted in Dublin and, in the main, sponsored by the newly formed Simon Community and other voluntary agencies (O'Cinneide and Mooney, 1972; Hart, 1978; Kennedy, 1985). Additional urban centres were the subject of research on homelessness from the 1980s onwards (Dillon *et al.*, 1990; O'Sullivan, 1993; Farrell, 1988; McCarthy, 1988; Murphy-Lawless and Dillon, 1992), and the five major urban centres (Cork, Dublin, Galway, Limerick and Waterford) have been the sites for the majority of research into homelessness in Ireland to date.

As noted above, what constitutes a state of homelessness and the extent of homelessness in Ireland is intensely contested. Since 1991, an initially bi-annual, and now tri-annual national assessment of the extent of homelessness was conducted by local authorities under the provisions of the Housing Act, 1988.[1] The Act also provides a definition of homelessness under section 2.[2] However, many providers of services to the homeless have contested these data, arguing that the local authorities undercount the extent of homelessness in their functional area.

Definitions of the 'rural are generally either descriptive or addressed in socio-cultural terms' (Halfacree, 1993). Although Halfacree argues for an alternative immaterial definition of the rural, for the purposes of this chapter, the two more common definitions of the rural will be used. In the first section of the chapter, an overview of these data will be provided. This will permit an assessment of the extent of homelessness in rural Ireland from this official data. The second section will then take a broader socio-historical-cultural perspective to explore the extent to which the structure of rural Ireland can contribute to homelessness rather than simply counting the numbers of homeless persons in rural Ireland. This section suggests that not only are there the usual risk factors for homelessness – poverty, deinstitutionalization, shortages of affordable accommodation, absence of, or poorly developed social services, etc.[3] – but, in addition, the historically constituted structure of rural Ireland produces its own unique risk factors.

Homelessness in rural Ireland

There are considerable variations in how 'rural' is defined by various actors. The Central Statistics Office provide data on 'aggregate rural areas', by which they mean the 'population residing in all areas outside clusters of 1,500 or more inhabitants' (2003: 164). On the other hand, a recent *White Paper on Rural Development* (1999) has a broader understanding of rural which effectively encompassed all areas outside of the five major urban areas. In broad historical terms, since the mid-1840s (as a consequence of the great Irish famine, 1845–50), the rural population had been in continuous decline, due primarily to emigration.[4] As the Commission on Emigration and Other Population Problems, which reported in 1954, noted, 'the striking feature revealed by the town–rural distribution statistics over the last 100 years is that the decline in total population was brought about entirely by a decline in rural population' (1954: 9). This trend continued during the 1950s and 1960s but was unevenly reversed during the 1970s (Commins, 1986).

Examining the more recent trends based on the first definition, the population of rural Ireland rose in real terms by 44,452 between 1986 and 2002, but as shown in Table 11.1, its share of the national population declined from 43 to 40 per cent over the same period. If we take rural Ireland to encompass all areas outside of the five major urban areas, the population increased slightly over that period. An even more restrictive definition might be outside of the greater Dublin region, but this shows virtually no change over the period in question.

As noted above, since 1991, local authorities, on behalf of the Department of Environment, Heritage and Local Government, have periodically conducted a national assessment of the extent of homelessness. In addition, the local authorities simultaneously assess housing need in their functional areas. Local authorities have

Table 11.1 'Rural' population of Ireland, 1986–2002 (%)

	1986	1991	1996	2002
Aggregate rural area	43.5	43.0	41.9	40.4
Outside the five urban areas	64.1	64.0	63.8	64.7
Outside Greater Dublin	71.9	71.7	71.5	72.0

Source: Central Statistics Office, *Census of Population*, various years.

Table 11.2 Number of homeless persons observed wandering on the public highways in a single night in November 1925

	Outside Metropolitan area			Metropolitan area		
	Men	Women	Children	Men	Women	Children
Travelling in search of work	248	33	44	116	18	0
Willing to undertake casual labour but unfit or unwilling to work continuously	238	48	58	120	18	0
Habitual tramps	652	416	614	34	7	0
Old and infirm persons	150	63	14	13	5	0
Bona-fide peddlers, hawkers etc.	141	77	122	7	1	0
Total	1,429	637	852	290	49	0

Source: Commission on the Relief of the Sick and Destitute Poor, Including the Insane Poor (1928).

assessed housing need since the 1960s, but only in the current format since 1989. Before the collection of these data, the only previous national survey of the extent of homelessness was carried out in 1925. The report of the Commission on the Relief of the Sick and Destitute Poor, Including the Insane Poor, requested the Garda Siochana (police force) to carry out 'a census of homeless persons observed wandering on the public highways in a single night in November, 1925' (1928: 27). They arrived at a figure of 3,257 homeless persons, of whom 90 per cent were outside the Metropolitan (i.e. Dublin) area (see Table 11.2).[5]

Tables 11.3 and 11.4 provide an overview of the extent of homelessness – a stock figure, rather than a flow figure – periodically recorded by local authorities on 31 March in various years between 1991 and 2002, disaggregated by local authority administrative areas.[6] It is not possible to match these areas with the aggregate rural areas defined by the CSO, but it is possible to provide a breakdown of the extent of homelessness outside of the five major urban areas. Recorded homelessness in the five major urban areas increased by 132 per cent between 1991 and 2002, with the capital city, Dublin, experiencing an increase of 162 per cent. In 1991, 76 per cent of recorded homelessness was reported in the five major urban areas; by 2002, this had increased to 87 per cent. Thus, based on

Table 11.3 Distribution of homelessness in Ireland, 1991–2002

	1991	1993	1996	1999	2002	% change, 1991–2002	% change, 1999–2002
County councils	400	385	260	439	415	3.8	−5.5
Town councils	171	129	177	130	234	36.8	80.0
Borough councils	89	33	70	76	72	−19.1	−5.3
City councils	2,091	2,120	1,994	4,589	4,860	132.4	5.9
Dublin	1,536	1,648	1,533	3,918	4,060	164.3	3.6
Totals	2,751	2,667	2,501	5,234	5,581	102.9	6.6

Source: Department of the Environment, Heritage and Local Government, *Annual Housing Statistics Bulletin*, various years.

Table 11.4 Distribution of homelessness in Ireland, 1991–2002 (%)

	1991	1993	1996	1999	2002
County councils	14.5	14.4	10.4	8.4	7.4
Town councils	6.2	4.8	7.1	2.5	4.2
Borough councils	3.2	1.2	2.8	1.5	1.3
City councils	76.0	79.5	79.7	87.7	87.1
Dublin	55.8	61.8	61.3	74.9	72.7
Total	100.0	100.0	100.0	100.0	100.0

Source: Department of the Environment, Heritage and Local Government, *Annual Housing Statistics Bulletin*, various years.

the data collected by the various local authorities, while the actual number of persons recorded as homeless outside the five major urban areas increased slightly from 660 to 721, as a proportion of the total number of homeless persons recorded, homelessness decreased in rural Ireland.

However, these data are highly problematic. First, a change in methodology between the 1996 assessment and the 1999 assessment renders it problematic to trace meaningful long-term patterns. The 1999 and 2002 assessment provided data on the total number of homeless persons (including child dependants), the number of homeless adults and the number of homeless households. As shown in Table 11.5, depending on the measure used, the extent of recorded homelessness can range from 3,773 to 5,581. The key difficulty in assessing long-term trends is what the data for the assessments in 1991, 1993 and 1996 actually measure. Do they measure homeless households, adult homelessness only or homeless adults and child dependants? This lack of clarity renders any comparison between 1996 and subsequent years very problematic.

Second, one of the leading social research agencies in Ireland, the Economic and Social Research Institute (ESRI), in conjunction with the Homeless Agency

Table 11.5 Assessments of homelessness, 1999 and 2002

	1999			2002		
	Homeless persons	*Homeless adults*	*Homeless households*	*Homeless persons*	*Homeless adults*	*Homeless households*
County councils	439	357	340	415	334	318
Town councils	130	95	85	234	168	156
Borough councils	76	64	63	72	67	65
City councils	4,589	3,476	3,255	4,860	3,607	3,234
Dublin	3,918	2,890	2,669	4,060	2,920	2,560
Total	5,234	3,992	3,743	5,581	4,176	3,773

Source: Department of the Environment, Heritage and Local Government, *Annual Housing Statistics Bulletin*, various years.

– a governmental body responsible for the planning, co-ordination and delivery of services to people who are homeless in the Dublin area – now conduct the assessment of homelessness on behalf of the local authorities in the greater Dublin area (Williams and Gorby, 2002; Williams and O'Connor, 1999). As a consequence of the robust methodology utilized, a more accurate quantification of homelessness is available for the Dublin region than for elsewhere, thus distorting the overall portrait.[7]

Third, many rural authorities have either never recorded a homeless person in the course of the five assessments to date or have only ever recorded single digit figures, while others have returned inconsistent results (O'Sullivan, 2004b, 2005). For example, the predominantly rural Offaly County Council recorded no homeless persons in 1991, then recorded 70 persons in 1993, and in the subsequent three assessments recorded no homeless persons; in Laois County Council, no homeless persons were recorded in the 1996 assessment, 36 persons in the 1999 assessment and 3 persons in 2002, while Longford County Council recorded 103 homeless persons in 1999, but none in 2002. More generally, the data collected provides no consistent information on the age, gender or duration of those recorded as homeless. This of course is not unique to Ireland, with Cloke *et al.* (2001) highlighting the variations in practice by rural local authorities in recording homelessness.

As noted above, in addition to the assessment of homelessness, local authorities simultaneously carry out an assessment of housing need.[8] This exercise is much broader in scope than the assessment of homelessness, but suffers from many of the same flaws. Considerable caution is therefore required before drawing too many conclusions from these data (see O'Sullivan, 2004a, for a critique of the recent data on housing need and Fahey and Watson, 1995, on the initial assessments). Nonetheless, it remains our only detailed source of information on those deemed by the local authorities to be inadequately or precariously housed in Ireland and, therefore, potentially at risk of homelessness.

One of the categories of housing need is 'homelessness', but the data on homelessness in the assessment of housing need includes only the homeless who are registered with local authorities as homeless, while the assessment of homelessness includes those on the register and others identified as homeless, but who for various reasons are not on the housing waiting list. In 2002, there were 2,468 homeless households – rather than individuals – enumerated in the assessment of housing need compared to 3,773 in the assessment of homelessness, a gap of 1,305 households. Ninety-seven per cent of the gap was found in the five major urban areas. Thus, in terms of rural homelessness, no significant difference was found between homeless households recorded in either the assessment of housing need or the assessment of homelessness. Rather curiously, some county councils, for example, Wicklow, Kilkenny and Cavan, recorded slightly more homeless households in their assessment of housing need than their assessment of homelessness. On the basis that the assessment of homelessness includes those homeless households on both the housing waiting list and those that are not, the figure for the assessment of homelessness should always be greater than the number of homeless households on the assessment of housing need. This is but a further illustration of the inadequacy of these data for either theoretical and policy related work.

Examining the total number of households recorded in the assessment of housing need, unlike the assessment of homelessness, those deemed to have a housing need (the alleviation of this housing need can be delivered through the various local authority housing programmes or by housing associations) on the basis that their existing accommodation is inadequate, overcrowded, excessively expensive relative to income etc., are more evenly distributed between rural and urban areas as shown in Tables 11.6 and 11.7. In 2002, 59 per cent of such households were recorded outside the five major urban areas and 70 per cent outside of Dublin. On average, over the five assessments since 1991, 58 per cent of those assessed as having a housing need under the terms of the Housing Act, 1988, were outside of the five major urban areas and 72 per cent were outside of Dublin. These aggregate figures do however conceal substantial decreases in some County Councils between 1999 and 2002, for example, Kerry (−32 per cent), Limerick (−22 per cent), Monaghan (−44 per cent) and Wicklow (−26 per cent). In total, 22 of the 90 local authorities recorded decreases in the number of households requiring housing, and analogous to the assessment of homelessness, considerable fluctuations – not convincingly explained by demographic trends, social housing output, stock of social housing etc. – are evident from assessment to assessment.

Thus, the data from the assessments of housing need ought to be treated with a high degree of scepticism. Despite these caveats, the very rapid escalation

Table 11.6 Distribution of housing need in Ireland, 1991–2002

	1991	1993	1996	1999	2002	% change, 1991–2002	% change, 1999–2002
County councils	9,309	11,700	11,308	15,603	16,978	82.4	8.8
Town councils	4,270	5,097	5,893	6,987	9,905	132.0	41.8
Borough councils	976	995	1,045	1,539	1,616	65.6	5.0
City councils	8,687	10,832	9,181	15,047	19,914	129.2	32.3
Dublin	6,346	7,890	6,543	11,510	14,697		
Total	23,242	28,624	27,427	39,176	48,413		

Source: Department of the Environment, Heritage and Local Government, *Annual Housing Statistics Bulletin*, various years.

Table 11.7 Distribution of housing need in Ireland, 1991–2002 (%)

	1991	1993	1996	1999	2002
County councils	40.1	40.9	41.2	39.8	35.1
Town councils	18.4	17.8	21.5	17.8	20.5
Borough councils	4.2	3.5	3.8	3.9	3.3
City councils	37.4	37.8	33.5	38.4	41.1
Dublin	27.3	27.6	23.9	29.4	30.4
Total	100.0	100.0	100.0	100.0	100.0

Source: Department of the Environment, Heritage and Local Government, *Annual Housing Statistics Bulletin*, various years.

of house prices in Ireland since 1995 and consequent 'affordability crisis' (Memery, 2001; Drudy and Punch, 2002),[9] has undoubtedly contributed to the growing number of households recorded as requiring direct housing either directly or indirectly from local authorities. However, as Fahey *et al.* (2004: 46) argue, the issue of 'affordability' is most acute amongst private rented tenants in the Dublin region where rents are twice as high as rents in rural areas.

This escalating cost of purchasing housing for first-time buyers resulted in an increased demand for both publicly and privately rented housing. Both the state and market responded to this demand sluggishly but, by 2002, the private rented housing sector had reversed its historic decline and now accounted for 11 per cent of all tenures in Ireland compared to 7 per cent in 1991. However, the bulk of the increase in private rented accommodation was located in urban, rather than rural areas, thus limiting the housing options of those living in rural areas. While new house prices have risen to a similar degree in both urban and rural areas (as shown in Table 11.8) in rural Ireland, Finnerty *et al.* argue 'as property

Table 11.8 Index of new house prices in Ireland, 1995–2003 (1995=100)

	1995	1997	1999	2001	2003
Dublin	100.0	137.2	217.6	273.3	327.9
Five major urban areas	100.0	142.4	202.8	250.0	312.3
Rest of country	100.0	147.5	213.4	260.0	316.5

Source: Department of the Environment, Heritage and Local Government, *Annual Housing Statistics Bulletin*, various years.

prices rise there are no viable alternatives for newly forming households unable to buy their own home' (2003: 133). However, one could also argue that, in rural areas, options such as the provision of sites for housing to newly married couples from existing family land holdings and the use of mobile homes while the house is undergoing construction on the site, which do not exist in urban areas, may balance out the relative range of options in rural and urban areas.

Local authority (or publicly rented) housing responded more slowly and the ongoing policy of selling properties to sitting tenants ensured that the total stock was never going to grow substantially despite increased output. Between 1995 and 2003, 35,903 units of local authority housing were constructed and 15,652 units were sold to sitting tenants, with a further 8,929 units of accommodation constructed by the non-profit social housing sector. Census 2002 enumerated 88,206 (7 per cent of total stock) housing units rented from local authorities, compared to 97,742 in 1991 (10 per cent of stock). However, local authorities claim to be renting 102,665 units of housing in 2002, a gap of 14,459. This gap is reasonably evenly spread between urban and rural areas and suggests a substantial undercount of local authority housing by the census enumerators in 2002. Based on the census data, local authority housing accounts for only 4 per cent of stock in aggregate rural areas in comparison to 9 per cent in aggregate urban areas (see Fahey, 1999, and Nolan *et al.*, 1998, for further discussion on local authority housing in rural Ireland). Thus, in the aggregate, the options for those households priced out of the new or second-hand housing market are considerably more restricted in rural rather than urban areas.

The tenure structure of Irish housing has deep rural roots and through a variety of state interventions, including extensive land redistribution,[10] state provision of housing in rural areas,[11] pioneering tenant purchase schemes,[12] etc. has resulted in comparatively very high rates of homeownership (Aalen, 1986, 1992, 1993; Daly, 1997; Dooley, 2004; Fahey, 2002; Fraser, 1996; Hooker, 1938; Walsh, 1999). By the mid-1990s, Ireland, along with Greece and Spain, topped the European league table of homeownership, with rates in excess of 75 per cent (Fahey *et al.*, 2004: 10). The high rates of homeownership in Ireland – between 70 and 80 per cent over the last three decades – is even more the case in rural Ireland as shown in Table 11.9. Reflecting the deeper roots of home-

Table 11.9 Rates of homeownership in Ireland, 1946–2002 (%)

	1946	1961	1971	1981	1991	2002
Aggregate town areas	23.2	38.0	55.6	68.3	74.6	71.5
Aggregate rural areas	69.3	77.4	85.6	85.7	87.9	86.7
Whole country	52.6	59.8	70.8	76.1	80.2	77.4

Source: Central Statistics Office, *Censuses of Population*, 1946–2002.

ownership in rural Ireland, 57 per cent of homeowners in rural Ireland owned their homes outright, having no loan or mortgage on the property compared to 38 per cent of homeowners in urban areas.

In summary, the limited available quantitative data suggests that homelessness in Ireland is predominately recorded in urban areas and more particularly in Dublin. The broader administrative category of 'housing need' is more evenly distributed between urban and rural areas, but in the case of both sets of data, inconsistencies in methodology and difficult to explain variations from year to year ensure that reliable indicators of homelessness and housing need are difficult to extract from the data.

Despite these substantial caveats, homelessness does not appear to be a serious problem (at least in quantitative terms) in rural Ireland, although some have suggested that considerable undercounting occurs in rural areas. For example, one such study suggested that the real extent of homelessness in three predominantly rural counties in the north-west of Ireland was some ten times the figure recorded in the assessment of homelessness (Irwin, 1998), although little substantive evidence was offered to support this proposition. In a review of the Homeless Action Plans,[13] Hickey *et al.* argued that, outside of the major urban areas, there was 'little sense from the non-metropolitan plans on the process for diminishing the incidence of homelessness in source areas outside of major urban areas' and that '(w)ithout appropriate strategies non-metropolitan local authorities will continue to "export" their homeless constituents to large cities' (2002: 91). Thus, a counterview to the thesis that homelessness is a relatively minor problem in rural Ireland is that homelessness is substantially undercounted in rural areas, perhaps more so than in urban areas, and where homelessness does occur in rural Ireland, an absence of services results in homeless persons migrating to urban areas to seek such services.

Homelessness and rural Ireland

The quantitative overview of homelessness in rural Ireland presented above does not tell us much about the dynamics of homelessness, or to what degree the structural features of rural Ireland either limit or exacerbate the risk or actualization of homelessness. As noted earlier, homelessness in Ireland is largely viewed as a consequence of urban (and largely Dublin) rather than rural 'disorder'. However, we also noted that, in the first count of homeless persons after independence, homelessness was considerably more prevalent outside of Dublin than within it. This is not to say that rural Ireland was always kind to the homeless. In his detailed study of the activities of the Irish Republic Army (IRA) in Cork, Hart (1998: 304) has shown that, at a minimum, 8 per cent of those shot by the IRA during the period 1919 to 1923 for allegedly informing were 'tinkers/tramps'. One possible explanation for the relatively large number of homeless persons in rural Ireland in the first half of the twentieth century was possibly the greater range of accommodation options in rural areas through the various 'casual wards', usually situated on the grounds of hospitals or county homes (former workhouses).[14] However, by 1950, the number of homeless persons (or casuals) recorded in county homes was only 139, of which 'approximately 70 were accommodated in Dublin, Cork and Galway' (Interdepartmental Committee Appointed to Examine the Question of the Reconstruction and Replacement of County Homes, 1949: 27). Despite these limited numbers, with the publication in 1968 of the report of the Inter-Departmental Committee on the Care of the Aged, a policy change was recommended with regard to the operation of casual wards. This report stated that:

> A number of persons, e.g. itinerants, seek accommodation in county homes for a short period because they have nowhere else to stay. At present most county homes make separate provisions for casuals. They constitute a social problem but the committee considers that it is not an appropriate problem for consideration in connection with the care of the aged.
> (Inter-Departmental Committee on the Care of the Aged, 1968: 87–8)

As a consequence of this report, the functions of the county homes changed substantially and many closed down or redirected their orientation. By 1982, 53 per cent of the county homes had either closed down their 'casual' facility or operated with a much-reduced service (Doherty, 1982). Nonetheless, as late as the mid-1980s, casual wards were still providing accommodation for homeless men in rural Ireland (Housing Centre, 1986), but this service had virtually disappeared by the 1990s. Thus, a process emerged from the late 1960s whereby services for homeless persons in rural areas gradually declined. This led to a concentration of homeless persons in urban areas where the same processes were not occurring, and indeed new services for the homeless were emerging (for example, on the emergence of the Simon Community in Dublin in 1969, see Hart, 1978; Coleman, 1990).

However, this explanation does not help explain whether the structural features of rural Ireland can lead to homelessness. To perhaps oversimplify a complex and contested history, it would seem that there is considerable agreement that the process of land redistribution initiated from the 1870s resulted in the construction of peasant proprietors, the stem-family in Ireland and the principle of impartibility of inheritance (for accessible overviews of these debates, see Hannan and Commins, 1992: McCullagh, 1991; Harris, 1988; Tovey, 2001). This contrasted with the earlier system of largely tenant farmers and land subdivision amongst heirs. The new system of inheritance resulted in a situation whereby only one child (usually a son, but not always, and not necessarily the eldest) would inherit the farm,[15] and the remaining (surplus) siblings, in a rough descending order, emigrated, primarily to England; were educated, particularly to acquire posts in the public service or in dioceses and congregations of the Catholic Church;[16] remain on the family farm in a celibate subordinate role to the heir or were institutionalized in the extensive network of psychiatric hospitals and other asylums that dotted rural Ireland. In addition, females were provided with a dowry that would allow marriage or entry to religious congregations (Delaney, 2000; O'Tuathaigh, 1982; Finnane, 1981, Fitzpatrick, 1985).[17] This system existed in a strong form until the late 1950s, but gradually faded during the 1960s, hastened by the gradual state-initiated industrialization of Ireland and agricultural changes resulting from membership of the European Union from the early 1970s (Tovey, 2001).

The previous paragraph, although simplifying a large and complex period of Irish history, has aimed to distill from the extensive research particular aspects that might inform our discussion of rural homelessness. For those who were not going to inherit the land or be given the opportunity for formal education beyond primary level and were unwilling to remain on the land as a non-owning assistant, emigration was, in many cases, the only remaining option, particularly in the west of Ireland, where both agricultural and non-agricultural employment opportunities were virtually non-existent until the 1960s. As we will see, many of those who did not 'voluntarily' emigrate were banished to a range of closed institutions. Until the Great Depression of the late 1920s when the Americans effectively closed their borders, the United States of America was the favoured destination for Irish emigrants, with England, Wales and Scotland dominating after that period. Emigration was crucial to the maintenance of the rural Ireland that was constructed after the famine. For Fitzpatrick,

> [i]t was, after all, emigration which made possible the virtual extinction of the farm labourer, the reduction of rural poverty, the realistic pursuit of tenant security – and also the elimination without homicide of deviants, informers and defeated factions.
>
> (Fitzpatrick, 1981: 141)

Surveys of the homeless in the countries traditionally associated with Irish emigration show high percentages of Irish persons included in their statistics on homelessness. For example, in a census of tramps in the United States in 1893, 'in order of nativity, America leads the list with 56.1 percent; Ireland is next with 20.3 percent' (McCook, 1893: 756). Over sixty years later, a study of homeless men in the United States found that

> 25 percent of the men were born in Ireland; 42 percent of their fathers and 44 percent of their mothers were also born in Ireland. We do not know how many second or third generation Irish-Americans were in our sample ... an estimated guess would be at least one third of them were of Irish descent.
>
> (Levinson, 1966: 168)

Similarly high numbers of Irish-born males are found in various surveys of homelessness in England and Wales. For example, in a study of London's Skid Row, the single largest ethnic group (37 per cent) in their sample was Irish (Edwards *et al.*, 1966: 449). Washbrook in his survey of 200 homeless offenders in London observed that 24 per cent were Irish (1970: 178), and Lodge-Patch in a survey of a London lodging house, found that 25 per cent of his sample were originally Irish (1970: 314). More recently, Drake *et al.*'s (1982) survey of an East End night shelter showed that 28 per cent of those in the shelter were originally Irish. Clearly, not all those recorded as Irish and homeless were originally from rural Ireland, but given the much higher rate of emigration from rural rather than urban Ireland, it is likely that a high percentage were of rural origin. Interestingly, most of these surveys of homelessness in the United States of America and England record homeless men of Irish origin rather than homeless women, despite the fact that slightly more than half of those who emigrated from Ireland were female (Lee, 1990; Clear, 2004). It is not clear whether this particular invisibility reflected the general invisibility of women in research into homelessness until recently (see O'Sullivan and Higgins, 2001, for an overview of the research on homeless women in Ireland) or that the emigrant experience rendered males more susceptible to homelessness than females.

The other key area where the structure of rural Ireland may have contributed to homelessness was the extensive utilization of institutionalization. For example, studies of those committed to psychiatric hospitals/asylums suggest that many families utilized these institutions as instruments to 'discipline unruly family members', particularly in rural Ireland (Malcolm, 1999, 2003). Similarly, mother and baby homes, Magdalen penitentiaries and industrial schools were used extensively by families to divest themselves of problematic, awkward and socially embarrassing kin (Finnegan, 2004; Luddy, 1995; Raftery and O'Sullivan, 1999). By the mid-1950s, some 1 per cent of the Irish population was contained within a range of carceral institutions (females slightly higher at risk than males), with the psychiatric hospitals dominating with nearly 20,000 inmates by the mid-1950s (see Kilcommins *et al.,* 2004, for further details). From the mid-1960s, the psychiatric hospital population gradually began to decline, prompted in part by the publication of the Commission on Mental Illness in 1966. By the early 1980s, the psychiatric hospital population was half what it had been in the early 1960s and again, following on the publication of a review of psychiatric services in 1984, the population continued to dwindle to its current figure of just over 3,500 patients. Those contained in other carceral institutions, industrial schools, mother and baby homes, etc. also showed a continuous decline from the early 1960s. The role of the Catholic Church in both managing many of these carceral institutions and inculcating the values that supported them is subject to much heated debate. Rather than rehashing these debates, Lee best articulates this complex relationship, pithily noting that:

> The sancity of property, the unflinching materialism of farmer calculations, the defence of professional status, depended on continuing high emigration and celibacy. The church did not invent these values. But it did baptize them.
>
> (Lee, 1989: 159)

Thus, it may be argued that the desire for the preservation of a particular type of rural Ireland, and a raw economic motivation for the maintenance of the stem family, effectively displaced those rendered superfluous by these processes. For those displaced, emigration or education may have ensured a more satisfying lifestyle outcome than for those who remained on the land, but as we saw in the case of emigration, this was not always the case. However, it was those who remained on the land and, in particular, those women who gave birth outside of marriage in rural Ireland that created obstacles to the smooth operation of impartible inheritance and the preservation of the stem family. In order to speed up the process of inheritance or rid the farm of unwanted relatives, large numbers of men and women were committed to psychiatric hospitals, a process facilitated by minimum statutory safeguards on preventing such 'socio-economic' committals. Illegitimate children had the potential to disrupt these inheritance practices, and raw economics rather than any concern with sexual morality ensured that many of the mothers of such children were incarcerated in various institutions for lengthy periods of time[18] and their children adopted, fostered, institutionalized in Ireland or exported to the United States of America (Milotte, 1997) and thus would have no claim on the land. That the number of adults and children so institutionalized declined as did rural Ireland is surely no coincidence. The preservation of rural Ireland required such institutions as much as it required emigration (see also McCullagh, 1991: 207–9).

Agencies working with the homeless have long suggested a link between desinstitutionalisation of long-stay patients from psychiatric units and homelessness and that a large proportion of the homeless suffered from psychiatric illnesses (Fernandez, 1995). For example, one study of long-term psychiatric patients in a large psychiatric hospital in the West of Ireland showed that 44 per cent of patients suitable for discharge, if discharged, had no home (Crehan *et al.*, 1987). However, overall the evidence is mixed on the contribution of deinstitutionalization from psychiatric hospitals to homelessness (see O'Sullivan, 2005). In relation to children raised in care, McCarthy's survey of residents of Simon Community hostels showed that 10 per cent of those using their facilities had been raised in care (1988: 114) and Collins and McKeown's data suggested that homeless people known to the Simon Community in Ireland were 45 times more likely to have been brought up in care than the national average (1992: 20). Thus, if one accepts the thesis that the social structure of rural Ireland contributed to the comparatively high rates of institutionalization in Ireland[19] and that such institutionalization has contributed to homelessness, rural Ireland has contributed to homelessness in an indirect manner.

Conclusion

This chapter has attempted to measure homelessness in rural Ireland and to explore tentatively the extent to which the socio-economic structure of rural Ireland may have contributed to homelessness. On both measures, the limited existing evidence suggests homelessness in contemporary Ireland is primarily located in urban areas, particularly in Dublin. However, many of those who are currently homeless in urban areas have rural origins and for those who experienced institutionalization as children or as adults, the social structure of rural Ireland may have been an important contributor to that institutionalization.

In contemporary Ireland, while recognizing the predominance of homelessness in urban areas, policy-makers have also acknowledged the existence of homelessness in rural areas. For example, the first national strategy published by the Irish state to address homelessness noted that:

> While homelessness is a greater problem in urban areas, it is still a problem in rural areas and this issue needs to be addressed. For this reason, a homeless forum should be established in every county, not just in the larger urban areas where homelessness is currently a problem.
>
> (Department of the Environment and Local Government, 2000: 26)

The broad principles enunciated by the strategy document were: a continuum of care from the time someone becomes homeless, with sheltered and supported accommodation, and where appropriate, assistance back into independent living in the community; emergency accommodation should be short-term; settlement in the community to be an overriding priority through independent or supported housing; long-term supported accommodation should be available for those who need it; support services should be provided on an outreach basis as needed and preventative strategies for at risk groups should be developed. To achieve these broad objectives, Homeless Forums were to be established in every county and three-year action plans prepared. Both the homeless forums and the action plans were to include input from both the statutory and non-profit sectors. In addition, under the Planning and Development Act, 2000, local authorities must prepare housing strategies. These strategies must ensure that: sufficient land is zoned to meet the housing requirements in the region; there is a mixture of house types and sizes to meet the needs of various households; that housing is available for people on different income levels; and provide for the need for both social and affordable housing.

In early 2002, a Homeless Preventative Strategy was published with the key objective of ensuring that 'no one is released or discharged from state care without the appropriate measures in place to ensure that they have a suitable place to live with the necessary supports, if needed' (Department of the Environment and Local Government *et al.*, 2002: 3). Specific proposals included the establishment by the Probation and Welfare Service of a specialist unit to deal with offenders who are homeless; the provision of transitional housing units by the Prison Service as part of their overall strategy of preparing offenders for release; and ensuring that all psychiatric hospitals have a formal and written discharge policy. In addition, the vexed question of which statutory agency had responsibility for the homeless was apparently clarified, with the strategy stating that

> it recognises that both local authorities and health boards have key central roles in meeting the needs of homeless persons. Local authorities have responsibility for the provision of accommodation for homeless adults as part of their overall housing responsibility and health boards are responsible for the health and care needs of homeless adults.
>
> (2002: 6)

These strategies have the potential to address many of the difficulties encountered by those currently homeless or at risk of homelessness. Crucially, the development of services in rural areas within the context of these strategies has the potential to minimize the period of homelessness for those who do become homeless and to prevent others from becoming homeless in the first instance. This in turn may have the effect of reducing the drift to urban areas where currently the majority of requisite services are located and consequently homeless persons are enumerated.

Acknowledgements

I would like to thank Hilary Tovey, Mary Higgins, Jarleth McKee, Tony McCashin, Paula Mayock and Paul Milbourne for their thoughtful and constructive comments on earlier drafts of this chapter.

Notes

1   The Housing Act 1988 specifies the local housing authority as the statutory agency with responsibility for the homeless, partly ending earlier confusion over which statutory body had responsibility for providing for the needs of the homeless. However, the Act can be described as permissive legislation in that it permits local housing authorities to assist the homeless, but does not place an obligation on them to house homeless people. In summary, in relation to homelessness, the Act provides a definition of homelessness; empowers housing authorities to provide assistance to voluntary organizations who are approved by the Department of the Environment for the provision or management of housing accommodation; obliges local authorities to conduct periodic assessments of housing need and homelessness; provides for the type of assistance that homeless people may be provided with from a Housing Authority; and requires housing authorities to develop a scheme of letting priority.

2   For the purposes of the Act, the homeless are those for whom: 'a – There is no accommodation available which, in the opinion of the authority, he, together with any other person who normally resides with him or who might reasonably be expected to reside with him, can reasonably occupy or remain in occupation of, or, b – He is living in a hospital, county home, night shelter or other such institution, and is so living because he has no accommodation of the kind referred to in the paragraph (a) and he is, in the opinion of the authority, unable to provide accommodation from his own resources'. The interpretation of this definition as provided by the Department of the Environment is as follows: 'The definition is drawn in broad terms and covers not only persons actually without Accommodation but also persons living in Hospitals, county homes, night shelters or similar institutions solely because they have no suitable alternative accommodation. Equally, persons who are unable to occupy or remain in occupation of otherwise suitable accommodation due, for example, to violence come within the scope of the definition ... It is a pre-requisite to being regarded as homeless for the purposes of the Act that a person is unable

to provide accommodation from his/her own resources. The determination of whether or not a person is homeless is a matter for the housing authority. This will necessitate a number of basic inquiries regarding the person's previous accommodation, marital status, family circumstances, dependants, income etc. Generally speaking, these particulars can best be obtained by arranging personal interviews; any such interviews should be conducted in a sensitive and helpful manner' (DOE, 1989: 8–9).

3   See the collection by Curtin *et al.* (1996) for discussion of some of these issues in relation to rural Ireland.

4   The consequences of the Irish famine on subsequent demographic trends and on shaping the social structures of rural Ireland are the subject of much debate. For excellent overviews on different aspects of the consequences of the famine, see Mjøset (1992), Guinnane (1997) and Whelan (1999).

5   It is not clear from the report whether or not members of the traveller community were included in this census of homeless persons. For a useful discussion of travellers (or as they were formerly known, intinerants or tinkers), see McCann *et al*, 1994.

6   There are 29 County Councils in Ireland, with at least one Council for each of the 26 counties, although Dublin county has 3 Councils and Tipperary 2. There are 5 City Councils: these are in effect the five major urban areas of Cork, Dublin, Galway, Limerick and Waterford. There are also 5 Borough Councils, including Clonmel, Drogheda, Kilkenny, Sligo, and Wexford and 75 Town Councils.

7   Despite the relative methodological sophistication of the Dublin assessment, a number of difficulties were reported. For example, the total number of homeless adult individuals recorded exceeded the total number of emergency beds available in Dublin and the number recorded as sleeping rough does not explain the difference. As the Director of the Homeless Agency has pointed out, this is largely attributable to the discrepancies in the administrative data maintained by the local authorities on the numbers of individuals recorded as homeless (Higgins, 2002: 15). It would appear that individuals and households recorded as homeless by the local authorities moved out of homelessness, but did not report this and thus were on the list and counted as homeless at the time of the assessment. Thus, the data on those using homeless and other services may be a more accurate reflection of the extent of homelessness. On this basis, the number of homeless households increased by 180 from 1,290 in 1999 to 1,470 in 2002. The difficulties encountered with the administrative data held by local authorities and by Homeless Agency/Economic and Social Research Institute researchers reiterates the point that the data provided by other local authorities on the extent of homelessness need to be treated with extreme caution. However, it does not necessarily follow that the overall

number of homeless persons enumerated by local authorities is exaggerated (although it may well be), but administrative data reflect bureaucratic procedures and priorities rather than an accurate extent of homelessness.

8   Section 9 of the Housing Act, 1988 requires housing authorities, not less frequently than every three years, to conduct an assessment of the need for the provision by the authority of adequate and suitable housing accommodation for persons whom the authority have reason to believe require, or are likely to require, accommodation from the authority, and who, in the opinion of the authority, are in need of such accommodation and are unable to provide it from their own resources. In doing so, the housing authority shall have regard to the need for housing of persons who (1) are homeless, (2) are persons to whom section 13 applies, i.e. travellers, (3) are living in accommodation that is unfit for human habitation or is materially unsuitable for their adequate housing, (4) are living in overcrowded accommodation, (5) are sharing accommodation with another person or persons and who, in the opinion of the housing authority, have a reasonable requirement for separate accommodation, (6) are young persons leaving institutional care or without family accommodation, (7) are in need of accommodation for medical or compassionate reasons, (8) are elderly, (9) are disabled or handicapped, or (10) are, in the opinion of the housing authority, not reasonably able to meet the cost of the accommodation which they are occupying or to obtain suitable alternative accommodation.

9   In 1990, the average cost of a new house in Ireland was €65,541. By 1995 the cost had modestly risen to €77,994, but rapidly spiralled to €169,191 by 2000 and to €224,567 in 2003.

10 As summarized by the Inter-Departmental Committee on Land Structure Reform, 'By a series of Land Acts dating from 1870, the landlord/tenant system which had obtained since the 17th century was eliminated and replaced by a system of owner-occupancy. In all, 414,000 tenants became full owners of their lands, totaling some 14 million acres' (1978: 19).

11 By 1900, over 15,000 cottages for rural labourers had been built in Ireland, compared to 14 cottages built in England and Wales (Aalen, 1992: 138).

12 In a review of housing policy in 1964, it was noted that of the 87,000 cottages built under the various Labourers Acts, four out of every five had been sold to sitting tenants at discounted rates (Minister for Local Government, 1964).

13 These are plans that local authorities are encouraged to produce under the recommendations of the 2000 government strategy to eliminate homelessness.

14 Prior to the passing of the Housing Act, 1988, statutory responsibility for the homeless was vested in the Health Act, 1953, which under section 54, obliged health authorities to provide institutional assistance to those who are unable to provide shelter for themselves.

15 For a detailed review on the evidence on forms of inheritance in rural Ireland, see Guinnane (1997: 151–6).

16 For example, Newman's study of vocations to the Maynooth seminary from 1956 to 1960 showed that 73% of those who entered were from rural families, generally large families, and he concluded that '(i)t is reasonable to suppose that the same holds for vocations in general' (1962: 89). In Lee's acerbic interpretation, the Irish clergy were 'strong farmers in cassocks' (1989: 159). Barry Coldrey, a Christian Brother, and author of a number of histories of the congregation, has argued that recruitment into the congregation 'was heavily rural in Ireland' (1992: 284).

17 Possibly the best known account of the use of psychiatric hospitals in rural Ireland is that provided by the American anthropologist Nancy Scheper-Hughes (1979). She attributes the high rate of institutionalization in such hospitals as resulting from the anomie associated with the decline of the population of rural Ireland. Her account, however, fails to take into account that rates of institutionalization were rapidly declining at the time of her research and that, contra her thesis, a vibrant rural Ireland would require such institutions more than a declining one would.

18 For example, as reported by a committee of enquiry in the late 1940s, 'the usual practice is to keep the mother and her child in the County Home for about two years at least. After that period the child is boarded out and the mother may be permitted to leave the home. This, however, is not the invariable rule. The mother may be retained much longer and the child may be boarded out much earlier' (Interdepartmental Committee Appointed to Examine the Queestion of the Reconstruction and Replacement of County Homes, 1949: 24).

19 For example, the Commission of Inquiry on Mental Illness noted that 'Statistics in respect of different countries may not be directly comparable, but, even if allowance is made for this, the number of in-patients in Ireland seems to be extremely high – it appears to be the highest in the world' (1966: 24–5). Earlier, Penrose had observed that in the 1930s, Ireland had the highest per capita number of patients 'under the care of institutions for the insane or the mentally defective' (1939: 4). On the comparatively high number of children contained in reformatory and industrial schools, see O'Sullivan (1997).

Chapter 12
Inhabiting the margins
A geography of rural homelessness in Australia

Neil Argent and Fran Rolley

Introduction

Little is known about the extent, pattern and nature of homelessness in rural Australia, a situation echoed by other authors in this volume in relation to other countries in North America, Europe and the UK. While acknowledging that homelessness does have a spatial or locational dimension, the conventional wisdom is that homelessness is spatially concentrated in 'large cities rather than rural towns and cities; in central city areas rather than the suburbs' (Burke, 1994: 33), where numbers are largest and the homeless population more visible. Homelessness in Australia has been typically represented as a metropolitan phenomenon and, as such, rural homelessness has received little specific attention from academics, policy makers or the media. Perhaps this is not surprising in one of the most urbanized countries in the world. Despite this situation, the rural homeless occupy a very special and highly visible role in Australian folklore and mythology. The de facto national anthem, 'Waltzing Matilda' tells the tale of a homeless male sleeping rough by the famed billabong who meets his demise at the hands of the colonial authorities for sheep stealing. Similarly, some of the nation's most famous poetry and painting of the colonial era is centrally concerned with itinerant male labourers (e.g. Lawson's 'Clancy of the Overflow') and nomadic older homeless men (commonly known as 'swaggies') (e.g. Frederick McCubbin's 'Down on His Luck').

The issue of rural homelessness in Australia has been, therefore, shrouded in cultural myopia and myth. Recent research and public policy interest in this field is, however, gradually dispelling some of these blinds and myths, and revealing the real spatial, social and institutional dimensions of rural homelessness in Australia. This chapter aims to contribute to the development of a clearer understanding of the extent and nature of homelessness in rural Australia by first examining its geographical dimensions at the 2001 Census, concentrating particularly on New South Wales, and, second, exploring the causes of homelessness in coastal and inland regions of that state, focusing specifically on the influence of key aspects of rural society and economy. To provide an appropriate context for this analysis, however, it is first necessary to review major trends in the nature of the homeless population over recent decades and the causes for their homelessness.

Homelessness in Australia

Although homelessness has long been part of Australia's social environment (AIHW, 2003), traditional notions of homelessness have changed over time, as have the populations of homeless people. The post-war economic boom which resulted in employment growth and increasing prosperity saw homelessness slip from the social policy agenda as the visible homeless population was, apparently, reduced to a core group of older, single men (Memmott *et al.*, 2003). However, over the past two decades, this caricature has been dispelled by the increasingly complex reality of the homeless in Australia. Joining the older single men in this picture are growing numbers of single young men and women, single parents with children, families and Indigenous people (Department of Family and Community Services (FACS), 2000: 5). In substantial part, this growing hetero-geneity of the homeless population can be explained by major structural change in the economy, coinciding with high and stubborn unemployment rates; significant shifts in Australian society, including the increasing propensity of family breakdown, an associated tendency for women and children to flee violent husbands and fathers; a long-term decline in the availability of relatively low-skilled work in both metropolitan and non-metropolitan areas; greater availability of illicit drugs; and the deinstitutionalization of people with disabilities and mental health patients (Human Rights and Equal Opportunity Commission, 1993; FACS, 2000; AIHW, 2003). Simultaneously, there has been a decrease in housing affordability and a decline in the number and geographical spread of boarding houses and other low-cost, non-private accommodation.

Most recent estimates of the homeless population in Australia suggest that on any one night between 60,000 and 105,000 people are without adequate and secure shelter, of whom almost half have experienced some form of chronic homelessness at some time (Berry, 2003). The most accurate estimates of the homeless population in Australia have been made by Chamberlain and MacKenzie (2003, 2004a, 2004b), who suggest that, for policy and planning purposes, it is reasonable to quote a figure of 100,000 people a night. While it is generally recognized that in Australia most homeless people are not forced to sleep rough, at the most recent census (August 2001), 14.2 per cent of those who were homeless were 'primary' homeless (that is, sleeping rough or in a tent or improvised dwelling) (Chamberlain and MacKenzie, 2003). As Robinson (2003: 7) suggests, however, homelessness is perhaps better thought of as 'the ongoing search for stable and safe shelter ... the most significant proportion of the homeless population in Australia are those moving from one form of temporary accommodation to another'. Of this 'secondary' homeless population at the 2001 Census, over half (56.7 per cent) were staying with friends and relatives, 26.7 per cent were enumerated in boarding houses, and the remainder were housed in some form of emergency accommodation, refuge or hostel (funded under the Federal Government's Supported Accommodation Assistance Scheme, SAAP). Although in absolute terms the largest numbers of homeless people are to be found in the state capitals, particularly in the inner-most central city areas, rates of homelessness are consistently higher outside metropolitan areas.

Chamberlain and MacKenzie (2003) suggest that, although it is clear that the population of homeless people has increased over the last four decades, there is no data available to quantify the rate of increase. What is clear, however, is that the pattern of homelessness is now more complex than that of the stereotypical, older male. There are now more women, young people and families comprising the contemporary homeless population in Australia. At the last census, women made up 42 per cent of the homeless population, and whilst more than half of all of the homeless people in 2001 were aged over 25 years, 36 per cent were aged 12–24 years and 10 per cent were children under 12 years of age. Indigenous Australians, in particular, are more likely to experience homelessness than other Australians, with the Indigenous population over-represented in all sections of the homeless population. While just over 2 per cent of the Australian population identify as being of Aboriginal or Torres Strait Islander (ATSI) origin, they comprise 9 per cent of the homeless population and 16 per cent of SAAP clients (Chamberlain and MacKenzie, 2003).

With the recognition of the increasing diversity of the Australian homeless population has come an acknowledgement of the complexity of the 'causes' of homelessness. Indeed, understanding of causes has shifted from a focus on the characteristics of the homeless person to an increasing acceptance of the importance of exogenous, structural forces acting in concert with a wide range of triggers which are known to have a role in precipitating those at risk of homelessness into incipient homelessness and producing or exacerbating a 'homeless career' as identified by Chamberlain and MacKenzie (2003).

In short, poverty, the changing characteristics of the housing market, health-related issues – including those at both an individual and/or societal level – social dislocation and domestic violence have all been identified as direct causes of homelessness (Burke, 1994). Triggered by a range of personal circumstances, such as leaving the parental home, marriage breakdown or deterioration of health, these factors often operate to compound 'joined-up' problems to produce and perpetuate homelessness (Robinson, 2003). Clearly, some people are more likely to become homeless than others. Those in financial housing stress (private renters, recipients of social security payments, single income units and women escaping domestic violence) and low income groups such as people of ATSI origin, itinerant workers and people who have been involved with the justice system are most vulnerable (Neil *et al.*, 1992; Mendes, 2002).

While there is now a growing body of Australian research examining the interaction of structural and individual factors causing homelessness (see, for example, Neil *et al.*, 1992; Crane and Brannock, 1996; Arthurson and Jacobs, 2003; Chamberlain and MacKenzie, 1998, 2003; Chamberlain and Johnson, 2003), an understanding of the 'iterative' nature of the experience of homelessness is less well developed. There is as yet limited research into the repetitive cycle of homelessness for people moving from one kind of 'stop-gap' accommodation to the next, despite the fact that the cycle is well understood by service providers dealing with the homeless (Robinson, 2003). Those most vulnerable to iterative homelessness, like those most at risk of initially becoming homeless, are young people leaving the parental home, those with mental health problems, with alcohol, drug or substance abuse issues, those exiting (or with a history of dealing with) the justice system and, in particular, the Indigenous population. Given the compounding of social, economic, health and educational disadvantage faced by the Indigenous population, it is not surprising that they are particularly vulnerable to chronic and iterative homelessness. Although there are similarities between the immediate causes of homelessness for ATSI people, there are some fundamental differences in the causes and contexts of this group's experience of homelessness. Indigenous Australians face considerable difficulties in accessing the private rental market, resulting in a heavy reliance on the public and community housing stock. This, together with the need for a large proportion of the Indigenous population to leave their local area in order to access services, results in considerable primary homelessness and severe overcrowding due to 'hidden' homelessness (Keys Young, 1999).

In Australia, recent recognition of the complexity of the 'web of causation' in relation to homelessness, combined with an increasing awareness of a lack of exit points from a homeless career has led to a variety of responses from government with a view to early intervention and prevention strategies. Although the Australian government provides a number of programmes and services that can be accessed by people in crisis, only the SAAP, Crisis Assistance Program (CAP) and Reconnect (a community-based early intervention programme for young people who are homeless or at risk of becoming so, and their families) are directed specifically at those who are homeless. CAP provides capital funds for the construction of dwellings to be used to accommodate the homeless or those in crisis, while SAAP assists the homeless through a range of support and accommodation programmes. SAAP service providers are a diverse mix of primarily non-government agencies, who deliver a range of emergency services such as crisis accommodation, referrals for transitional housing, domestic violence support and health-related assistance. The most recent SAAP agreement between the Commonwealth and State and Territory governments (SAAP IV) has specifically identified Aboriginal and Torres Strait Islander homelessness and homeless people with complex needs as priorities (AIHW, 2001).

Many other government programmes, however, address some aspects of the circumstances of people at risk of or experiencing homelessness.[1] In response to coordination problems related to service delivery for the homeless, the Commonwealth Government launched the National Homeless Strategy in 2000, which seeks to provide a strategic framework for policies to prevent, reduce and respond to homelessness in Australia (AIHW, 2001). In addition, state and local governments operate a variety of programmes targeting the homeless and those at risk of homelessness. In New South Wales, for example, the State Department of Housing's ' Partnership Against Homelessness' strategy brings together a network of government agencies to help address the wider causes of homelessness (Robinson, 2003).

Is rural homelessness essentially the same as urban homelessness, except set in a different landscape? There are many reasons for suspecting that this is not the case.

Homelessness in rural Australia: an overview

Although the pattern of rural settlement in Australia varies greatly between the closer settled agricultural districts of the coast and the inland areas of extensive agricultural and pastoral activity, the hallmark of rural areas is typically large distances, inaccessibility and low population thresholds which operate to constrain human activity and influence the provision of essential services (Humphreys *et al.*, 1996). Rural areas, despite their diversity, share the common characteristic of population dispersion which leads to relatively low levels of demand for goods and services. Combined with the impacts of recent economic restructuring within the farm sector, rationalization and centralization of public and private services, and the associated processes of rural depopulation, many rural communities are at risk of falling below the critical threshold for maintaining existing services. Even in the high rural population growth areas of the coastal belt, service provision often lags behind the needs of the regional population.

So, despite the general invisibility of the rural homeless, there is no necessary 'philosophical dissonance' (Lawrence, 1995) between homelessness and rurality in the Australian context. Nor are the homeless 'out-of-place' in a 'purified' rural space as is the situation in rural Britain (Cloke *et al.*, 2000). Indeed, much recent research has demonstrated the anti-idyllic aspects of Australian rural life (Walmlsey and Weinand, 1997; Vinson, 1999, 2004; Pritchard and McManus, 2000; Lloyd *et al.*, 2001).

The two most recent national population censuses – 1996 and 2001 – have seen the Australian Bureau of Statistics (ABS) adopt concerted efforts to include the homeless in its quinquennial winter snapshot of the Australian population. For many years, the ABS has included questions in the census on the dwelling type in which residents were enumerated, including categories such as 'improvised dwellings, campers, sleepers out' and 'homeless refuge'. However, these categories provide an altogether too crude measure of the homeless because, for instance, they included ordinary holiday makers in tents in the ranks of the primary homeless yet did not count at all those people without a permanent home sleeping on a friend's or relative's floor. In other words, prior to 1996 and 2001, censuses were constructed in such a way that the homeless – in rural and urban settings – were rendered invisible. Even disaggregation of the 1996 Census could not readily give reliable data on homelessness due to problematic question wording.

In the context of a growing recognition amongst academics, policy makers and service providers that a more standardized and rigorous approach to counting the homeless was required, the ABS devised a 'special enumeration strategy' (Chamberlain, 1999: 15). This involved both a change in question wording and special training for census collectors. The strategy was ultimately focused on allowing the census results to be interrogated in such a way that homeless people could be placed in a four-fold categorization of homelessness designed by Chamberlain and MacKenzie (1992; see Table 12.1). Although homelessness may be experienced by an individual in an iterative (Robinson, 2003), incipient (Kearns *et al.*, 1993) and episodic fashion, as Chamberlain (1999: 3) emphasizes, the census snapshot of the number and type of homelessness is more important to policy makers than data on the number of people who become homeless over a year.

The ABS's special enumeration strategy was further refined for the 2001 Census, with more effort devoted to training census collectors to identify typical homeless 'haunts' and the refuges and private hostels located within residential areas which are often indistinguishable from a normal detached house. Another change went to the heart of the cultural definitions of 'adequate shelter or housing'. For the 1996 Census, collectors recorded any form of shelter without a working toilet and bathroom as an 'improvised dwelling', thereby allocating its residents to the ranks of the primary homeless. This was culturally inappropriate because, in some situations, Aboriginal communities share communal toilet and bathroom facilities (Chamberlain and MacKenzie, 2003: 22). For the 2001 Census, therefore, census collectors only needed to satisfy themselves that 'a dwelling was fit for the purpose of housing people' (Chamberlain and MacKenzie, 2003: 22). The change in collection methodology saw the number of 'improvised dwellings' in Aboriginal communities decline from 8,727 in 1996 to 823 in 2001, and the number of Indigenous people in such dwellings drop from 9,751 to 2,681 over the same period (Chamberlain and MacKenzie, 2003: 22).

Despite these incremental advances, the census remains a largely opaque database on the homeless. While primary homelessness (Table 12.1) is relatively

Table 12.1 A continuum of homelessness

Culturally recognised exceptions: where it is inappropriate to apply the minimum standard – for example, seminaries, gaols, student halls of residence etc.	*Marginally housed:* people in housing situations close to the minimum standard*
	Tertiary homelessness: people living in single rooms in private boarding houses, without their own bathroom, kitchen or security of tenure
	Secondary homelessness: people moving between various forms of temporary shelter including: friends, emergency accommodation, youth refuges, hostels and boarding houses
	Primary homelessness: people without conventional accommodation – sleeping rough, living on the streets, in improvised dwellings etc.

Source: Chamberlain and MacKenzie, 1992: 291.
Note: * minimum community standard – equivalent to a small rented flat with a bedroom, living room, kitchen and bathroom.

easily obtained via the census category 'improvised homes, tents and sleepers out' (after those who record another address are removed: Chamberlain and MacKenzie, 2003), secondary and tertiary homelessness is much more difficult to ascertain – impossible without specialist knowledge and access to other databases.[2] Using the combined census, SAAP and homeless school student census data, Chamberlain and MacKenzie (2001) estimated that there were 105,300 homeless persons on Census night 1996, nearly 20,000 of whom were in the primary homeless category. A further 13,000 and 23,000 were categorized as secondary and tertiary homeless, respectively (Chamberlain and MacKenzie, 2001).

Although Chamberlain and MacKenzie extended their analysis to each of the States and Territories, little commentary was made on the differentials between urban and rural areas. However, in a report to the Victorian Department of Human Services for that State's Homelessness Strategy, Chamberlain (2000) used disaggregated 1996 Census data to produce a snapshot of homelessness across rural and metropolitan parts of Victoria. This revealed that, apart from inner Melbourne, rural Victoria had overall higher rates of homelessness than the State's capital. Using his and MacKenzie's four categories of homelessness, Chamberlain (2000) found that homeless rates across rural Victoria ranged from 40 to 60 per 10,000 residents (with a peak of 67 per 10,000 in East Gippsland), compared to a State mean of 41 per 10,000, and a suburban Melbourne mean of 28 per 10,000.

As noted above, the 2001 Census saw some refinement to the 'special enumeration strategy' for counting the homeless used at the 1996 Census. Nevertheless, undercounting of the homeless population would almost certainly have occurred at this census also. At the level of the States and Territories, the analysis of the 2001 Census results confirmed Chamberlain and MacKenzie's (1999) findings for the 1996 Census: that homelessness rates are highest in the north and north-west (Queensland, Northern Territory and Western Australia) – where significant Aboriginal and Torres Strait Islander populations reside – compared to the south-eastern States of New South Wales, Australian Capital Territory, Victoria, Tasmania and South Australia (see Figure 12.1). A series of State- and Territory-specific reports produced by Chamberlain and MacKenzie on the basis of the 2001 Census results provided quite a detailed examination of the geography of homelessness in Australia at a range of scales.

Figure 12.1 shows that homelessness is not only higher in the north and west of the country relative to the south-east, but that homelessness appears to be strongly and positively correlated with remoteness. While most non-metropolitan Statistical Divisions[3] recorded higher rates of homelessness than their respective State or Territory means, extreme levels of homelessness tended to be found in the remotest SDs of Western Australia, the Northern Territory and Queensland. The Kimberley SD recorded the highest homelessness rate in the nation with 555 per 10,000 (Chamberlain and MacKenzie, 2004a: 68), with one of its constituent local government areas (Wyndham-East Kimberley) recording a rate of 772 per 10,000 (Chamberlain and MacKenzie, 2004a: 51). As Chamberlain and MacKenzie (2004a: 51) note, this entire, vast region experiences a surge in its 'floating' population during the southern winter months (the 'dry' season in the northern Australian tropics) with many visitors seeking casual work in the tourism and agricultural industries and/or passing through to region on the way to, or from, other work destinations. The lack of affordable private rental accommodation in most of the key localities forces large numbers of people to 'room' with others or 'sleep rough'. This region is unusual, though, in that the non-Indigenous homelessness rate is much greater than the Indigenous rate.[4] Throughout most of the remainder of the country, this relationship is reversed.

As in the national picture, homelessness rates across New South Wales vary widely (see Figures 12.2 and 12.3). However, rural areas, with few exceptions, record higher than average rates than the metropolitan area of Sydney and its satellite cities of Newcastle and Wollongong.[5] Particularly high rates are observable (see Figure 12.3) within the Far North Coast and South Coast, where the spatially selective counter-urbanization process has been maintained (Burnley and Murphy,

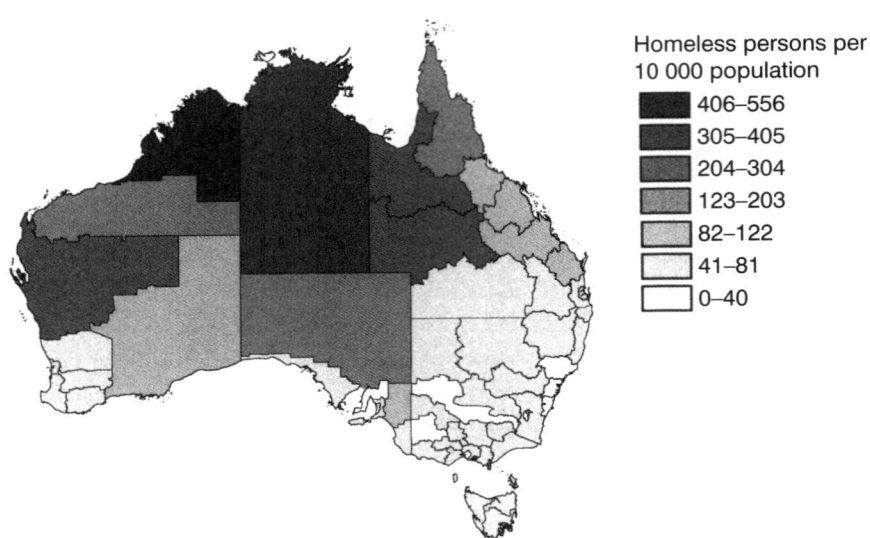

12.1 Homeless rates in rural Australia by statistical division, 2001.
Source: Chamberlain and McKenzie, 2004a, b, c, d, e, f, g, h.

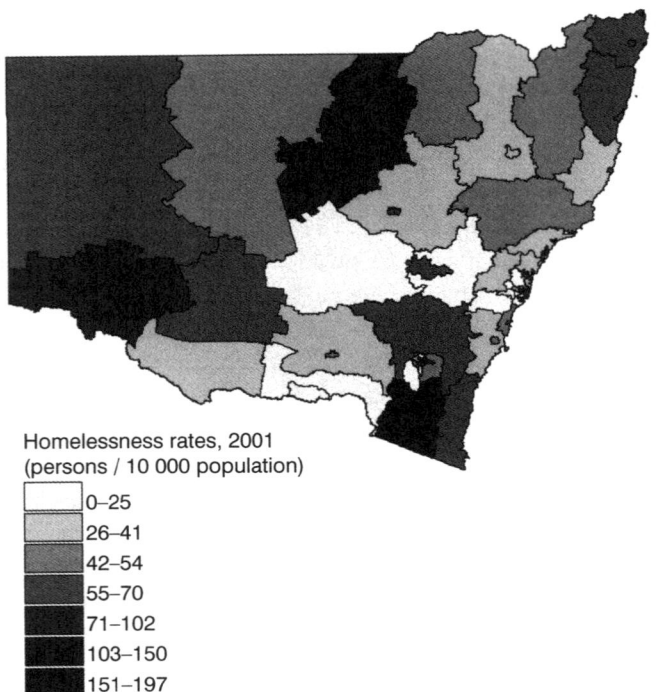

12.2 Homelessness in New South Wales by statistical subdivision, 2001.
Source: Chamberlain and McKenzie, 2004, Appendix 1.

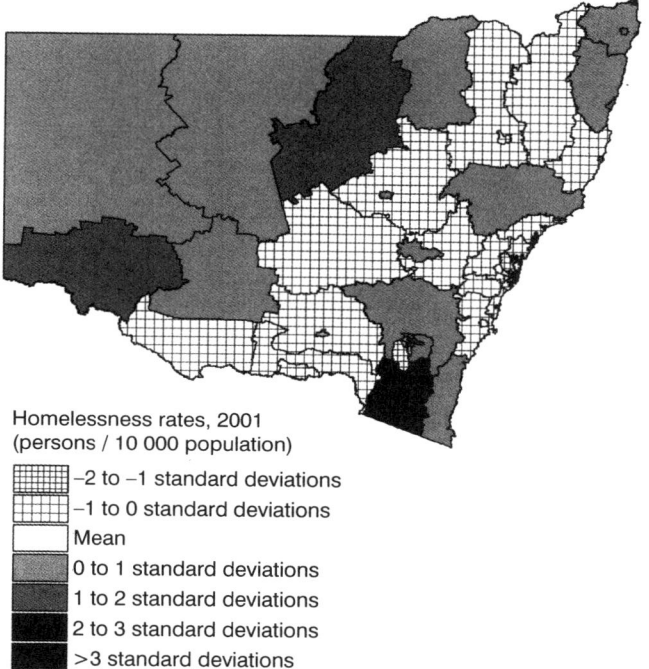

Homelessness rates, 2001
(persons / 10 000 population)

-2 to -1 standard deviations
-1 to 0 standard deviations
Mean
0 to 1 standard deviations
1 to 2 standard deviations
2 to 3 standard deviations
>3 standard deviations

12.3 Homelessness in New South Wales by statistical subdivision, 2001 (standard deviations from the mean). Source: Chamberlain and McKenzie, 2004, Appendix 1.

2004); the Snowy Mountains and Southern Tablelands to the south-west of Sydney; the upper Hunter Valley; and most of the vast portion of the State west of the Great Dividing Range. While there is not a strong visible correlation between homelessness and remoteness from major service centres, there is apparently a strong positive correlation between rural homelessness and Aboriginality, or the proportion of the population identifying as Indigenous. Not only are Indigenous people overrepresented within the homeless population at a national and State level, but in the zones just mentioned above, they also comprise a higher than average proportion of the overall homeless population (Chamberlain and MacKenzie, 2004b; see Table 12.2).

It is important to remember, though, that the extent and depth of homelessness mapped in Figures 12.1, 12.2 and 12.3 are mere snapshots of what is usually a highly mobile population – in real spatial as well as categorical terms. Therefore, depending upon what time of year a census is conducted, 'hot spots' on a chloropleth map of homelessness may well shift to other areas. For example, the high homelessness rates shown in the Snowy Statistical Subdivision (Figures 12.2 and 12.3) can be attributed to large numbers of itinerant vegetable pickers

Table 12.2 Indigenous homelessness as a proportion of total homeless: Statistical Divisions and selected Statistical Subdivisions, Western Australia and New South Wales, 2001

WA–SDs	% Indigenous of total homeless[a]	NSW–SDs and selected SSDs	% Indigenous of total homeless[a]
Perth	7.9	Sydney	3.7
South West	4.1	Hunter	5.2
Lower Great Southern	3.0	Illawarra	5.8
Upper Great Southern	8.5	Richmond-Tweed	6.4
Midlands	4.8	Mid-North Coast	7.7
South Eastern	18.7	Coffs Harbour	9.7
Central	14.0	Port Macquarie	7.0
Pilbara	9.9	Clarence (excl. Coffs)	6.5
Kimberley	10.3	Hastings (excl. Port M)	8.6
		Northern	13.1
		Tamworth	14.2
		Northern Slopes	0.0
		Northern Tablelands	9.0
		North Central Plain	31.6
		North Western	18.5
		Central West	7.3
		South Eastern	5.3
		Murrumbidgee	5.3
		Murray	1.6
		Far West	13.3
Total[b]	9.0	Total[b]	5.2

Source: Chamberlain and MacKenzie 2004a; 2004b.
Notes: a) Estimated number adjusted for missing data on Indigenous status; b) Includes missing data.

operating out of Cooma, together with a substantial number of people staying in boarding houses that once housed labourers employed in the post-Second World War Snowy Mountains Hydroelectric Scheme (Chamberlain and MacKenzie, 2004b: 59–60). If the census had been held during the cotton chipping season, it is highly likely that other regions in the State's west would show up as 'hot spots' of homelessness.

This quantitative overview demonstrates clearly the dimensions of rural homelessness in Australia and provides some clues as to its causes – both at an individual and a regional-specific level. However, in order to develop a better understanding of how rurality shapes, or even causes homelessness, we now explore the nature and causes of homelessness, as well as the institutional responses to it, in two New South Wales case study areas: one within the Mid-North Coast SD, centred on Coffs Harbour; and the other within the Northern SD and containing the major towns of Moree and Narrabri (see Figure 12.4). We do this through the lens of local service providers to the homeless: the various SAAP agencies represented at a local level and who comprise both the frontline in dealing with the rural homeless as well as the critical buffer between the homeless individual and public and private welfare, housing and health institutions.[6]

Homelessness in coastal and inland rural New South Wales

The two case study areas are markedly different regions across a wide range of criteria. In demographic terms, the Mid-North Coast has experienced sustained population growth over the past twenty years as one of the most popular zones for counter-urbanization-associated in-migration. By contrast, the mixed farming/ extensive cropping region of the Northern SD has undergone a sustained slow process of demographic decline, with almost all local government areas experiencing net losses of population over the past two decades. While the economic base of the Mid-North Coast has become increasingly dependent upon the services sector, with agriculture becoming progressively less important as an employer and source of gross regional product, the Northern SD still depends

12.4 The study areas

quite heavily upon farming, even though agriculture employs proportionally many fewer workers now than it did two decades ago (Table 12.3).

Both the Mid-North Coast and Northern SDs reported above average (NSW mean = 42/10,000) rates of homelessness at the 2001 Census, though in numerical terms the size of the homeless population in each SD was relatively small: 1,513 in the Mid-North Coast and 749 in the Northern SD (Chamberlain and MacKenzie, 2004b). Interestingly, primary homelessness (rough sleeping, sleeping in improvised dwellings) was much higher in both SDs relative to the State mean (10.6 per cent) and the proportion recorded in inner Sydney (7.1 per cent). In most of the SSDs that make up both SDs, the primary homeless

Table 12.3 Selected socio-demographic indicators – Coffs Harbour and North Central Plain SSD, 2001

Indicator	Coffs Harbour SSD	North Central Plains SSD
Total population[a]	46,338	29,558
Population change, 1996–2001	+4.0%	−0.2%
Population change, 1991–6	+15.9%	−6.2%
Population density (people/sq. km)	214.8	0.95
Population aged less than 15 years	20.7%	23.8%
Population aged over 65 years	16.5%	10.7%
ATSI population	1,423	3,891
ATSI population as proportion of total	3.1%	13.2%
Overseas born as proportion of total	10.8%	4.7%
Median age (years)	39	34
Mean household size (persons)	2.5	2.7
Median weekly household income	$300–399	$700–799
Median weekly individual income	$300–399	$300–399
Industry of employment (% of workforce)		
Agriculture, forestry and fishing	0.3	26.8
Manufacturing	0.5	5.9
Construction	7.6	5.6
Retail trade	20.4	13.5
Accommodation, cafes, restaurants	8.9	4.6
Property and business services	9.0	6.9
Education	7.4	6.1
Health and community services	11.2	6.8
Government administration and defence	4.1	3.7

Source: ABS 2002.
Note: a) Includes overseas visitors.

comprised around one-quarter of all homeless people and, in one extreme case – the North Central Plain SSD, in which two of our case study towns, Moree and Narrabri, are located – accounted for over one-third of the regional homeless population. However, most homeless people in these two regions slept on the floors of friends and relatives. Relatively few people stayed in boarding houses or SAAP accommodation, though this did vary between SSD, reflecting, in part, the relative availability of each kind of service in each area.

As across most of the rest of the nation, Indigenous people are heavily over-represented in the homeless population of both regions, ranging from at least double the rate of homelessness of the non-Indigenous population, to triple in Coffs Harbour and North Central Plain SSDs and quadruple the rate in Port Macquarie SSD (Chamberlain and MacKenzie, 2004b: 79). In each of the case study regions the overall numbers of Indigenous people homeless on Census night 2001 was relatively small.

Using data collected from the SAAP agencies in each region[7] it is possible to develop a profile of the broad socio-economic and demographic groups seeking shelter for 1997/8 and 2002/3. Because the data is collected from SAAP agencies, it does not necessarily describe the situations of those who fall into other categories of homelessness, as many of the homeless tend to appear in different 'categories' in a cyclical and episodic fashion. In the Mid-North Coast region, single people accounted for just over half of all homeless people in both 1997/8 and 2002/3. Single women with children comprised a further third, suggesting high rates of domestic violence and abuse as an important contributor to service demand. Interestingly, single homelessness is much more prevalent on the Northern Tablelands, Ranges and Plains, with three-quarters of all people seeking SAAP homeless support services falling into this category. By contrast, women with children made up less than one-quarter of all homeless people (AIHW, 2000: 20). In the Northern SD it is possible that some women and children seek out family and friends in higher proportions than similarly placed women on the Mid-North Coast when escaping domestic violence. These proportions do not mirror the level and focus of SAAP agencies in each region. Young people's refuges and related services (presumably catering for homeless youth) account for nearly one-half of all SAAP services in the Mid-North Coast, and just over one-quarter in the Northern SD. Single men's refuges account for a further 10 per cent of Northern SD SAAP services. Domestic violence refuges and related services comprise nearly 40 per cent of Northern SD SAAP services but only one-quarter of Mid-North Coast SAAP agencies (AIHW, 2000: 20).

Interviews with SAAP agency operators in both regions highlighted three broad categories relating to the causes and nature of homelessness: housing; families and the multi-generational reproduction of poverty and marginal housing conditions; and rurality. We expand upon each category in detail below.

Housing

While housing is usually cheaper in rural than metropolitan areas – thus offering a potential haven for the housing disadvantaged and marginalized – housing choice is often narrower (Beer *et al.*, 2003). For example, rural housing markets are often characterized by an awkward combination of low provision of private rental accommodation, limited public rental and emergency accommodation and higher costs of construction. Housing is only cheaper in depressed areas, where access to housing must be traded off against lack of employment opportunities, reduced access to services and increased costs of living (Neil *et al.*, 1992: 44).

Therefore, homeless people generally experience marginal housing conditions on a regular basis, because of the combination of individual characteristics with the inherent nature of capitalist housing markets. Over the past three years, most of Australia's capital cities have experienced a sustained housing price boom. Australia's 'negative gearing' laws provide lucrative tax benefits to homeowners who purchase additional properties for rental. This boom has also been felt in regional centres as investor interest has rippled out from the metropolitan areas to seek out more affordable investment properties, driving up local housing and rental prices.

Not surprisingly, then, almost all SAAP agencies in both regions expressed concern at the difficulty in placing clients in private rental accommodation. Some agencies even suggested that local real estate agents had lifted rents across all rental categories in order to keep 'undesirable' people out of their properties. According to one crisis accommodation provider on the coast, this made the search for housing particularly difficult, especially for 'young single mothers and Koori (Indigenous) women'. One women's refuge in Coffs Harbour stated that a prominent local real estate agent was refusing to accept single mothers as tenants so as to avoid violent partners or spouses damaging their property and/or disturbing other residents. This was a worrying trend for this refuge as they had experienced a noticeable increase in demand for their services, having been forced to turn away almost as many women and children as they had been able to provide temporary, crisis accommodation to in a recent four-month period.

So, it is clear that it is not just a shortage of affordable private rental housing in both regions that is contributing to rural homelessness; it is also the way in which that housing is allocated to particular subgroups of the population by 'gate keepers'. In Moree, two SAAP agencies described the great difficulties they experience in securing temporary accommodation for homeless people, yet in almost the same breath commented upon the local abundance of available private rental stock. In this case, local landlords were prepared to keep housing vacant rather than rent it out to suspect tenants. Both agencies remarked upon how regularly rental properties – public and private – were vandalized by tenants. Of course, this further reduces the available pool of local housing for rent.

Relatedly, local real estate agents in both Moree and Narrabri have resorted to requesting rent references from up to as many as three previous landlords before considering renting a property to prospective tenants. It was clear that this 'policy' was not applied to all enquiring tenants but just to those about whom the real estate agent had suspicions. While all agencies contacted in Narrabri and Moree could appreciate real estate agents' desire to police tenants more strictly in the context of high rates of property damage, they also highlighted its discriminatory effects upon those groups most vulnerable to homelessness. For those (primarily Indigenous) people growing up and remaining in extended family situations, it is virtually impossible to gain access to rental accommodation for independent living under this regime. The same is true for people who have a chequered housing career and who, through rent defaults, late payment and/or property damage, have gained a poor reputation as a tenant. The 'rent references' scheme in these towns thus operates to keep some groups in, or close to, homelessness. Of course, it would be far easier for real estate agents and other landlords to make decisions about who is a reliable tenant if there was some central database containing historical and personal records of all tenants. This is no Orwellian fantasy. Almost all agencies in both regions discussed the role of TICA – a tenancy registry and database operated for Australian and New Zealand landlords – in keeping their clients out of private rental housing (TICA, 2004).

However, it is not just private sector gate keepers with their geodemographic surveillance tools who the rural homeless must confront. The New South Wales Department of Housing has recently resorted to using very short tenancies to avoid being left with violent or disruptive tenants on a long-term basis. In addition, public housing waiting lists can be extremely long, even in a rural setting. This can perpetuate the marginal housing position of vulnerable groups. In Moree, those on the public housing list can expect to wait up to six years to be housed. An Indigenous homeless support service in Moree regularly assists people on the local public waiting list who move cyclically from friend or relative to friend or relative until their welcome wears out and they need emergency housing support. Approximately one-third of this service's client base is 'revolving door' homeless – in need of crisis accommodation on a regular basis.

The family and generational issues in entrenched homelessness

There is a sizeable literature concerning the individual-level causal factors under-lying homelessness (e.g. mental health issues, alcohol abuse). However, in our discussions with SAAP agency operators in Coffs Harbour, Moree and Narrabri it became increasingly obvious that the family – sometimes reaching back several generations – played a substantial role in many people's pathway into homelessness.

For example, the growing youth homelessness issue on the Mid-North Coast was highlighted as being attributable to, in many cases, a combination of an adolescent's own mental health problems, and their parents' inability to deal with their child's psychoses. Often, such children are too young, by legislation, to stay in a local refuge, should one be available, and so end up on the street. A Coffs Harbour youth refuge worker stated that, 'These young streetwise kids are more likely to fall through the cracks, both in terms of housing and health services and being counted as part of the local homeless population.' Others who ended up in youth refuges were escaping abusive, violent family situations caused by drug and/or alcohol abuse of parents.

In the Northern SD, where the Indigenous population forms a higher proportion of the entire population and the regional homeless population relative to the rest of the State, homelessness appears strongly related to the multi-generational reproduction of poverty and suboptimal living skills. In Moree and Narrabri, all SAAP agencies interviewed commented upon the large number of clients that came from families with a history of alcohol abuse, physical violence (both within and outside the home), long-term unemployment and marginal housing conditions. The children (and there are often many) of these families essentially reproduced these conditions for themselves and their own children by dropping out of school very early, having children as teenagers themselves and becoming involved in drug and alcohol abuse and, inevitably, falling into a pattern of periodic homelessness. This is a particularly important issue as Indigenous families are usually larger – partly because they include extended family members – compared with non-Indigenous families. The manager of a local women's refuge observed, for example, that her service is beginning to provide crisis accommo-dation to the children – now young women with their own children – of women that they gave refuge to a (short) generation earlier. As a worker at a women and children's refuge in Moree observed, 'We're now seeing kids of mums that came to us escaping domestic violence a few years ago turning up here with kids of their own escaping DV – refuge kids breeding refuge kids.' In recognition that one of the key causes of these entrenched poor living skills is the lack of appropriate role models, at least one of SAAP agency in Moree runs an outreach service to teach 'life skills' (e.g. how to develop and maintain a household budget) to families in marginal housing situations.

Rurality

Rural homelessness is clearly not metropolitan homelessness in a rural environment: there are some distinct features of rural communities and their physical settings that make the experience of rural homelessness qualitatively different to urban homelessness. This is not to suggest, however, that rural homelessness is experienced in the same way in all rural regions or towns, for as the following reveals, differences exist between regions in the causes and contexts of homelessness.

A key locational factor that affects virtually all rural regions and localities relative to the capital cities and their conurbations can be described as an 'urban hierarchy' effect – the fact that the number and functional complexity of private and public sector services is generally lower in rural than in the metropolitan areas. Nor do markets for key public and private goods and services operate in the same way in all rural areas as they do in the cities, with rural housing generally much cheaper for equivalent housing stock in the capitals (Hugo and Bell, 1998). As suggested by Hugo and Bell's (1998) 'hypothesis of welfare-led counter-urbanisation', cheap housing in scenically attractive coastal areas – relative to Sydney – together with Australia's system of portable welfare payments sees large numbers of ex-urban migrants flowing into key coastal zones annually. However, for some of these people, their move to cheaper and more salubrious surroundings is a large trade-off for the abandonment of a denser support network of mental health and other welfare services.

One issue discussed by all SAAP agencies both on the coast and on the tablelands and ranges was the large number of homeless people with obvious mental health problems. Yet, with the 'deinstitutionalization' of Australia's mental health services (HREOC, 1993), and with the general decline and retraction of medical and mental health services from rural areas, the vast majority of rural towns lack the facilities and staff to provide adequately for these people's needs. This means that, at times, mentally ill people are housed inappropriately, abandoned to crisis accommodation. This combination of a paucity of mental health services in rural areas and the lure of cheap housing in high amenity coastal settings works to ensure that certain subgroups of the population continually circulate and reappear as part of the rural homeless. A homelessness support worker summed up the problems of the mentally-ill homeless person in anywhere other than a metropolitan or major regional centre:

> We used to be able to get (mental health) assessments done here but then it was shut down and now the nearest place that we can get someone assessed is Tamworth (two-and-a-half hours drive north-east of Tamworth). It's a real problem because you've got to get them there, you take them away from their social networks here, and these people (mentally-ill homeless persons awaiting assessment) are usually forced to wait around, staying in God knows what accommodation … It's a real problem out here …

Until relatively recently, rurality was also equated with tight, close-knit communities in which deep social bonds developed between residents in a

Gemeinschaft conception of social space (Wolstenholme, 1995; Philo, 1997; Sibley, 1997). A growing number of authors have also highlighted the potential – and reality – for rural communities to be riven with social conflict and for practices of exclusion and marginalization to occur (Wild, 1974; Poiner, 1990). In our discussions with SAAP agencies, both aspects of rural communities were identified as influencing the nature of homelessness in rural areas, as well as responses to it. In Coffs Harbour, the stark and high visibility of rough sleeping in the town triggered a reasonably widespread reaction amongst the community, including the local council, to try and do something about the issue.

Additionally, social networks are generally smaller and tighter in rural compared with metropolitan communities, meaning that the information 'grapevine' often operates rapidly. This may work for or against homeless people. In Narrabri, a homeless support worker noted that local business people and others often fed important information back to his service on the movements of particular clients. Equally, though, information on perceived disorderly behaviour could make its way to key local gate keepers, such as real estate agents or Federal welfare agency officers, with negative consequences for the alleged perpetrator. Rurality can be a double-edged sword for homeless people, therefore: it can offer support and invisibility, but it can just as easily take it away.

One of the critical differences between inland and coastal rural communities – though this can be overstated – is the generally high level of dependence of inland and remote towns upon a narrow economic base, dominated by farming. This situation also influences the degree and character of homelessness in a number of ways. First, with the ongoing restructuring of broadacre farms into larger and more capital-intensive units, the demand for farm workers has declined, ensuring that those with little training and/or skills remain in the ranks of the structurally long-term unemployed (or unemployable). In Moree and Narrabri, this problem has been compounded by the general shift from wool production, which had a high demand for year-round seasonal work such as shearing, crutching, lamb marking and the like, to cotton and beef, which have low demands for seasonal labour. Thus, the opportunities for people most vulnerable to marginal housing situations to earn extra cash and, for example, pay off rent arrears, has diminished.

In largely unprotected agricultural systems such as Australia's, international commodity price and currency fluctuations, together with more localized perturbations like drought, have a rapid and pervasive effect on rural towns. Through the peak of a recent drought, Narrabri has experienced a surge in the number of local homeless people as a number of live-in caretakers on local properties – often living in farmhouses abandoned after farm amalgamation – were retrenched by cash-poor farmers. These caretakers usually earn very little income but work mainly for their 'keep' and hence have few resources once forced into town.

Another crucial issue relating to homelessness in the broadacre farming belt that includes Narrabri and Moree relates to the itinerant workers who flow into the region every year. 'Cotton chipping' attracts seasonal labourers from around the country who, through their experience in following seasonal work around the country (e.g. fruit picking), are well-prepared for all aspects of the job, including finding their own accommodation. However, there are also many who join the cotton chipping gangs with little or no experience of rural life, let alone the rigours of hoeing weeds all day under the sun. Unemployed, welfare-dependent people are often provided with an advance on their unemployment pension (the 'dole') by the Federal Government's welfare agency to facilitate their travel 'out west' to the chief cotton farming zones to make money. However, once in town, temporary accommodation is often in tight supply and these people find it difficult to organize housing, having exhausted their resources, and with a fortnight to wait until the next dole payment. The potential difficulties of housing these 'cotton chippers' were highlighted recently when local cotton farmers advertised nationally that 700 cotton shipping jobs were available in the Narrabri region. Around 4,000 people arrived in response. No arrangements had been made locally to provide accommodation for the expected influx of people and many found themselves homeless for a considerable period. As a result, a special itinerant labourers' accommodation programme has been established in Narrabri.

Finally, one of the defining characteristics of the settlement pattern in the broadacre farming belts is remoteness. Most major service centres are at least one hour's drive (at 100 km/h) from each other. Therefore, it is very difficult, given poor or non-existent public transport, for marginalized individuals to escape their homelessness or poor housing situation by simply moving to the nearest town.

Conclusion

Rural homelessness is a little recognized, poorly understood and under-researched issue in Australia, a situation not dissimilar to those described in many other chapters in this volume. This chapter has aimed to foster a better appreciation of the extent, nature, causes and geographical dimensions of rural homelessness in this country by mapping it using the most reliable data from the national census and other data sources and then identifying – in coastal and inland case study regions – some of the critical factors and forces that shape pathways into homelessness and which perpetuate it. Recent innovations in the Australian Bureau of Statistics' methodology for collecting the quinquennial Census, in collaboration with Chamberlain and MacKenzie and the SAAP National Data Collection Authority, are providing researchers and policy makers with an increasingly rich and reliable database on the Australian homeless population. This snapshot of the 'stock' of homeless people reveals clearly that the stereotypical down-and-out male 'drifter' is only a relatively small component of an increasingly heterogeneous group in which women, with and without children, and children and older youth form significant components. Typically, homelessness in rural Australia affects the most marginalized subgroups of society, and those most vulnerable to becoming marginalized: Indigenous people; the mentally ill; victims of violence and abuse; those suffering from drug and/or alcohol dependence; and those in marginal housing and employment situations. Of course, it is not uncommon for homeless people to suffer from two or more of these maladies simultaneously, emphasizing the fact that disadvantage and homelessness are mutually constitutive. Importantly for the focus of this volume, though, we have shown that homelessness is almost ubiquitous across rural Australia and in many regions occurs at much higher rates than in metropolitan areas.

However, to acquire a more accurate picture of the causes of homelessness in rural Australia, and to appreciate the particular pathways into and through it, requires greater attention to 'flow' data and a more qualitative approach. In investigating the issues facing SAAP service operators in two contrasting rural regions, we have identified three key aspects of Australian rural society that give particular nuances to the causes and experiences of homelessness: housing, the family and rurality. These draw together quite neatly the dialectics of structure and agency relating to homelessness: homeless individuals and the regulatory networks which impinge upon their movement through different levels of housing adequacy and classificatory systems; the homeless individual and his/her family; and the regional economies, housing and labour markets with which they must interact on a daily basis. In combination, these three broad factors reinforce the notion that homelessness is one aspect – a key aspect – of the experience of marginalization, compounded by living in often marginal communities. In this sense, homelessness is mutually constitutive of social exclusion in rural areas. The case study research demonstrates the varying nature of homelessness in different rural regions and the challenges posed to service providers and, indeed, whole communities depending upon where they are located. While many rural regions appear under-resourced to deal adequately and appropriately with the various faces of homelessness it seems that in some communities – and for some individuals – homelessness is but a surface manifestation of deeper, more entrenched processes of alienation that potentially threaten the very fabric of social cohesion in these areas.

Acknowledgements

We are extremely grateful to Associate Professor Chris Chamberlain in helping us gain access to the 2001 homelessness data and for discussions on its use. Thanks are also due to Allan Raisin, Judy Addleton, Pam Brunner and Helen Moore for their timely aid in introducing us to relevant SAAP service providers. We also sincerely thank the many SAAP agency representatives who deal with the 'coalface' on a daily basis and made time to speak to us. Thank you also to Michael Roach, who drew Figures 12.1 and 12.4. Finally, we are grateful to the editorial team for their constructive comments on an earlier draft of this chapter.

Notes

1   For example, housing assistance programmes coordinated under the Common-wealth State Housing Agreement, Commonwealth Rent Assistance scheme and various income support payments which, apart from general transfer payments, include benefits such as those for young people in housing crisis and a range of emergency financial support.

2   As Chamberlain and MacKenzie (2003: 19–20) state, numbers of primary, secondary and tertiary homeless cannot be directly obtained from the raw census figures. In their analysis of the levels and distribution of the homeless using the 2001 Census, Chamberlain and MacKenzie adjusted and supplemented the census figures with SAAP data and information from the second national census of homeless school students to help derive the number of secondary homeless.

3   The Australian Standard Geographical Classification (ASGC) is a hierarchy of nested spatial units for which official statistics, including census data, are disseminated. The Statistical Division (SD) is the largest spatial unit below the States and Territories. All lower levels in the ASGC are devised to fit within the SD boundaries. The SD has no administrative function but is a large spatial unit encompassing broadly similar land uses, environmental gradients and communities of interest.

4   Lu Fox, one of the central characters in Tim Winton's novel, *Dirt Music*, sleeps rough on beaches in this region with numerous other backpackers, holidaymakers and 'drifters'. The high proportion of non-Indigenous people in this region's homeless population does not mean that homelessness is not an important issue for local Indigenous people, however. Innifer (2001) describes how large numbers of local Aboriginal people are forced into Broome, Kununurra and Wyndham during the cyclone season to seek shelter only to find little in the way of suitable accommodation. Many are forced into 'long grass' or 'fringe dweller' camps on the outskirts of the major towns.

5   Of course, these centres contained the greatest overall *number* of homeless people, accounting for nearly two-thirds of New South Wales's homelessness on the 2001 Census night (Chamberlain and MacKenzie, 2004b: 82).

6   The information for the case study section of this chapter was derived from structured interviews with key stakeholders in several SAAP agencies and allied

service providers in Coffs Harbour, Narrabri and Moree during early 2004.

7   See AIHW (2000) for a discussion of methodological issues related to the SAAP data collection strategy.

Chapter 13
Homelessness amongst young people in rural regions of Australia

Andrew Beer, Paul Delfabbro, Kristin Natalier, Susan Oakley, Jasmin Packer and Fiona Verity

In common with many other developed economies, public perceptions of homelessness in Australia do not focus on persons without housing in the countryside (Cloke *et al.*, 2002). As many of the chapters within this volume have noted, homelessness is usually associated with people 'living rough' in the cities. Moreoever, the stereotypes of homelessness tend to generate an image of older persons – commonly males – who are homeless. Such attitudes ignore the reality of homelessness in rural areas (Beer *et al.*, 2003a) and the over-representation of young people amongst the homeless in Australia. Almost one-third of the homeless population in Australia are under 25 years of age. Rural homelessness is a particularly pressing problem in Australia because Indigenous Australians are more likely to be homeless than the non-Indigenous population (Allwood and Rogers, 2001) and they are over-represented in the non-metropolitan parts of the nation (Hugo and Maher 1995).

This chapter considers the issues confronting homeless young people in rural regions of Australia. The challenges faced by this group may be more acute than those evident in many other, more densely settled, nations. Low population density and the distances within Australia mean that the homeless are often 500–600 kilometres from the nearest large city. It is in these large cities that services for the homeless are concentrated but rural young people moving to gain access to these supports lose the family and friendship ties that have supported them in the past. Moreover, even provincial centres often lack significant supports for the homeless – young or old.

In this chapter we will attempt to draw out the distinctive features of homelessness amongst young people in rural Australia but also to examine those issues that are common with other nations. Increasingly Australia's policy makers are looking to European solutions to dealing with homelessness and this chapter considers the potential applicability of one model – foyers. The chapter begins with a discussion of the nature, incidence and factors that give rise to homelessness amongst young people in rural areas before considering two case studies: Bunbury-Busselton in Western Australia and Mt Gambier in South Australia. The chapter then examines recent policy debates on meeting the needs of homeless young people before concluding with a discussion of lessons from other nations.

Understanding homelessness in Australia

Despite several decades of research into homelessness in Australia there is still considerable debate around the precise definition of the term 'homelessness', and how many people fall into this category. Perhaps the most widely accepted definition of homelessness is the so-called 'cultural' or 'conventional' definition first articulated by Chamberlain and MacKenzie (1992), and applied by the Australian Bureau of Statistics (ABS) in the both the 1996 and 2001 National Censuses. According to this definition, homelessness is not an objectively defined construct or benchmark, but a relative concept defined with reference to society's understanding of the minimum accommodation to which they believe each citizen is entitled (Chamberlain and MacKenzie, 2001). With a few exceptions this minimum accommodation is thought to consist of any living arrangement where people have sufficient facilities to undertake the basic functions of everyday living, such that their safety and physical health is not compromised (Centrepoint, 1995; Neil and Fopp, 1992). Such facilities include a connection to utilities, adequate living space, a bathroom, food preparation areas, sleeping space, and where their tenure is secured by a lease or other similar arrangement (Badcock and Beer, 2000). At the same time, it is recognized that this definition is subject to variation depending upon the particular circumstances prevailing (for example, family size), or the cultural beliefs or expectations of the people concerned.

In Chamberlain and MacKenzie's view, three forms of suboptimal living arrangement can be classified as homelessness. The first, termed 'primary homelessness' is generally uncontroversial, and refers to situations where people are literally without any form of conventional accommodation. This includes people living rough on the streets, in caravans, derelict buildings, squats, tents, cars, or any other improvised structure or arrangement. The second form of homelessness refers to people who are living in insecure or short-term accommodation, where there is no lease or arrangement in place to provide security or stability. Common examples include people living with friends or relatives, and those living in hostels, boarding houses, or shelters. The third and final form refers to people who live in private boarding houses for extended periods (usually three months or longer), where the accommodation is deemed suboptimal either because of the absence of basic amenities in the rooms (e.g. bathroom, kitchen), or because there is no formal lease in place to provide stability and security. This final category is considered controversial because it is more strongly defined with reference to culturally agreed definitions of acceptable accommodation and because there may be variations in the nature of the amenities available (Chamberlain and MacKenzie, 2001; Crane and Brannock, 1996).

This chapter draws upon the 'cultural' definition of homelessness and makes use of its insights to understand the circumstances of homeless young people in rural Australia. In particular it recognizes the validity of the primary, secondary and tertiary definitions of homelessness and the understanding that homeless young people often move from one form of homelessness to the next.

Pathways into homelessness for young people

Young people have different pathways into homelessness compared to adults and it is important to understand the processes that result in homelessness for this group. MacKenzie and Chamberlain (2002) suggest that homeless young people are placed across a spectrum of homelessness, ranging from occasional tertiary or secondary homelessness with infrequent exposure to risky behaviours (such as illicit drugs, crime or prostitution) through to chronic homelessness comprised of periods of 'sleeping rough', immersion in street culture and adoption of risky behaviours. While adopting MacKenzie and Chamberlain's framework, Farrin (2003) suggests that homeless young people from rural regions have a slightly different pathway into homelessness, with a longer early 'transition' period into homelessness – as the young adult remains in contact with their family and friends – but a more significant break from their past once they enter chronic homelessness. In large measure this break represents their movement from their region of birth to one of the capital cities. It is therefore important to understand the factors that contribute to homelessness amongst young Australians if we are to understand the unique features of homelessness amongst young people in rural regions.

Personal circumstances

Numerous national and international studies have documented the many factors that contribute to youth homelessness (Bridgman, 2001; Ensign and Panke, 2002; Morgan and Vincent, 1987; Neil and Fopp, 1992). Although caution must be applied in not confusing correlation with causation (Fopp, 1995), or over-estimating the importance of the personal characteristics of homeless young people, a consistent set of situational factors have emerged in the literature (Crane and Braddock, 1996). Situational factors are those relating primarily to young people's interactions with others, most notably their family and peers. One of the most commonly identified issues is abuse. Studies in Australia (Kamieniecki 2001; Zabar and Angus, 1994), the United Kingdom (Centrepoint, 1993) and in the United States (Auerswald and Eyre, 2002; Pfeifer and Oliver, 1997) reveal that a substantial proportion of homeless youth are victims of multiple forms of abuse, including sexual, physical, emotional and neglect, or general domestic violence. In Australia, Howard and Zilbert (1992), for example, found that 75 per cent of homeless people were victims of domestic violence; Levesley (1984) reported that 44 per cent of cases involved neglect, whereas the Centrepoint study in the UK found that a third had experienced either physical or sexual abuse. Studies have shown that sexual abuse is often a greater risk factor for homeless girls (Hendessi, 1992), and that this abuse often has a history extending back many years (O'Connor, 1989).

A second very common finding is that the decision for young people to leave home frequently coincides with significant family conflict (O'Connor, 1989) particularly between married partners. Young (1987) found that this was by far the most significant factor identified by young people who had left home. In many cases, this involved conflicts with existing biological parents, but research has also consistently documented the elevated risk of conflict in families involving separation and the establishment of new family structures, as might occur when a new partner enters the household (Ochiltree, 1990). Mitchell (1994), in Canada, for example, showed that among 2,033 homeless young people aged 15–24 years, those with step-parents were two and a half times more likely to leave home due to conflict, and that step-parents are frequently the perpetrators of abuse (Angus and Woodward, 1995). Maas (1995) points out, however, that the significance of these factors varies according to children's age. Abuse is much more likely to be a longer term cause of children leaving home, or being placed into state care in the interests of child protection, whereas conflicts with parents and child-initiated departures from the home are much more likely to be a relevant factor for children aged 15–17 years (Delfabbro *et al.*, 2002).

Studies of young people who have spent time in out-of-home care (foster or residential care) until the age of 18 have found that most enter care because of significant abuse, parental problems such as substance abuse, domestic violence, or mental illness (Cashmore and Paxman, 1996). Until these children are 18, care is provided by the relevant state government. However, once orders expire, care is withdrawn and young people must fend for themselves, often with inadequate preparation. Unlike other young people who can rely upon family support when they leave home (Jones, 1995), former state wards do not have such supports, and very often have little ongoing contact with their former foster carers (Cook and Lindsey, 1996). They have few practical living skills (e.g. how to budget, apply for accommodation, undertake basic household chores), and often continue to bear the psychological and emotional effects of previous abuse, separation and dislocation.

Older teenagers tend to leave home largely at their own volition, or as a result of a breakdown in the relationship with their parents. In such situations, the pathway into homelessness may be more gradual, and involve multiple short-term departures before the final decision to leave. Furthermore, in situations where parents have separated, the departure may involve a departure from more than one home (i.e. that of the father and the mother). Smith (1995), Plass and

Hotaling (1994) and Tasker (1995) found that approximately a third to 60 per cent of young people leaving home go from home to live with friends, approximately 20 per cent go to live with relatives, whereas others seek government shelters, or begin living on the streets. Thus, the transition to homelessness can vary significantly across individuals, and does not always involve a progression from less severe (secondary) to the most severe form of homelessness (primary). There are those who proceed immediately to primary homelessness, and others who experience secondary homelessness when they first leave home. As discussed below, this finding is likely to have significant implications for the nature of possible intervention strategies.

Personal factors

Young homeless people are significantly more likely to have mental health problems than their peers (Kamieneicki, 2001); to have a greater incidence of substance abuse (Unger *et al.*, 1997; Diaz *et al.*, 1997); to be more sexually at-risk both in terms of susceptibility to STDs and their involvement in prostitution (Johnson *et al.*, 1996); to be more socially isolated (McCarthy *et al.*, 2002); to have poorer physical health (Ensign, 2003); and to have a greater involvement in offending behaviour (Bessant, 2001).

It is likely that these findings are attributable both to the experience of homelessness, and also a 'selection effect', whereby young people with a higher prevalence of psychosocial difficulties are more likely to become homeless. Evidence from the studies above clearly shows that homelessness significantly increases the likelihood of young people being exposed to social groups and circumstances conducive to the development of high-risk behaviours. At the same time, given the significant over-representation of former state wards in homeless populations (Cashmore and Paxman, 1996; Maunders *et al.*, 1999), it is clear that many young people with *previous* histories of abuse, family disruption and emotional problems become homeless. Australian research by Delfabbro *et al.* (2002) and Bath (1998) shows that young people in out-of-home care score significantly worse than their peers on measures of psychosocial adjustment, and have a greater incidence of offending behaviour, school disruption and substance abuse.

The challenges of youth homelessness in rural Australia

The limited literature on homelessness in rural Australia suggests that homelessness in non-metropolitan Australia raises a different set of issues from those attached to homelessness in urban areas. In rural areas private rental markets can be very small and public rental housing entirely absent, particularly in the sparsely settled agricultural regions and the remote localities that make up the bulk of the Australian land mass (Beer *et al.*, 2003b). People often face high rental costs due to competition for scarce housing and the stock may be substandard (Yardy and Thompson, 2003). There are significant housing problems in Australia's rural or non-metropolitan regions (Beer, 1998; Minnery and Greenhalgh, 1999) and these include relatively high construction costs (Beer *et al.*, 1994), the 'redlining' of rural areas by some financial institutions (Office of Regional Development, 2002) and lower housing standards when compared with metropolitan regions (Burbridge and Winter, 1995). Many of the housing problems in rural regions arise out of the lower incomes and reduced job prospects in rural regions, as well as the more limited housing opportunities. There are simply fewer resources – accommodation options, support services, etc. – and this may severely limit an individual or household's ability to meet their housing needs.

Access to the housing stock

Access to the housing stock is one of the critical issues affecting homeless people in rural areas. While declining rural areas may have excess housing stock, many non-metropolitan regions have a shortage of housing, especially rental housing (Beer *et al.*, 2003b). Work by O'Dwyer (2002) suggests there has been growing pressure on rental housing markets in many parts of rural Australia, especially in the more densely settled areas. Yardy and Thompson (2003: 27) articulate this situation in a forthright manner:

> So what about this housing drought? The simple fact in CQ (Central Queensland) is that there is not enough accommodation; there is a chronic lack of affordable housing, and increasing issues about the standards of existing houses. CQ is not unique in experiencing these issues; they are common throughout rural Australia. There is a declining investment in building houses in rural areas, declining standards of some houses and diminishing resources for the provision of social and public housing. Yet at the same time across the region there is an increase in population, in some areas a slow and steady build, in some a slow decline, some are boom/bust and others are just BOOM.

Moreover, recent economic growth projections for Australia's regions (Adams, 2002) suggest that all of Australia's non-metropolitan regions will continue to grow over the period leading up to 2008, thereby placing extra pressure on non-metropolitan housing markets. The shortage of affordable housing options in rural areas and regional cities has important implications for young people who leave home or other care arrangements. They may be forced into homelessness because affordable accommodation simply is not available. They are then faced with the alternatives of sleeping rough, 'couch surfing', returning to unacceptable circumstances in their parental home or previous living arrangement, or being forced to leave the region.

Caravan parks are one potential low cost source of housing. Greenhalgh (2003) examined the role of caravan parks in meeting the needs of low income households in search of long-term accommodation. While her work was based in the Central West of Queensland, there are strong resonances between her findings and more anecdotal evidence about the nature of caravan park accommodation in other parts of rural Australia. She reported a number of problems with caravan park accommodation as a low cost solution to the housing needs of people in need or at risk. These difficulties included: first, the relatively high cost of caravan park accommodation, with many residents spending more than half their income on rent. People at risk of becoming homeless therefore may not be able to afford caravan park accommodation. Second, there was the reluctance of caravan parks to take on long-term tenants. A large and growing percentage of caravan parks focus on the more lucrative short-term and holiday markets. Park managers may be unwilling to provide accommodation for persons outside the paid workforce, thereby excluding most people at risk of homelessness. Third, in rural areas the number of caravan parks appears to be contracting. In many rural areas there simply may not be space in a caravan park for persons at risk of homelessness. Fourth, management practices in many caravan parks are seen to be restrictive and unwelcome by tenants. As Mowbray (1994) has noted previously, caravan park managers may impose rigid controls on tenants, who may have few if any rights under tenancy or other legislation. Homeless people may therefore be deterred from using this accommodation source. Fifth, caravan parks may be unsafe and insecure, especially for vulnerable groups.

Place and home: what role the region?

To date, our discussion of rural housing has focused on the problems confronting young people seeking affordable accommodation in rural areas. Migration to a capital city is one potential solution to the housing problems confronting this group. If housing is not available locally they could move to one of the capitals where the stock of housing is larger and there are more opportunities for employment.

There are a number of significant barriers stopping young people from rural areas moving to the cities. There are often strong emotional and other ties that bind to their region young people raised in a country town or regional city. There is empirical evidence to suggest that social capital is more strongly developed in Australia's rural areas than in the cities (Onyx and Bullen, 2000) and there is a considerable body of work on the strength of community ties in rural areas (see, for example, Kenyon and Black, 2001). Young people often place a high value on being able to live in the communities they were raised in and may be reluctant to move. In addition, while the employment prospects of unskilled young people in rural areas may be poor, they may be little better in the cities. Rural regions have lower levels of educational attainment than the cities and young people whose schooling has been disrupted are unlikely to have the formal skills sought in urban labour markets. Poor job prospects in the cities may deter some homeless young people from migrating. Third, young people from rural areas may lack the social networks and/or skills needed to successfully negotiate a transition to life in a capital city. Farrin (2003) notes from her work on the Eyre Peninsula that young people reported concern about the absence of support networks in the city for those moving for employment or education; the lack of available accommodation in these areas, poor knowledge on how to gain access to services; and a general lack of information on the resources and facilities available in cities. Fourth, Indigenous youth from a rural region would be reluctant to leave their 'country' and moving to a capital city would necessarily entail occupying the 'country' of another Indigenous people.[1] This would serve as a significant disincentive to moving (Allwood and Rogers, 2001).

Clearly there are strong practical and emotional reasons why homeless young people in rural areas are reluctant to move to the capitals. Being homeless is more than being without shelter. Homeless young people living in rural areas are able to maintain the broader community or locality dimensions of 'home' and moving to a larger urban centre may not be a realistic option. Policy development therefore needs to focus on developing solutions in the regions and places where homelessness is expressed.

Case studies of homelessness in rural Australia

Rural youth homelessness needs to be examined in detail in order to understand how multiple and complex processes shape the experience of being homeless in a rural region of Australia. This section examines two regional cities – Mount Gambier in South Australia and Bunbury-Busselton in Western Australia – in order to understand the social, economic, demographic and policy factors that affect rural youth homelessness. The two case studies highlight many of the themes discussed in earlier sections, including the problems young people confront in gaining access to the housing stock, the limited options available with respect to government-provided assistance, poor labour market opportunities and the very real contradictions between the perception of country areas as a 'rural idyll' and the reality of a rural society that may offer higher levels of social capital, but may also be less tolerant of difference in others.

The experience of homelessness in Mt Gambier

Mt Gambier is a regional city of 23,000 persons approximately 400 kilometres south-east of Adelaide in South Australia (Figure 13.1). The city derives most of its income from intensive primary production in the form of logging and wood-chipping, market gardening and dairy products. Its proximity to southern Victoria as well as many local features has made it a popular tourist destination, as well as a hub for transport and farm equipment companies.

As part of our research we conducted focus groups with representatives from government and non-government agencies as well as with approximately 15 young people aged 15–20 years. Agency representatives indicated that at least 50 young people were persistently homeless in the area, but that very few were living rough on the streets. Almost all were 'couch surfing' with friends or living in temporary or supported accommodation. Most of these young people had left home because of domestic violence or abuse, conflict with parents, new partners entering the home or their parents' unwillingness to deal with their absences or behaviour in the family home.

The young people involved in our focus groups had a very localized perception of territory: they defined their 'place' as Mt Gambier alone and expressed strongly negative sentiments about other towns within the region.

13.1 The two regional case studies

The nearby town of Millicent, for example, was linked in their minds with crime and drug addiction while the town of Naracoorte 60 kilometres to the north was largely unknown to them. In large measure their perception of the world was limited to Mt Gambier and its environs and this reflected both the spatial distribution of friends and relatives who helped support them in a period of considerable vulnerability and the very limited public transport in the region. Some of those who participated in the focus groups came from the smaller settlements and farms around Mt Gambier. Young people were drawn to the city by a mix of processes including school catchments, child support arrangements including foster care, access to income support and friendship networks that offered the prospect of a roof over their head for at least one night. Most of the young people we met with, however, came from families who lived within Mt Gambier.

Ongoing difficulties in finding stable accommodation were generally attributed to three principal factors. The first of these was the very limited supply of affordable accommodation in the area for young people. Mt Gambier has no state government-funded Supported Accommodation Assistance Program (SAAP)[2] accommodation, an expensive private rental market, while public rental housing is restricted to those aged 18 years and older. Supported accommodation options tend to be restricted to young families rather than individual young people. Caravan parks generally refuse to take young homeless people, and boarding houses or hostels are considered undesirable because they are used by recently released prisoners from Mt Gambier gaol. A second problem was that there were too few support workers and outreach services to assist the transition to independent living. Young people often do not have the necessary skills to live independently, allowed the houses to fall into neglect, or allowed other young people to use the house as a 'drop-in' centre.

A third difficulty was that young people often did not have the financial resources to live independently. Connection fees for utility bills were considered excessive; young people were unable to secure insurance on their possessions; and many reported difficulties in obtaining sustained employment. Although supermarket and shop work was available, young men reported that they were seldom able to take advantage of these opportunities. At the same time, the sawmills offered little alternative employment because they did not regard young people as having sufficient maturity to undertake high-risk factory or lumber work, while the Coonawarra wine-growing region required reliable private transport each morning and night.

In response to these concerns both young people and agency representatives expressed an urgent need for an emergency youth shelter in Mt Gambier with 24-hour services to respond to crises. There was also a need for a supervised 'drop-in' centre where young people could socialize, network, and become aware of the services that were available. Indeed, this idea of a service directory had been specifically identified in a recently initiated Integrated Community Youth Service (ICYS) programme located in the Mt Gambier region. More broadly, agencies called for greater state support for SAAP housing in the region and recognition that Mt Gambier, despite its reputation for wealth, also contained significant pockets of social disadvantage. As one agency reported, the difficulties experienced in Mt Gambier have in some cases led to referrals to services on the south coast of Victoria, where youth accommodation services were seen to be better developed. In other instances the only assistance youth workers could provide was a bus ticket to Adelaide where the young person *might* receive housing assistance. In many cases the young people resisted the option of moving to the capital city and returned to their family home.

The experience of homelessness in Bunbury and Busselton

In Western Australia we investigated two regional centres, Bunbury and Busselton in the South West of that state. In 1996 the Greater Bunbury region, which includes Bunbury and Busselton, had a population of approximately 24,885.

Many of the young people we interviewed as part of our research discussed tensions and abuse within the home as reasons for being homeless. Some of the circumstances the young people raised included living with abuse as well as family conflict and tensions emerging from 'blended' families. Other young people left home because they wanted to be independent earlier than their parents were willing to accept. In addition, service providers identified an increase in the incidence of homeless young males who have experienced abuse; young pregnant woman and/or mothers; and young people without positive role models in their lives. An increasing trend of young people being violent to their parents was another trigger to homelessness observed by agency workers.

One of the key issues to emerge in discussions with homeless young people was the importance of their own capacity for self-definition. In the main, 'homelessness' was seen to be much more than the absence of bricks and mortar. In response to questions about what it is to be 'homeless', a recurring theme emerged. Being homeless was:

- not having a roof over their head, not having a safe and secure accommodation, not having an emotional attachment to home, not having a choice about where home is, not having enough food to eat,
- having to live portably – eating packaged food, restrictions on clothing and possessions, not being able to have pets and not belonging.

In common with Mt Gambier, young people in the South West of Western Australia adopted very parochial views about other towns and places. Some of the young people in Bunbury had never visited Busselton, despite the fact that it was only 40 kilometres away and the largest neighbouring town within the region. The parochialism evident in both of the case studies discussed here suggests that young homeless people in rural areas are constantly confronted by a sense of vulnerability or powerlessness, and identifying with one place – and the associated support networks – is one way they can exercise a degree of control over the external environment.

Some respondents identified 'generational homelessness' or situations where their parents experienced homelessness and now the young people were seen to reproduce similar experiences. An example was of parents who grew up in state care. This has affected their sense of 'place' and/or 'home' and the level of personal skills and knowledge gained by them. This in turn has made bringing up their children more challenging. In other places service workers have reported inter-generational discrimination within the housing market. Landlords and real estate agents may refuse to rent properties to young people on the basis of the 'reputation' of their families. In this instance, small housing markets and tight-knit communities are a considerable disadvantage.

Lesbian and gay young people were considered to be particularly vulnerable in rural areas. According to some of the agency workers interviewed, lesbian and gay young people inevitably leave and move to the city in the belief that they will experience acceptance and be able to express their sexuality openly and safely. Bullying as well as problems at school were raised as triggers into homelessness by both focus group participants and service providers.

The young homeless people who participated in this study engaged in a range of ways of ensuring they had a place to sleep. It was not uncommon for young people to 'bed-hop' or 'couch surf'. Some reside in short-term accommodation offered by the Bunbury Youth Accommodation Program (BUNYAP) who also operate a crisis accommodation service for people aged between 15 and 19 years. Others move from friend to friend, find an older adult to take them in, or move from place to place as opportunities arise, for example, backpacker lodgings and caravan parks in the off-season. While there was evidence of a capacity by young people to be mobile, many more young people were 'place-bound' because they preferred to stay in their own community. For example, some young people in Busselton did not want to relocate to accommodation in Bunbury because this was not a place they were familiar with.

The experiences of young homeless people were gendered. More young women were likely to be taken in by other families, whereas there was a perception that young males are capable of looking after themselves on the streets. However, young males and females do share common experiences. The preparedness to engage in illicit activity to gain either money or lodging, for example drug dealing or living with older people for sex, was increasing according to service workers.

The lack of housing options, restricted employment opportunities as well as low incomes was a significant problem for young people. Young people revealed that finding suitable housing was made even more difficult with the increasing cost of the rental market and the shrinking of the size of the public housing stock. Securing employment to pay for accommodation was made more difficult by an increasingly segmented and restricted labour market. As one young person commented: 'Finding a job in this town is difficult. There is a catch 22 operating – to get a job you need experience, to get experience you need a job.' The absence of education qualifications was a further barrier to gaining a job and an income. Education was seen as critically important to breaking the cycle of homelessness and in the words of one young person 'Education is the beginning and the end'. For those young people relying on income support, the difficulties of navigating and negotiating mutual obligation arrangements and understanding changes to the youth allowance have contributed to many not receiving income through Centrelink, the Federal Government's income support agency.

Stereotypical images of young people not being reliable or trustworthy tenants were seen to hinder young people gaining access to the private rental housing stock. There was a stigmatization about how young people behave: young people are often constructed as 'trouble' or 'irresponsible'. For example, one young couple interviewed were expecting a child and had been living in a caravan in the local caravan park. They were asked to leave by the manger once it was revealed that they were both under 18 years old. This was despite them paying the rent on time and not attracting trouble or disturbing other caravan occupants. According to one service provider, young people in lesbian and gay relationships often find it difficult to access the private rental market. Local real estate agents will not let properties to same sex couples.

Based on the findings from Bunbury and Busselton it is evident that there are unique challenges confronting homeless young people in rural areas compared with those in urban centres. At one level there is a lack of services and infrastructure. For example, there is limited public transport and a lack of specialist services available (for example, mental health and support services for gay and lesbian young people). There is also a limited range of accommodation/referral options available for young people when crisis accommodation services are full. Some of the difficulties associated with young people being able to obtain rental accommodation have been raised previously. It was seen that real estate agents/ landlords were reluctant to rent to young people under 18 years of age and this was compounded in small communities where young people are 'well-known' for the wrong reasons, or are associated with certain family reputations. Youth unemployment is also high in rural areas and limited access to transport makes finding work and fulfilling the job search requirements of Centrelink more difficult.

On another level there are issues derived from the nature of 'place'. Young people identified isolation in rural places as constraining. Low levels of activity and stimulation in rural areas were connected to poor mental health. Living on a farm and feeling isolated could lead to depression and/or to drug involvement. A common perception expressed during the interviews was that rural areas are conservative and mirror conservative views of society. Alongside these conservative and seemingly intolerant views was a perception that living in the country was a safe and welcoming place. Examples were given of young people moving from the city to the country in the belief that this could remove them from a cycle of homelessness and drug taking. They believed that they would find work, obtain affordable housing and develop and belong to social networks that were safe and nurturing, and not based on drugs or abuse.

Lessons from the case studies

The two case studies have emphasized some of the distinctive features of youth homelessness in rural areas compared with the youth homelessness in the major urban areas. Homeless young people in the rural regions of Australia have strong feelings of attachment to the places where they have grown up and these feelings are reinforced by supportive networks, as reflected in the prevalence of 'couch surfing'. Rural Australia is also seen to be more judgemental and less accepting of difference amongst homeless young people, as reflected in the attitudes to, and experience of, gay young people. Finally, resource constraints exert an acute influence on homeless young people in rural regions; this includes a more limited stock of housing, poor access to employment, and limited services. It is worth noting that the two case studies discussed above would not be perceived as 'rural' by many Australians as each is a major urban centre by national standards. However, the complete absence of services in smaller towns drives young people to the larger centres for support.

Policy issues and challenges

Policies that deal with youth homelessness generally may not be appropriate or feasible when applied to rural settings. This is a major challenge for policy makers, especially given the low priority awarded to rural issues in many areas of social policy within Australia. This section considers the direction of youth homelessness policies in Australia generally and their links with policy evolution in some of the other nations discussed in this volume. It outlines some of the general policy directions at the national level and considers the potential application of foyers for addressing rural youth homelessness in Australia.

Major policy directions

According to Crane and Brannock (1996), there has been a significant change in Australian homelessness policy over the last decade, and this has significantly influenced the nature of services that have been developed. As encapsulated in the Human Rights and Equal Opportunity Commission report on homeless children in 1989, the House of Representatives or (Morris) Report (1995), and Prime Ministerial Taskforce on Youth Homelessness (1996), the fundamental direction of this change has been a switch away from a sole emphasis on *ad hoc* (or tertiary) interventions, to a greater emphasis on early, or primary and secondary intervention strategies. Essentially, these involve attempts to target services either to those at greatest risk of homelessness (secondary intervention), or to examine ways of identifying and assisting children before they come to be at risk (primary intervention). Further coinciding with this policy change has been a movement towards case-management as a preferred strategy for interventions, and an emphasis on family preservation in out-of-home care policy. This has led to a greater focus on interventions involving families, schools, or other educational bodies because of their potentially strategic role in prevention and/or early intervention.

Interestingly, this change in policy focus is mirrored by almost identical policy changes in other Commonwealth countries such as the United Kingdom, which are outlined in the Homelessness Act (2002) and the report 'More than a Roof'. In this report it is recognized that authorities are unlikely, in the near future, to be able meet the needs of the growing population of homeless people in Britain, and that the emphasis should switch from a concentration on housing market failures to social exclusion, and the causes of homelessness. Indeed, one requirement of the new Homelessness Act is the requirement that all local council authorities provide a documented response to how they are dealing with homelessness. The aim is to address the long-term causes of homelessness, to develop early intervention and pre-crisis prevention strategies, and to target families at risk of homelessness. Not surprisingly, many of the strategies recommended as part of the most recent innovation documents in the UK (for example, 'The Safe in the City' report produced by Centrepoint and the Peabody Trust) are almost identical to those in Australia.

Chamberlain and MacKenzie (2001) report that the Prime Ministerial Taskforce has funded 26 pilot projects at a cost of $8 million and provided $22 million in funding to programmes such as Reconnect, and the Full Service Schools Program that was introduced in conjunction with the establishment of the Youth

Allowance. The Federally funded Reconnect project involves over 90 services Australia-wide and has assisted over 6,000 young people (Reconnect Data Report 2001). This programme has been targeted at young people at risk while they are still living with their parents and has reported a 75 per cent success rate. Reconnect is designed to reduce homelessness by reconciling relationships between young people and their families, predominantly via the use of counseling and mediation services (Evans and Shaver, 2001).

Notes

1   This can be a relatively difficult concept for Europeans (including non-Indigenous Australians). To place this in context, Adelaide, the capital of South Australia, is on the traditional lands of the Kuarna people, whereas an Indigenous Australian from Goolwa, 100 km to the south east, would be a Nararnjirri person. Moving to the capital, therefore, involves both leaving their own 'country' and occupying the 'country' of another Aboriginal nation.

2   The Supported Accommodation Assistance Program (SAAP) is the primary vehicle for delivering assistance to homeless people in Australia. SAAP services may be State Government funded, Federal Government funded, or receive financial support from both tiers of government. In Australia, local governments have little role in meeting the needs of homeless people.

Chapter 14

Places to stand but not necessarily to dwell

The paradox of rural homelessness in New Zealand

Robin Kearns

Introduction

A decade earlier than the recent promotion of New Zealand as 'Middle Earth' (thanks to Peter Jackson's *Lord of the Rings* trilogy), the film *Once Were Warriors* offered a more down-to-earth vista on life in Aotearoa. The opening sequence begins by focusing on what appears to be a classically 'clean green' image of empty green fields and mountains. However, as the camera pans away, this scene turns into a tourist promotion-style billboard high above an Auckland motorway passing a gritty, ghetto-like neighbourhood. This parody of the 'calendar' style representation of New Zealand reminds the viewer of what lies behind and beyond promotional images (Wall, 1997; Le Heron, 2004).

This visual sequence also reflects dimensions of the paradox of homelessness in New Zealand. First, and notwithstanding the literature on the downstream effects of the so-called 'New Zealand experiment' (Kelsey, 1995), New Zealand is regarded internationally as a well-housed nation. While true in relative terms, the contrast between face-value perceptions of 'paradise' and the behind-the-scenes reality of those living on the 'margins' is stark (Kearns *et al.*, 1991). At a second level, the grittiness of the city depicted in *Once Were Warriors* that contrasts with the idyllic and pastoral rural billboard in the opening sequence mirrors the discourse of homelessness in New Zealand: the homeless are regarded as being an urban 'problem', and only recently has the rural population been recognized as including, if not homeless people, then at least significant numbers of people in serious housing need.

These 'numbers' are not a cross-section of the population; rather New Zealand's indigenous Maori population that comprises 14 per cent of the national population are disproportionately represented among the poorly housed. This chapter surveys the context for this level of Maori representation among the poorly housed in rural areas of New Zealand, and asks to what extent the term 'homeless' is applicable to people who often experience a sense of home that is stronger than their status as being adequately housed.

Homelessness and the New Zealand rural idyll

A search for media articles on the theme of 'rural homelessness' in New Zealand's major daily newspapers over recent years produces no results. Although the references to homelessness that do appear in the media are never qualified as exclusively 'urban', by default cities are assumed to be the sites where homelessness is problematized and politicized. This prominence can likely be accounted for by the sheer visibility of the relatively few street people in major cities as opposed to their rural counterparts who dwell in dilapidated or overcrowded housing 'off the beaten track'.

Examples of the prominence of the urban in discourses of homelessness in New Zealand abound. For instance, Wellington City Council recently proposed to outlaw camping and sleeping in public places, ending a long-standing unwritten policy to leave the homeless alone unless they were causing problems. Mayor Prendergast reports Wellingtonians as being intimidated by homeless people, even when they are not legally causing problems (*Dominion Post*, 2003). Further north in Auckland, Mayor Banks claims that 'many people ... sleeping rough have been doing it for too long'. As a consequence, the city council will work through its law and order committee to 'make government-funded agencies accountable for them' (*Sunday Star Times*, 2004).

The central parts of New Zealand's major cities are therefore sites where the lives of homeless people are being legislated and constrained in an attempt to purify public space. Those affected by such rulings are, however, but the most visible subset of those lacking shelter (Cooper, 2000). Emergency houses and overcrowded rental accommodation hide the more widespread face of serious housing need in the South Auckland suburbs fictionalized in *Once Were Warriors* (Cheer *et al.*, 2002).

Beyond the cities, however, the less publicized phenomenon of rural housing need is accounted for by estimate and anecdote. While accurate counts remain as elusive as in other countries, two studies in the late 1980s offered informed estimates of between 17,000 and 20,000 (Waldegrave and Sawrey, 1994; Percy and Johnson, 1988). Roberts reports these figures as having 'widespread acceptance as the actual level of homelessness' (1988: 160). Percy and Johnson (1988) offered the more comprehensive set of estimates, breaking the data down according to region and ethnicity (Table 14.1). Two observations from this data are notable: first, that the major ethnic representation among the households deemed to be homeless was Maori; and, second, that while most were urban, a nonetheless significant proportion of the distribution was located in rural regions.

Although comprising estimates, the data may well have been conservative, given that a key marker of those people in 'urgent housing need' (i.e. a proxy for being homeless) was their status as being waitlisted for state housing. However, this measure of demand is directly linked to the supply of state housing. Given

Table 14.1 Approximate distribution and ethnicity of households with children in serious housing need by regions covered

	Maori	Pacific Island Polynesian	Pakeha	Total
Central and Southern Auckland	3,150	5,250	2,100	10,500
Christchurch	–	–	200	200
Rotorua/Whakatane	800	–	200	1,000
Wellington Region	400	400	200	1,000
Hamilton	60	–	40	100
Palmerston North	30	–	70	100
Nelson/Motueka	–	–	100	100
Northland	2,500	–	–	2,500
East Coast	2,000	–	–	2,000
All areas covered	8,940	5,650	2,910	17,500
% of total	51	32	17	100

Source: Percy and Johnson, 'Serious Housing Need', Chapter 5, in National Housing Commission Five Yearly Report (1988)

that there is minimal public housing in rural areas, the prevalence of *rural* homelessness may well have therefore been underestimated in this data.

It is noticeable, however, that Table 14.1 in fact reports 'serious housing need' not homelessness per se. This usage conforms to a persistent pattern of categorization: homeless persons are deemed to be those people who are visible in their embodied proneness *on* the street, whereas others who are (albeit precariously) sheltered are considered to have housing needs (of varying degrees of seriousness). The arbitrariness of this distinction is arguably more the case in rural areas where there are no streets for homelessness persons to be 'on'. If, therefore we take the state of homelessness to be dependent on the existence of 'the street' in the discursive construction of the social order in New Zealand, then there is, and can be, no homelessness beyond settlements with streets.

However, there is another, more local logic that undermines the utility and applicability of the 'homeless' category in New Zealand. This is the fact that the group most vulnerable to 'incipient homelessness' in rural New Zealand (i.e. Maori), generally have a strong sense of home even when they are poorly housed or even lacking shelter. By way of example, those living precariously in rural New Zealand are less likely to be identified in media reports or by welfare agencies as being homeless than is the case with their urban counterparts. Rather, the *consequences* of dwelling in marginal conditions are frequently constructed as an abdication of responsibility (rather than a convergence of precarious circumstances). For instance in 1977, three young children, the eldest only 11, died when the shack where they were living in the remote Northland community of Matauri Bay caught fire. A candle had started the fire in their 'home' that had neither electricity nor running water. This is but an indicative example of a not infrequent occurrence.

Roots of belonging

What are the determinants of such precarious living? During the 1990s, a significant counterurbanization among Maori became apparent (see Waldegrave and Stuart, 1997). This movement was both a reflection of and contributor to, rural housing need and homelessness (e.g. Davey and Kearns, 1994; Murphy and Urlich-Cloher, 1996; Saville-Smith and Thorns, 2001). The limited literature linking population movement to housing outcomes generally sees housing as being closely linked to other cultural and socio-economic determinants of well-being for Maori (National Health Committee, 1998).

From a cultural vantage point, moves from cities back to rural areas may be prompted as much by a sense that a locality is 'home' rather than any immediate prospect of gaining a dwelling to call home (Kearns and Smith, 1994). Extending the metaphor of 'home', it is reasonable to suggest that 'return migration' might involve some individuals and families coming home to where they spent their childhood, and others 'coming home' to family-owned land that they have never lived on before. Being able to feel so deeply at home in a place is possible because Maori regard themselves as *tangata whenua* (literally, people of the land), a status they acquired by living entirely off the land within their tribal territories for generations prior to European contact. In the foregoing name, the word *whenua* has especial significance, carrying two meanings: land and placenta. These otherwise disparate referents are tangibly linked in a Maori practice (now adopted by some Pakeha, or European New Zealanders). This practice involves the burying of the placenta after a child is born on land where there is some pre-existing significance. Thus, people and land become inextricably linked through the materiality and spirituality of life itself. As Smith lyrically puts it:

> the phrase *tangata whenua* has a deeper, more significant meaning of being 'composed of' the elements of that place through generations and centuries of occupation; for the people not only passed 'through' or over the land but the land passed 'through' and made up the substance of the people both physically and metaphysically.
>
> (Smith, 2004)

To say that a precariously housed Maori family is homeless may, therefore, have some currency using internationalised or secular terminology, but is something of a contradiction in terms when it is acknowledged that a deep sense of belonging and 'being at home' pervades their residence within a rural landscape. This recognition has resonances in acknowledgement of the problematic conflation of the ontological notion of 'home' with the materiality of 'housing' in the homelessness literature (cf. Veness, 1993). The difference in constructs between home and housing is thus acutely apparent with respect to Maori whose connections with their *turangawaewae* (site of belonging, literally 'a place to stand') may be latent, yet nonetheless potent. Indeed prominent commentators such as Durie (1998) have advocated the nurturing of this dimension of belonging and its linkage to mental health and general well-being, thus adding a breadth to housing and health debates that in western scientific discourse largely centre on the material dwelling itself.

Routes back home

Over the last 15 years, specific regions have witnessed significant return migration of Maori population. This movement has partially restored a balance that was upset in the mid-twentieth century. Until this time, 75 per cent of the national Maori population lived in rural areas. However, by 1981, 80 per cent of Maori were urban dwellers (Metge, 1995). The 1990s saw a reversal, beginning with the Northland region, for instance, having the highest regional influx of Maori between 1986 and 1991, with a net gain of 1,700. Most Maori returning to Northland came from Auckland and many may have moved because of unemployment brought about by economic and service sector restructuring (Le Heron and Pawson, 1996). In particular, corporatization in the state sector from 1984 onwards led agencies such as the Post Office, Railways and New Zealand Forestry Service to reduce their workforces significantly, resulting in many Maori in rural as well as urban areas becoming unemployed. Heavy job losses also occurred in manufacturing industries. The restructuring which led to reduction of the labour force and the general liberalization of the national economy thus offset the gains made from the return of resources to Maori (Spoonley, 1996).

Evidence suggests that rural return migration has continued as welfare benefit cuts, market rentals for state housing and other economic hardships have encouraged families to return to *turangawaewae*. In the 1950s, Metge argued that Auckland Maori knew that if 'worst came to worst, they could always go home' (1959: 176). Four decades later, this opportunity identified by Metge was seized upon by many, with families and older people returning to rural areas (Gardiner, 1997). While, to some degree, this trend of return migration was driven by cultural considerations (i.e. a facet of the so-called Maori 'renaissance') involving a return to tribal areas and home *marae* (meeting places, spiritual homes), there were also strong economic imperatives involved (Butterworth, 1991). Indeed, 25 years ago, Stokes (1979: 36) found that

> the desires of many urban Maori to return to ancestral land are genuine and strongly felt but ... such aspirations are often thwarted by the practical necessities of rural living.

Housing is one central 'practical necessity'. While the migration decisions of many were tempered by housing availability, for others the imperative to return to rural areas was stronger than the realization that housing options were severely limited.

Conceptualizing rural homelessness

Notwithstanding difficulties with the cultural appropriateness of the 'homeless' term, there are clear and persistent housing issues related to residence in, and increasing return to, rural areas by Maori. Arguably, 'sleeping rough' is a more viable activity in rural areas than in cities, yet rarely are people in the country found to be visibly homeless in New Zealand. Rather, after a long period in which New Zealand congratulated itself on being one of the 'best housed countries in the world', reports in the 1980s and 1990s began to appear arguing that Maori were experiencing crises with respect to housing (Douglas, 1986; Maori Women's Research Project, 1991). Issues such as crowding, structural unsoundness and excessive cost relative to income were being noted, yet on the whole, these issues were considered 'on the margins' both geographically (mainly within the Northland and East Coast regions) and demographically (affecting only a small proportion of very low income New Zealanders). Indeed, Maori home ownership rates remain high in these regions (Te Puni Kokiri, 2004). As Saville-Smith and Thorns (2001) note, this perceived marginality of 'the Maori housing problem' was one factor that allowed the occurrence of the housing reforms of the 1990s which involved the enactment of a series of radical measures. These measures included: market rents being applied to public housing stock, the sale of a large proportion of state houses, the disposal of the public mortgage portfolio and housing assistance being moved away from direct provision of houses to the granting of an 'accommodation supplement' that could be paid to either state or private landlords (Murphy and Kearns, 1994). In sum, this policy package

> was predicated on the notion that housing problems in New Zealand were demand-side problems rather than supply-side problems and that the quality, quantity and distribution of the housing stock was largely adequate.
>
> (Saville-Smith and Thorns, 2001: 11)

The material condition, and actual numbers, of dwellings in the rural regions that are most populated by Maori provide evidence that the demand-side, single-market assumptions of the housing reforms have been overly simplistic. Rather 'there are profound supply-side problems in some localities and for some segments of the housing market' (Saville-Smith and Thorns, 2001: 11).

Supply-side problems relate not only to the number of dwellings available, but also issues that have tended to undermine the ability of New Zealand housing stock to provide, or amplify, a sense of home. First, New Zealand housing tends to be poorly maintained, a trend that is naturally exacerbated in household and localities characterized by receipt of low incomes (Clark *et al.*, 2000). Newer dwellings in some rural areas have also been noted as being of poor construction, design and finishing (Saville-Smith, 1999). Second, the largely uniform size and design of New Zealand houses has frequently meant that there is a mismatch between dwelling and household size that disproportionately occurs within Maori and Pacific households. The mix of crowded, expensive and poor quality dwellings is mirrored in stresses including food poverty (Cheer *et al.*, 2002), elevated rates of infectious disease (Baker *et al.*, 2000) and heightened dampness with associated respiratory ill-health (Matheson *et al.*, 2001).

These issues are compounded in regions to which there has been return migration (Scott and Kearns, 2001; Waldegrave and Stuart, 1997). Frequently, return to a tribal area prior to gaining a house to rent or buy leads to the occupation of temporary and makeshift dwellings, or staying with *whanau* (extended family). Both situations may result in overcrowding and comprise an expression of 'incipient homelessness' (Kearns *et al.*, 1992). In combination, overcrowding and substandard housing have been linked to not only physical but mental health problems. Indeed, a leading commentator on Maori health, Mason Durie sees poor housing as one of a set of socio-economic issues that 'are more relevant to health than ... strategies for delivering health services' (1998: 191).

Policy responses to precarious housing

In the decade since the market-based housing reforms of the National Government in the 1990s, a number of policy responses have been designed in acknowledgement of demand-side problems and the absence of real housing markets in some rural areas. In a decade when increasing recognition of Maori aspirations has occurred across the social policy spectrum, the paradox of Maori being both at home yet precariously housed in tents, shacks or abandoned vehicles has been increasingly recognized. A major stumbling block to usual forms of assisted lending for the construction of new dwellings (in the face of near-absent rental markets) has been the fact that much Maori land remains collectively owned and not in individual title (Kearns, 2001). One intervention designed to arrest the vulnerability of Maori families to incipient homelessness is the *Papakainga* Lending Scheme, first introduced under the fourth Labour government in 1986. Deriving from a term loosely meaning 'where the family gathers', *Papakainga* lending was introduced nationally following a brief pilot period in Northland and on the East Coast of the North Island. The scheme is a means for the state to remove legal impediments to Maori building houses on multiply owned ancestral land through the issuing of occupation licenses and loans secured against the house rather than the house *and* land, as in standard mortgage agreements. Two fundamental conditions of the scheme are: that the house in question must be easily removable from the land should the mortgagor default on their loan; and that permission must be obtained from the land trustees. The rationale is that most private sector lending institutions are unwilling to provide finance to people wanting to build on Maori land with multiple owners. However, under the *Papakainga* programme, the government provides finance to low-income earners to enable them to build on collectively owned land on terms and conditions that exclude the land from the security required for the loan. The effect of this arrangement is that, in the event of a mortgagee sale, the land is not at risk. Loans are dependent on the house being transportable to cover the situation when there is a default on the mortgage (Davey and Kearns, 1994).

Other solutions designed to address the demand for rural housing involved local people more closely. In the mid-1980s, Ministry of Housing officials and regional Maori *runanga* (tribal councils) identified the 'deposit gap' – the inability of impoverished households to attain the required deposit for *Paapakainga* scheme participation – as an explanation for the decline in its popularity (from 264 loans being issued in 1990/1 to only 31 in 1995/6). *Runanga* representatives also pointed to problems including a general lack of awareness among Maori of information on housing options, opportunities and responsibilities (Kearns, 2001). In 1994, the government announced a commitment to addressing Maori rural housing problems, especially in these regions, with the goal of collaboration between Ngapuhi and Ngati Porou *iwi* (tribes) and Housing Corporation (HCNZ) executives. New HCNZ lending programmes were devised to address problems inherent in existing finding arrangements such as the deposit requirement of 20 per cent for general lending and 15 per cent for *Papakainga* lending. These initiatives reflected an acceptance by the government of the extent of Maori rural housing problems and the limits of demand-side assistance.

While the needs of Maori *have* been recognized in the regions such as Northland, Ferguson (1994) argues that policy responses aimed at incorporating Maori values such as the desire to live on ancestral land have been peripheral to the wider housing objectives of the state in New Zealand. Schemes tailored to Maori values remained tied to market mechanisms such as floating interest rates, making housing inaccessible to the majority of applicants, most of whom are dependent on welfare payments (Kearns, 2001). A change occurred through the development of the Low Deposit Rural Lending Scheme, which was targeted at Maori, although anyone in rural areas could apply. Through this scheme the Minister of Housing and the relevant *runanga* agreed to a programme in which, among other things, a relaxed deposit requirement of 5 per cent will apply where the proposed borrower has successfully completed a series of 12 workshop courses on home ownership skills run by the *runanga* with supervision and content provided by HCNZ. *Iwi* are also funded to provide on-going advice for participants and graduates. These initiatives represent new partnerships between local Maori and the state, consistent with the broader imperatives of 'collaborative problem-solving' in social services (Fougere, 2001).

Notwithstanding these innovations, rates of uptake have been modest. Following one such scheme in Northland, only 10 per cent of those who had graduated from a course in 1998 had succeeded in obtaining a mortgage. This failure was attributed to the difficulty of raising the required 5 per cent deposit (Scott and Kearns, 2001). It also seems likely that people who have been long-term social welfare beneficiaries would not be able to afford to maintain mortgage repayments and other costs associated with home ownership. This situation indicates that 'incipient homelessness' must be remedied by not only easing the pathways to housing provision, but also by generating work opportunities that can assist people to move beyond the 'breadline'.

More recently, the controversial 'Closing the Gaps' report of the Labour-led government of 2000 highlighted the urgent need for government to work more closely with rural communities to improve outcomes for Maori. One outcome was Special Housing Action Zones, a joint programme between Te Puni Kokiri (TPK – the Ministry of Maori Development) and the renamed Housing New Zealand Corporation (HNZC). Recognizing the deeply concerning issues of poor repair and affordability, this programme provided funding and services for Maori communities to repair existing houses or build new houses. While the programme has operated throughout New Zealand, high priority is given to Maori communities occupying their *papakainga* (original home base) or living on land in multiple-ownership in Northland, Eastern Bay of Plenty and Tairawhiti (the East Coast). In terms of process, TPK works with the community and housing agencies to establish a Community Housing Plan. HNZC then puts this plan into action, building new homes or carrying out repairs (TPK, 2004). More recently, Special Housing Action Zones have been established in which TPK will develop 'comprehensive housing plans' which 'identif(y) exactly what your housing needs are, what resources your community can contribute, and how your housing needs can be met', by paying the costs associated with planning the building of new housing (TPK, 2004).

The foregoing survey of issues relating to housing opportunities for rural Maori raises a number of questions. First, if prospects for housing are limited, why do people still 'come home', risking the occupation of precarious dwelling places? Second, how do Maori who have returned to rural areas feel about their moves after resettlement and how have they adjusted to 'coming home'? I turn to narrative evidence to address these questions.

At home on the margins: voices from a valley

In this section of the chapter, I focus on the Northland locality of Mangakahia to examine the reasons for, responses to and implications of population movement with respect to housing and homelessness. The case study draws on narratives collected in 1996 from 16 Maori respondents who had returned to the Mangakahia Valley over the previous decade, supplemented by interviews and participant observation and originally reported in Scott and Kearns (2001; see also Scott *et al.*, 1997). In conveying the challenges faced by residents who 'came home', we inevitably confront the spectre of homelessness and the limits of local housing initiatives. Specifically, we must turn to narratives from the people themselves to understand why return migration has been undertaken, what have been the experiences of residents after resettlement and how they perceived state policy in light of their moves.

By way of introduction, the Mangakahia Valley (1996 population: 2,907, of whom 579 or 20 per cent were Maori) is situated in the middle of the Northland region of New Zealand, to the west of the city of Whangarei (population 43,000). The Mangakahia River is an important geographical as well as symbolic focus for the valley. Pastoral farming predominates, with dairy farms having been enlarging through the 1990s, with the amalgamation of neighbouring farms. In the south-east, volcanic soils which formerly supported dairy farming have been subdivided into horticultural and 'lifestyle' blocks. There are small pockets of collectively owned Maori land in the district, most of which is leased out to farmers or remains covered in native bush.

As described by Scott and Kearns (2001), the Mangakahia Valley can be regarded as a microcosm of rural issues in Northland. In common with other parts of the region, there is widespread evidence of in-migration and the dramatic changes in the supply and organization of rural services. These factors have contributed to a changing community fabric. Residents talked of the movement of individuals and families back to the valley as being both a source of concern and a basis for the revitalization of Maori communities. Most of those people interviewed stated that 'returning home' was a permanent move. A key factor precipitating a return to this area was disillusionment with city life. For many, the employment and educational opportunities as well as general quality of life in urban centres had not lived up to their expectations. All interviewees had returned during the preceding decade and all expressed a strong sense of belonging to the valley. For them, ancestral and present-day *whanau* (family) connections to the area made Mangakahia a preferred place to live. People valued the sense of belonging that came with such connections, together with the support of *whanau* and the ability to live on ancestral land. In most cases, those who had returned had spent some of their childhood in the Mangakahia, but this was not always the case. For example, one woman was the first of her generation to live there and spoke of 'coming home' to family land where one parent had grown up (Scott and Kearns, 2001).

Several respondents said that they returned because it was time for them to become involved in their *marae* or local community. Along with such 'pull' factors, 'push' factors were also reported. Return migration was, for most, a choice made in response to becoming dependent on social welfare benefits. Faced with living on state benefits, returning home was seen as the best option. Social workers and teachers spoke of their concerns that some Maori who had returned to the valley were living in extremely substandard conditions. In some cases, this involved crowded or makeshift conditions:

> [In the Mangakahia Valley] a family were living in a cowshed with open walls for a while … a family were living in a tin shack by a river, just a lean-to that they had put up themselves. People coming back to small country cottages devoid of windows and power and things like that, they just move in, and the place is overcrowded. (Social service worker)

For such people, 'coming home' to live in a lean-to by the river for the summer and be, in one sense, homeless may well be preferable to living in crowded urban conditions. Based on the stories reported in Scott and Kearns (2001), most research participants were living in substandard conditions not by choice but out of necessity and a sense of alienation from 'the system'. Based on research in the nearby Hokianga district (Kearns and Reinken, 1994), it is likely that some of these people are not included in national census statistics, and the under-enumeration means that the local Maori population is unlikely to be adequately provided for in forecasted social service budgets. Thus, following Cloke *et al.* (2000), these people who 'come home' are hidden from view by both the ordinariness of their temporary dwellings (e.g. 'just a lean-to that they had put up') and their (intentional or otherwise) avoidance of the gaze of the state.

Many of the Maori who returned to the Mangakahia Valley sought to establish a dwelling on family land, despite constraints in terms of money and access to land. There was clearly a need for housing provision in the valley at the time, as many Maori had already begun to return to the area. One woman explained their living conditions prior to getting a *Papakainga* housing scheme (PHS) home:

> The Health Department and the district nurse and all them got on our case, 'oh you can't bring up children with no running water and no power and no flush toilet' … there were rats and in your sleep they're jumping over your head …

Another commented on the net effect of the new *Papakainga* schemes in the 1990s:

> The most exciting thing I guess happened in terms of Papakainga which was in the late 80s … those people got homes, even though they struggle to pay for them. And so I guess that saw the returning, by that stage, from the cities, of others who all of a sudden were made aware that they had land that could be of some use to them in terms of building a whare [house] and bringing up children, because the cost of living in the north is so much cheaper of course than living in Auckland.

In one valley, the foregoing narratives speak to the tenuous housing circumstances embraced by returnees, yet the hope and practical assistance provided by interventions like the *Papakainga* scheme. While affordability problems remain for families opting for this type of housing, the key breakthrough was that new housing was at last possible on communal land and otherwise poorly housed families could achieve robust shelter, having left the city, moved north and acted on their homing instinct.

Conclusion

There are two rural New Zealands. First, there are the largely unpeopled landscapes of breathtaking beauty, an example of which was ironically depicted on a billboard that cleverly opens the movie *Once Were Warriors*. Second, there are the rural regions less travelled by tourists that reveal materially deprived, yet spiritually rich, Maori communities. This chapter has focused on the latter rural New Zealand. Here, I have argued, rural homelessness must be considered within the context of the recent and pervasive effects of restructuring in New Zealand which 'can never be wholly contained, either sectorally or geographically'(Knight and Joseph, 1999: 6). In other words, incipient, if not actual, homelessness (in the sense of people bereft of adequate dwellings) can be seen as an outcome of restructuring processes that have cut across institutional and geographical boundaries and profoundly altered the face of rural New Zealand. Changes in employment opportunities, welfare benefit eligibility and housing policy have, for instance, synergistic effects that ripple between the urban and the rural in terms of human experience (Kearns and Joseph, 1997). However, for Maori, the counterurbanization trend that has led to the repopulation of certain remote rural areas of the North Island has also been spurred by a re-valuation of community and traditional values. As the foregoing narratives illustrated, this trend is as much about people seeking home as leaving home.

Compared to the 'purified space' of the English countryside, the rural regions of Northland and East Cape in New Zealand are perceived, at least in part, as feral areas where productive activity is limited, and activities at odds with the urban order occur (e.g. Walker et al., 1998; Ryks, 2002). Thus, although homelessness is predominantly coded an urban problem, the phenomenon of being precariously housed in certain (predominantly Maori) rural regions is recognized as a problem, but connected to a persistent discourse of culpability (North and South, 1994). In other words, people living in poor housing are easily perceived to have made choices to move to and live in remote rural regions. What political commentary and public opinion invariably miss is the 'structure' component of the structure/agency equation: that constrained opportunities often strongly influence migration decisions and structure lives relocated on ancestral land.

This willingness to risk *becoming homeless* for the sake of *being at home* raises a terminological paradox that is particularly evident in the New Zealand case. For many Maori, belonging constitutes a complex anchoring in time and place expressed in both the recitation of *whakapapa* (genealogy) and identification of significant landscape features (e.g. *maunga* – hills or mountains) (Smith, 2004). Thus while the authorities in cities like Wellington propose regulatory mechanisms to banish 'camping out' in order to purify their streets of homeless persons, in rural districts the more effective solution to Maori homelessness has been found: the stabilization of communities through satisfying people's quests for roots through interventions like the *Papakainga* and low deposit lending schemes.

The New Zealand case leads to the conclusion that, as elsewhere in western countries, homelessness is predominantly constructed in political and media-generated discourse as an 'urban' problem. This chapter has shown, using a combination of evidence (e.g. quantitative estimates, ground-level narratives), that the rural experience of homelessness is less one of abject lack of shelter and more to do with the occupation of poor quality, crowded or unaffordable housing. While the presence of this 'incipient homelessness' has been recognized within social policy for some time, it was subsumed in housing policy driven by demand-side solutions in the 1990s and has only recently been creatively addressed as an expression of crisis in housing supply.

Acknowledgement

The Mangakahia case study draws on ethnographic work published in Scott and Kearns (2001) and undertaken by Kathryn Scott as part of the project 'Definition and Analysis of Sustainable Land-based Production', funded by the Foundation for Research, Science and Technology.

Chapter 15

Writing/righting rural homelessness

Paul Cloke and Paul Milbourne

Homelessness and rurality

Although by no means an exhaustive survey of current knowledge about and understandings of homelessness as it occurs in rural areas of the 'developed' world, the preceding chapters suggest thematic discourses which offer vital clues to the next phase of research into rural homelessness. It is immediately obvious from these accounts that the previously reported propensity to regard homelessness as an *urban* phenomenon is by no means restricted to the UK and the US where the bulk of research on this issue has so far been carried out. Throughout the book, authors refer to the widespread perception that homelessness is an urban problem, and that where it occurs in rural areas it is unseen, unacknowledged and largely unattended. The overlooking and underestimation of rural homelessness is linked to a broad assumption that if rural people become homeless they will gravitate to the cities where infrastructure exists to meet their needs. Homelessness, then, becomes conflated with out-migration. Whether because a nation as a whole carries the reputation of being 'well-housed' (as is reported here in the cases of Canada and New Zealand), or whether rural areas themselves are seen as housing-rich, or spaces of community and well-being, the very idea of there being homelessness in rural areas can turn into the literally unthinkable.

Yet evidence abounds in these chapters that we need to think the unthinkable; that even in housing-rich nations and in prosperous rural regions, as well as in more depressed rural areas with seemingly plenty of spare housing, homelessness exists in various forms and is not automatically exported to the cities. One important strand of further analysis, then, is to investigate more closely the ways in which the state is imposing order on the complexity of everyday life by making homelessness *legible* in certain spaces and amongst certain social groups, yet *illegible* elsewhere. Geisler and George in Chapter 3 suggest that regimes of legibility serve to blot out the contradictions and compromises of state histories of resource allocation. In the context of their study of American Indians, they argue that both the legibility and illegibility of rural homelessness require emphasis if ways are to be found for Native Indians to be 'at home' rather than homeless in current society.

Authors have regularly begged important questions in their chapters about how homelessness is defined, and how it is measured. Both definitions and data are tools of legibility and illegibility. Contestations of how homelessness should/ could be defined serve to provide critical appreciation of the issues involved, but at the same time they muddy the waters of how to know homelessness *conceptually*. In the US, homelessness tends to be defined in terms of a person lacking fixed, regular and adequate residence – a definition which Geisler and George regard as of limited use in rural areas because it fails to take account of culturally divergent attitudes towards housing, home-place and tenure rights. As Calrera and Ruiz write in the Spanish context, any definition of homelessness focusing on a *situation* characterized by lack of adequate housing tends to omit important variations in personal conduct. They refer instead to a conceptualization of homelessness which emphasizes those people who cannot access adequate housing that suits their personal situation.

Defining homelessness is therefore, in O'Sullivan's words, 'problematic, contested and emotionally charged'. At worst it can reduce homelessness to houselessness (see Hanninen's introduction to Chapter 10), and at very worst it can be mixed with moral representations to suggest 'acceptable' forms of homeless people (local, settled, invisible) and more 'culpable' discourses of a kind of homelessness that is non-local, passing through, and visibly the consequence of people's own choices (see Kearns's discussion of 'feral' homelessness in Chapter 14). In many cases previous folklores of rural homelessness, suggesting the nomadic life of rough sleeping men (tramps, hobos, swaggies), continue to dominate how rural homelessness is known. The authors in this book are clear in their insistence that rural homelessness must render legible a wider range of people – experiences relating to lack of adequate housing, and a fuller range of people-practices (such as disablement, dispossession and so on – see Chapter 10) which assemble to discriminate against various different social groups and types. Here, Hanninen's chapter is again helpful to the cause, emphasizing not only that homelessness is performatively brought to life through efforts to define it, but also that homelessness is a relational consequence of the different practices which constitute it as an assemblage. Recognizing these practices necessitates situational perspectives which will differ significantly within the category 'rural'.

It follows that attempts to render homelessness legible through measurement will also be contested and politicized. Some of the chapters in this book offer a serious attempt to use available data in the US (Chapter 2), UK (Chapter 6), and Australia (Chapter 12) to gain insight into the scale, extent and trajectory of housing need and homelessness in rural areas. Given the seductive persuasiveness of numbers as 'evidence' by which policy-makers can attempt to change things, such analyses can be both politically progressive and entirely necessary in any task of regulating rural homelessness. Yet the necessity to work with official data which are not fit-for-purpose, or which are so contested as to raise doubts about their practical and political validity, raises crucial questions about how homelessness in rural areas is 'known'. In some contexts, data bases are interpreted simply but forcefully as obscurantist (Chapter 2); allowing particular groups of rural people to 'fall through the cracks' of state agencies can be viewed as systematic omission by which states deliberately choose not to make legible the welfare needs of others. Elsewhere, attempts to provide data on rural homelessness are acknowledged as useful if flawed mechanisms of enumeration.

Overall, it is clear that nowhere do we have a clear picture of the degree of homelessness in rural areas. The range of chapters in this book offer varying degrees of omission, obscurity and potential picturing. In New Zealand, for example, Kearns suggests that knowledge about rural housing need and homelessness is informed by 'estimate and anecdote'. Elsewhere, the principal source of enumeration draws on the activities of local authorities in assessing and responding to housing need. In some cases (see Chapters 6, 10 and 11) systematic recording of how authorities accept certain numbers of rural people as homeless (variously defined) has allowed both spatial and time-series variation to be analysed. Inevitably these seemingly authoritative measurements become instrumental in policy analysis and process, yet this book is littered with cautionary tales of how these enumerations entail undercounting, variations in what is recorded and how, and how rates of acknowledgement of homelessness can be tied, practically and politically, to the scope which authorities have to respond, for example in terms of available stocks of social housing. So while these data can be used to suggest that rural homelessness compares with, or even exceeds (see Chapter 12), national averages, they can also have the reverse political impact in fuelling interpretations that rural homelessness is insignificant. O'Sullivan's analysis of the Irish context is a case in point. Data on housing needs can support the conclusion that homelessness does not appear to be a serious problem (at least in quantitative terms) in rural Ireland, but an equally valid conclusion would be that rural homelessness is substantially undercounted in Ireland's rural areas. More generally with these variations in how definition and data produce so many different ways of knowing – of rendering legible and illegible – rural homelessness, it is difficult to reach an overall conclusion about the extent of rural homelessness. The conclusion must be, first, to acknowledge that rural homelessness is universally *more significant* than it is acknowledged to be in public and political discourses and, second, to insist that a greater degree of research effort is required to investigate the between-spaces and the invisible people not dealt with in official statistics.

How, then, can we make homelessness known in our rural areas? The excellent research reported on here offers a number of starting points. In some nations now the official gaze has turned to enumeration by headcount, using a census of sightings of on-street homeless people to assess the problem of rooflessness or rough sleeping. O'Sullivan reminds us that headcounts of homeless people in rural areas are nothing new – he refers to counts of 'homeless persons observed wandering on the public highways' in the 1920s in Ireland. However, there are two immediate problems with headcounts in rural settings. First, homelessness in rural areas is usually not 'on-street', and without a framework of dedicated temporary accommodation in these areas (an obvious point of congregation for 'head-counting') homelessness often takes a far less visible form than its urban counterpart. Second, headcounts – even in city locations – are thought to be flawed as enumeration measures (see Cloke *et al.*, 2000a) and especially so in smaller places (Cloke *et al.*, 2000b). As Hanninen confirms in Chapter 10, the standard presupposition that in small rural municipalities the homeless are personally well known to local authorities cannot always be taken for granted.

Rather, an initiative for further research into rural homelessness needs more intensive methods of thick description. In the UK context, research has turned to interviews with people who are, or have recently been, homeless in a rural context. Such interviews require a considerable commitment of time and service because of obvious questions about access to such people and about the ethics of close interaction with people who are often in a desperate plight (see Cloke *et al.*, 2000c). Elsewhere, fruitful research has focused on posing questions to service providers (see, for example, Chapters 2 and 9). Even though many rural areas are devoid of targeted homelessness services, narratives about rural homelessness can be drawn from regional case files and from interviews with local generic welfare service providers or with more specific homelessness service providers further along the settlement network. Many authors have fruitfully adopted a case study approach, in which data sources can be interconnected with more ethnographic materials, and case studies can either be spatial or social (see for example Salamon and MacTavish's analysis in Chapter 4) or both.

These various processes of legibility and illegibility are inevitably overlain by axes of moral coding which are actively shaping the practices and processes which make homeless people knowable. As we argue in Chapter 8, the process of making known the rural homeless vacillates between an under-determination and an over-determination. Homeless people can become a shadowy and uncertain absence, hidden away or ignored, or they can become an over-determined caricature, ripe for vilification through discourses of culpability. Such moral order is neither fixed nor similar throughout different studies of rurality. However, both the wilderness of under-determination and the visibility of over-determination conspire against appropriate discursive recognition of rural homelessness.

Rurality and homelessness

If how we 'know' homelessness can be seen to shape our understanding of rural homelessness, then so too does how we 'know' rurality. This book has deliberately focused on research undertaken in a series of so-called 'developed' nations. Throwing our gaze onto the wider rural regions of the two-thirds world would have forced us to engage with other, perhaps in some ways more closely acknowledged, forms of rural homelessness and landlessness. Indeed one conclusion that is prompted by this book is the potential fruitfulness of a rural study which crosses over the boundary so often established between 'developed' and 'developing' contexts. In the case of indigenous peoples, for example, we can still learn much from the postcolonial critiques of how colonial modernism traps such peoples into forced conditions of dependency, deprivation and landlessness. Even so the different ruralities represented in and by the nations discussed in this book present us with considerable complexity and difference rather than any sense of homogeneity of space, culture or network.

As Aron and others make clear, defining rurality is as contested a process as defining homelessness. Moving beyond the mechanics of how definition prompts legibility, it will also be clear from this book that we are talking here about very different material and cultural spaces of rurality. In the UK, rural spaces have been subject to social constrictions of idyll-ism, suggesting places where communities are close-knit, and which offer the benefits both of a proximity to nature and an escape from urban-based problematics. Rural life somehow becomes characterized as problem-free in such places; indeed rural communities work actively to purify their space by establishing orthodoxies and expectations which preclude the othernesses presented by poor or broken people. As Robinson puts it, the symbolic markers of contemporary homelessness are absent from rural areas in the UK. Consider then rural Ireland – somewhat similar but very significantly different. According to O'Sullivan, rural Ireland is vested with symbolic invocations of the superiority of rural life – an Arcadian utopia for both nationalism and Catholicism – and despite economic regeneration, counterurbanization and important European in-migration over the last 30 years or so, a sentimentality about the positive attributes of rurality lingers in contemporary discourses. So too does a welfare history which is integrally associated with the strength of religious institutions in rural settings.

Compare these ruralities with that in parts of Spain (Chapter 9) where high levels of ageing population and continuing rampant depopulation suggest not only a sustained demographic recession but also the abandonment of some settlements. Again here, the strength of religious presence has been significant in informal welfare provision, and state-sector welfare is in its infancy and is seen by Cabrera and Ruiz to be 'continually forgotten and postponed'. On a much larger scale, Argent and Rolley's picture of inland rural Australia carries some of the same markers. Economic restructuring of the farm sector, rationalization of public and private sector services and the associated processes of rural depopulation have placed whole communities at risk. Rural life in such places has significant anti-idyllic aspects. Even New Zealand, which carries symbologies of paradise and space-for-all, can be seen as a place of stark contrast between such perceptions and the behind-the-scenes realities of living on the margins (see Chapter 14). As Kearns tells us, compared to the 'purified space' of the English countryside, the rural regions of Northland and East Cape in New Zealand are perceived at least in part in terms of 'feral' ruralities.

So, we need to reiterate that there is no one rurality, but rather many ruralities. In the huge land masses of North America and Australia, these varying ruralities occur within single nations, while elsewhere nations seem to be more uniform, even if this perception is usually false, as in Chapter 6 where homelessness in rural Wales and rural Scotland is differentiated from the so-called rural English idyll. Equally some of the contexts discussed in this book reflect the significant presence of nations within nations, posing important questions about how for example Maori, Aboriginal, Native Indian and Inuit peoples experience particular forms of homelessness.

The point of emphasizing these many ruralities is surely to argue that rurality and homelessness couple differentially in different contexts. In the UK, research suggests a tendency for the *non-coupling* of rurality and homelessness, partly because homelessness is often performed invisibly, and partly because idyll-ized constructions of rural living tend to cloak out social problems such as poverty, crime and homelessness which would otherwise challenge these hegemonic discourses. As Hanninen puts it in the Finnish context, rurality can be presented in terms of a space in which homeless people as 'others' are easily out-of-sight, hidden in multiple folds of spatial and social complexity. Elsewhere, there is no necessary philosophical dissonance between homelessness and rurality; rather than being out-of-place in purified space, homeless people represent an under-appreciated part of the normality of the anti-idyll – neglected in terms of being known not as homeless but by some other discursive category, whether social or cultural.

Variations in rurality also present other, more material benchmarks for how rural homelessness becomes known. For example, there is a strong sense throughout this book that a homeless existence built around rough sleeping is much more difficult in rural settings than in the city. As Aron notes, because there are few or no shelters in rural areas, and settlement patterns are so dispersed, living on the street may not be possible, and as Kearns so cogently argues, rural areas are effectively places where there are no streets to be homeless on. Although rural rough sleeping has been encountered in UK research, this tends to be influenced by weather conditions, and therefore restricted to summer months, a trend which is exaggerated in most of rural Canada, for example, where Bruce tells us that particularly unfriendly weather and climate are simply not conducive to living on the streets, with the consequence that the risk of becoming homeless for an individual or household is a really frightening prospect. Different rural contexts present different material landscapes and conditions which shape the likely and even possible configurations of 'being homeless'. We need to know much more about these materialities, and how they are negotiated by rural people. The 'habitus' of rural homelessness is a major research void.

Equally, and perhaps more obviously, the differential state, quality, affordability and accessibility of local housing markets will also influence localized manifestations of rural homelessness. There is sporadic evidence throughout the book of very significant local housing conditions. Aron observes that, while housing costs are often lower in rural areas, so too are services, meaning that rent burdens in rural communities can actually be higher than in urban places. These conditions deserve close attention both in terms of the potential overall effect on homelessness, and for the inevitable spatial differentials within that overall picture. The varying availability of rented housing, and in some cases the low utilization of available rental dwellings suggest complex and nuanced frameworks of housing opportunity and housing desirability in particular places.

If we are to draw an overall conclusion about rurality and homelessness from the evidence presented in this book it would be that there is little indication of significant *absolute* homelessness in rural areas. Despite the suggestion that rough sleeping does occur (see, for example, Chapter 8), researchers have not as yet uncovered any rural equivalent of the city-based rough sleeping phenomenon. There is evidence from longitudinal studies of homeless people who end up in cities that the lack of services in small towns and rural areas does dictate that emergency absolute homelessness is often catered for in urban centres where shelters, drop-ins and soup-runs 'support' an experience of sleeping rough. This does not mean, however, that homelessness is absent from rural places; it is merely the case that informal networks of care (families doubling up, sofa surfing with friends, various forms of temporary accommodation and so on) in rural areas serve, as Bruce puts it, to keep people 'off the roads' and 'out of the woods'. The short-term presence of absolute homelessness is thereby masked, and rural areas appear to be characterized only by at-risk forms of homelessness. Much more detailed research evidence is required to clarify these relations between absolute and at-risk forms of homelessness in rural settings.

Rural homelessness as an assemblage of practices

Contemporary accounts of homelessness in western society suggest that people become homeless both because of a general background of impoverishment and because of specific life-crises associated with the loss of work or income, the breakdown of personal relations, the occurrence of various forms of deinstitutionalization, the onset of debilitating addiction or dependency, and the gap between the cost and availability of affordable housing and state welfare payments. Evidence from different chapters varies as to how particular characteristics of susceptibility figure in any national or local picture. In Chapter 6, for example, it is suggested that homeless people in rural areas of the UK are less likely than those in urban settings to comprise vulnerable groups, such as people experiencing domestic violence or living with physical or mental disability. Instead, 90 per cent of recorded cases of homelessness were associated with a loss of rented or tied accommodation, a relative being unable or unwilling to 'double up' two households in one dwelling, a relationship breakdown or an inability to keep up with mortgage payments. Bruce's case study of St Stephen in Canada also characterizes at-risk population, in this instance the elderly, social welfare benefit recipients (including those with long-term disabilities) and the working poor. Other chapter authors zero in on other vulnerable and at-risk groups, including Native Americans (Chapter 3), trailer-park residents (Chapter 4), 'foreign' seasonal workers, asylum seekers and gypsies (Chapter 9), deinstitutionalized outcasts (Chapter 11), indigenous Australians (Chapters 12 and 13), lesbian/gay couples (Chapter 13), single women with children (Chapter 12) and indigenous Maori populations (Chapter 14). Clearly, alongside the need for urgent exploration of the habitus of homelessness in rural areas, there is an equally urgent need to investigate how specific social groups become particularly at-risk in particular habitus-places.

These specificities of habitus and 'at-riskness' lend credence to Hanninen's contention (Chapter 10) that situations of homelessness should be regarded as complex assemblages of practices, characterized in different ways by a lack of connectivity and/or a lack of stability. Hanninen identifies four dynamic aspects of these assemblages which we use here to summarize some of the principal findings from the book as a whole. Each of the four can be interconnected in multiple ways and can elicit different power effects, and so they should not be regarded as separate or mutually exclusive.

Disablement

Here we recognize a set of practices which inhibit or pre-empt the capacity of a homeless person to care for him- or herself, to regulate their conduct and to avoid risk. In broad terms, disablement refers most commonly to alcohol or drug dependency, illness and young people who escape from their families at an immature age with no affordable alternative means of dwelling. These practices are often less than visible in a rural setting, but close research examination of individual biographies of mobility begins to reveal that not all such practices lead inexorably to an outmigration to the service- and market-rich spaces of the city. In Chapters 7 and 8 for example, we read of individual cases of disablement: Matt's early disablement due to breakdown of his family security; Elsa's alcohol addiction and related psychiatric illness; Dave and Suzy's connections between alcohol and criminality. We suspect that practices of disablement are amongst the most under-researched aspects of being at risk of homelessness in rural communities.

Dispossession

Practices associated with dispossession thwart homeless people's self-recognition as part of a social entity, whether that be society, nation, state or market-society. This book offers evidence of highly significant cultural dispossession experienced by First Nation peoples in North America and Australasia. Geisler and George in Chapter 3 highlight the landlessness of Native peoples in the US as a vital but unrecognized practice of de facto homelessness, which is likely to continue unabated so long as the appropriation of Indian Country lands by non-Indians remains unchallenged, with Indians alienated materially and culturally, and placed into positions of landless homelessness in their own homes. Similarly Aboriginal Canadians living on reserves designated by the federal government for collective Aboriginal settlement experience an inevitable lack of security of tenure due to the inability to own land or property, which can only be held collectively (Chapter 5). Practices of dispossession are also graphically illustrated in the New Zealand context by Kearns (Chapter 14), who charts the 'moving back' of Maori people from the city to rural localities which they regard as home. Often such return migration is practised without any immediate prospect of gaining access to a dwelling which they could call 'home', necessitating occupation of temporary and makeshift dwellings (such as tents, shacks or abandoned vehicles), or staying with extended family (*whenau*) and contributing to incipient homelessness in the rural area concerned. Thus the willingness to risk becoming homeless for the sake of being at home points to a broader practice of being dispossessed of appropriate habitation rights in home territory.

Displacement

Displacement refers to practices of territorial transformation by which homeless people find it impossible to find their place, to dwell in it and to hold onto it. They therefore engage in cycles of moving somewhere else, transforming into something else, and continually being in-between places, out-of-place, and generally unable to become at home where they are. Such displacement is recognizable in the mobilities of many homeless people. In Chapter 8, we emphasized a range of different mobilities practised by people who at some stage were homeless in a rural area. These include the classic 'moving out' of the rural to gain access to city-based services and opportunities, but also the restless mobility of homeless people within rural areas, adjusting their circumstances temporarily by staying with friends/family or inhabiting temporary or makeshift dwellings in the hope of re-establishing themselves in the area. We also noted the possibility of displacement into and through rural areas by people seeking their answers to homelessness away from the problematic temptations and dangers of the city. Some are attracted by seasonal employment or by New Age traveller sites. Some may settle in the area concerned, but mostly there is a restlessness which militates against putting down roots – a restlessness which is exacerbated and sometimes shaped by the refusal of local communities to accept such people as in-place. Where indigenous peoples are culturally nomadic (see, for example, Chapters 12 and 13 on Australia), similar kinds of displacement, and therefore placelessness can occur.

Disaffiliation

Rural homelessness is also co-constituted by practices of disaffiliation which bring about a dissociation of social bonds resulting in an inability to achieve social belonging, integration or even sometimes interaction. Disaffiliation can be brought about by a range of mobilities or in-site differences. For example, Salamon and MacTavish's account of the owners and renters of mobile homes on trailer parks in the US identifies a very significant set of quasi-homeless risks and practices. Because trailer-park residents do not own the land on which their trailer is parked, they are at risk of homelessness. Because the sites of trailer parks are segregated from adjacent communities – often on the edge of town – residents will rarely mix with people in that local community. Indeed trailer-park living is often associated with stigmatizing representations such as 'Trailer Trash'. Mobile home owners and renters often identify themselves as rural or small town people, but lack attachment to the place where they live, despite its being rural. Their sense of transience, otherness and spatial distinction adds up to disaffiliation. In similar vein, Cabrera and Ruiz's study of homelessness in rural Spain emphasizes the position of itinerant workers providing seasonal labour for agricultural harvesting. Here, the transience of these workers is compounded by their experiences as foreigners, immigrants, asylum seekers or gypsies. These combinations of identities and practices result in disaffiliation from local communities.

These different sets of practices variously constitute the complex assemblage which is homelessness in rural areas. They help identify the significant disadvantage that occurs when people are unable to or prevented from making use of society's relations and institutions. Particular social groups will be involved in the power relations of multiple practices – dispossession, for example, will often be linked with disaffiliation, and disablement with displacement. This understanding of rural homelessness in terms of the complex assemblage of practices begs important questions about both the governing of the society in which homelessness is practised, and the governing of the homeless self. It also, perhaps, offers some kind of agenda for governmentalities which emphasize enablement, repossession, replacement and affiliation as key practices for addressing rural homelessness.

Righting rural homelessness?

Although it was not the intention for this book to identify progressive policies, schemes or practices for dealing with rural homelessness, many authors have nevertheless begun to identify existing and potential policy responses which are worth noting here. What we can suggest from the conclusions reached by individual chapter authors is that there are three broad but important principles which should be applied to the task of responding to homelessness in rural areas. First, habitus matters. There are no global answers to rural homelessness because both rurality and homelessness exhibit important variations when examined at a local scale. Responses, then, need to be tailored to the specific needs of people in particular rural settings. Second, and related to the first principle, responses to rural homelessness need to focus on at-risk people occupying the in-between spaces of culture and society in these habitus settings. Third, responses to rural homelessness should seek to reverse the 'practices of assemblage' discussed above; that is, anti-homelessness policies should practise enablement, repossession, replacement and reaffiliation for the at-risk or homeless groups concerned.

Authors in this book allude to a range of existing and potential programmes of response to conditions and circumstances experienced by homeless people in rural settings. Perhaps the most obvious sector of response is that of housing provision for those who are homeless and at risk of homelessness. In Chapter 2, for example, Aron outlines a federal initiative in the US aimed at ending chronic street homelessness. Here available emergency shelters, and other short-term solutions (such as hotel vouchers) are reserved for people with acute needs, who are homeless for the first time or as the result of life-crises such as job-loss or eviction from housing. By contrast, transitional settings are provided for people under legal supervision, for example by the legal justice or child welfare systems, or for those who have been victims of family violence. Other groups of homeless people, including those with chronic needs, are moved directly from the streets into permanent supportive housing. As Aron points out, there remain very significant challenges in rural areas in developing systems of permanent supportive housing even though the costs of real estate may be advantageous in rural locales.

Using this US model as a litmus test for the problems associated with responding to rural homelessness, we can suggest a number of potential difficulties. As this book has clearly demonstrated, most rural homelessness is not of the 'chronic street' variety, and in most of the rural areas described in the various chapters there is little evidence of an effective system of emergency shelters or programmes of short-term alternative emergency housing. There may be a case for proposing urgent investment in such programmes, perhaps using the idea of foyers described in Chapter 13. Foyers do appear to represent an idea which can be responsive to different social and cultural conditions in different rural localities. Equally, there is little evidence here that 'housing first' programmes would be underwritten by sufficient available housing in many types of rural settings. Not only would such programmes require supportive political will and resourcing – factors which do not seem to be the stock-in-trade of rural governance – but there is a danger that low-grade rented housing opportunities in rural areas can place people in a kind of quasi-homelessness. Salamon and MacTavish's account of living in trailer parks is an extreme case in point (see Chapter 4). Here, the rural poor are given an opportunity to climb out of homelessness, but their ongoing financial, structural and social insecurities are likely to lead to a circling in and out of homelessness, rather than a solution to it. So while housing-first programmes are appealing in rural areas which lack elaborate homeless-specific systems of response, they are capable of maintaining 'at-risk' people in 'in-between' spaces and of reinforcing rather than counteracting the practices of homelessness assemblage.

What, then, can be done for the rural homeless besides provision of emergency infrastructure? Three responsive themes emerge tentatively in this book. First, there is potential for programmes of *early intervention* amongst particular groups of rural people who are at risk of homelessness. Bruce's account of the Canadian Regional Homelessness Fund describes the funding and support given there to help small communities to establish local support services to prevent at-risk individuals and families from becoming homeless and to help stabilize their living conditions. Second, there is potential for programmes to target specific *at-risk* groups. One of the core themes of this book has been the extreme problems of tenure experienced by landless indigenous peoples in their home territories. These complex bundles of need require specific priority response, not only identifying native peoples as at-risk, but affording them comprehensive repossession of land as well as living rights. Third, there is the less tangible but equally significant issue of promoting core values of *compassion* for disadvantaged others in rural settings. Although rural communities are apt to be presented as sites of mutual aid and self-help, and accepting that indeed some rural places clearly exhibit characteristics of charity and generosity, it remains the case that rurality can also be intertwined with political conservatism, moral individualism and cultural tendencies to blame the victim. Given these propensities, it seems that the promotion, enablement and replacement of spaces of compassionate reaffiliation in rural areas will be a vital prerequisite to the righting of rural homelessness. If the cloying conservatisms of the purifying idyll or the feral anti-idyll can be counteracted in rural areas, then politically costly programmes of welfare support for homeless people are much more likely to take root, and compassionate spaces of care will enable at-risk groups to enjoy a belonging and affiliation in rural areas which is currently denied them.

References

Chapter 1

Cairns, L. (2002) Rural homelessness, *Creative Resistance*, http://www.creativeresistance.ca/awareness01/2002-nov10-rural-homelessness-leslie-cairns (accessed 2 Sept. 2005).

Cloke, P., Milbourne, P. and Widdowfield, R. (2000a) The hidden and emerging spaces of rural homelessness, *Environment and Planning A*, 32: 77–90.

Cloke, P., Milbourne, P. and Widdowfield, R. (2000b) Homelessness and rurality: out of place in purified space, *Environment and Planning D: Society and Space*, 18(6): 715–35.

Cloke, P., Milbourne, P. and Widdowfield, R. (2001a) The local spaces of welfare provision: responding to homelessness in rural England, *Political Geography*, 20(4): 493–512.

Cloke, P., Milbourne, P. and Widdowfield, R. (2001b) The geographies of homelessness in rural England, *Regional Studies*, 35(1): 23–37.

Cloke, P., Milbourne, P. and Widdowfield, R. (2001c) Interconnecting rurality and homelessness: evidence from local authority homelessness officers in England and Wales, *Journal of Rural Studies*, 17: 99–111.

Cloke, P., Milbourne, P. and Widdowfield, R. (2001d) Homelessness and rurality: exploring connections in local spaces of rural England, *Sociologia Ruralis*, 41(4): 438–53.

Cloke, P., Milbourne, P. and Widdowfield, R. (2002) *Rural Homelessness: Issues, Experiences and Policy Responses*, Bristol: Policy Press.

First, R., Rife, J. and Toomey, B. (1990) Homelessness in rural areas – causes, patterns and trends, *Social Work*, 39: 97–108.

Fitchen, J. (1991) Homelessness in rural places: perspectives from upstate New York, *Urban Anthropology*, 20(3): 177–210.

Fitchen, J. (1992) On the edge of homelessness: rural poverty and housing insecurity, *Rural Sociology*, 57(2): 173–93.

Hutin, J. and Wright, T. (eds) (1997) *International Critical Perspectives on Homelessness*, London: Routledge.

Lambert, C., Jeffers, S., Burton, P. and Bramley, G. (1992) *Homelessness in Rural Areas*, London: Rural Development Commission.

Patton, L (1998) The rural homeless, in the Committee on Health Care for Homeless People (eds) *Homelessness, Health and Human Needs*, Washington, DC: National Academy Press.

Robinson, D. (2002) *Estimating Homelessness in Rural Areas*, Sheffield: Sheffield Hallam University.

Streich, L., Havell, C. and Spafford, J. (2002) *Preventing Homelessness in the Countryside … What Works?*, Cheltenham: Countryside Agency.

Wright, T. (1997) Introduction, in J. Hutin and T. Wright (eds) *International Critical Perspectives on Homelessness*, London: Routledge.

Chapter 2

Andrews, D. (2002) Farm health care as a social justice issue: the role of faith-based organizations, Wisconsin, Madison: Wisconsin Farm Health Summit, University of Wisconsin at Madison. Available online at http://www.ncrlc.com/web02_ncrlcRP.html (1 May 2004).

Beale, C. L. (1996) Rural prisons: an update. *Rural Development Perspectives*, 11(2): 25–7. Available online at http://www.ers.usda.gov/publications/rdp/rdp296/rdp296d.pdf (1 May 2004).

Beale, C. L. (2004) Anatomy of nonmetro high-poverty areas: common plight distinctive in nature, *Amber Waves*, Washington, DC: Economic Research Service, US Department of Agriculture.

Burt, M. (1996) *Rural Homelessness: A Report on the Findings and Implications of RECD's Rural Homelessness Conferences*, Washington, DC: US Department of Agriculture, Rural Economic and Community Development.

Burt, M. R. (2001) *What Will It Take to End Homelessness?* Urban Institute Brief. Washington, DC: Urban Institute. Available online at http://www.urban.org/UploadedPDF/end_homelessness.pdf (1 May 2004).

Burt, M., Aron, L. and Lee, E. (2001) *Helping America's Homeless: Emergency Shelter or Affordable Housing?* Washington, DC: Urban Institute Press.

Burt, M., Aron, L., Douglas, T., Valente, J., Lee, E., and Iwen, B. (1999) *Homelessness: Programs and the People they Serve, Findings of the National Survey of Homeless Assistance Providers and Clients, Technical Report*, Washington, DC: Interagency Council on the Homeless. Available online at http://www.huduser.org/publications/homeless/homeless_tech.html (1 May 2004).

Burt, M., Hedderson, J., Zweig, J., Ortiz, M.J., Aron-Turnham, L., and Johnson, S.M. (2004) *Strategies for Reducing Chronic Street Homelessness*, Final Report, Washington, DC: US Department of Housing and Urban Development, Office of Policy Development and Research. Available online at http://www.huduser.org/Publications/PDF/ChronicStrtHomeless.pdf (1 May 2004).

Castle, E. N. (2001) Wanted: a rural public policy, *Choices: The Magazine of Food, Farm and Resource Issues.* Available online at http://articles.findarticles.com/ p/articles/mi_m0HIC/is_1_16/ai_75477928 (1 May 2004).

Community Shelter Board (2002) *Preventing Homelessness: Discharge Planning from Corrections Facilities,* Columbus, OH: Community Shelter Board. Available online at http://www.csb.org/What_s_New/FinalReportAug2002/Final%20 Report%20August%202002.pdf (1 May 2004).

Countryside Agency (2002) *Rural Proofing: Policymakers' Checklist,* Cheltenham, England: Countryside Agency. Available online at http://www.countryside. gov.uk/Images/CA%2035_tcm2-12127.pdf (1 May 2004).

Cromartie, J. B. and Swanson, L. L. (1997) Census tracts more precisely define rural populations and areas, *Rural Development Perspectives,* 11(3): 31–9. Available online at http://www.ers.usda.gov/publications/rdp/rdp696/ rdp696e.pdf (1 May 2004).

Culhane, D. P., Metraux, S., and Hadley, T. (2002) Public service reductions associated with placement of homeless persons with severe mental illness in supportive housing, *Housing Policy Debate,* 13(1):107–63. Available online at http://www.fanniemaefoundation.org/programs/hpd/pdf/hpd_1301_ culhane.pdf (1 May 2004).

DARD Rural Proofing Unit (n.d.) *Rural Proofing: A Guide to Considering the Needs of Rural Areas and Communities,* Belfast: Department of Agriculture and Rural Development. Available online at http://www.ofmdfmni.gov.uk/iia/ pdfs/rural.pdf (1 May 2004).

Duncan, C. (1999) *Worlds Apart: Why Poverty Persists in Rural America,* New York and London: Yale University Press.

Economic Research Service (2003a) *Measuring Rurality: What is a Micropolitan Area?,* Washington, DC: US Department of Agriculture. Available online at http://www.ers.usda.gov/Briefing/Rurality/MicropolitanAreas/ (1 May 2004).

Economic Research Service (2003b) *Measuring Rurality: What is Rural?,* Washington, DC: US Department of Agriculture. Available online at http:// www.ers.usda. gov/Briefing/Rurality/WhatisRural/ (1 May 2004).

Economic Research Service (2003c) *Measuring Rurality: Urban Influence Codes,* Washington, DC: US Department of Agriculture. Available online at http:// www.ers.usda.gov/briefing/rurality/UrbanInf/ (1 May 2004).

Economic Research Service (2004) *Measuring Rurality: Rural–Urban Continuum Codes,* Washington, DC: US Department of Agriculture. Available online at http://www.ers.usda.gov/briefing/rurality/RuralUrbCon/ (1 May 2004).

First, R. J., Toomey, B. G., Rife, J. C., and Stasny, E. A. (1994) *Outside of the City: A Statewide Study of Homelessness in Nonurban/Rural Areas,* Final Report for NIMH Grant # RO1MH46111, Columbus, OH: College of Social Work, Ohio State University.

Fitchen, J. M. (1992) On the edge of homelessness: rural poverty and housing insecurity, *Rural Sociology*, 57(2): 173–93.

Hewitt, M. (1989) *Defining Rural Areas: Impact on Health Care Policy and Research*, Washington, DC: Office of Technology Assessment, Congress of the United States. Available online at http://www.wws.princeton.edu/cgi-bin/byteserv.prl/~ota/disk1/1989/8912/8912.PDF (1 May 2004).

Housing Assistance Council (2002a) *Continua of Care Best Practices: Comprehensive Homeless Planning in Rural America*, Washington, DC: Housing Assistance Council. Available online at http://www.ruralhome.org/pubs/hsganalysis/continua.pdf (1 May 2004).

Housing Assistance Council (2002b) *Taking Stock: Rural People, Poverty, and Housing at the Turn of the 21st Century*, Washington, DC: Housing Assistance Council. Available online at http://www.ruralhome.org/pubs/hsganalysis/ts2000/ (1 May 2004).

Kentucky Housing Corporation (2001) *2001 Kentucky Homeless Survey Report*, Morehead, KY: Institute for Regional Analysis and Public Policy, Morehead State University. Available online at http://www.kyhousing.org/Publications/resources/2001HomelessReport.pdf (1 May 2004).

Kilborn, P. T. (2001) Rural towns turn to prisons to reignite their economies, *The New York Times* (1 Aug.) Available online at http://grassrootsleadership.org/Articles/article4_spr2002.html (1 May 2004).

Koebel, C. T., Murphy, M., and Brown, A. (2001) *The 2001 Virginia Rural Homeless Survey*, Blacksburg, VA: Center for Housing Research, Virginia Polytechnic and State University. Available online at http://www.arch.vt.edu/caus/research/vchr/pdfreports/VaRuralHomeless_sum.pdf (1 May 2004).

Kondratas, A. (1991) Estimates and public policy: the politics of numbers, *Housing Policy Debate*, 2(3): 631–47. Available online at http://www.fanniemaefoundation.org/programs/hpd/pdf/hpd_0203_kondratas.pdf (1 May 2004).

Lawrence, M. (1995) Rural homelessness: a geography without a geography, *Journal of Rural Studies*, 11(3): 297–307.

Lipton, F. R., Siegel, C., Hannigan, A., Samuels, J., and Baker, S. (2000) Tenure in supportive housing for homeless persons with severe mental illness, *Psychiatric Services*, 51(4): 479–86. Available online at http://ps.psychiatryonline.org/cgi/reprint/51/4/479 (1 May 2004).

Miller, K. K. and Weber, B. A. (2004) Persistent poverty and place: how do persistent poverty dynamics and demographics vary across the rural-urban continuum?, *Measuring Rural Diversity RUPRI Policy Brief*, Corvallis, OR: Rural Policy Research Institute, Rural Poverty Research Center, Oregon State University. Available online at http://www.rupri.org/rprc/miller_weber.pdf (1 May 2004).

National Advisory Committee on Rural Health and Human Services (2004) *The 2004 Report to the Secretary: Rural Health and Human Service Issues*, Rockville, MD: Office of Rural Health Policy, Health Resources and Services Administration. Available online at ftp://ftp.hrsa.gov/ruralhealth/NAC04web.pdf (1 Sept. 2004).

National Alliance to End Homelessness. (2000) *A Plan, Not a Dream: How to End Homelessness in Ten Years*, Washington, DC: National Alliance to End Homelessness. Available online at http://www.endhomelessness.org/pub/tenyear/index.htm (1 May 2004).

National Coalition for the Homeless (1999) *Rural Homelessness*, NCH Fact Sheet #13, Washington, DC: National Coalition for the Homeless. Available online at http://www.nationalhomeless.org/rural.html (1 May 2004).

National Health Care for the Homeless Council (2003) *Mainstreaming Health Care for Homeless People*, Nashville, TN: National Health Care for the Homeless Council. Available online at http://www.nhchc.org/Publications/Mainstreaming.pdf (1 May 2004).

Post, P. A. (2002) *Hard to Reach: Rural Homelessness and Health Care*, Nashville, TN: National Health Care for the Homeless Council. Available online at http://www.nhchc.org/Publications/RuralHomeless.pdf (1 May 2004).

Rosenheck, R., Kasprow, W., Frisman, L., and Liu-Mares, W. (2003) Cost-effectiveness of supported housing for homeless persons with mental illness, *Archives of General Psychiatry*, 60(9): 940–51.

Rural Welfare Policy Panel (1999) *Rural America and Welfare Reform: An Overview and Assessment*, Columbia, MO: Rural Policy Research Institute. Available online at http://www.rupri.org/publications/archive/old/welfare/p99-3/p99-3.pdf (1 May 2004).

Shern, D. L., Felton, C. J., Hough, R. L., Lehman, A. F., Goldfinger, S. M., Valencia, E., Dennis, D., Straw, R., and Wood, P. A. (1997) Housing outcomes for homeless adults with mental illness: results from the Second-Round McKinney Program, *Psychiatric Services*, 48(2): 239–41.

Summers, G. F. and Sherman, J. (1997) *Who's Poor in Rural America? Working Together for a Change*, Madison, WI: Rural Sociological Society.

Tsemberis, S. and Eisenberg, R. F. (2000) Pathways to housing: supported housing for street-dwelling homeless individuals with psychiatric disabilities, *Psychiatric Services*, 51(4): 487–93. Available online at http://psychservices.psychiatryonline.org/cgi/reprint/51/4/487 (1 May 2004).

US General Accounting Office (2000) *Homelessness: Barriers to Using Mainstream Programs*, GAO/RCED-00-184, Washington, DC: US General Accounting Office. Available online at http://www.gao.gov/new.items/rc00184.pdf (1 May 2004).

Wilkins, C., Greiff, D. and Proscio, T. (2003) *Laying a New Foundation: Changing the Systems that Create and Sustain Supportive Housing*, New York, NY: Corporation for Supportive Housing. Available online at http://documents. csh.org/documents/pubs/LayingANewFoundation.pdf (1 May 2004).

Chapter 3

Berg, S. (2003) *Punishing Poverty: The Criminalization of Homelessness, Litigation and Recommendations for Solutions*, Washington, DC: National Alliance to End Homelessness.

Burt, M. R. (1996) Rural homelessness: a report on the findings and implications of RECD's Rural Homelessness Conference, in USDA, *Rural Homelessness: Focusing on the Needs of the Rural Homeless*, pp. 11–37, Washington, DC: United States Department of Agriculture.

Burt, M. R. and Aron, L. Y. (2000) *America's Homeless II*, Washington, DC: The Urban Institute.

Champagne, D. (1989) *American Indian Societies*, Cambridge, MA: Cultural Survival.

Churchill, W. (1993) *Struggle for the Land*, Monroe, ME: Common Courage Press.

Clifton, J. (1987) Wisconsin death march: explaining the extremes of old northwest Indian removal, *Transactions of the Wisconsin Academy of Sciences, Arts, and Letters*, 75: 1–39.

Cloke, P. M., Milbourne, P. and Widdowfield, R. (2002) *Rural Homelessness: Issues, Experiences, and Policy Responses*, Bristol: Policy Press.

Collier, J. (1934) Indians at work, *Survey Graphic*, 23: 261–72.

Collier, J. (1947) *Indians of the Americas*, New York: Mentor Books.

Corday, D. S. and Pion, G. M. (1997) What's behind the numbers? Definitional issues in counting the homeless, in D. Culhane and S. Hornburg (eds) *Understanding Homelessness: Definitional Issues in Policy Research Perspectives*, Washington, DC: Fannie Mae Foundation, pp. 69–99.

De Toqueville, A. (1938) *Democracy in America*, vol. 1, New York: Vintage.

Dove, M. and Kammen, D. M. (2001) Vernacular models of development: an analysis of Indonesia under the 'New Order', *World Development*, 29: 619–39.

Fitchen, J. (1981) *Poverty in Rural America: A Case Study*, Boulder, CO: Westview.

Fitchen, J. (1995) Spatial redistribution of poverty through migration of poor people to depressed rural communities, *Rural Sociology*, 60: 416–36.

Gallent, N., Shucksmith, M. and Tewdwr-Jones, M. (2003) *Housing in the European Countryside*, London: Routledge.

GAO (1998) *Native American Housing: Homeownership Opportunities on Trust Lands Are Limited*, Washington, DC: General Accounting Office Report to the Committee on Indian Affairs, US Senate (Feb.).

GAO (1999) *Homelessness: Coordination and Evaluation of Programs are Essential*, Washington, DC: Report to Congressional Committees, US Government Accounting Office (Feb.).

Geisler, C. (1988) Homelessness and landlessness: an American condition, *Earth Matters* (Winter): 12–16.

Gibson, A. M. (1980) *The American Indian: Prehistory to the Present*, Toronto: D. C. Heath & Co.

HAC (1987) A decent home: a history of federal rural housing programs, unpublished, Washington, DC: Housing Assistance Council.

HAC (1999) *Cost-Based Appraisals on Native American Trust Lands*, Washington, DC: Housing Assistance Council.

HAC (2002) *Taking Stock: Rural People, Poverty, and Housing at the Turn of the 21st Century*, Washington, DC: Housing Assistance Council.

Hamilton, C. (1997) Indians to tackle housing crisis – on their own, *Christian Science Monitor*, 8 August: 12.

Harvard Joint Center (2003) *State of the Nation's Housing*, Cambridge, MA: Joint Center for Housing Studies, Graduate School of Design, J. F. Kennedy School of Government, Harvard University.

Hensen, E. and Taylor, J. B. (2002) *Native America at the New Millennium*, Cambridge, MA: Harvard University, J. F. Kennedy School of Government, Project on American Indian Economic Development (Nov.).

Hobbs, F. and Stoops, N. (2002) *Demographic Trends in the 20th Century: Census 2000 Special Reports*, Washington, DC: US Census Bureau, CENSR-4.

Hombs, M. E. (1994) *American Homelessness: A Reference Handbook*, Santa Barbara, CA: ABC-Clio.

HUD (1996) *Assessment of American Indian Housing Needs and Programs: Final Report,* Washington, DC: US Department of Housing and Urban Development and Urban Institute (May).

Hurt, R. D. (1987) *Indian Agriculture in America,* Lawrence, KS: University of Kansas Press.

Hurtado, A. L. and Iverson, P. (eds) (1994) *Major Problems in American Indian History*, Toronto: D. C. Heath.

Kalt, J. (1987) *The Redefinition of Property Rights in American Indian Reservations: A Comparative Analysis of Native American Economic Development,* Cambridge, MA: Harvard Project on American Indian Economic Development, J. F. Kennedy School of Government.

Kelley, K. B. (1979) Federal Indian land policy and economic development in the United States, in *Economic Development in American Indian Reservations*, pp. 30–42, Native American Studies Development Series, 1, Albuquerque, NM: University of New Mexico.

Kickingbird, K. and Ducheneaux, K. (1973) *One Hundred Million Acres,* New York: Macmillan.

Kingsley, T. G., Spencer, V., Simonson, J., Herbig, C., and Kay, N. (1996) *Assessment of American Indian Housing Needs and Programs: Final Report*, Washington, DC: Urban Institute.

Kroeber, A. (1925) *Handbook of the Indians of California, 1876-1960*, Washington, DC: Smithsonian Institute, Bureau of American Ethnology Bulletin 78.

Kruekeberg, D. A. (1995) The difficult character of property: to whom do things belong?', *Journal of the American Planning Association,* 61: 301–9.

Lawson, M. L. (1994) *Dammed Indians,* Norman, OK: University of Oklahoma Press.

Mason, D. (2000) *Indian Gaming: Tribal Sovereignty and American Politics,* Norman, OK: University of Oklahoma Press.

Mattison, R. H. (1955) The Indian reservation system on the Upper Missouri, 1875–1890, *Nebraska History,* 36 (Sept.): 141–72.

McDonnell, J. A. (1991) *The Dispossession of the American Indians, 1887–1934,* Bloomington, IN: Indiana University Press.

Meyer, M. (1991) We can not get a living as we used to: dispossession and the White Earth Anishinaaleg, 1889–1920, *American Historical Review*, 96: 368–94.

Mitchell, L. C. (1981) *Witnesses to a Vanishing America*, Princeton, NJ: Princeton University Press.

Nabakov, P. (ed.) (1999) *Native American Testimony*, New York: Penguin.

NAIHC (2001) *Too Few Rooms: Residential Crowding in Native American Communities and Alaska Native Villages,* Washington, DC: National American Indian Housing Council.

NARF (1996) 300,000 Indians sue federal government for mismanaging their money, *NARF Legal Review*, 21 (Summer/Fall): 1–11.

NLIHC (2003) *Native American Housing Assistance and Self-Determination Act (NAHASDA): 2003 Advocates' Guide to Housing and Community Development Policy*, Washington, DC: National Low Income Housing Coalition.

Ortiz, D. S. (1973) *The Dawes Act and the Allotment of Indian Land*, Norman, OK: University of Oklahoma Press.

Peacock, T. and Wisuri, M. (2002) *Ojibwe Waasa Inaabidaa: We Look in All Directions,* Afton, MN: Afton Historical Society Press.

Rice, M. (1999) *Appraisal of Single Family Homes on Native American Lands* (Working Paper), Washington, DC: HUD (Dec.).

Rodgers, W. H. Jr, Bean, M. J., Burgess, H., Fairfax, S. K., Geisler, C. C., Hagenstein, P. R., Harris, L. D., Healy, R. G., Lovejoy, T. E., McMahon, J. P., Slazar, D. J., Shaw, W. W., Stanton, N. L., Turner, M. G., and Vandermoer, C. (1993)

Setting Priorities for Land Conservation, Washington, DC: NRC, National Academy Press.

Ross, A. (1999) *The Celebration Chronicles*, New York: Ballantine Books.

Scott, J. (1998) *Seeing like a State*, New Haven, CT: Yale University Press.

Seymour, F. W. (1926) Our Indian land policy, *Journal of Land and Utility Economics*, 2: 93–108.

Sheehan, B. W. (1973) *Seeds of Extinction: Jeffersonian Philanthropy and the American Indian*, New York: Norton.

Shumway, M. and Jackson, R. (1995) Native American population patterns, *Geographical Review*, 85: 185–201.

Smith, H. N. (1957) *Virgin Land*, New York: Vintage Press.

Spence, M. D. (1999) *Dispossessing the Wilderness: Indian Removal and the Making of the National Parks*, New York: Oxford University Press.

Sutton, E. (1971) *Indian Land Tenure*, New York: Clearwater Publishing Co.

Task Force (1990) *Persistent Poverty in Rural America: Rural Sociological Society Task Force on Persistent Rural Poverty*, Boulder, CO: Westview Press.

Terrell, J. U. (1972) *Land Grab*, New York: Dial Press.

US Bureau of the Census (1980) *Characteristics of American Indians by Tribes and Selected Areas*, PC80-2-1D, Washington, DC: Bureau of the Census.

US Commission on Civil Rights (2003) *A Quiet Crisis: Federal Funding and Un-met Needs in Indian Country*, Washington, DC: US Commission on Civil Rights (July).

USDA (1999) *502 Direct Loans Obligated for American Indians and Alaska Natives*, RHS Data, Washington, DC: US Department of Agriculture, Rural Housing Service (Dec.).

US Department of Commerce (1973) *1970 Census of Population and Housing: Subject Report, American Indians*, Washington, DC: Bureau of the Census (June).

US Department of Commerce (2002) *Economics and Statistics Administration, Technical Documentation: Summary File 3, 2000 Census of Population and Housing*, Washington, DC: US Bureau of the Census, A-4 to A-24.

Wagoner, P. L. (1998) An unsettled frontier: property, blood and US federal policy, in C. M. Hann (ed.) *Property Relations: Renewing the Anthropological Tradition*, pp. 124–41, London: Cambridge University Press.

Wallace, A. F. C. (1993) *The Long, Bitter Trail: Andrew Jackson and the Indians*, ed. Eric Foner. New York: Hill & Wang.

Wellman, P. (1954) *The Indian Wars of the West*, Garden City, NY: Doubleday.

Williams, T. B. and Leatherman, R. D. (1975) *Indian Housing in the United States. A Staff Report on the Indian Housing Effort in the United States with Selected Appendixes*, Washington, DC: US Government Printing Office.

Wolf, P. (1981) *Land in America: Its Value, Use, and Control*, New York: Pantheon.

Chapter 4

Apgar, W., Calder, A., Collins, M. and Duda, M. (2002) *An Examination of Manufactured Housing as a Community- and Asset-Building Strategy*. A report to the Ford Foundation by Neighborhood Reinvestment Corporation, in collaboration with the Joint Center for Housing Studies of Harvard University. Available online at http://www.jchs.harvard.edu/publications/communitydevelopment/W02-11_apgar_et_al.pdf.

Berenson, A. (2001) A boom built upon sand, gone bust: trailer owners and Conseco are haunted by risky loans, *New York Times* (25 Nov.): section 3: 1, 7.

Brown, D. L. and Lee, M. A. (1999) Persisting inequality between metropolitan and nonmetropolitan America: implications for theory and policy, in P. Moen, D. Dempster-McClain, and H. A. Walker (eds) *A Nation Divided: Diversity, Inequality, and Community in American Society*, pp. 107–51, Ithaca, NY: Cornell University Press.

Cloke, P., Milbourne, P. and Widdowfield, R. (2002) *Rural Homelessness: Issues, Experiences and Policy Responses*, Bristol: Policy Press.

Consumer Reports (1998) Dream home ... or nightmare? (Feb.): 30–5.

Consumers Union (2002) Paper tiger, missing dragon: Poor service and worse enforcement leave manufactured homeowners in the lurch. Southwest Regional Office, Nov. Available online at http://www.consumersunion.org/other/mh/paper-info.htm

Copeland, G. (1997) *From Heatless to Homeless*, St Paul, MN: Energy CENTS Coalition.

Dean, E. (1999) Dialing America: paradise, yeah, *Talk*, 1 (Sept.): 133–8.

Edwards, M. L. K. (2004) We're decent people: constructing and managing family identity in rural working-class communities, *Journal of Marriage and Family*, 66 (May): 515–29.

Eley, M. (2004) Going mobile in the rural South: informal household strategies of African-American trailer-park families, unpublished Ph.D. dissertation, University of Illinois at Urbana-Champaign.

Fitchen, J. M. (1991) *Endangered Spaces, Enduring Places: Change, Identity, and Survival in Rural America*, Boulder, CO: Westview.

Fitchen, J. M. (1992) On the edge of homelessness: rural poverty and housing insecurity, *Rural Sociology*, 57(2): 173–93.

Fuguay, D. (2001) *Lending Perspectives: Doing it the Right Way*, Arlington , VA: Manufactured Housing Institute. Available online: http://www.manufacturedhousing.org/lending_news/default.asp?id=1&article=16.

Geisler, C. C. and Mitsuda, H. (1987) Mobile-home growth, regulation, and discrimination in upstate New York, *Rural Sociology*, 52: 532–43.

Goffman, E. (1963) *Stigma: Notes on the Management of Spoiled Identity*, New York: Simon & Schuster.

HAC (2003) *Rental Housing in Rural America*, Washington, DC: Housing Assistance Council.

Heskin, A. D. (1983) *Tenants and the American Dream: Ideology and the Tenant Movement*, New York: Praeger.

Howell, J. T. (1990) *Hard Living on Clay Street: Portraits of Blue Collar Families*, Longrove, IL: Waveland Press; originally published 1973.

HUD (2004) *Utility Bills Burden the Poor and Can Cause Homelessness*, Housing and Urban Development Department, retrieved 10 June 2004, from http://www.hud.gov:80/offices/cpd/energyenviron/energy/homelessness.cfm.

Hummon, D. M. (1990) *Commonplaces: Community Ideology and Identity in American Culture*, Albany, NY: State University of New York Press.

Hurley, A. (2001) *Diners, Bowling Alleys and Trailer Parks: Chasing the American Dream in Postwar Consumer Culture*, New York: Basic Books.

Huss-Ashmore, R. and Behrman, C. (1999) Transitional environments: health and the perception of permanence in urban micro-environments, in L. M. Schell and S. J. Ulijaszek (eds) *Urbanism, Health and Human Biology in Industrialised Countries*, pp. 67–84, Cambridge: Cambridge University Press.

Jarrett, R. (1995) Growing up poor: the family experiences of socially mobile youth in low-income African-American neighborhoods, *Journal of Adolescent Research*, 111: 121–3

Jewell, K. (2001) *Can We Trust Information from the Manufactured Housing Association? Expected Life-span of Manufactured Homes*, Austin, TX: Consumers Union.

Kefalas, M. (2003) *Working-Class Heroes: Protecting Home, Community, and Nation in a Chicago Neighborhood*, Berkeley, CA: University of California Press.

Kloppenburg, J. R. and Geisler, C. C. (1985) The agricultural ladder: agrarian ideology and the changing structure of U.S. agriculture, *Journal of Rural Studies*, 1(1): 59–72.

Knox, M. L. (1993) Why mobile homeowners want landlords to hit the road, *Business and Society Review*, 85 (Spring): 39–42.

Leland, J. (2003) Trying to stay put in Florida mobile homes, *New York Times* (2 June): 1, 21.

Liu, K. S., Huang, F. Y., Hayward, S. B., Wesolowski, J. and Sexton, K. (1991) Irritant effects of formaldehyde exposure in mobile homes. *Health Perspectives*, 94: 91–4.

Logan, J. R. (1978) Growth, politics, and the stratification of places, *American Journal of Sociology*, 84(2): 404–16.

Low, S. M. and Altman, I. (1992) Place attachment: a conceptual inquiry, in I. Altman and S. M. Low (eds) *Place Attachment*, pp. 1–12, Human Behavior and Environment, Advances in Theory and Research, vol. 12, New York: Plenum Press.

MacTavish, K. (2001) Going mobile in rural America: the community effect of rural trailer parks on child and youth development, unpublished Ph.D. dissertation, University of Illinois at Urbana-Champaign.

MacTavish, K. and Salamon, S. (2001) Mobile home park on the prairie: a new rural community form, *Rural Sociology*, 66(4): 487–506.

Meeks, C. (1998) *Manufactured Home Life: Existing Housing Stock Through 1997*, Arlington, VA: Manufactured Housing Institute.

Mobley, C., Sugarman, J.R., Deam, C., and Giles, L. (1994) Prevalence of risk factors for residential fire and burn injuries in an American Indian community, *Public Health Reports*, 109(5): 702–5.

NEADA (2004) *National Energy Assistance Director's Association Survey Report*, Washington, DC: NEADA.

Nelson, M. K. and Smith, J. (1999) *Working Hard and Making Do: Surviving in Small Town America*, Berkeley, CA: University of California Press.

Newby, H. (1980) The rural sociology of advanced capitalist societies, in F. H. Buttel and H. Newby (eds) *The Rural Sociology of Advanced Societies*, pp. 1–30, Montclair, NJ: Allanheld, Osmun.

O'Hare, W. and O'Hare, B.C. (1993) Upward mobility, *American Demographics* 15: 26–34.

Parker, D. J., Sklar, D. P., Tandberg, D., Hauswald, M. and Zumwalt, R. E. (1993) Fire fatalities among New Mexico children, *Annals of Emergency Medicine*, 22: 517–22.

Perin, C. (1977) *Everything in its Place: Social Order and Land Use in America*, Princeton, NJ: Princeton University Press.

Putnam, R. (2000) *Bowling Alone: The Collapse and Revival of American Community*, New York: Simon & Schuster.

Ritzer, G. (2001) *Explorations in the Sociology of Consumption*, London: Sage.

Ruditsky, H. (1994) New life for old mobile home parks: investing in parks through real estate investment trusts, *Forbes*, 154 (7 Nov.): 44–5.

Runyan, C. W., Bangdiwala, S. I., Linzer, M. A., Sacks, J. J. and Butt, J. (1992) Risk factors for fatal residential fires, *New England Journal of Medicine*, 327(12): 859–88.

Salamon, S. (1992) *Prairie Patrimony: Family, Farming, and Community in the Midwest*, Chapel Hill, NC: University of North Carolina Press.

Salamon, S. (2003) *Newcomers to Old Towns: Suburbanization of the Heartland*, Chicago, IL: University of Chicago Press.

Salamon, S. (2004) The rural household as a consumption site, in P. Cloke, T. Marsden and P. Mooney (eds) *Handbook of Rural Studies*, London: Sage, pp. 330–43.

Shanklin, M. (2003) Fatalities took place in mobile home built pre-fire retardants, *Orlando Sentinel* (10 June), retrieved 10 June 2004, from http://0-search.

epnet.com.oasis.oregonstate.edu:80/direct.asp?an= 2W64059191998&db
=nfh.

Spillman, W. J. (1919) The agricultural ladder, *American Economic Review Supplement*, 9(1): 170–9.

Stone, M. E. (1993) *Shelter Poverty: New Ideas on Housing Affordability*, Philadelphia, PA: Temple University Press.

Tickamyer, A. R. (2000) Space matters! Spatial inequality in future sociology, *Contemporary Sociology*, 29(6): 805–13.

Tilly, C. (1999) *Durable Inequality*, Berkeley, CA: University of California Press.

Tremblay, Jr., K. R. and Dillman, D. A. (1983) *Beyond the American Housing Dream: Accommodation to the 1980s*, Lantham, MD: University Press of America.

US Census Bureau (2001a) *American Housing Survey for the United States: 2001*, TAble 4-13: Selected Housing Costs – Renter Occupied Units. Available online http://www.census.gov/hhes/www/housing/ahs/ahs01_2000wts/tab413.html.

US Census Bureau (2001b) *American Housing Survey for the United States: 2001*, Table 4-1: Introductory Characteristics – Renter Occupied Units. Available online http://www.census.gov/hhes/www/housing/ahs/ahs01_2000wts/tab41.html.

US Census Bureau (2001c) *American Housing Survey for the United States in 2001*, Table 4-3: Size of Unit and Lot – Renter Occupied. Available online http://www.census.gov/hhes/www/housing/ahs/ahs01_2000wts/tab43.html.

US Census Bureau (2003) *Structural and Occupancy Characteristics of Housing: 2000* (Nov.). Available online athttp://www.census.gov/prod/2003pubs/c2kbr-32pdf.

Williams, F. (1998) Living out the trailer dream, *High Country News*, 30(15):http://www.hcn.org/article_id=4363.

Wilson, W. J. (1987) *The Truly Disadvantaged*, Chicago, IL: University of Chicago Press.

Ziebarth, A., Prochaska-Cue, K. and Shrewsbury, B. (1997) Growth and locational impacts for housing in small communities, *Rural Sociology*, 62: 111–25.

Zuckman, J. (1990) New fight likely over change in mobile home standards, *Congressional Quarterly* (2 June): 1732.

Chapter 5

Beavis, M., Klos, N., Carter, T. and Douchant, C. (1997) *Literature Review: Aboriginal Peoples and Homelessness*, Winnipeg: Institute of Urban Studies, University of Winnipeg.

Bentley, D. (1995) *Measuring Homelessness: A Review of Recent Research*, Winnipeg: Institute of Urban Studies, University of Winnipeg.

Bruce, D. (2000a) *The Changing Rural Rental Market in Atlantic Canada*, Ottawa: CMHC.

Bruce, D. (2000b) *Housing Opportunities Study for Charlotte County*, Report to the Charlotte County Aquaculture and Fish Processors Adjustment Committee. Sackville, NB: Rural and Small Town Programme.

Bruce, D. (2003) *Housing Needs of Low Income Persons Living in Rural Areas*, Ottawa: CMHC.

Callaghan, M. (1999) *Understanding Homelessness in Muskoka*, Muskoka: District of Muskoka.

Canada Mortgage and Housing Corporation (1991) *Core Housing Need in Canada*, Ottawa: CMHC.

Canada Mortgage and Housing Corporation (1994) *Technical Guide to Understanding 1991 Core Housing Need Databases and Estimate*, Ottawa: CMHC.

Canada Mortgage and Housing Corporation (1995) *Inventory of Projects and Programs Addressing Homelessness*, Ottawa: CMHC.

Canada Mortgage and Housing Corporation (2000) *Housing in Canada: Electronic Data Series Database*, Ottawa: CMHC.

Carter, T. (1997) Current practices for procuring affordable housing: the Canadian context, *Housing Policy Debate*, 8(3): 593–631.

du Plessis, V., Beshiri, R., Clemenson, H. and Bollman, R. (2001) *Definitions of Rural*, Rural and Small Town Canada Analysis Bulletin, 3(3).

Family and Community Services (2002) Social assistance recipient profile, unpublished special tabulations, Fredericton.

Frankish, C. J., Hwang, S. and Quartz, D. (2003) *The Relations between Homelessness and Health in Canada: Research Lessons and Priorities*, Ottawa: Discussion Paper prepared for the International Think Tank on Reducing Health Disparities and Promoting Equity for Vulnerable Populations.

Government of Canada (2003a) *National Homelessness Initiative: Supporting Communities Partnership Initiatives;* online, http://www21.hrdc-drhc.gc.ca/partners/communitypartnersindex_e.asp (3 March 2004).

Government of Canada (2003b) *National Homelessness Initiative: Regional Homelessness Fund;* online, http://www21.hrdc-drhc.gc.ca/initiative/rhf_e.asp (3 March 2004).

Homelessness Working Group, National Housing Research Committee (2000–3) Meeting notes.

Marshall, J. and Bollman, R. (1999) *Rural and Urban Household Expenditure Patterns for 1996*, Rural and Small Town Canada Analysis Bulletin, 1(4).

Rostum, H. (1987) *Human Settlements in Canada: Trends and Policies, 1981–1986*, Ottawa: CMHC.

Rupnik, C., Thompson-James, M. and Bollman, R. (2001) *Measuring Economic Well-being of Rural Canadians Using income Indicators,* Rural and Small Town Canada Analysis Bulletin, 2(5).

Spurr, P. (2001) *Special Studies on 1996 Census Data: Housing Conditions of Native Households,* Socio-Economic Research Highlight 55-6, Ottawa: CMHC.

Statistics Canada (2003) *Population of Canada: The 2001 Census,* Ottawa: Statistics Canada.

Tota, K. (2004) *Homelessness in Halifax Regional Municipality (HRM): A Portrait of Streets and Shelters,* Halifax: Halifax Regional Municipality, Planning and Development Services.

VisionLink Consulting (2002) *Faces of Homelessness in a Rural Area: Housing Issues and Homelessness in the West Kootenay Boundary Region,* Nelson, British Columbia: Advocacy Centre.

Chapter 6

Ambrose, P. (1974) *The Quiet Revolution,* London: Chatto and Windus.

BBC News (2004) Big rise in rural homeless, http://news.bbc.co.uk/2/hi/uk_news/wales/mid_/3227855.stm

Bramley, G. (1992) Explaining the incidence of statutory homelessness in England, *Housing Studies,* 8: 128–47.

Clark, D. (1990) *Affordable Rural Housing,* Cirencester: ACRE.

Cloke, P., Milbourne, P. and Thomas, C. (1994) *Lifestyles in Rural England,* London: Rural Development Commission.

Cloke, P. Goodwin, M. and Milbourne, P. (1998) Cultural change and conflict in rural Wales: competing constructs of identity, *Environment and Planning A,* 30: 463–80.

Cloke, P., Goodwin, M. and Milbourne, P. (1997) *Rural Wales: Community and Marginalization,* Cardiff: University of Wales Press.

Cloke, P., Milbourne, P. and Widdowfield, R. (2000a) !The hidden and emerging spaces of rural homelessness, *Environment and Planning A,* 32: 77–90.

Cloke, P., Milbourne, P. and Widdowfield, R. (2000b) Partnership and policy networks in rural local governance, *Public Administration,* 78(1): 111–33.

Cloke, P., Milbourne, P. and Widdowfield, R. (2000c) Homelessness and rurality: 'out of place' in purified space, *Environment and Planning D: Society and Space,* 18(6): 715–35.

Cloke, P., Milbourne, P. and Widdowfield, R. (2001a) The local spaces of welfare provision: responding to homelessness in rural England, *Political Geography,* 20(4): 493–512.

Cloke, P., Milbourne, P. and Widdowfield, R. (2001b) The geographies of homelessness in rural England, *Regional Studies,* 35(1): 23–37.

Cloke, P., Milbourne, P. and Widdowfield, R. (2001c) Interconnecting rurality and homelessness: evidence from local authority homelessness officers in England and Wales, *Journal of Rural Studies*, 17: 99–111.

Cloke, P., Milbourne, P. and Widdowfield, R. (2001d) Homelessness and rurality: exploring connections in local spaces of rural England, *Sociologia Ruralis*, 41(4): 438–53.

Cloke, P., Milbourne, P. and Widdowfield, R. (2001e) *Tackling Homelessness in Rural Areas*, Cardiff: Cardiff University, School of City and Regional Planning.

Cloke, P., Milbourne, P. and Widdowfield, R. (2002) *Rural Homelessness: Issues, Experiences and Policy Responses*, Bristol: Policy Press.

Cochrane, A. (1994) Restructuring the local welfare state, in R. Burrows and B. Loader (eds) *Towards a Post-Fordist Welfare State?*, London: Routledge.

Countryside Agency (2004) *The State of the Countryside*, London: The Countryside Agency.

Dunn, M., Rawson, M. and Rogers, A. (1981) *Rural Housing: Competition and Choice*, London: Allen and Unwin.

Evans, A. (1999) *They Think I Don't Exist: The Hidden Nature of Rural Homelessness*, London: Crisis.

Everitt, G. and Wright, J. (1996) Small town, big problem, *Roof*, March–April: 11.

Fitchen, J. (1992) On the edge of homelessness: rural povert and housing insecurity, *Rural Sociology*, 57(2): 173–93.

Hutson, S. and Clapham, D. (eds) (1999) *Homelessness: Public Policies and Private Troubles*, London: Cassell.

Kennett, P. and Marsh, A. (eds) (1999) *Homelessness: Exploring the New Terrain*, Bristol: Policy Press.

Lambert, C., Jeffers, S., Burton, P. and Bramley, G. (1992) *Homelessness in Rural Areas*, London: Rural Development Commission.

Larkin, A. (1979) Rural housing and housing needs, in J. Shaw (ed.) *Rural Deprivation and Planning*, Norwich: GeoBooks.

McLaughlin, B. (1986) The rhetoric and reality of rural deprivation, *Journal of Rural Studies*, 2: 291–307.

Milbourne P. (1998) Local responses to central state social housing restructuring in rural areas, *Journal of Rural Studies*, 14(2): 167–84.

Milbourne, P. (2005) Rural housing and homelessness, in P. Cloke, T. Marsden and P. Mooney (eds) *The Handbook of Rural Studies*, London: SAGE.

Newton, J. (1991) *All in One Place: The British Housing Story 1971–91*, London: CHAS.

Pahl, R. (1966) *Urbs in Rure*, London: LSE.

Robinson, D. (2002) *Estimating Homelessness in Rural Areas*, Sheffield: Sheffield Hallam University.

Robinson, D. and Coward, S. (2003) *Your Place, Not Mine: Homeless People Staying with Family and Friends*, London: Crisis/The Countryside Agency.

Rogers, A. (1976) Rural housing, in G. Cherry (ed.) *Rural Planning Problems*, London: Leonard Hill.

Rogers, A. (1984) Housing, in M. Pacione (ed.) *Rural Geography*, London: Harper and Row.

Rogers, A. (1985) Rural housing: an issue in search of a focus, *Journal of Agirucltural Economics*, 36(1): 87–9.

Scottish Housing (2000) *Homelessness in Rural Scotland*, Edinburgh: Scottish Housing.

Shelter (2004) *Priced Out: The Rising Cost of Rural Homes*, London: Shelter.

Shucksmith, M., Chapman, P., Clark, G., with Black, S. and Conway, E. (1996) *Rural Scotland Today: The Best of Both Worlds*, Avebury: Aldershot.

Streich, L., Havell, C. and Spafford, J. (2002) *Preventing Homelessness in the Countryside … What Works?*, Cheltenham: Countryside Agency.

Chapter 7

Burrows, R. (1997) The social distribution of the experience of homelessness, in R. Burrows, N. Pleace and D. Quilgars (eds) *Homelessness and Social Policy*, London: Routledge.

Byers, S. (2002) A Response to 'More than a Roof' from the Rt. Hon. Stephen Byers MP, Secretary of State for Transport, Local Government and the Regions, London: Office of the Deputy Prime Minister (13 March).

Centrepoint (2000a) *Homelessness in Cumbria*, London: Centrepoint Cumbria.

Centrepoint (2000b) Memorandum submitted to the Select Committee on Social Security. Minutes of Evidence, 19 July (www.publications.parliament.uk).

Centrepoint Eden Valley (1998) *A Study into a Rural Network of Supported Housing for Young People*, Leeds: Centrepoint.

Chapman, P., Phimister, E., Shucksmith, M., Upward, R. and Vera-Toscano, E. (1998) *Poverty and Exclusion in Rural Britain: The Dynamics of Low Income and Employment*, York: Joseph Rowntree Foundation.

Cloke, P. (1995) Rural poverty and the welfare state: a discursive transformation in Britain and the USA, *Environment and Planning A*, 27: 1001–16.

Cloke, P., Milbourne, P. and Widdowfield, R. (2000) The hidden and emerging spaces of rural homelessness, *Environment and Planning A*, 32: 71–90.

Cloke, P., Milbourne, P. and Widdowfield, R. (2001a) The geographies of homelessness in rural England, *Regional Studies*, 35(1): 23–37.

Cloke, P., Milbourne, P. and Widdowfield, R. (2001b) Making the homeless count? Enumerating rough sleepers and the distortion of homelessness, *Policy and Politics*, 29(3): 259–79.

Cloke, P., Milbourne, P. and Widdowfield, R. (2003) The complex mobilities of homeless people in rural England, *Geoforum*, 34: 21–35.

Countryside Agency (2004) *State of the Countryside*, London: Countryside Agency.

Crane, M. and Warnes, A. M. (2003) *Homelessness Research Review 2003: Research Summaries and Bibliography Update*, London: CRASH.

Diaz, R. and Colman, B. (1997) *Who Says there's No Housing Problem? Facts and Figures on Housing and Homelessness*, London: Shelter.

DTLR (2001a) Government meets target on reducing rough sleeping, Department for Transport, Local Government and the Regions, Press Release, 3 Dec.

DTLR (2001b) *Preventing Tomorrow's Rough Sleepers: A Good Practice Handbook*, London: Department for Transport, Local Government and the Regions.

DTLR (2002) *More than a Roof: A Report into Tackling Homelessness*, London: Department of Transport, Local Government and the Regions.

Evans, A. (1999) *They Think I Don't Exist: The Hidden Nature of Rural Homelessness*, London: Crisis.

Fitzpatrick, S. and Lynch, E. (2002) *Homelessness Research Review 2002: Research Summaries and Bibliography Update*, London: CRASH.

Fitzpatrick, S., Kemp, P.A. and Klinker, S. (2000) *Single Homelessness: An Overview of Research in Britain*, Bristol: Policy Press

Ford, J., Quilgars, D., Burrows, R. and Pleace, N. (1997) *Young People and Housing*, London: Rural Development Commission.

Hilditch, S. (2002) A new approach to homelessness, *Property People* (2 May): 8–9.

Hutson, S. and Liddiard, M. (1994) *Youth Homelessness: The Construction of a Social Issue*, London: Macmillan.

Kemp, P. and Rugg, J. (1998) *The Single Room Rent: Its Impact on Young People*, York: Centre for Housing Policy.

Lockwood, J. (1996) View without a room? *Housing Association Weekly*, 30(10): 10–11.

Natress, H. (2000) *Rough Sleepers Research in Scunthorpe*, Northern Consortium of Housing Associations.

Pleace, N., Burrows, R. and Quilgars, D. (1997) Homelessness in contemporary Britain: conceptualisation and measurement, in R. Burrows, N. Pleace and D. Quilgars (eds) *Homelessness and Social Policy*, London: Routledge.

Reeve, K. and Coward, S. (2004) *Life on the Margins: The Experiences of Homeless People Living in Squats*, London: Crisis.

Robinson, D. (1998) Health selection in the housing system: access to council housing for homeless people with health problems, *Housing Studies*, 13(1): 23–41.

Robinson, D. (2002) *Estimating Homelessness in Rural Areas: A Step-by-Step Guide and Sourcebook of Information and Ideas*, Sheffield: CRESR, Sheffield Hallam University, Countryside Agency and North Lincolnshire Council.

Robinson, D. (2003) *Hidden Homelessness in Rural England: Homeless People Staying with Family and Friends*, Research Note CRN 74 December, London: Countryside Agency.

Robinson, D. (2004) Rough sleeping in rural England: challenging a problem denied, *Policy and Politics*, 32(4): 471–86.

Robinson, D. and Coward, S. (2003) *Your Place, Not Mine: The Experiences of Homeless People Staying with Family and Friends*, London: Crisis.

Robinson, D. and Hawtin, M. (2002) *Preventing Homelessness: The Role of Housing Management*, Edinburgh: Communities Scotland.

Robinson, D. and Reeve, K (2002) *Homelessness and Rough Sleeping in North Lincolnshire*, Sheffield: CRESR, Sheffield Hallam University.

Rugg, J. and Jones, A. (1999) *Getting a Job, Finding a Home: Rural Youth Transitions*, Bristol: Policy Press.

Sawtell, M. (2002) *Rural Homelessness: Experiences of Homeless Pregnant Women and New Families in Rural Areas*, London: Maternity Alliance.

Shucksmith, M. (1990) *House Building in Britain's Countryside*, London: Routledge.

Shucksmith, M., Roberts, D., Scott, D., Chapman, P. and Conway, E. (1996) *Disadvantage in Rural Areas*, London: Rural Development Commission.

Smith, J. and Ing, M. (2001) *Making Youth Homelessness Visible: Young People Homeless in the Cotswolds*, Stoke-on-Trent: Housing and Community Research Unit, Staffordshire University.

Sterling, T. and Fitzpatrick, S. (2001) *A Review of Single Homelessness Research: Research Summaries and Bibliography Update 1999–2000*, London: CRASH.

Streich, L. (2000) Rural homelessness in the South West: recent research findings, in P. Cole, P. Milbourne and R. Widdowfield (eds) *Tackling Homelessness in Rural Areas,* Conference proceedings, Stoke Rochford Hall, Grantham, 11–12 Nov. 1999.

Townsend, A. (1991) New forms of employment in rural areas: a national perspective, in A. Champion and C. Watkins (eds) *People in the Countryside*, London: Paul Chapman.

White, V. and Levison, D. (1999) *Housing Benefit and the Private Rented Sector*, London: Department of the Environment, Transport and the Regions.

Wright, J. and Everitt, G. (1995) *Homelessness in Boston*, Sleaford: Shelter.

Chapter 8

Cloke, P. (2005) Conceptualising rurality, in P. Cloke, T. Marsden and P.Mooney (eds) *Handbook of Rural Studies*, London: Sage.

Cloke, P., Goodwin, M., Milbourne, P. and Thomas, C. (1995) Deprivation, poverty and marginalisation in rural lifestyles in England and Wales, *Journal of Rural Studies*, 11: 351–65.

Cloke, P., Milbourne, P. and Widdowfield, R. (2000a) Homelessness and rurality 'out of place' in purified space? *Environment and Planning D: Society and Space*, 18: 715–35.

Cloke, P., Milbourne, P. and Widdowfield, R. (2000b) The hidden and emerging spaces of rural homelessness, *Environment and Planning A*, 32: 77–90.

Cloke, P., Milbourne, P. and Widdowfield, R. (2000c) Change but no change: dealing with homelessness under the 1996 Housing Act, *Housing Studies*, 15: 739–56.

Cloke, P., Milbourne, P. and Widdowfield, R. (2001a) The geographies of homelessness in rural England, *Regional Studies*, 35: 23–37.

Cloke, P., Milbourne, P. and Widdowfield, R. (2001b) Interconnecting housing, homelessness and rurality, *Journal of Rural Studies*, 17: 99–111.

Cloke, P., Milbourne, P. and Widdowfield, R. (2002) *Rural Homelessness: Issues, Expenses and Policy Responses*, Bristol: Policy Press.

Cloke, P., Milbourne, P. and Widdowfield, R. (2003) The complex mobilities of homeless people in rural England, *Geoforum*, 34: 21–35.

Crane, M. (1999) *Understanding Older Homeless People: Their Circumstances, Problems and Needs*, Buckingham: Open University Press.

Cresswell, T. (1996) *In Place, Out of Place: Geography Ideology and Transgression*, Minneapolis: University of Minnesota Press.

Deacon, A., Vincent, J. and Walker, R. (1995) Whose choice hostels or houses? Policies for single homeless people, *Housing Studies*, 10: 345–63.

Hetherington, K. (2000) *New Age Travellers: Vanloads of Uproarious Humanity*, London: Cassell.

Lukes, S. (1974) *Power: A Radical View*, London: Macmillan.

May, J. (2000) Of nomads and vagrants: single homelessness and narratives of home and place, *Environment and Planning D: Society and Space*, 18: 737–59.

May, J., Cloke, P. and Johnson, S (2005) Re-phasing neo-liberalism: New Labour and Britain's crisis of street homelessness, *Antipode*, 37: 703–30.

Pleace, N., Burrows, R. and Quilgars, D. (1997) Homelessness in contemporary Britain: conceptualisation and measurement, in R. Burrows, N. Pleace and D. Quilgars (eds) *Homelessness and Social Policy*, London: Routledge.

Scott, J. (1998) *Seeing like a State*, New Haven: Yale University Press.

Takahashi, L. (1998) *Homelessness, AIDS and Stigmatisation the NIMBY Syndrome at the End of the Twentieth Century*, Oxford: Oxford University Press.

Chapter 9

Abad, C. and Naredo, J. M.(2002) Sobre la modernización de la agricultura española; de la agricultura tradicional hacia la capitalización agraria y la dependencia asistencial, in Cristobal Gómez Benito and Juan J. Gomez (eds) *Agricultura y Sociedad en el cambio de siglo*, Madrid: UNED and McGrawHill.

Alguacil Gómez, J. *et al.* (2000) Las características de la pobreza desde la perspectiva territorial, in Victor Renes Ayala (ed.) *Las condiciones de vida de la población pobre desde la perspectiva territorial; pobreza y territorio,* Madrid: Cáritas Española and Fundación Foessa.

Avramov, D. (1995) *Homelessness in the European Union: Social and Legal Context of Housing Exclusion in the 1990s. Fourth Research Report of the European Observatory on Homelessness,* Brussels: FEANTSA.

Cabrera Cabrera, P. J. (1998) *Huéspedes del aire: Sociología de las personas sin hogar,* Madrid: Universidad Pontificia Comillas.

Cabrera Cabrera, P. J. (2000) *La acción social con personas sin hogar en España,* Madrid: Foessa-Cáritas.

Cabrera Cabrera, P. J. and Rubio, M.J. (2003) *Personas sin techo en Madrid: Diagnóstico y propuestas de actuación,* Madrid: General Administration of Social Services. Community of Madrid.

Cabrera Cabrera, P. J., Malgesini, G. and López Ruiz, J. A. (2000) Informe sobre la situación de las personas sin hogar en La Rioja, unpublished report.

Camarero Rioja, Luis A. (2002) Pautas y tendencias demográficas del medio rural en la última década del siglo XX, in Cristobal Gómez Benito and Juan J. Gomez (eds) *Agricultura y Sociedad en el cambio de siglo,* 63–00, Madrid : UNED and McGrawHill.

Castel, R. (1995) *Les Métamorphoses de la question sociale: Une chronique du salariat,* Paris: Fayard.

EDIS *et al.* (1998) *Las condiciones de vida de la población pobre en España,* Madrid: Foessa Foundation-Cáritas.

Esping-Andersen, G. (2000) *Fundamentos sociales de las economías postindustriales,* Barcelona: Ariel.

García Roca, J. (1998) *Exclusión social y contracultura de la solidaridad: Prácticas, discursos y narraciones,* Madrid: HOAC.

García Serrano, C., Malo, M. Á. and Toharia, L. (2001) *La pobreza en España: Un análisis crítico basado en el panel de hogares de la Unión Europea (PHOGUE),* Madrid: Ministry of Labor and Social Affairs.

Hervieu, B. (1996) *Los campos del futuro,* Madrid: MAPA.

INE (1991) National Census 1991, Madrid: National Institute of Statistics.

INE (2001) National Census 2001, Madrid: National Institute of Statistics.

INE (2004) *Encuesta sobre las personas sin hogar (Centros),* Madrid: National Institute of Statistics.

Izcara Palacios, Simón Pedro (2002) Jornaleros desocupados e inmigrantes sobreexplotados: las nuevas infraclases rurales, in Cristobal Gómez Benito and Juan J. Gomez (eds) *Agricultura y Sociedad en el cambio de siglo,* pp. 459–80, Madrid: UNED and McGraw-Hill.

Jansa, J.M., Puigpinos, R. and Borrel, C. (1999) La salut de la població sense sostre a la ciutat de Barcelona, *Barcelona societat: Revista d'informació i estudis socials,* 46–54.

Juarez, M. (1994) *Informe sociológico sobre la situación social en España*, Madrid: Fundación FOESSA.

Moreno Rebollo, J. L., Muñoz García, J. and Pascual Acosta, A. (2003) *Estudio sobre la Población de Personas Sin Hogar*, Seville: Centro Andaluz de Prospectiva. Government of Andalusia.

Muñoz Lopez, M., Vazquez Valverde, C. and Cruzado Rodríguez, J. A. (1995) *Personas sin hogar en Madrid: Informe psicosocial y epidemiológico*, Madrid: Department of Social Integration. Community of Madrid.

Muñoz, M., Vázquez, C. and Vázquez, J. J. (2003) *Los límites de la exclusión: Estudio sobre los factores económicos psicosociales y de salud que afectan a las personas sin hogar en Madrid*, Madrid: Ediciones Témpora; Obra Social Cajamadrid.

Pereira Jerez, D. (2004) *Las zonas rurales en España: Un diagnóstico desde la perspectiva de las desigualdades territoriales y los cambios sociales y económicos*, Madrid: Foessa Foundation–Cáritas.

Ramos, E. and Romero, J.J. (2000) Evolución y perspectivas del desarrollo rural en Europa, *Juventud rural*, Revista de Estudios de Juventud, 48: 45–58, Madrid; Instituto de la Juventud.

Renes Ayala, V. (ed.) (2000) *Las condiciones de vida de la población pobre in España*, Madrid: Foessa Foundation–Cáritas.

Renes Ayala, V. (ed.) (2000) *Las características de la pobreza desde la perspectiva territorial*, Madrid: Foessa Foundation–Cáritas.

Rural Europe (2000) Lucha contra la exclusión social en el medio rural. http://www.rural-europe.aeidl.be/rural-es/biblio/exclusion

Vega González, L. S. (1996) *Salud mental en población sin hogar*, Asturias: Edita Servicio de Publicaciones del Principado de Asturias.

Zarraga Moreno, J.L. (2000) Medio rural y sociedad de la informatión, *Juventud rural*, Revista de Estudios de Juventud, 48: 59–68, Madrid; Instituto de la Juventud.

Chapter 10

Asunnottomuuden vähentämisohjelma 2001–2003 (The Programme for the Reduction of Homelessness), Ympäristöministeriön moniste, 73 (Helsinki, 2001).

Asunnottomuustyöryhmä. Tutkimusryhmä. 15.1.2001. Moniste (Ad hoc committee on Houselessness. Research group. A memo).

Berkel, R. van and Roche, M. (2002) Activation policies as reflexive social policies, in R. van Berkel and I. H. Møller (eds) *Active Social Policies in the EU: Inclusion through Participation?*, Bristol: Policy Press.

Brandt, P. (1992) Yngre hjemlöse i Köbenhavn (Disputats) (Young homeless in Copenhagen – thesis), Copenhagen: Fadl's forlag.

Castel, R. (2000) The roads to disaffiliation: insecure work and vulnerable relationships, *International Journal of Urban and Regional Research*, 24(3): 519–35.

Christensen, P., Hockey, J. and Allison, J. (1998) 'You just get on with it': questioning models of welfare dependency in a rural community, in I. R. Edgar and A. Russel (eds) *The Anthropology of Welfare*, London: Routledge.

Cloke, Paul (1997) Poor country: marginalisation, poverty and rurality, in P. Cloke and J. Little (eds) *Contested Countryside Cultures. Otherness, Marginalisation and Rurality*, pp. 252–71, London and New York: Routledge.

Cloke, P., Milbourne, P. and Widdowfield, R. (2000) Homelessness and rurality: 'out-of-place' in purified space? *Environment and Planning D: Society and Space*, 18: 715–35.

Cloke, P., Milbourne, P. and Widdowfield, R. (2001) Homelessness and rurality: exploring connection in local spaces of rural England, *Sociologia Ruralis*, 41(4): 438–53.

Cruikshank, B. (1999) *The Will to Empower: Democratic Citizens and Other Subjects*, Ithaca, NY and London: Cornell University Press.

Deleuze, G. (1993) *The Fold. Leibniz and the Baroque*, foreword and trans. Tom Conley, London: Athlone Press.

Displacement of politics by responsabilization (2003) The research project (Sakari Hänninen) funded by the Academy of Finland 1.8.2002 –31.12.2003.

Edgar, B., Doherty, J. and Meert, H. (2003) Review of Statistics on Homelessness in Europe, European Federation of National Organisations Working with the Homeless, European Observatory on Homelessness, Nov.

Finnish Red Cross (2003) Suomen Punaisen Ristin arkistot, Epävirallisen avun hakemukset 2003 (Finnish Red Cross Archives, Applications for unofficial assistance of the Finnish Red Cross in 2003).

Foucault, M. (1988) *Technologies of the Self: A Seminar with Michel Foucault*, ed. L. H. Martin, H. Gutman and P. H. Hutton, London: Tavistock Publications.

Haatanen, P. (1968) *Suomen maalaisköyhälistö tutkimusten ja kaunokirjallisuuden valossa*, Helsinki: Werner Söderström.

Haraway, D. J. (1991) *Simians, Cyborgs, and Women: the Reinvention of Nature*, New York: Routledge.

Hirschman, A. O. (1970) *Exit, Voice, and Loyalty: Responses to Decline in Firms, Organizations, and States*, Cambridge, MA: Harvard University Press.

Ihmisen maaseutu – tahdon maaseutupolitiikka. Maaseutupoliittinen kokonaisohjelma vuosille 2001–2004. Maaseutupolitiikan yhteistyöryhmä. Helsinki, 2000.

Jokinen, A. and Juhila, K. (1991) *Pohjimmaiset asuntomarkkinat. Diskurssianalyysi kuntatason: viranomaiskäytännöistä. Sosiaaliturvan Keskusliitto, Asunto-hallitus,* Helsinki: Sosiaaliturvan keskusliitto – Asuntohallitus.

Kärkkäinen, S.-L. (1998) Services for homeless people: the policy context from 1960s until the present day and two examples of innovative services, The National Research and Development Centre for Welfare and Health, *Themes,* 2.

Kärkkäinen, S.-L. (1999) Annual survey on homelessness in Finland: definitions and methodological aspects, in Dragana Avramov (ed.) *Coping with Homelessness: Issues to be Tackled and Best Practices in Europe,* Aldershot and Brookfield: Ashgate.

Kärkkäinen, S.-L. (2003) Regulations guiding the services for homeless people in Finland: the changing role of the public sector, manuscript, 18 pp.

Kärkkäinen, S.-L. (2004) Statistical update on homelessness 2004 Finland, a memorandum, The National Research and Development Centre for Welfare and Health (20 Sept.).

Kärkkäinen, S.-L. and Tiitinen, V. (1989) Asuinolot ja niiden kehitys, in S.-L. Kärkkäinen, T. Matala, V. Tiitinen and A.Tyrkkö, *Asunto-olot ja asumisen tuki. Tilastokeskus.* Tutkimuksia (Studies), 155, Helsinki: Tilastokeskus.

Karvonen, S. and Rintala, T. (2004) Alueellisten hyvinvointierojen kasvu jatkuu (The growth of regional differences in welfare continues), *Yhteiskuntapolitiikka,* 69(2): 159–70.

Kysely asuntoasioista (1998) Suomen Kuntaliiton kysely asuntoasioista. Suomen Kuntaliitto.

Latour, B. (1986) The powers of association, in J. Law (ed.) *Power, Action and Belief. A New Sociology of Knowledge?,* London: Routledge.

Latour, B. (1991) The impact of science studies on political philosophy, *Science, Technology and Human Values,* 16(1): 3–19.

Latour, B. (1992) One more turn after the social turn..., in E. McMullin (ed.) *The Social Dimensions of Science,* Notre Dame, IN: University of Notre Dame Press.

Latour, B. (1993) *We Have Never Been Modern,* Cambridge, MA: Cambridge University Press.

Lehtonen, Turo-Kimmo (2000) Montako meitä on? Kollektiivin koettelua kolmessa Bruno Latourin tutkimuksessa, *tiede & edistys,* 4: 276–95.

MacKenzie, D. (2004) Social connectivities in global financial markets, *Environment and Planning D: Society and Space,* 22: 83–101.

Ministry of Environmental Affairs (2001) *'Pidot voivat parantua väen vähetessä': Väestöltään supistuvien alueiden asuntopolitiikkaa selvittäneen Pidot-työryhmän raportti* ('The Party can start when some people leave': the report on the housing policy of the out-migration regions), Helsinki: Ministry of Environmental Affairs.

National Action Plan against Poverty and Social Exclusion for 2003–2005. Working Group Memorandum of the Ministry of Social Affairs and Health 2003: 23eng. Helsinki 2003, 74 pp.

Pihlajaniemi, Toivo (2003) The changing roles of the state and municipalities, *Finnish Local Government Studies (Kunnallistieteellinen Aikakausikirja)*, 4: 263–70.

Pitkänen, S., Rissanen, P. and Mattila, K.(2004) Ihmisen arvoista asumista: Y-säätiön ja Asumispalvelusäätiö Aspan tuki- ja palveluasumismallien arviointi (Housing worth Human Living. Evaluation of the models of supported and sheltered housing of Y-Foundation and ASPA Housing Services Foundation), *Avustustoiminnan raportteja*, 13 (Helsinki: RAY).

Rakennukset, asunnot ja asuinolot 2002 (Buildings, Dwellings and Housing Conditions 2002), *Tilastokeskus: Asuminen*, 9 (Helsinki, 2003).

Rose, N. (1999) *Powers of Freedom: Reframing Political Thought*, Cambridge: Cambridge University Press.

Silvasti, T. (2003) Alueellinen kehitys ja sosiaalinen tasa-arvo (Regional development and social equality), *Sosiaalinen politiikka* (Helsinki, WSOY).

Seutukunta- ja maakuntakatsaus 2003. Tilastokeskus. Oulu 2003.

Taipale, I. (1982) Asunnottomuus ja alkoholi: Sosiaalilääketieteellinen tutkimus Helsingissä vuosilta 1937–1977, *Alkoholitutkimussäätiön julkaisuja*, 32 (Jyväskylä).

Thompson, M. and Wildavsky, A. (1986) A poverty of distinction: from economic homogeneity to cultural heterogeneity in the classification of poor people, *Policy Sciences,*19: 163–99.

Tiitinen, V. (2004) Miksi asunnottomuus on edelleen ongelma? (Why homelessness is still a problem?), *Aratieto: Valtion asuntorahaston asiakaslehti*, 1.

Tiitinen, V. and Ikonen, M.-L. (2003) Asunnottomat 2002: Valtion Asuntorahasto, *Selvityksiä*, 7.

Tiitinen, V. and Ikonen, M.-L. (2004) Asunnottomat 2003: Valtion Asuntorahasto, *Selvityksiä*, 6.

Urry, John (1995) *Consuming Places*, London and New York: Routledge.

Valtion asuntorahasto: väestö ja asuntomarkkinatietoja 1992–2003 (Housing Market Surveys conducted by the National Housing Board in 1992–1993 and by the Housing Fund of Finland in 1994–2003).

Valtion asuntorahasto: Täyttöohjeet kunnan asuntomarkkinaselvitys-lomakkeeseen 15.10.2002 (Instructions to complete the municipal housing market survey 15 Oct. 2002).

Valtion asuntorahasto: Asuntomarkkinaselvitykseen liitetyt kommentit. Valtion asuntorahasto 2003.

Vesanen, P. (1988) Puutteellisen asumisen parantaminen kunnissa vuosina 1987–1991. Asuntohallitus, Tutkimus- ja suunnitteluosasto julkaisuja, 1.

Chapter 11

Aalen, F. H. A. (1986) The rehousing of rural labourers in Ireland under the Labourers' Acts, 1883–1919, *Journal of Historical Geography*, 12(3): 287–306.

Aalen, F. H. A. (1992) Ireland, in C. G. Pooley (ed.) *Housing Strategies in Europe, 1880–1930*, Leicester: Leicester University Press.

Aalen, F. H. A. (1993) Constructive unionism and the shaping of rural Ireland, c.1880–1921, *Rural History*, 4(2): 137–64.

Byrne, A., Edmondson, R. and Varley, T. (2001) Arensberg and Kimball and anthropological research in Ireland: introduction to the third edition, in C. Arensberg and S. Kimball (eds) *Family and Community in Ireland*, pp. 1–101, Ennis: CLASP.

Central Statistics Office (2003) *Census 2002,* vol. 1, *Population Classified by Area,* Dublin: Stationery Office.

Clear, C. (2004) 'Too fond of going': female emigration and change for women in Ireland, 1946–1961, in D. Keogh, F. O'Shea and C. Quinlan (eds) *The Lost Decade: Ireland in the 1950s*, Cork: Mercier Press.

Cloke, P., Milbourne, P. and Widdowfield, R. (2001) The geographies of homelessness in rural England, *Regional Studies*, 35(1): 23–37.

Coldrey, B. (1992) 'A most unenviable reputation': the Christian Brothers and school discipline over two centuries, *History of Education*, 21(3): 277–89.

Coleman, U. (1990) *It's Simon: The Story of the Dublin Simon Community*, Dublin: Glendale Press.

Collins, B. and McKeown, K. (1992) *Referral and Resettlement in the Simon Community*, Dublin: Simon Community (National Office).

Commins, P. (1986) Rural social change, in P. Clancy, S. Drudy, K. Lynch and L. O'Dowd (eds) *Ireland: A Sociological Profile*, Dublin: Institute of Public Administration.

Commission of Inquiry on Mental Illness (1966) *Report*, Dublin: Stationery Office.

Commission on Emigration and Other Population Problems (1954) *Report,* Dublin: Stationery Office.

Commission on the Relief of the Poor, Including the Insane Poor (1928) *Report*, Dublin. Stationery Office.

Crehan, J., Lyons, N. and Laver, M. (1987) *The Effects of Self-Care Skills and Homelessness on the Independent Living Potential of Long-Stay Psychiatric Patients*, Galway: Social Sciences Research Centre, University College Galway.

Crowley, E. (2003) The evolution of the common agricultural policy and social differentiation in rural Ireland, *Economic and Social Review*, 34(1): 65–85.

Curtin, C., Haase, T. and Tovey, H. (1996) *Poverty in Ireland: A Political Economy Perspective*, Dublin: Oaktree Press/Combat Poverty Agency.

Cusack, T. (2001) A 'countyside bright with cosy homesteads': Irish nationalism and the cottage landscape, *National Identities*, 3(3): 221–38.

Daly, M. E. (1985) An alien institution? Attitudes towards the city in nineteenth and twentieth century Irish society, *Études Irlandaises*, 10: 181–94.

Daly, M. E. (1997) *The Buffer State: The Historical Roots of the Department of the Environment*, Dublin: Institute of Public Administration.

Delaney, E. (2000) *Demography, State and Society: Irish Migration to Britain, 1921–1971*, Liverpool: Liverpool University Press.

Department of Environment (1989) *Assessment of Housing Needs*, Dublin: Department of the Environment.

Department of the Environment and Local Government (2000) *Homelessness: An Integrated Strategy*, Dublin: Department of the Environment and Local Government.

Department of Environment and Local Government, Department of Justice, Equality and Law Reform, Department of Health and Children, Department of Education and Science (2002) *Homeless Preventative Strategy*, Dublin: Stationery Office.

Devereux, E. (1991) Saving rural Ireland: Muinter na Tire and its anti-urbanism, 1931–1958, *Canadian Journal of Irish Studies*, 17(2): 23–30.

Dillon, B., Murphy-Lawless, J. and Redmond, D. (1990) *Homelessness in Co. Louth: A Research Report*, Dundalk: SUS Research for Dundalk Simon Community and Drogheda Homeless Aid.

Doherty, G. and Keogh, D. (eds) (2003) *De Valera's Irelands*, Cork: Mercier Press.

Doherty, V. (1982) *Closing down the County Homes*, Dublin: Simon Community (National Office).

Dooley, T. (2004) *'The Land for the People': The Land Question in Independent Ireland*, Dublin: UCD Press.

Drake, M., O'Brien, M. and Biebuyck, T. (1982) *Single and Homeless*, London: HMSO.

Drudy, P. J. and Punch, M. (2002) Housing models and inequality: perspectives on the recent Irish experience, *Housing Studies*, 17(4): 657–72.

Edgar, B., Doherty, J. and Meert, H. (2003) *Review of Statistics on Homelessness in Europe*, Brussels: European Observatory on Homelessness.

Edwards, G., Hawker, A., Williamson, V. and Hensman, C. (1966) London's Skid Row, *The Lancet* (29 Jan.): 249–52.

Fahey, T. (ed.) (1999) *Social Housing in Ireland: A Study of Success, Failure and Lessons Learned*, Dublin: Oaktree Press.

Fahey, T. (2002) The family economy in the development of welfare regimes: a case study, *European Sociological Review*, 18(1): 51–64.

Fahey, T. and Watson, D. (1995) *An Analysis of Social Housing Need*, Dublin: Economic and Social Research Institute.

Fahey, T., Nolan, B. and Maitre, B. (2004) *Housing, Poverty and Wealth in Ireland*, Dublin: Institute of Public Administration/Combat Poverty Agency.

Farrell, N. (1988) *Homelessness in Galway*, Galway: Galway Social Service Council.

Fernandez, J. (1995) Homelessness: an Irish perspective, in D. Bhugra (ed.) *Homelessness and Mental Health*, Cambridge: Cambridge University Press.

Finnane, M. (1981) *Insanity and the Insane in Post-Famine Ireland*, London: Croom Helm.

Finnegan, F. (2004) *Do Penance or Perish: A Study of Magdalen Asylums in Ireland*, Oxford: Oxford University Press.

Finnerty, J., Guerin, D. and O'Connell, C. (2003) Ireland, in N. Gallent, M. Shucksmith and M. Tewdwr-Jones (eds) *Housing in the European Countryside: Rural Pressure and Policy in Western Europe*, London: Routledge.

Fitzpatrick, D. (1981) Review of 'Social Origins of the Irish Land War', *Irish Economic and Social History*, 8: 139–42.

Fitzpatrick, D. (1985) Marriage in post-famine Ireland, in A. Cosgrove (ed.) *Marriage in Ireland*, pp. 116–31, Dublin: College Press.

Fraser, M. (1996) *John Bull's Other Homes: State Housing and British Policy in Ireland, 1883–1922*, Liverpool. Liverpool University Press.

Gibbon, P. (1973) Arensberg and Kimball revisited, *Economy and Society*, 2(4): 479–98.

Government of Ireland (2002) *Homeless Preventative Strategy: A Strategy to Prevent Homelessness among Patients Leaving Hospital and Mental Health Care, Adult Prisoners and Young Offenders Leaving Custody, Young People Leaving Care*, Dublin: Stationery Office.

Guinnane, T. W. (1997) *The Vanishing Irish: Households, Migration and the Rural Economy in Ireland, 1850–1914*, Princeton: Princeton University Press.

Halfacree, K. H. (1993) Locality and social representation: space, discourse and alternative definitions of the rural, *Journal of Rural Studies*, 9(1): 23–7.

Hannan, D. F. and Commins, P. (1992) The significance of small-scale landholders in Ireland's socio-economic transformation, in J. H. Goldthorpe and C. T. Whelan (eds) *The Development of Industrial Society in Ireland*, Oxford: Oxford University Press.

Harris, R. (1988) Theory and evidence: the 'Irish stem family' and field data, *Man*, NS 23(3): 417–34.

Hart, I. (1978) *Dublin Simon Community 1971–1976: An Exploration*, Dublin: Economic and Social Research Institute.

Hart, P. (1998) *The I.R.A. and its Enemies: Violence and Community in Cork, 1916–1923*, Oxford: Clarendon Press.

Hickey, C., Bergin, E., Punch, M. and Buchanan, L. (2002) *Housing Access for All? An Analysis of Housing Strategies and Homeless Action Plans*, Dublin: Focus Ireland/Simon Communities of Ireland/Society of St Vincent de Paul/Threshold.

Higgins, M. (2002) Counted in 2002, *Cornerstone: The Magazine of the Housing Agency*, 14: 14–15.

Hooker, E. R. (1938) *Readjustments of Agricultural Tenure in Ireland*, Chapel Hill: University of North Carolina Press.

Housing Centre (1986) *National Directory of Hostels, Night Shelters, Temporary Accommodation and Other Services for Homeless People*, Dublin: Housing Centre.

Inter-Departmental Committee Appointed to Examine the Question of the Reconstruction and Replacement of County Homes (1949) *Report*, Dublin: Stationery Office.

Inter-Departmental Committee on the Care of the Aged (1968) *Report*, Dublin: Stationery Office.

Inter-Departmental Committee on Land Structure Reform (1978) *Final Report*, Dublin: Stationery Office.

Irwin, G. (1998) *Linking to Meet the Needs of the Homeless: A Cross-Border Research Study into Homelessness in Counties Armagh, Cavan, Donegal, Fermanagh, Leitrim, Monaghan and Tyrone*, Dublin: Simon Community Northern Ireland/Simon Community of Ireland.

Jacobs, K., Kemeny, J. and Manzi, T. (1999) The struggle to define homelessness: a constructivist approach, in S. Hutson and D. Clapham (eds) *Homelessness: Public Policies and Private Troubles*, London: Cassell.

Kearns, K. C. (1984) Homelessness in Dublin: an Irish urban disorder, *American Journal of Economics and Sociology*, 43(2): 217–33.

Kennedy, S. (1985) *But Where Can I Go? Homeless Women in Dublin*, Dublin: Arlen House.

Kilcommins, S., O'Donnell, I., O'Sullivan, E. and Vaughan, B. (2004) *Crime, Punishment and the Search for Order in Ireland*, Dublin: Institute of Public Administration.

Lee, J. J. (1989) *Ireland 1912–1985: Politics and Society*, Cambridge: Cambridge University Press.

Lee, J. J. (1990) Emigration: a contemporary perspective, in R. Kearney (ed.) *Migrations: The Irish at Home and Abroad*, Dublin: Wolfhound Press.

Levinson, B. M. (1966) Subcultural studies of homeless men, *Transactions of the New York Academy of Sciences*, 29 (Dec.): 165–82.

Lodge-Patch, I. C. (1970) Homeless men: a London survey, *Proc. Roy. Soc. Med.*, 63: 437–46.

Luddy, M. (1995) *Women and Philanthropy in Nineteenth-Century Ireland*, Cambridge: Cambridge University Press.

McCann, M., O'Siochain, S. and Ruane, J. (eds) (1994) *Irish Travellers: Culture and Ethnicity*, Belfast: Institute of Irish Studies.

McCarthy, P. (1988) A *Study of the Work Skills, Experience and Preferences of Simon Community Residents*, Dublin: Simon Community (National Office).

McCook, J. J. (1893) A tramp census and its revelations, *Forum*, 15: 753–66.

McCullagh, C. (1991) A tie that blinds: family and ideology in Ireland, *Economic and Social Review*, 22(3): 199–212.

McCullagh, C. (1999) Rural crime in the Republic of Ireland, in G. Dingwall and S. R. Moody (eds) *Crime and Conflict in the Countryside*, Cardiff: University of Wales Press.

McDonagh, J. (1998) Rurality and development in Ireland: the need for debate? *Irish Geography*, 31(1): 47–54.

Mac Neela, P. (1999) *Homelessness in Galway: A Report on Homelessness and People Sleeping Rough in Galway City*, Galway: Galway Simon Community.

Malcolm, E. (1999) 'The house of strident shadows': the asylum, the family and emigration in post-famine rural Ireland, in E. Malcolm and G. Jones (eds) *Medicine, Disease and the State in Ireland, 1650–1940*, Cork: Cork University Press.

Malcolm, E. (2003) 'Ireland's crowded madhouses': the institutional confinement of the insane in nineteenth- and twentieth-century Ireland, in R. Porter and D. Wright (eds) *The Confinement of the Insane: International Perspectives*, Cambridge: Cambridge University Press.

Memery, C. (2001) The housing system and the Celtic tiger: the state response to a housing crisis of affordability and access, *European Journal of Housing Policy*, 1(1): 79–104.

Milotte, M. (1997) *Banished Babies: The Secret History of Ireland's Baby Export Business*, Dublin: New Island Books.

Minister for Local Government (1964) *Review and Report on Progress in Housing*, Dublin: Stationery Office.

Mjøset, L. (1992) *The Irish Economy in a Comparative Institutional Perspective*, Dublin: National Economic and Social Council, Report No. 93.

Murphy-Lawless, J. and Dillon, B. (1992) *Promises, Promises. An Assessment of the Effectiveness of the Housing Act 1988, in Housing Homeless People in Ireland*, Dublin: Nexus/National Campaign for the Homeless.

Newman, J. (1962) The priests of Ireland: a socio-religious survey, II, patterns of vocations, *Irish Ecclesiastical Record*, 5th series, 98: 65–92.

Nolan, B., Whelan, C. T. and Williams, J. (1998) *Where are Poor Households? The Spatial Distribution of Poverty and Deprivation in Ireland*, Dublin: Oaktree Press/Combat Poverty Agency.

O'Cinneide, S. and Mooney, P. (1972) *Simon Survey of the Homeless*, Dublin: Simon Community of Ireland Supported by the Medico-Social Research Board (Aug.).

O'Donnell, I. and O'Sullivan, E. (2001) *Crime Control in Ireland: The Politics of Intolerance*, Cork: Cork University Press.

O'Donnell, I. and O'Sullivan, E. (2003) The politics of intolerance – Irish style, *British Journal of Criminology*, 43(1): 41–62.

O'Dowd, L. (1987) Town and country in Irish ideology, *Canadian Journal of Irish Studies*, 13(2): 43–54.

O'Sullivan, E. (1993) Identity and survival in a hostile environment: homeless men in Galway, in C. Curtin, H. Donnan and T. Wilson (eds) *Irish Urban Cultures*, Belfast: Institute of Irish Studies.

O'Sullivan, E. (1997) 'Restored to virtue, to society and to God': juvenile justice and the regulation of the poor, *Irish Criminal Law Journal*, 7(2): 171–94.

O'Sullivan, E. (2003) Marxism, homelessness and the state, in M. Adshead and M. Millar (eds) *Public Administration and Public Policy in Ireland: Theory and Methods*, pp. 37–53, London: Routledge.

O'Sullivan, E. (2004a) How much housing need? *Cornerstone* (Magazine of the Homeless Initiative), 19: 17–19.

O'Sullivan, E. (2004b) Welfare regimes, housing and homelessness in the Republic of Ireland, *European Journal of Housing Policy*, 4(3): 323–43.

O'Sullivan, E. (2005) Homelessness, in D. Redmond and M. Norris (eds) *Housing Contemporary Ireland: Economy, Society, Space and Shelter*, Dublin: Institute of Public Administration.

O'Sullivan, E. and Higgins, M. (2001) Women, the welfare state and homelessness in the Republic of Ireland, in B. Edgar, J. Doherty and A. Mina-Couell (eds) *Women and Homelessness in Europe*, pp. 77–90, Bristol: Policy Press.

O'Tuathaigh, M. A. G. (1982) The land question, politics and Irish society, 1922–1960, in P. J. Drudy (ed.) *Ireland: Land, Politics and People*, Cambridge: Cambridge University Press.

Penrose, L. S. (1939) Mental disease and crime: outline of a comparative study of European statistics, *British Journal of Medical Psychology*, 18(1): 1–15.

Raftery, M. and O'Sullivan, E. (1999) *Suffer the Little Children: The Inside Story of Ireland's Industrial Schools*, Dublin: New Island Books.

Scheper-Hughes, N. (1979) *Saints, Scholars and Schizophrenics: Mental Illness in Rural Ireland*, Berkeley, CA: University of California Press.

Tovey, H. (1992) Rural sociology in Ireland: a review, *Irish Journal of Sociology*, 2: 96–121.

Tovey, H. (1999) Rural poverty: a political economy perspective, in D. G. Pringle, J. Walsh and M. Hennessy (eds) *Poor People, Poor Places: A Geography of Poverty and Deprivation in Ireland*, Dublin: Geography Society of Ireland/Oaktree Press.

Tovey, H. (2001) Creating and re-creating modernity: peasantisation and de-peasantisation in Ireland, in L. Granberg, I. Kovach and H. Tovey (eds) *Europe's Green Ring*, Aldershot: Ashgate.

Tovey, H. (2002) Rethinking urbanisation: struggles around rural autonomy and fragmentation, in M. P. Corcoran and M. Peillon (eds) *Ireland Unbound: A Turn of the Century Chronicle*, Dublin: Institute of Public Administration.

Walsh, A.-M. (1999) Root them in the land: cottage schemes for agricultural labourers, in J. Augusteijn (ed.) *Ireland in the 1930s*, Dublin: Four Courts Press.

Washbrook, R.A. (1970) The homeless offender: an English study of 200 cases, *International Journal of Offender Therapy and Comparative Criminology*, 14(3): 176–84.

Whelan, K. (1999) Economic geography and the long-run effects of the Great Irish Famine, *Economic and Social Review*, 30(1): 1–20.

Williams, J. and Gorby, S. (2002) *Counted in 2002: The Report of the Assessment of Homelessness in Dublin*, Dublin: Homeless Agency/Economic and Social Research Institute.

Williams, J. and O'Connor, M. (1999) *Counted In: The Report of the 1999 Assessment of Homelessness in Dublin, Kildare and Wicklow*, Dublin: ESRI/Homeless Initiative.

Chapter 12

Arthurson, K. and K. Jacobs (2003) *Social Exclusion and Housing*, Brisbane: AHURI Southern Research Centre.

Australian Bureau of Statistics and MapInfo Pty. Ltd (2002) *CData2001*, Belconnen: Australian Bureau of Statistics.

Australian Institute of Health and Welfare (1999) *Australia's Welfare*, Cat. No. AUS16, Canberra: AGPS.

Australian Institute of Health and Welfare (2001) *Australia's Welfare*, AIHW Cat. No. AUS24, Canberra: AGPS.

Australian Institute of Health and Welfare (2003) *Australia's Welfare*, AIHW Cat. No. AUS41, Canberra: AGPS.

Australian Institute of Health and Welfare (2003) *Homeless People in SAAP: SAAP National Data Collection Annual Report 2002–03*, New South Wales supplementary tables, AIHW Cat. No. HOU 92, Canberra: AIHW.

Beer, A. (1998) Overcrowding, quality and affordability: critical issues in non-metropolitan rental housing, *Rural Society*, 8(1): 5–15.

Beer, A., Delfabro, P., Natalier, K., Oakley, S. and Verity, F. (2003) *Developing Models of Good Practice in Meeting the Needs of Homeless Young People in Rural Areas*, Adelaide: AHURI.

Berry, M. (2003) *Counting the Cost of Homelessness*, Brisbane: AHURI Research and Policy Bulletin.

Burke, T. (1994) *Homelessness in Australia: Causal Factors*, Canberra: AGPS.

Burnley, I. and P. Murphy (2004) *Sea Change: Movement from Metropolitan to Arcadian Australia*, Sydney: UNSW Press.

Chamberlain, C. (1999) *Counting the Homeless: Implications for Policy Development*, Occasional Paper, Canberra: Australian Bureau of Statistics.

Chamberlain, C. (2000) *Homelessness in Victoria: A Report Prepared for the Victorian Homelessness Strategy*, Melbourne: Department of Human Services.

Chamberlain, C. and Johnson, D. (2003) *The Development of Prevention and Early Intervention Services for Homeless Youth: Intervening Successfully*, Brisbane: AHURI-RMIT-NATSEM Research Centre.

Chamberlain, C. and MacKenzie, D. (1992) Understanding contemporary homelessness: Issues of definition and meaning, *Australian Journal of Social Issues*, 36: 35–50.

Chamberlain, C. and MacKenzie, D. (1998) *Youth Homelessness: Early Intervention and Prevention*, Sydney: Australian Centre for Equity Through Education.

Chamberlain, C. and MacKenzie, D. (2003) *Counting the Homeless 2001*, Australian Census Analytic Program, Canberra: ABS.

Chamberlain, C. and MacKenzie, D. (2004a) *Counting the Homeless 2001: Western Australia*, Cat. No. 2050.0, Hawthorn: Swinburne University and RMIT University.

Chamberlain, C. and MacKenzie, D. (2004b) *Counting the Homeless 2001: New South Wales*, Cat. No. 2050.0, Hawthorn: Swinburne University and RMIT University.

Chamberlain, C. and MacKenzie, D. (2004c) *Counting the Homeless 2001: Victoria*, Cat. No. 2050.0, Hawthorn: Swinburne University and RMIT University.

Chamberlain, C. and MacKenzie, D. (2004d) *Counting the Homeless 2001: Tasmania*. Cat. No. 2050.0. Hawthorn, Swinburne University and RMIT University.

Chamberlain, C. and MacKenzie, D. (2004e) *Counting the Homeless 2001: South Australia*, Cat. No. 2050.0, Hawthorn: Swinburne University and RMIT University.

Chamberlain, C. and MacKenzie, D. (2004f) *Counting the Homeless 2001: Queensland*, Cat. No. 2050.0, Hawthorn: Swinburne University and RMIT University.

Chamberlain, C. and MacKenzie, D. (2004g) *Counting the Homeless 2001: Northern Territory*, Cat. No. 2050.0. Hawthorn: Swinburne University and RMIT University.

Chamberlain, C. and MacKenzie, D. (2004h) *Counting the Homeless 2001: Australian Capital Territory*, Cat. No. 2050.0, Hawthorn: Swinburne University and RMIT University.

Cloke, P., Milbourne, P. and Widdowfield, R. (2000) Homelessness and rurality: 'out-of-place' in purified space? *Environment and Planning D: Society and Space*, 18: 715–35.

Crane, P. and Brannock, J. (1996) *Homelessness Among Young People in Australia*, Hobart: National Clearinghouse for Youth Studies.

Department of Family and Community Services (2000) *National Homelessness Strategy: A Discussion Paper*, Canberra: Department of Family and Community Services.

Hugo, G. and Bell, M. (1998) The hypothesis of welfare-led migration to rural areas: the Australian case, in P. Boyle and K. Halfacree (eds) *Migration into Rural Areas. Theories and Issues*, Chichester: John Wiley, 107–33.

Human Rights and Equal Opportunities Commission (1993) *Human Rights & Mental Illness*, Vol. 2, Canberra: Australian Government Publishing Service.

Humphreys, J., Matthews-Cowey, S. and Rolley, F. (1996) *Health Frameworks for Small Rural and Remote Communities*, Armidale: Department of Geography and Planning, University of New England.

Innifer, C. (2001) A brief insight into homelessness in the Kimberley, *Parity*, 14(6): 20–1.

Kearns, R., Smith, C. and Abbott, M. (1992) The stress of incipient homelessness, *Housing Studies*, 17: 280–98.

Lawrence, M. (1995) Rural homelessness: a geography without a geography, *Journal of Rural Studies*, 11(3): 297–307.

Lloyd, R., Harding, A. and Hellwig, O. (2001) Regional divide? A study of income inequality in Australia, *Sustaining Regions*, 1: 1–14.

Marchingo, K. (1998) Rural homelessness – what's the difference? *Parity*, 11(2): 10–11.

Memmott, P., Long, S. and Chambers, C. (2003) *Categories of Indigenous Homeless People and Good Practice Responses to Their Needs*, Brisbane: AHURI Research Centre.

Mendes, P. (2002) Leaving care and homelessness, *Parity*, 15(1): 4–5.

Neil, C., Fopp, R., McNamara, R. and Pelling, M. (1994) *Homelessness in Australia: Causes and Consequences*, Melbourne: CSIRO and Victorian Ministerial Advisory Committee on Homelessness and Housing.

Robinson, C. (2003) *Understanding Iterative Homelessness: The Case of People with Mental Disorders*, AHURI Postioning Paper. Sydney: AHURI.

Vinson, T. (1999) *Unequal in Life: The Distribution of Social Disadvantage in Victoria and New South Wales*, Richmond: The Ignatius Centre.

Vinson, T. (2004) *Community Adversity and Resilience: The Distribution of Social Disadvantage in Victoria and New South Wales and the Mediating Role of Social Cohesion*, Richmond: The Ignatius Centre.

Walmsley, D. J. and Weinand, H. C. (1997) Is Australia becoming more unequal? *Australian Geographer*, 28(1): 69–88.

Young, K. (1999) *Homelessness in the ATSI Context and its Possible Implications for the SAAP: Final Report*, Canberra: Department of Health and Aged Care.

Chapter 13

Adams, P. (2002) Prospects for Australian regions, *Sustaining Regions*, 1(2): 4–17.

Agencies for South West Accommodation (2002) *Annual Report*, Bunbury: Agencies for South West Accommodation.

Aldridge, R. (2001) Women and homelessness in the United Kingdom, in B. Edgar and J. Doherty (eds) *Women and Homelessness in Europe*, Bristol: Policy Press.

Allen, C. (2001) Criticism of foyers is being stifled, *Guardian*, London, 19 June.

Allwood, D. and Rogers, N. (2001) *Moving Yarns: Aboriginal Youth Homelessness in Metropolitan Adelaide*, Adelaide: South Australian Government Printer.

Anderson, I. (2001) *Housing and Support Services for Young People: Are Foyers an International Model?*, Sydney: UWS Urban Frontiers Program.

Angus, G. and Woodward, S. (1995) *Child Abuse and Neglect: Australia 1993–94*, Australian Institute of Health and Welfare Child Welfare Series, 13, Canberra: AGPS.

Auerswald, C. L. and Eyre, S. L. (2002) Youth homelessness in San Francisco: a life cycle approach, *Social Science and Medicine*, 54: 1497–1512.

Badcock, B. and Beer, A. (2000) *Home Truths: Property Ownership and Housing Wealth in Australia*, Melbourne: Melbourne University Press.

Bath, H. (1998) *Missing the Mark: Contemporary Out of Home Care Services for Young People with Intensive Support Needs*, Canberra: Child and Family Welfare Association of Australia.

Beer, A. (1998) Overcrowding, quality and affordabilty: critical issues in non-metropolitan rental housing, *Rural Society*, 8(1): 5–17.

Beer, A., Bolam, A. and Maude, A. (1994) *Beyond the Capitals: Urban Growth in Regional Australia*, Canberra: Australian Government Publishing Service.

Beer, A., Delfabbro, P., Natalier, K., Oakley, F., Packer, J. and Verity, F. (2003a) Developing models of good practice in meeting the needs of homeless young people in rural Australia, positioning paper, www.ahuri.edu.au/research.

Beer, A., Maude, A. and Pritchard, P. (2003b) *Developing Australia's Regions: Theory and Practice*, Kensington: UNSW Press.

Bessant, J. (2001) From sociology of deviance to sociology of risk: youth homelessness and the problem of empiricism, *Journal of Criminal Justice*, 29: 31–43.

Bisset, H., Campbell, S. and Goodall, J. (1999) *Appropriate Responses for Homeless People whose Needs Require a High Level and Complexity of Service Provision*, Canberra: Department of Family and Community Services.

Bridgman, R. (2001) I helped build that: a demonstration employment training program for homeless youth in Toronto, Canada, *American Anthropologist,* 103: 779–95.

Burbridge, A. and Winter, I. (1995) Housing and living standards, Report 4, in C. Kilmartin, H. Brownlee, T. Weston, I. Winter, A. Burbridge, C. Millward and G. Snider (eds) *Aspects of Living Standards: A Study of Families in Two Rural Areas,* Melbourne: AIFS.

Cashmore, J. and Paxman, M. (1996) *Wards Leaving Care: A Longitudinal Study,* Sydney: New South Wales Department of Community Services.

Centrelink (2003) Australian Government www.centrelink.gov.au/internet/ internet.nsf/payments/ pay_how_yal.htm.

Centrepoint (1993) *Housing our Children,* London: Centrepoint.

Centrepoint (1995) *Tackling Youth Homelessness in South East London,* London: Centrepoint.

Chamberlain, C. and MacKenzie, D. (2001) *Youth Homelessness 2001,* Melbourne: Royal Melbourne Institute of Technology.

Clay, N. and Coffey, M. (2003) Foyers: in the Australian context, *Parity,* 16(7): 7–9.

Cloke, P. Milbourne, P. and Widdowfield, R. (2002) *Rural Homelessness: Issues, Experiences and Policy Responses,* Bristol: Policy Press.

Commonwealth Department of Family and Community Services (2003) Welfare Reform, www.facs.gov.au/internet/facsinternet.nsf/abo.../esp-welreform_ backgroundofwr.ht.

Cook, P. and Lindsey, M. (1996) *Approaching Adulthood: Quality Standards in Planning Services for Young People who are Leaving Care,* Glasgow: Centre for Residential Care.

Crane, P. and Brannock, J. (1996) *Homelessness among Young People in Australia: Early Intervention and Prevention,* Canberra: National Youth Affairs Research Scheme (NYARS).

Crinall, K. (1995) The search for a feminism that could accommodate homeless young women, *Youth Studies,* 14(3): 42.

Delfabbro, P. H., Barber, J. G. and Cooper, L. (2002) A profile of children entering out-of-home care in South Australia: baseline analyses for a 3-year longitudinal study, *Children and Youth Services Review,* 24: 917–32.

Department of Family and Community Services (2000) *National Homelessness Strategy: A Discussion Paper,* Canberra: Department of Family and Community Services.

Diaz, T., Dusenbury, L., Botvin, G. J. and Farmer Huselid, R. (1997) Factors associated with drug use among youth living in homeless shelters, *Journal of Child and Adolescent Substance Abuse,* 6: 91–110.

Ensign, J. (2003) Illness experiences of homeless youth: age and gender differences, *Journal of Adolescent Health,* 32:127–37.

Ensign, J. and Panke, A. (2002) Barriers and bridges to care: voices of homeless female adolescent youth in Seattle, Washington, USA, *Journal of Advanced Nursing*, 37: 166–72.

Evans, C. and Shaver, S. (2001) *Youth Homelessness: Case Studies of the Reconnect Program*, Sydney: Social Policy Research Centre, University of New South Wales.

Farrin, J. (2003) Rural youth homelessness: has the bough broken? Presentation to the National Housing Conference, Adelaide, 7 Nov.

Fopp, R. (1995) The causes of homelessness: clearing the path, *National Housing Action*, 11: 11–16.

Goodall, J., Mackinnon, D. and Thomson, J. (2001) *Statewide Assessment and Referral in Homelessness Services Project: Final Report*, Melbourne: Victorian Department of Human Services.

Greene, J. M. and Ringwalt, C. L. (1996) Youth and familial substance use's association with suicide attempts among runaway and homeless youth, *Substance Use and Misuse*, 31: 1041–58.

Greenhalgh, E. (2003) Principal place of residence? Long term caravan park residents in rural Australia, unpublished masters thesis, Queensland University of Technology, Brisbane.

Hendessi, M. (1992) *4 in 10: Report on Young Women Who Become Homeless as a Result of Sexual Abuse*, London: CHAR.

House of Representatives Standing Committee on Community Affairs (1995) *Inquiry into Aspects of Youth Homelessness (The Morris Report)*, Canberra: House of Representatives.

Hugo, G. and Maher, C. (1995) *Atlas of the Australian People – 1991 Census, National Overview*, Canberra: Australian Government Publishing Service.

Job Placement Employment and Training (2003) Australian Government, www.jpet.facs.gov.au/index.asp.

Jones, G. (1995) *Leaving Home*, Birmingham: Open University.

Johnson, T. P., Aschkenasy, J., Herbers, M. R. and Gillenwater, S. A. (1996) Self-reported risk factors for AIDS among homeless youth, *Aids Education and Prevention*, 8: 308–22.

Kamieniecki, G. (2001) Prevalence of psychological distress and psychiatric disorders among homeless youth in Australia: a comparative review, *Australian and New Zealand Journal of Psychiatry*, 35: 352–8.

Kenyon, P. and Black, A. (2001) *Small Town Renewal: Overview and Case Studies*, Canberra: Rural Industries Research and Development Corporation.

Kidd, S. A. and Kral, M. J. (2002) Suicide and prostitution among street youth: a qualitative analysis, *Adolescence*, 37: 411–30.

Levesley, S. (1984) *The Police Role in Child Protection in Queensland*, Brisbane: Queensland Police Department.

Maas, F. (1995) *Finding a Place*, National Youth Housing Strategy Final Report, Canberra: Commonwealth Department of Housing and Regional Development.

MacKenzie, D. and Chamberlain, C. (2002) The second national census of homeless school students, *Youth Studies Australia*, 21(4): 24–31.

Maginn, A., Frew, P., O'Regan, R. and Kodz, J. (2000) *Stepping Stones: An Evaluation of Foyers and Other Schemes Serving the Housing and Labour-Market Needs of Young People*, Department of Environment, Transport and the Regions, London: HMSO.

Maunders, D., Liddell, M., Liddell, M. and Green, S. (1999) *Young People Leaving Care and Protection*, Hobart: National Youth Affairs Research Scheme (NYARS).

McCarthy, B., Hagan, J. and Martin, M.J. (2002) In and out of harm's way: violent victimization and the social capital of fictive street families, *Criminology,* 40: 381–86.

McCaskill, P. A., Toro, P. A. and Wolfe, S. M. (1998) Homeless and matched housing adolescents: a comparative study of psychopathology, *Journal of Clinical Child Psychology*, 27: 306–19.

Minnery, J. and Greenhalgh, J. (1999) Housing beyond the capitals, *Urban Policy and Research*, 17(4): 309–22.

Mitchell, B. (1994) Family structure and leaving the nest: a social resource perspective, *Sociological Perspectives*, 37: 652–69.

Morgan, E. and Vincent, C. (1987) Youth housing needs: housing questions, *Youth Studies and Abstracts*, 6: 21–3.

Mowbray, M. (1994) *Transforming the Great Australian Dream: The Quarter vs the 30th of an Acre Block*, Urban Research Program Monograph, Canberra: ANU.

Ochlitree, G. (1990) *Children in Step Families*, New York: Prentice Hall.

O'Connor, I. (1989) *Our Homeless Children: Their Experiences*, Sydney: Human Rights and Equal Opportunity Commission.

O'Dwyer, L. (2002) *Rental Housing Markets*, www.ssn.flinders.edu.au/geog/staff/spirtmaps.

Office of Regional Development (2002) *Regional Workforce Accommodation Solutions Study*, Adelaide: ORD.

Onyx, J. and Bullen, P. (2000) Sources of social capital, in I. Winter (ed.) *Social Capital and Public Policy in Australia*, pp. 105–35, Melbourne: AIFS.

Neil, C. and Fopp, R. (1992) *Homelessness in Australia: Causes and Consequences*, Melbourne: Australian Housing and Urban Research Institute, CSRIO.

Nyamathi, A., Leake, B. and Gelberg, L. (2000) Sheltered versus nonsheltered homeless women, *Journal of General Internal Medicine*, 15: 565–72.

Pfeifer, R. W. and Oliver, J. (1997) A study of HIV seroprevalence in a group of homeless youth in Hollywood, California, *Journal of Adolescent Health*, 20:

339–42.

Plass, P. and Hotaling, G. (1994) The intergenerational transmission of running away: childhood experiences of the parents of runaways, *Journal of Youth and Adolescence*, 24: 335–48.

Prime Ministerial Taskforce on Youth Homelessness (1998) *Putting Families in the Picture: Evaluating Early Interventions into Youth Homelessness*, Canberra: Department of the Prime Minister and Cabinet.

Randolph, B., Pang, L. and Wood, H. (2001) *Evaluating the Miller Live 'n' Learn Campus Pilot*, Australian and Housing Urban Research Institute, positioning paper, www.ahuri.edu.au/research.

Rohde, L. A., Ferreira, M. H. M., Zomer, A., Foster, L. and Zimmerman, H. (1998) The impact of living on the streets on latency children's friendships, *Revista de Saude Publica*, 32: 273–80.

Shelter (1992) *The Foyer Project: A Collection of Background Papers*, Part I and Part II, London: Shelter.

Smith, J. (1995) *Being Young and Homeless: Analysis and Discussion of Young People's Experience of Homelessness*, Melbourne: Salvation Army.

Tasker, G. (1995) *Moving on: Austudy and the Lives of Unsupported Secondary Students*, Melbourne: Brotherhood of St Laurence.

Unger, J. B., Kipke, M. D., Simon, T. R., Montgomery, S. B. and Johnson, C. J. (1997) Homeless youths and young adults in Los Angeles: prevalence of mental health problems and the relationship between mental health and substance abuse disorders, *American Journal of Community Psychology*, 25: 371–94.

Wade, P. and Maher, A. (2003) Living and earning, *Grapevine* (April): 1–4.

Webber, R. (2002) Generation gaps and fault lines: Vietnamese-Australian young people and illicit drug use in Melbourne, *Youth Studies Australia*, 21(3): 17–24.

Williams, F. and Popay, J. (1999) Balancing polarities: developing a new framework for welfare research, in F. Willliams, J. Popay and A. Oakley (eds) *Welfare Research: A Critical Review*, pp. 156–84, London: UCL Press.

Yardy, W. and Thompson, W. (2003) Housing drought in Central Queensland, *Parity*, 16(2): 27.

Young, C.M. 1987 *Young People Leaving Home in Australia: The Trend Towards Independence*, Melboourne: Australian Institute of Family Studies.

Zabar, P. and Angus, G. (1994) *Child Abuse and Neglect: Reporting and Investigation Procedures in Australia*, Australian Institute of Health and Welfare Studies, Child Welfare Series, 8, Canberra: AGPS Canberra.

Chapter 14

Baker, M. A., McNicholas, A. and Garrett, N. (2000) Household crowding: a major risk factor for epidemic meningococcal disease in Auckland children, *Pediatric Infectious Diseases Journal*, 19: 983–90.

Butterworth, G. V. (1991) *Nga Take I Neke Ai Te Maori: Maori Mobility*, Wellington: Manatu Maori/Ministry of Maori Affairs.

Cheer, T., Kearns, R. and Murphy, L. (2002) Housing policy, poverty and culture: 'discounting' decisions among Pacific peoples in Auckland, New Zealand, *Environment and Planning C: Government and Policy*, 20: 497–516.

Clark, S. Page, I., Bennett, A. and Bishop, S. (2000) *New Zealand House Condition Survey*, Poirirua: Building Research Association of New Zealand (BRANZ).

Cloke, P., Milbourne, P. and Widdowfield, R. (2000) Homelessness and rurality: 'out-of-place' in purified space? *Environment and Planning D: Society and Space*, 18: 715–35.

Cooper, R. (2000) The intersection of space and homelessness in central Auckland, MA thesis, School of Geography and Environmental Science, University of Auckland.

Davey, J. A. and Kearns, R. A. (1994) Special needs versus the 'level playing field': recent developments in housing policy for indigenous people in New Zealand, *Journal of Rural Studies*, 10: 73–82.

Dominion Post (2003) Hardline homeless 'unreformed and unrepentent', http://www.cleansafeworldwide.org/doc.asp?doc=523&cat=98, accessed 6 June 2004.

Douglas, E. (1986) *Fading Expectations: The Crisis in Maori Housing*, Wellington: Board of Maori Affairs.

Durie, M. (1998) *Whai Ora: Maori Health Development*, 2nd edn, Auckland: Oxford University Press.

Ferguson, G. (1994) *Building the New Zealand Dream*, Palmerston North: Dunmore Press.

Fougere, G. (2001) Transforming health sectors: new logics of organising in the New Zealand health system, *Social Science and Medicine*, 52: 1233–42.

Gardiner, W. (1997) Population change and Maori development, *Proceedings, The Population Conference: People, Communities, Growth*, Wellington, http://www.executive.govt.nz/96-99/minister/bradford/population/content/pnldis3a_1.htm.

Kearns, R. A. (2001) Colonised by policy? Housing opportunities for indigenous peoples on collectively-owned land in Canada and New Zealand, *Australian–Canadian Studies*, 19: 65–80.

Kearns, R. A. and Joseph, A. E. (1997) Restructuring health and rural communities in New Zealand, *Progress in Human Geography*, 21: 18–32.

Kearns, R. A. and Reinken, J. (1994) Out for the count? Questions concerning the population of the Hokianga, *New Zealand Population Review*, 20(1–2): 19–30.

Kearns, R A. and Smith, C. J. (1994) Housing, homelessness and mental health: mapping an agenda for geographical inquiry, *Professional Geographer*, 46(4): 418–24.

Kearns, R. A., Smith, C. J. and Abbott, M. W. (1991) Another day in paradise? Life on the margins in urban New Zealand, *Social Science and Medicine*, 33: 369–79.

Kearns, R. A., Smith, C. J. and Abbott, M. W. (1992) The stress of incipient homelessness, *Housing Studies*, 7: 280–98.

Kelsey, J. (1995) *The New Zealand Experiment: A World Model for Structural Adjustment*, Wellington: Bridget Williams Books.

Knight, D. and Joseph, A. (eds) (1999) *Restructuring Societies*, Ottawa: Carleton University Press.

Le Heron, E. (2004) Placing geographical imagination in film: New Zealand filmmakers' use of landscape, *New Zealand Geographer*, 60(1): 60–6.

Le Heron, R. and Pawson, E. (1996) *Changing Places: New Zealand in the Nineties*, Auckland: Longmans.

Maori Women's Research Project (1991) *For the Sake of Decent Shelter*, Wellington: Maori Women's Housing Research Project.

Matheson, A. and Howden-Chapman, P. (2001) *Housing, Energy and Health: Working Paper*, Wellington: Department of Public Health, Wellington School of Medicine, University of Otago.

McLeod, R. (1992) The slow picturesque death of the Hokianga, *North and South*, March: 42–59.

Metge, J. (1959) Maori population trends, *New Zealand Geographer*, 15: 98–9.

Metge, J. (1964) *A New Maori Migration: Rural and Urban Relations in Northern New Zealand*, London School of Economics Monographs in Social Anthropology, 27, London: Athlone Press.

Metge, J. (1995) *New Growth from Old: The Whanau in the Modern World*, Wellington: Victoria University Press.

Murphy, L. and Kearns R. A. (1994) Housing New Zealand Ltd: Privatisation by Stealth, *Environment and Planning A*, 26: 623–37.

Murphy, L. and Urlich-Cloher, D. (1996) Economic restructuring, housing policy and Maori housing in Northland, New Zealand, *Geoforum*, 26: 325–36.

National Health Committee (1998) *The Social, Economic and Cultural Determinants of Health*, Wellington: NHC.

Percy, A. and Johnson, A. (1988) Serious housing need, in Housing New Zealand, *National Housing Commission (NHC) Five Yearly Report*, Wellington: NHC.

Poulsen, M. F. and Johnston, R. J. (1973) Patterns of Maori migration, in R. J. Johnston (ed.) *Urbanisation in New Zealand: Geographical Essays*, pp. 150–74, Wellington: Reed.

Roberts, C. (1988) Housing, in *The April Report*, vol. 4, *Social Perspectives*, pp. 151–94, Wellington: Royal Commission on Social Policy (RCSP).

Ryks, J. (2002) Land/seascapes of exclusion, Ph.D. thesis, Department of Geography, University of Waikato, Hamilton, NZ.

Saville-Smith, K. (1999) The condition of Opotiki's rural housing stock: a survey of three communities, unpublished report, Centre for Research, Evaluation and Social Assessment (CRESA), Wellington.

Saville-Smith, K.and Thorns, D. (2001) *Community-Based Solutions for Sustainable Housing*, Wellington: Centre for Research, Evaluation and Social Assessment.

Scott, K. and Kearns, R. A. (2001) Coming home: return migration by Maori to the Mangakahia Valley, Northland, *New Zealand Population Review*, 26: 21–44.

Scott, K., Park, J., Cocklin, C. and Blunden, G. (1997) '*A Sense of Community*': An *Ethnography of Rural Sustainability in the Mangakahia Valley, Northland*, Auckland: Department of Geography, University of Auckland, Occasional Publication, 33.

Smith, A. (2004) A Mori sense of place? Taranaki Waiata Tangi and feelings for place, *New Zealand Geographer*, 54: 12–17.

Spoonley, P. (1996) Mahi Awatea? The racialisation of work in Aotearoa/New Zealand, in P. Spoonley, C. Macpherson and D. Pearson (eds) *Nga Patai: Racism and Ethnic Relations in Aotearoa/New Zealand*, pp. 55–78, Palmerston North: Dunmore Press.

Stokes, E. (1979) Population change and rural development: the Maori situation, in R. D. Bedford (ed.) *New Zealand Rural Society in the 1970s*, pp. 23–44, Studies in Rural Change, 1, Christchurch: Department of Geography, University of Canterbury.

Sunday Star Times (2004) Let's shelter the homeless – Banks, 9 April: 3.

Te Puni Kokiri (2004) Awhina Noho Whare/Housing Assistance, http://www.tpk.govt.nz/community/housing/SHAZ.asp (accessed 25 May 2004).

Veness, A. R. (1993) Neither homed nor homeless: contested definitions and the personal worlds of the poor, *Political Geography*, 12: 319–40.

Waldegrave, C. and Sawrey, R. (1994) *The Extent of Serious Housing Need in New Zealand 1992–1993*, Lower Hutt: Family Centre Social Policy Research Unit.

Waldegrave, C. and Stuart, S. (1997) Out of the rat race: the migration of low income urban families to small town Wairarapa, *New Zealand Geographer*, 53(1): 22–9.

Walker, L., Cocklin, C., Blunden, G., Davis, P., Kearns, R. and Scott, K. (1998) *Cannabis Highs and Lows: Sustaining and Dislocating Rural Communities in*

Northland, Auckland: Department of Geography, University of Auckland, Occasional Publication, 36.

Wall, M. (1997) Stereotypical constructions of the Maori 'race' in the media, *New Zealand Geographer*, 53: 40–5.

Chapter 15

Cloke, P., Milbourne, P. and Widdowfield, R. (2000a) Change but no change, dealing with homelessness under the 1996 Housing Act, *Housing Studies*, 15: 739–56.

Cloke, P., Milbourne, P. and Widdowfield, R. (2000b) Partnerships and policy networks in rural local governance, homelessness in Taunton, *Public Administration*, 78: 111–34.

Cloke, P., Milbourne, P. and Widdowfield, R. (2000c) Ethics, reflexivity and research: encounters with homeless people, *Ethics, Place and Environment*, 3: 133–54.

Index